# The First Indian Author in English

## Dean Mahomed (1759–1851) in India, Ireland, and England

# The First Indian Author in English

## Dean Mahomed (1759–1851) in India, Ireland, and England

MICHAEL H. FISHER

DELHI
OXFORD UNIVERSITY PRESS
BOMBAY   CALCUTTA   MADRAS
1996

*Oxford University Press, Walton Street, Oxford* OX2 6DP

*Oxford   New York*
*Athens   Auckland   Bangkok   Bombay*
*Calcutta   Cape Town   Dar es Salaam   Delhi*
*Florence   Hong Kong   Istanbul   Karachi*
*Kuala Lumpur   Madras   Madrid   Melbourne*
*Mexico City   Nairobi   Paris   Singapore*
*Taipei   Tokyo   Toronto*
and associates in
*Berlin   Ibadan*

© Oxford University Press 1996

ISBN 0 19 563899 9

*Typeset by Rastrixi, New Delhi 110070*
*Printed in India at Pauls Press, New Delhi 110020*
*and published by Manzar Khan, Oxford University Press*
*YMCA Library Building, Jai Singh Road, New Delhi 110001*

*Dedicated to Roswita and James,*
*Nikki, Noah, and Emily*

# Contents

# List of Illustrations

# Acknowledgements

Over his long life, Dean Mahomed (1759–1851) travelled widely within the growing British empire: in India, Ireland, and England. Unique among Indians during this period, he wrote and published books and other autobiographical writing in English, directly for the Anglo-Irish and English people among whom he lived. My research for this volume thus drew on sources in India, Ireland, England, and the United States.

Dean Mahomed grew to manhood in India from 1759–84. He later wrote about his travels through Indian society, as a camp follower and then subaltern officer in the English East India Company's Bengal Army. His *Travels of Dean Mahomet*[1] is republished for the first time since its original edition in 1794 as Chapter Two of this volume. Our knowledge of the lives of Indians and Britons in the Bengal Army, and of Indian society generally, during this period has hitherto rested on three other kinds of sources. First, voluminous records of the East India Company survive in the National Archives of India (NAI), New Delhi, and the Oriental and India Office and Records (IOL), London. This range of official records enables us to trace the growth and activities of the East India Company, its Bengal Army, and their relationships with Indian society. These records also convey the values of their almost exclusively British authors. Very few Indian voices appear in these records; reconstructing the lives of Indians from these records thus remains difficult.[2]

Second, various Europeans wrote histories, memoirs, journals, and letters about their lives in India. A number of such accounts by British army officers contemporary to Dean Mahomed and from a slightly later period have survived.[3] The works of many Company civil officials also provide British views of the army and Indian society.[4] A variety of European travellers and settlers living in India, but not attached to the Company, also described their own lives during this period.[5] Sarah Shade, a camp follower, presented a less elite European view of army life.[6] Not until the early nineteenth century do we have an account about daily life within Indian society by a European: an Englishwoman married into a Muslim elite family.[7] The British Library, Institute for Historical Research, National Army Museum, and School of Oriental and African Studies Library each proved valuable in my research into these sources. Each of these European accounts, however, presents us with a quite different perspective on the Bengal Army and Indian society from that of Dean Mahomed.

The third type of source material relevant here consists of accounts by Asians from this period. A number of histories in Persian and Indian regional languages, often following a well-established Islamic genre of 'tarikh', described late eighteenth century politics in India.[8] The autobiographical account of Joseph Emin, an Armenian in the Company's Bengal Army at the time of Dean Mahomed, presented a fascinating West Asian view of life in London but included little on his life in India.[9] During the nineteenth century, as British authority spread, an increasing number of Indians wrote—often under British patronage—about their lives and society.[10] The second work (after *Travels*) by an Indian in the Bengal Army only appeared in print in 1873, covering events *c.* 1812–60; the English translator and editor of this autobiographical memoir attributed it to a soldier, Sita Ram, who rose to the rank of subedar.[11] Thus, Dean Mahomed's *Travels* comprises a singular Indian account of the Bengal Army and Indian society in the eighteenth century.

After he immigrated to Europe in 1784, Dean Mahomed shaped his own career and autobiographical writings in innovative and entrepreneurial ways. During this period, many Europeans wrote fictional accounts of the lives and travels of Asians.[12] Dean Mahomed worked among Europeans but he never lost his own distinctive voice. His writings and his careers as an Indian settled in colonial Ireland and then in England reveal much about the increasing heterogeneity of social life within the British empire.

Significantly, the most extensive account about Dean Mahomed during the quarter century he spent in Ireland comes from a travelling Indian dignitary, Abu Talib.[13] The latter met Dean

Mahomed only due to a fantastic conjunction of circumstances including adverse winds and chance meetings with old European friends at a local inn in Cork. The Cork Public Reference Library, University College Cork Library, the National Library of Ireland, and the Trinity College (Dublin) Library contain the thousands of newspapers contemporary to Dean Mahomed in Cork that I read. These newspapers also provide an excellent picture of Irish, and especially Anglo-Irish, society at the time. The Public Record Office of Ireland has a few tantalizing records about his unconventional marriage in 1786 to Jane Daly. Fires at key archives during the time of the Irish Nationalist movement, however, destroyed the original records of their marriage, although an index has survived. The records of the Representative Church Body Library and local Church of Ireland parishes revealed little further information about their lives. To my knowledge, only one complete copy of *Travels* exists in Ireland: at the Ursuline Convent, Blackrock. The Duke University, Shantiniketan, Wellcome Institute, and British Libraries each contains a complete—or nearly complete—copy of *Travels*.

Dean Mahomed lived in England from about 1807 until his death in 1851. His accomplishments in London (to 1813) and thereafter in Brighton inserted his name into a variety of records and publications. Church of England parish records contain vital statistics about him and his family. We can obtain a detailed picture of his life in England through his own continued newspaper advertisements and other writings; tax rate books, victualler licenses, court records, decadenal censuses, and other official documents; and frequent references to him in the works of European writers. Among the archives and libraries particularly valuable to me in London were the British Library, Family History Centre (Chancery Lane), Greater London Record Office, Guildhall Library, Office of Population Censuses and Surveys (St Catherine's House), Principle Registry of the Family Division (Somerset House), Public Record Office, Society of Genealogists Library, Wellcome Institute, and Westminster and Marylebone Public Libraries. For Dean Mahomed's thirty-five years in Brighton, much material exists. The Brighton Reference Library, Pavilion Art Gallery and Museum, and East Sussex Record Office (Lewes) all hold remarkable collections which I consulted extensively.

The assistance I have received in researching and writing this volume has been generous. I am grateful to the staffs of all the above-mentioned institutions for access to their collections. I would particularly like to thank other scholars who have shared their knowledge of, and enthusiasm for, Dean Mahomed and his descendants in Britain: Ms Rozina Visram, Dr J. Stewart Cameron, Mr Prabhu Guptara and Sir Asa Briggs. Oberlin College provided me with the time and support to complete this work and its library and reference staff proved particularly valuable. I thank Paula Richman, Roswita Fisher, James Fisher, and the anonymous reader at Oxford University Press for their careful suggestions for revision of drafts. I am, of course, responsible for the material in this book, including any errors or omissions.

## Notes

1. Except in direct quotes, I use the spelling of his name which he most often used in the second half of his life: Dean Mahomed.
2. Some efforts to recover Indian biographies from these records are: S.C. Hill, *Yusuf Khan* (1914) and 'Old Sepoy Officer', *English Historical Review* (April, July 1913) and Michael H. Fisher, *Indirect Rule* (1991), pp. 316–74.
3. Journals of Alexander Champion, Allan Macpherson and John Macpherson in William Charles Macpherson, ed. *Soldiering* (1928); 'Bengalee' [Albert Fenton], *Memoirs of a Cadet* (1839); Albert Hervey, *Soldier* (1988 edition); John Moodie, *History* (1788) and *Remarks* (1788); Thomas Dean Pearse, 'Memoir, *Bengal Past and Present*, vols 2–7 (1908–11); James Rennell, *Marches* (1792) and *Journals* (1910 edition); Richard Scott, 'Journal', *Naval and Military Magazine*, vols 1–4 (1827–28); John Shipp, *Memoirs* (1829); John Williams, *Historical Account* (1817; 1970 reprint); Thomas Williamson, *East India Vade Mecum* (1810).
4. See Charles Caraccioli, *Life of . . . Clive* (1775–77); John Henry Grose, *Voyage* (1766); Warren Hastings, *Memoirs*, ed. G.R. Gleig (1841); Mrs [Jemima] Kindersley, *Letters* (1777); Innes Munro, *Narrative* (1789); Robert Orme, *History* (1780); Henry Strachey, *Narrative* (1773); Henry Vansittart, *Narrative* (1766); Harry Verelst, *View* (1772); C.R. Wilson and W.H. Carey, *Glimpses*, ed. Amarendranath Mookerji (1968).
5. E.g. Eliza Fay, *Original Letters* (1817; 1925); William Hickey, *Memoirs* (1919–25 reprint); William Hodges, *Travels* (1793).
6. Sarah Shade, *Narrative* (1801).
7. Mrs Meer Hassan Ali, *Observations* (1832).
8. Examples (English translation) include Sayid Ghulam Husain Khan, *Seir*

*Mutaqherin* (1902 reprint) and Salim Allah, *Narrative*, tr. Francis Gladwin (1788).

9.  Joseph Emin, *Life* (1792; 1918 edition).

10. E.g. Lutfullah, *Autobiography*, ed. Edward B. Eastwick (1857; 1987 reprint); Jaffur Shurreef, *Qanoon-e-Islam*, tr. G.A. Herklots (1832).

11. Sita Ram, *Sepoy to Subedar*, ed. J. Norgate (1873). Many scholars have seen more of Northgate than Sita Ram in this text. The original manuscript, from which Norgate claims to have worked, no longer exists.

12. E.g. Eliza Hamilton, *Translation of the Letters of a Hindoo Rajah* (1796); James Moirer, *Adventures of Hajji Baba* (1824); Charles de Secondat Montesquieu, *Lettres persanes* (1721).

13. Abu Talib Khan, 'Masir Talibi fi Bilad Afranji', BM Add 8145–47, IOL and Abu Taleb Khan, *Travels*, tr. Charles Stewart (1810; 1814).

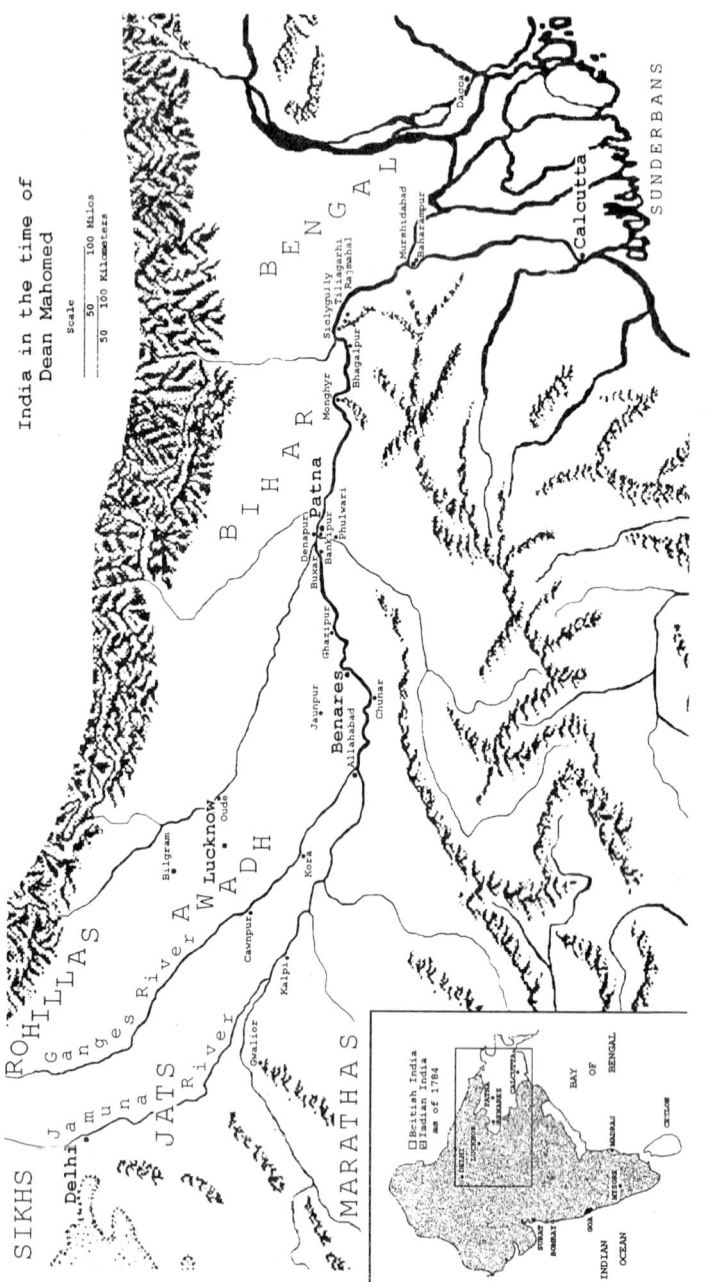

India at the time of Dean Mahomed

# Chapter One

# A Text and a Life

## Dean Mahomed's *Travels* and Life (1759–1851)

Dean Mahomed's writings and his life history reveal the complexity of social interactions within the developing British empire. Dean Mahomed spent his youth in India during a disorienting period of transition from Mughal to English East India Company rule. Born in 1759 into a family claiming traditions of service to the Mughal Empire, in 1769 Dean Mahomed followed his father and brother into the English East India Company's Bengal Army. Over the next fifteen years, he travelled up and down the Ganges as a camp follower and then subaltern officer in that colonial army. Through his words, we can see his conception of what being Indian meant, and the implications of that identity in terms of his loyalties and sense of self during this period of the establishment of British colonial rule over India.

Dean Mahomed also lived for two-thirds of a century in Europe, writing about himself and India throughout that period. In 1784, at age twenty-five, he emigrated from India to colonial Ireland, where he soon married a young Anglo-Irish woman and created a place for himself in the Protestant Ascendancy in Cork. In 1794, to represent himself and the changes he had observed in Indian society as the East India Company established its rule there, he brought out *The Travels of Dean Mahomet*: the first book ever written and published by an Indian in English.

In his late forties (around 1807), Dean Mahomed immigrated once again, this time to London. In the metropolis, he built several careers: as medical practitioner and then restaurateur. Finally, in his mid-fifties (1814), he settled in the English coastal resort town of Brighton. There, his repeated efforts to market himself and his reputedly Indian medical therapies to English royalty and the public eventually brought him fame, if not fortune. By the time of his death in 1851, however, Victorian England had relegated him to the margins of society. By republishing Dean Mahomed's first book, *Travels* (as Chapter Two) and by reconstructing his life history, this volume reveals his views on, and place in, the contested interactions among peoples and cultures brought about by the British empire in India, Ireland and England.

## Dean Mahomed's Travels in India (1769–84)

Dean Mahomed began his autobiographical travel narrative, *Travels*, with 1769 and his departure from the world of his childhood among the Muslim service elite of Patna. As the diverse provinces of the Mughal Empire broke away and the English East India Company began to conquer each in turn, families such as his had to make hard choices about their futures and their loyalties. Dean Mahomed recounted the entry of his father, his elder brother, and then himself into the East India Company's Bengal Army. At age eleven, he attached himself to a teenage Anglo-Irish patron: Ensign Godfrey Evan Baker. The power relationships in the colonial process become clear from Dean Mahomed's self-perceived need—in order to advance his career in India—for a British patron. Over their fifteen years together in the Company's Bengal Army, Dean Mahomed rose from camp follower to become a market master and then subaltern officer as Baker rose to his captaincy and independent command.

Through Dean Mahomed's words, we can follow his journey with the Bengal Army as it passed up and down the Ganges River and as it forced north India into the English East India Company's colonial administration. His marches with this army took him perhaps as far west as Delhi and certainly as far east as Dhaka; later he sailed to Madras (see map).

Dean Mahomed's narrative of his journeys through the cities and countryside of India, and his interactions with the peoples living there, enables us to understand the complexity and internal divisions within Indian society of the time. This diversity of Indian society meant that each city and region which he encountered struck him as distinct and worthy of notice. His relationship to other Indians remained ambivalent. He stood as both an insider to the domestic rituals of his Muslim relatives and also an outsider to their world. We can also note the specificity with which he described his own natal community's internal social organization and domestic customs, in contrast to his more limited knowledge of other Indian communities.

Dean Mahomed's ventures across India also brought him into a series of colonial contexts. Living as a camp follower in the English Company's army, and then rising through its Indian officer corps, Dean Mahomed fostered British rule. He fought against Indian rulers and to subdue the Indian countryside to British colonialism. Reading Dean Mahomed's *Travels*, we should consider the attitude he—and tens of thousands of other Indians in that army—held toward this British conquest of India. In part, he presented the views of people of his class toward the variety of Indian regional rulers as they submitted to, and/or resisted, English Company rule. We can also see why a career serving the British might seem so attractive, in comparison to a traditional career serving the nominal Mughal Emperor or one of the surviving Muslim or Hindu regional rulers.

During the second half of the eighteenth century, the English East India Company shifted from being a private company of merchants to the administrator of huge areas of India, with a strong military presence. The Company, as a de facto regional state, carried out diplomatic negotiations with other Indian polities. It was also moving toward a formal position as an official of the Mughal Empire (which it accepted as Diwan of Bengal in 1772). In London, the Company increasingly assumed political roles beyond its commercial ones. The Court of Directors was not just a body representing shareholders who sought returns on their capital investments, but also a political body whose membership overlapped with Parliament and held political clout. The Directors, especially from 1773 onward, accepted Parliamentary oversight in exchange for financial guarantees and subsidies that financed Company wars in India. While trade (especially in cotton cloth and opium) continued, English administration of the revenue system of Bengal garnered much larger sums for the British.

Europeans joined the Company's service for a variety of reasons. Britons who returned from India as 'Nabobs' dazzled European society with their wealth, garnered not from their relatively small salaries but from private trade and looted Indian treasure. The lure of adventure and possible glory motivated young British officer cadets—such as Dean Mahomed's patron, Baker—to make careers in the Company's army rather than the King's. Many of the Company's private European soldiers were driven by poverty or enticed by glib recruiters into its army. Death from disease, alcohol, and battle, however, put an end to the lives of dauntingly large numbers of these Europeans. Indian accusations of extortion against him put a premature end to Baker's military career.

The Company's European officer corps comprised an amalgam of British men whose values increasingly limited the authority of non-whites within the army. At the time Dean Mahomed lived in India, strong racial lines were developing which distinguished between white officers and Indian subordinates. By this time, the Company allowed Indians into its service only as subaltern officers, soldiers, and servants. From Dean Mahomed's perspective in this army's camp, he clearly revealed the tensions inherent in the imperial process, a process which created contact zones: 'social spaces where disparate cultures meet, clash and grapple with each other, often in highly asymmetrical relations of domination and subordination.'[1] Despite their subordinated position, Indians did much to shape virtually every aspect of the British presence in India.

Scholars today are beginning to overcome the tendency to regard European imperialism as a one-way flow of peoples and power. Clearly, relations between the European rulers and the Asians they ruled were unequal. Nevertheless, through our examination of Dean Mahomed's life and words, we can see the vital role played by Indians in the colonial process. The English Company used remarkably few Europeans to conquer and rule India. The Company's civil administration in Bengal Presidency in 1771, for example, had only 187 British officials but thousands of Indian officials carried out the actual work of administration.[2] This relatively minuscule number of Europeans administered a population in Bengal and Bihar of some thirty million people. Similarly, the Company's armies which extended and enforced British rule consisted of 6–8 times as many Indians as Europeans. Dean Mahomed's perspective as an Indian member of that army thus stands as particularly valuable.

## A Guide to This Volume

Dean Mahomed's *Travels* provides a singular entree into the world of eighteenth century India. Relatively little other specific evidence has survived about modestly placed Muslim families such as his. Dean Mahomed's accounts of his family's rituals and practices provide a unique, first-person description of Muslim domestic customs, ordinarily closed to outsiders. His remarks on his own family's history, while somewhat elliptical, provide us with vital clues to his background. Finally, we can use his own autobiographical narrative to reconstruct aspects of life as an Indian in the Bengal Army during a crucial phase of British colonialism.

In republishing Dean Mahomed's *Travels*, I have made no changes in his text or organization, although I have placed modern spellings in brackets where necessary and deleted his List of Subscribers. Nevertheless, the historical context of this publication of his work at the end of the twentieth century is quite different from its original appearance in colonial Cork in 1794.

Much of my contribution has been to contextualize the words and deeds of Dean Mahomed. Since no standard transliteration system existed at the time, he simply made up or copied idiosyncratic spellings. This has made some of the terms he used difficult to identify, even for an Indian and/or historian of India today. The Glossary/Index at the end of this volume contains brief definitions of key words and persons he mentioned, providing their modern and more familiar spellings.

We cannot today specifically identify Dean Mahomed's immediate family in other surviving sources. Families such as his did not retain a traditional family name, in either the male or female lines. Further, as was conventional, Dean Mahomed himself always referred to his father, mother, and elder brother by their kinship relationship to him, rather than by personal name. From Dean Mahomed's own passing references to the more illustrious relatives he claimed, however, we can deduce his social class and putative descent.

Similarly, we must rely on Dean Mahomed himself for most of our specific knowledge of his own life. In this period in India, the state collected or preserved little demographic information on Indians. While Dean Mahomed explained that a Brahmin astrologer cast horoscopes for the members of his family at the time of birth (XII),[3] his own horoscope has not—to our knowledge—survived. The extant records of the English East India Company refer mostly to its European employees, except where an Indian employee in some way came peculiarly to the attention of the Company, for example, in pension petitions at retirement after many years of official employment or else in judicial investigations into their alleged criminal acts. Since Dean Mahomed himself neither served the Company long enough in an official capacity to qualify for a pension nor fell subject to accusations of malfeasance or criminality, no specific record of his own service to the Company has survived.

Nonetheless, we can follow his life in India indirectly, via his various military units, as well as through the checkered career of his patron, Baker. (In contrast, once Dean Mahomed reached England early in the nineteenth century, he appeared almost continually both in the official records of the state and in unofficial sources as well.) Supplementing his unique auto-ethnographic and autobiographical account with other historical evidence, I have written a life history of the man. Chapter Three reconstructs the social, cultural, and political context of his family (to 1769). Chapter Four traces his life with the Company's army (1769–84). Some readers less familiar with India may wish to begin with Chapters Three and Four and then return to read Chapter Two: Dean Mahomed's *Travels*.

## Dean Mahomed's Travels in Europe (1784–1851)

Following the abrupt and disgraceful end of his patron Baker's military career in 1784, Dean Mahomed began yet a more distant journey, as an immigrant to the world of colonial Ireland. Chapter Five of this volume examines the historical evidence that may enable us to understand what it was to be an Indian living in Cork at the end of the eighteenth century. Sufficient attention has not yet been paid to Asian influences on Britain. Much of the culture that is today generally regarded as British stems from Indian origins. Dean Mahomed was only one of thousands of Asians living in Britain who formed a counter-flow to the mainstream of colonialism. As he settled in Cork, Dean Mahomed determined to write the account of his travels. He published his book, *Travels,* in 1794, in the form of a series of letters to a fictive friend. Readers of his *Travels* can note the ways in which he appropriated the English genre of the eighteenth century travel narrative—the only Indian to do so. Yet, his particular reactions to the peoples and environments of India distinguished him from those of his European contemporaries. The ways and extent to which his book both imitated and also stood distinct from the works of European authors remains worthy of study; I present some comparisons and contrasts between his account and those of contemporary European writers. Dean Mahomed's accurate command of detail so long after the events he described must strike us as remarkable. I explore the reasons why he wrote and the influences on his writing. I also consider the reasons why he, and his growing Anglo-Irish-Indian family, left Ireland and emigrated to London around 1807.

Early nineteenth-century London offered both opportunities and also constraints to Dean Mahomed and his family. Chapter Six examines his life in London. What resources could they call upon to make their way in this world? Dean Mahomed worked for a time as a medical practitioner in the fashionable mansion of a rich Scottish veteran of the Company. Then, he opened a coffee house and restaurant, serving Indian cuisine and ambience to the British elite. After a few years in the metropolis, however, Dean Mahomed exhausted his financial capital. Searching around for yet another career, he struck upon a profession that would bring him his greatest success.

Emigrating yet again at age fifty-five, Dean Mahomed moved to the resort town of Brighton on England's south coast. There, by 1814, he created a market for his medical arts as a therapeutic masseur. Through skilful publicity and the patronage of the British elite, including the Royal Family, he rose high in this professional world. Dean Mahomed's later autobiographical writings both asserted and revised his background as an Indian and an immigrant. He negotiated his place in society with the British public and his rivals. His words are available to us through his extensive newspaper advertisements, architectural and medical expressions, and his second autobiographical work, all presented in Chapter Seven. There we also examine the attitudes of his British contemporaries toward him.

As the Victorian era proceeded, his ability to retain control over his life, and his role in British society, diminished. In his final years, Dean Mahomed reverted to the margins of society. We can explore the reasons for his decline, due to changes both in his own condition and in British society itself. As we examine in Chapter Eight, his legacies remain contested down to the present.

## Notes

1. Mary Louise Pratt, *Imperial Eyes* (London, 1992), p. 4.
2. This was the number of active .covenanted British officials. Compiled from East India Company, *List* (1771).
3. All references to Dean Mahomed's *Travels* will consist of the Roman numeral of the Letter in parenthesis.

Chapter Two

# Republication of
# *The Travels of Dean Mahomet*

*The Travels of Dean Mahomet, A Native of Patna in Bengal, Through Several Parts of India, While in the Service of The Honorable The East India Company Written by Himself, In a Series of Letters to a Friend*
Cork: Printed by J. Connor,
At the Circulating Library, No. 17, Corner of Castle-street,
opposite the Square
1794
In two volumes
[Subscribers Names Omitted]

Dedication

To William A. Bailie, Esq., Colonel in the Service of
*The Honourable the East India Company*

Sir,

*Your distinguished character both in public and private life, is a powerful incitement for soliciting your patronage; and your condescension in permitting me to honour my humble production with your name, claims my best acknowledgements.*

*Though praise is a kind of tribute due to shining merit and abilities; yet, Sir, even envy must confess, that your well-earned laurels, the meed of military virtues, obtained in the service of the Honourable the East India Company, have been too eminently conspicuous, to receive any additional lustre from the language of Encomium.*

*Your respectable name prefixed to these pages, cannot fail to shield them with the armour of security, as the judicious must be highly gratified with the peculiar propriety of inscribing them to a Gentleman so perfectly conversant with scenes, which I have attempted to describe.*

*Allow me to request, Sir, your indulgence for any inaccuracies of style, or other imperfections, that may arrest your judgment in glancing over this Work, as my situation in life, and want of the literary attainments, that refine and polish the European, preclude me from embellishing it, with that elegance of expression, and those fine touches of the imagination, which always animate the performance of cultivated genius.*

*However, Sir, I have endeavoured, at least, to please; and the sincerity of my intention, will, I trust, in some degree, make even an inadequate compensation for my deficiency in learning and refinement. I have the Honor to remain.*

Sir, with the most profound veneration, your much obliged, and devoted, humble servant, Dean Mahomet, *Cork, South-Mall,* Jan. 15, 1794.

## Contents of Volume the First

some tents and marquees: carry off the Author in a palanquin which is described: rob him: some resolve to take his life, others against it, obtain his freedom: he returns to the camp: some of the villagers taken and punished: jackals infest the camp: the army marches towards Chrimnasa: the natives venerable regard for their wells accounted for.

*Letter VII.*

The Army arrive at Chrimnasa, and after a few months stay there, receive orders to march to Monghere [Monghyr]: description of a Faquir and hermitage near it: arrival there: fort and barracks described: ingenuity and manufactures of the inhabitants.

*Letter VIII.*

Description of the seats and villages round Monghere: character of Mr Bateman: account of the monument on the hill Peepaharea [Pirpahar]: imprudence of a Lieut. of the artillery: his untimely fate: the army receive orders to proceed to Calcutta: seven baths or wells near Sitakund described: the army halt at Bohogolpore [Bhagalpur]: account of it's situation, military strength, and manufactures: of Captain Brook [Brooke]: the Pahareas, and the punishment inflicted on them.

*Letter IX.*

March continued from Bohogolpore towards Calcutta: reach Rajamoul [Rajmahal]: ferocity of the Pahareas: skirmish with them, in which two hundred are taken prisoners and punished: encamp at Gouagochi [Godagarhi]: it's pleasant situation: arrive at Dumdumma [Dumdum]: grand review there: Governor Cottier [Cartier] is entertained by the Officers &c.: scene of their convivial meeting.

*Letter X.*

Arrival at Calcutta: description of it: of the old fort, and Fort William: of the docks, hospital, villas, gardens, and canal outside the town.

*Letter XI.*

Departure from Calcutta: arrival at Barahampore [Baharampur]: situation of the cantonments there: of Muxadabad [Murshidabad]: it's suburbs; Nabob's Palace: his grand procession to the mazide or temple, with all his retinue.

*Letter XII.*

Description of the different baptisms and circumcision of a Mahometan child, which the Author attended.

*Letter XIII.*

Account of the Mahometan ceremony of marriage.

*Letter XIV.*

Of the temperance of the Mahometans: their resignation at the approach of death: account of their funerals: sketch of their religion.

*Letter XV.*

Of the dancing girls: their manners and dress: remarkable instance of the generosity of one.

*Letter XVI.*

March from Barahampore to Denapore: of the brigades on the Bengal establishment: of the Seapoys: their military dress: explanation of Persian and Indian terms.

*Letter XVII.*

March from Denapore to Belgram [Bilgram]: the army halt at Benaras: description of it: of the beautiful country about it: description of the city continued: it's buildings, gauts or slips: sarai: pagodas: tanks: manufactures; Raja's palace.

*Letter XVIII.*

Of the religion of the Hindoos: their food, and manner of burying their dead.

*Letter XIX.*

March continued towards Belgram: description of the country: of the fort and palace of Alahabad [Allahabad]: climate, soil, flowers, fruits, &c.

*Letter XX.*

The army arrive at Belgram: dispute between the Nabob Aspadoulah [Asaf al-Daula] and the Fouzdars Maboub and Cossi-bussant [Faujdars Mahbub Ali Khan and Khwaja Basant Ali Khan]: Maboub invites our Officers to dine and previously poisons the provisions intended for them: his intentions disclosed: a detachment is sent from Gen. Stibbert to assist the Nabob against Maboub and his confederate: the former is taken, the latter escaped with his vanquished forces: Capt. Gravely receives a wound, of which he dies at Belgram, where he is interred.

Reproduction of the letters of Vol. I

*Letter I*

Dear Sir,

Since my arrival in this country, I find you have been very anxious to be made acquainted with the early part of my Life, and the History of my Travels: I shall be happy to gratify you; and must ingenuously confess, when I first came to Ireland, I found the face of every thing about me so contrasted to those *striking scenes* in India, which we are wont to survey with a kind of sublime delight, that I felt some timid inclination, even in the consciousness of incapacity, to describe the manners of my countrymen, who, I am proud to think, have still more of the innocence of our ancestors, than some of the boasting philosophers of Europe.

Though I acknowledge myself incapable of doing justice to the merits of men, whose happy manners are worthy the imitation of civilized nations, yet, you will do me the justice to believe, that the gratification of your wishes, is the *principal* incitement that engages me to undertake a work of this nature: the earnest entreaties of some friends, and the liberal encouragement of others, to whom I express my acknowledgements, I allow, are *secondary* motives.

The people of India, in general, are peculiarly favoured by Providence in the possession of all that can cheer the mind and allure the eye, and tho' the situation of Eden is only traced in the Poet's creative fancy, the traveller beholds with admiration the face of this delightful country, on which he discovers tracts that resemble those so finely drawn by the animated pencil of Milton. You will here behold the generous soil crowned with various plenty; the garden beautifully diversified with the gayest flowers diffusing their fragrance on the bosom of the air; and the very bowels of the earth enriched with inestimable mines of gold and diamonds.

Possessed of all that is enviable in life, we are still more happy in the exercise of benevolence and goodwill to each other, devoid of every species of fraud or low cunning. In our convivial enjoyments, we are never without our neighbours; as it is usual for an individual, when he gives an entertainment, to invite all those of his own

profession to partake of it. That profligacy of manners too conspicuous in other parts of the world, meets here with public indignation, and our women, though not so accomplished as those of
Europe, are still very engaging for many virtues that exalt the sex.

As I have now given you a sketch of the manners of my country;
I shall proceed to give you some account of myself.

I was born in the year 1759, in Patna, a famous city on the
north [south] side of the Ganges, about 400 miles from Calcutta,
the capital of Bengal and seat of the English Government in that
country. I was too young when my father died, to learn any great
account of his family; all I have been able to know respecting him,
is, that he was descended from the same race as the Nabobs of
Moorshadabad [Murshidabad]. He was appointed Subadar in a
battalion of Seapoys commanded by Captain Adams, a company
of which under his command was quartered at a small district not
many miles from Patna, called Tarchpoor [Tajpur], an inconsiderable fort, built on the side of a little river that takes its rise a
few miles up the country. Here he was stationed in order to keep
this fort.

In the year 1769, a great dearth overspread the country about
Tarchpoor, where the Rajas Boudmal [Budhmal], and his brother
Corexin [Kora Singh] resided, which they took an advantage of
by pretending it was impossible for them to remit the stipulated
supplies to the Raja Sataproy [Shitab Rai], who finding himself
disappointed in his expectations, sent some of his people to compel
them to pay: but the others retired within their forts, determined
on making an obstinate defence. My father having received others
to lead out his men to the scene of dispute, which lay about twelve
miles from the fort he was quartered in, marched accordingly, and
soon after his arrival at Taharah [Telarha], took the Raja Boudmal
prisoner, and sent him under a strong guard to Patna, where he
was obliged to account for his conduct. My father remained in
the field, giving the enemy some striking proofs of the courage of
their adversary; which drove them to such measures, that they
strengthened their posts and redoubled their attacks with such
ardour, that many of our men fell, and my lamented father among
the rest; but not till he had entirely exhausted the forces of the
Raja, who, at length, submitted. The soldiers, animated by his
example, made Corexin a prisoner, and took possession of the
fort.

Thus have I been deprived of a gallant father, whose firmness and resolution was manifested in his military conduct on several occasions.

My brother, then about sixteen years old, and the only child my mother had besides me, was present at the engagement, and having returned home, made an application to Capt. Adams who, in gratitude to the memory of my father, whose services he failed not to represent to the Governor, speedily promoted him to his post. My mother and I suffered exceedingly by his sudden yet honourable fate in the field: for my Brother was then too young and thoughtless, to pay any great attention to our situation.

I was about eleven years old when deprived of my father, and though children are seldom possessed of much sensibility or reflection at such immature years, yet I recollect well no incident of my life ever made so deep an impression on my mind. Nothing could wear from my memory the remembrance of his tender regard. As he was a Mahometan, he was interred with all the pomp and ceremony usual on the occasion. I remained with my mother some time after, and acquired a little education at a school in Patna.

*Letter II*

Dear Sir,

In a few months after my father's fate, my mother and I went to Patna to reside: she lived pretty comfortable on some of the property she was entitled to in right of her husband: the rest of his substance, with his commission, came into the hands of my brother: our support was made better by the liberality of the Begum and Nabob, to whom my Father was related: the Begum was remarkably affectionate and attentive to us.

The Raja Sataproy had a very magnificent palace in the centre of the city of Patna, where he was accustomed to entertain many of the most distinguished European Gentlemen, with brilliant balls and costly suppers. My mother's house was not far from the Raja's palace; and the number of Officers passing by our door in their way thither, attracted my notice, and excited the ambition I already had of entering on a military life. With this notion, I was always on the watch, and impatiently waited for the moment of their passing by our door; when, one evening in particular, as they went along, I seized the happy opportunity, and followed them directly to the palace, at the outward gates of which there, are sentinels placed, to keep off the people and clear the passage for the Gentlemen; I however got admittance, on account of the respect the guards paid my father's family. The Gentlemen go to the palace between seven and eight o'clock in the evening, take tea and coffee, and frequently amuse themselves by forming a party to dance; when they find themselves warm, they retire to the palace yard, where there are marquees pitched for their reception; here they seat themselves in a circular form, under a semiana, a sort of canopy made of various coloured double muslin, supported by eight poles, and on the ground is spread a beautiful carpet; the Raja sits in the centre; the European Gentlemen on each side; and the Music in the front. The Raja, on this occasion, is attended by his Aid-du-Camps and Servants of rank. Dancing girls are now introduced, affording, at one time, extreme delight, by singing in concert with the Music, the softest and most lively airs; at another time, displaying such loose and fascinating attitudes in their various dances, as would warm the bosom of an Anchoret: while the servants of the Raja are employed in letting off the fireworks, displaying, in the most astonishing variety, the forms of birds, beasts, and other animals, and far surpassing any thing of the kind I ever beheld in Europe: and to give additional brilliancy to the splendour of the scene, lighted branches blaze around, and exhibit one general illumination. Extremely pleased with such various entertainment, the Gentlemen sit down to an elegant supper, prepared with the utmost skill, by an Officer of the Raja, whose sole employ is to provide the most delicious viands on such an occasion: ice-cream, fowl of all kinds, and the finest fruit in the world, compose but a part of the repast to which the guests are invited. The Raja was very happy with his convivial friends; and though his religion forbids him to touch many things handled by persons of a different profession, yet he accepted a little fruit from them; supper was over about twelve o'clock, and the company retired, the Raja to his palace, and the Officers to their quarters.

I was highly pleased with the appearance of the military Gentlemen, among whom I first beheld Mr Baker, who particularly drew my attention. I followed him without any restraint through every part of the palace and tents, and remained a spectator of the entire scene of pleasure, till the company broke up; and then returned home to my mother, who felt some anxiety in my absence. When I described the gaiety and splendour I beheld at the entertainment, she seemed very much dissatisfied, and expressed, from maternal tenderness, her apprehensions of losing me.

Nothing could exceed my ambition of leading a soldier's life: the notion of carrying arms, and living in a camp, could not be easily removed: my fond mother's entreaties were of no avail: I grew anxious for the moment that would bring the military Officers by our door. Whenever I perceived their route, I instantly followed them; sometimes to the Raja's palace, where I had free access; and sometimes to a fine tennis court, generally frequented by them in the evenings, which was built by Col. Champion, at the back of his house, in a large open square, called Mersevil-lekeebaug [Mir Afzal ka Bagh]: here, among other Gentlemen, I one day, discovered Mr Baker, and often passed by him, in order to attract his attention: he, at last, took particular notice of me, observing that I surveyed him with a kind of secret satisfaction; and in a very friendly manner, asked me how I would like living with the Europeans: this unexpected encouragement, as it flattered my hopes beyond expression, occasioned a very sudden reply: I therefore told him with eager joy, how happy he could make me, by taking me with him. He seemed very much pleased with me, and assuring me of his future kindness, hoped I would merit it. Major Herd [Heard] was in company with him at the same time: and both these Gentlemen appeared with distinguished eclat in the first assemblies in India. I was decently clad in the dress worn by children of my age: and though my mother was materially affected in her circumstances, by the precipitate death of my father, she had still the means left of living in a comfortable manner, and providing both for her own wants and mine.

### Letter III

Dear Sir,

My mother observing some alteration in my conduct, since I first saw Mr Baker, naturally supposed that I was meditating a separation from her. She knew I spoke to him; and apprehensive that I would go with him, she did everything in her power to frustrate my intentions. Notwithstanding all her vigilance, I found means to join my new master, with whom I went early the next morning to Bankeepore [Bankipur], leaving my mother to lament my departure. As Bankeepore is but a few miles from Patna, we shortly arrived there, that morning. It is a wide plain, near the banks of the Ganges, on which we encamped in the year of 1769. It commands a most beautiful prospect of the surrounding country. Our camp consisted of four regiments of Seapoys, one of Europeans, two companies of Cavalry, and one of European Artillery: the Commander in Chief was Col. Leslie; and next to him in military rank was Major Morrison; Capt. Lundick [Landeg] had the direction of the Cavalry; and Capt. Duff of the Artillery. The camp extended in two direct lines, at Patna side, along the river, on the banks of which, for the convenience of water, were built the Europeans' bangaloes: at one extremity of the line, was Col. Leslie's; at the other, Major Morrison's. The second line was drawn in a parallel direction with the first, at a about a quarter of a mile from the river; the front was the residence of the Officers; the rere a barrack for the soldiers; and the intermediate space was left open for the purpose of exercising the men, a duty which was, every day, performed with punctuality. Near a mile farther off, was the Seapoys' chaumnies; and a short space from them, the horse barrack. Thus was the situation of the camp at Bankeepore.

The Officers' bangaloes were constructed on a plan peculiar to the taste of the natives. They were quite square; the sides were made of mats, and the roof, which was supported by pillars, thatched with bamboes and straw, much after the manner of the farmer's houses in this country [Ireland]: their entrance was wide, and opened to a spacious hall that contained on each wing, the servants' apartments, inside which, were the gentlemen's dining-rooms and bed-chambers, with large frames in the partitions, and purdoes, that answered the same end as our doors and windows fastened to those frames.

Purdoes are a contrivance made of coarse muslin, ornamented with fancy stripes and variegated colours, and so well quilted that they render the coolest situations agreeably warm: they are let up and down occasionally, to invite the refreshing breeze, or repel the sickly sunbeam. Inside is a kind of screen called cheeque, made of bamboes as small as wire, and interwoven in a curious manner, with various coloured thread, that keeps them together: it is let up and down like the purdoe, when occasion requires, and, admirable to conceive! precludes the prying eye outside from piercing through it, though it kindly permits the happy person within to gaze on every passing object.

The Colonel and Major had larger and more commodious bangaloes, than the other Officers, with adjacent outhouses, and stables. On the left angle, fronting the road, was the Colonel's guardhouse, and stood diametrically opposite to his bangaloe; between which and those of the Officers, is situate an ever-verdant grove inclosed with a brick wall: overshadowed by the spreading trees inside, a few grand edifices built by the Nabobs, made a fine appearance; among which was the Bank of Messieurs Herbert and Halambury [Hollingberry], the dwelling of Mr Barry [Berrie], Contract Agent, and a powder magazine.

The barrack of the European soldiers, was a range of apartments, whose partitions were made of mats and bamboes, and roofs thatched with straw. The chaumnies of the Seapoys were on the same plan; and such of them as had families, built dwellings near the chaumnies.

There are but few public buildings at Bankeepore: the only remarkable one that appeared in its environs, was the house of Mr Goolden, who lived about a mile from the camp: it was a fine spacious building, finished in the English style; and as it stood on a rising ground, it seemed to rear its dome in stately pride, over the aromatic plains and spicy groves that adorned the landscape below, commanding an extensive prospect of all the fertile vales along the winding Ganges flowery banks. The happy possessor of this finely situated mansion, was in high esteem among the Officers, for his politeness and hospitality.

At some distance from Mr Goolden's, lived Mr Rumble [Rumbold], a Gentleman who received the Contracts of the Company, for the supply of Boats and other small craft. Mr Baker had the utmost esteem for this Gentleman, for his many good qualities, and frequently visited him. For the honour of my country, I cannot help observing here, that no people on earth can be more attentive or respectful to the European Ladies residing among them, than the natives of all descriptions in India.

In gratitude to the revered memory of the best of characters, I am obliged to acknowledge that I never found myself so happy as with Mr Baker: insensible of the authority of a superior, I experience the indulgence of a friend; and the want of a tender parent was entirely forgotten in the humanity and affection of a benevolent stranger.

I remember to have seen numbers perish by famine this year: the excessive heat of the climate, and want of rain, dried up the land; and all the fruits of the earth decayed without moisture.

Numbers of people have dropped down in the streets and highways: none fared so well as those whose plantations were watered by wells. The proprietors, some of whom were Nabobs, and other European Officers, distributed as much rice and other food as they could possibly spare, among the crowds that thronged into their court-yards and houses: but the poor creatures, quite spent and unable to bear it, fell down and expired in their presence: some endeavoured to crawl out and perished in the open air. Little did the treasures of their country avail them on this occasion: a small portion of rice, timely administered to their wants, would have been of more real importance than their mines of gold and diamonds.

*Letter IV*

Dear Sir,

When six or seven months had elapsed from the time I was first received by Mr Baker, my mother unhappy at the idea of parting with me, and resigning her child to the care of a European, came to him, requesting, in the language of supplication, that I might be given up to her: moved by her entreaties, he had me brought before her, at the same time observing, that it was so remote from his intentions to keep me from her, he was perfectly reconciled to part with me, were it my inclination. I was extremely affected at her presence; yet my deep sense of gratitude to a sincere friend conquered my duty to an affectionate parent, and made me determine in favour of the former: I would not go, I told her—I would stay in the camp; her disappointment smote my soul—she stood silent—yet I could perceive some tears succeed each other, stealing down her cheeks—my heart was wrung at length, seeing my resolution fixed as fate, she dragged herself away, and returned home in a state of mind beyond my power to describe. Mr Baker was much affected, and with his brother Officers, endeavoured to find amusement for me. I was taken out, every morning, to see the different military evolutions of the men in the field, and on such occasions, I was clad myself in suitable regimentals. Capt. Gravely in particular, was very fond of me, and never passed by without calling to know how I was. This kind attention gradually dispelled the gloom which, in some pensive moments, hung over my mind since the last tender interview. My poor mother under all the affliction of parental anxiety, and trembling hope for my return, sent my brother as an advocate for her to Mr Baker, to whom he offered four hundred rupees, conceiving it would be a means of inducing him to send me back: but Mr Baker had a soul superior to such sordid purposes, and far from accepting them, he gave me such a sum to bestow my mother. Having given his people the necessary directions to conduct me to her, he provided for me his own palankeen, on which I was borne by his domestics.

When I arrived at my mother's, I offered her the four hundred rupees given me by my disinterested friend to present to her; but could not, with all my persuasion, prevail on her to receive them, until I told her she should never see me again, if she refused this generous donation. Thus, by working on her fears, I, at length, gained my point, and assured her that I would embrace every opportunity of coming to see her: after taking my leave of her, I returned on the palankeen to the camp.

We lay in Bankeepore about six months, when we received orders from Col. Leslie to march to Denapore [Denapur], where we arrived in the year of 1770, and found the remaining companies of the Europeans and Seapoys, that were quartered there for some time before. Our camp here, consisted of eight regiments; two of Europeans, and six of Seapoys. Denapore is eight miles from Bankeepore, and has nothing to recommend it but a small mud fort, on which some cannon are planted, fronting the water. Inside the fort is a very fine barrack, perhaps the first in India; and when it was ready to receive the number of men destined to serve in that quarter, we marched into it. 'Tis a fine square building, made entirely of brick, on the margin of the Ganges, and covers both sides of the road; on the east side, opposite the river, were the Captain's apartments, consisting of two bed chambers and a dining room, with convenient out-offices, stables, and kitchen, at the back of the barrack: a little distance farther out on the line, was the General's residence, an elegant and stately building, commanding a full view of the country many miles round. It was finished in the greatest style, and furnished in a superb manner: the ascent to it was by several flights of marble steps, and the servants about it were very numerous. In the north angle, on the same line, was the hospital, at a convenient distance from the barrack. In the other angles were planted some cannon, which were regularly discharged every morning and evening, as the flag was hoist up or pulled down. At one end of the fourth side, was the Artillery barrack; at the other, their stores: on the west, lay the companies of the brigade; on the north, the Doctors and inferior Officers had their apartments. About a mile thence, were the chaumnies of the Seapoys.

No situation in the world could be more delightful than that of the General's mansion; at the front and back of which, were gravel walks, where the soldiers and servants, at leisure hours, were accustomed to take recreation. A mud battery is drawn round the whole; and from north to south is a public road for travellers, which is intersected by another from east to west. Country seats and villas were dispersed through the neighbouring country, which was highly cultivated with fertile plantations and beautiful gardens. At one end of the avenue leading to the barrack, stood the markets or bazars of the Europeans; at the other, near their chaumnies, were those of the natives. Colonels Morgan, Goddard, and Tottingham, commanded here this year; and the army was mostly employed in going through the different manoeuvres in the field, as there happened no disturbances of any consequence in the country, that interfered with this duty. I called now and then to see my mother, who, at last, became more reconciled to my absence; and received some visits from my brother while I was in camp.

*Letter V*

Dear Sir,

I felt great satisfaction in having procured the esteem of my friend, and the other Officers, and acquired the military exercise, to which I was very attentive. We lay about eight months in

Denapore, when Col. Morgan having received intelligence of the depredations committed by some of the Morattoes [Marathas], gave orders to the army to make the necessary preparations for marching to Chrimnasa [Karamnasa], at a moment's warning. The baggage was immediately drawn out, and the cattle tackled with the utmost expedition. The Quarter Masters provided every necessary accommodation for the march: some of the stores they sent before them by water; the rest was drawn in hackeries and wagons, by bullocks. Mr Baker, who was also Quarter Master, and his brother Officers in the same line, had each a company of Seapoys, as a piquet guard along the road, and about seven hundred attendants, who were occasionally employed, as the army moved their camp, in pitching and striking the tents, composed of the lowest order of the people residing in the country, and forming many distinct tribes, according to their various occupations. We had a certain number of these men appointed to attend the garrison, which was usually augmented on a march, and distinguished under the various appellations of Lascars, Cooleys, Besties, and Charwalleys. They set out with us, a day before the main body of the army, accompanied by several classes of tradesmen, such as shoe-makers, carpenters, smiths, sail-makers, and others capable of supplying the camp; and were ranged into four departments, in order to perform the laborious business of the expedition without confusion. To each department was assigned it's respective duty: the employment of the Lascars, who wore mostly a blue jacket, turban, sash, and trousers, was to pitch and strike the tents and marquees; load and unload the elephants, camels, bullocks, waggons &c. The Cooleys were divided into two distinct bodies for different purposes; to carry burthens, and to open and clear the roads through the country, for the free passage of the army and baggage: The Besties were appointed to supply the men and cattle with water: and the Charwalleys, who are the meanest class of all, were employed to clean the apartments, and do other servile offices. Thus equipped, we marched in regular order from Denapore, early in the morning, in the month of February and the year of 1771. We enjoyed a pleasant cool breeze the entire day; while the trees, ever blooming and overshadowing the road, afforded a friendly shelter and an agreeable view along the country. The road was broad and smooth, and in places contiguous to it, we found several refreshing wells to allay the thirst of the weary traveller. In a few hours we reached Fulwherea [Phulwari], a spacious plain adapted for our purpose, where the Quarter Masters ordered out the Lascars to pitch the tents and marquees on the lines formed by them. Our camp, which made a grand military appearance, extended two miles in length: it was ranged into nine separate divisions, composed of two battalions of Europeans, six regiments of Seapoys, and one company of European Artillery. On the front line, the standards of the different regiments were flying: it consisted of a number of small tents called beltons [bell-tents], where they kept their fire arms: the central ones belonged to the Europeans; near them, were those of the Artillery; and on each wing, the Seapoys. The several corps were encamped behind their respective beltons, close to which, were first the tents of the privates; about twenty feet from their situation, were the larger and more commodious ones of the Ensigns and Lieutenants; next to them the Captains' marquees; a little farther back, the Major's; at some distance behind the two battalions, and in a middle direction between them, was the Colonel's, which lay diametrically opposite the main guard, situate outside the front line in the centre: a small space from the Colonels' marquees was the stop line, where the Quarter Masters, Adjutants, Doctors and Surgeons, were lodged: and between the stop line and bazars, was the line for the cattle. Every company of European privates occupied six tents and one belton: an Ensign, Lieutenant, and Captain, each a tent: such Officers as had jenanas or wives, erected tomboos, a kind of Indian marquees, for them, at their own expense. A Major had two marquees, one store, one guard tent, and one belton; a Colonel, three marquees, two store, two guard tents, and one belton; the Quarter Masters, Adjutants, Doctors and Surgeons, had each one marquee. On account of their peculiar duty in furnishing the camp, the Quarter Masters had, besides their own, other tents for their Serjeants, Artificers, and stores. The Seapoys lay behind their beltons, in the same position as the Europeans, and their Officers, according to rank, were accommodated much in the same manner. The hospital was in a pleasant grove not remote from the camp, about half a mile from which were the magazine and other stores for ammunition and military accoutrements; and on an eminence, at some distance, over the wide plain, where we encamped, arose in military grandeur, the superb marquees of the general Officers. In the rere of the entire scene, were the bazars or markets, belonging to the different regiments, on a direct line with each, and distinguished from one another, by various flags and streamers that wantoned in the breeze. Our camp, notwithstanding its extent, number of men, equipage, and arrangements, was completely formed in the course of the evening we arrived at Fulwherea, which is about twelve miles from Denapore.

*Letter VI*

Dear Sir,

We had scarcely been one night at Fulwherea, when some straggling villagers of the neighbouring country, stole unperceived into our camp, and plundered our tents and marquees, which they stripped of every thing valuable belonging to Officers and privates. It happened, at the same time, that they entered a store tent, next to Mr Baker's marquee, where I lay on a palankeen, a kind of travelling canopy-bed, resembling a camp bed, the upper part was arched over with curved bamboo, and embellished with rich furniture, the top was hung with beautiful tassels and adorned with gay trappings; and the sides, head, and foot were decorated with valuable silver ornaments. In short, it was elegantly finished, and worth, at least six hundred rupees; for which reason, such vehicles are seldom kept but by people of condition. Every palankeen is attended by eight servants, four of whom, alternately, carry it, much in the same manner as our sedan chairs are carried in this country [Ireland]. But to return—the villagers having entered the store-tent above mentioned, bore me suddenly away to a field about half a mile from the camp, on the conveyance I have just described to you, which they soon disrobed of its decorations, and rifled me of what money I had in my pocket, and every garment on my body, except a thin pair of trousers. So cruel were the merciless savages, that some were forming the barbarous resolutions of taking away my life, lest my escape would lead to a discovery of them; while others less inhuman, opposed the measure, by observing I was too young to injure them, and prevailed on their companions to let me go. I reached the camp with winged feet, and went directly to Mr Baker, who was much alarmed when he heard of my dangerous situation, but more astonished at my arrival; and when I related by what means my life was spared, and liberty obtained, he admired such humanity in a savage breast.

A few of those ravagers, who loitered behind the rest, were first detected by the guard, pursued, and taken: the track of others was, by this clew, discovered; many of whom were apprehended, and received the punishment due to their crimes, for such wanton depredations. They were flogged through the camp, and their ears and noses cut off, as a shameful example to their lawless confederates. Their rapacity occasioned us to delay longer at Fulwherea, than we intended. We had scarcely suppressed those licentious barbarians, when our quiet was again disturbed by the nocturnal invasion of the jackals that infest this country, ferocious animals not unlike the European fox; they flocked into our camp in the silent midnight hour, carried off a great part of the poultry, and such young children as they could come at. It was in vain to pursue them; we were obliged to endure our losses with patience.

Having dispatched the proper people to supply the markets, we left Fulwherea early on the eighth morning after our arrival, and proceeded in our march towards Chrimnasa, which lay about ninety miles farther off. We reached Turwherea, on the first day's march, where we had a river to cross, which retarded us three days, on account of our numbers. As the weather was very warm, we advanced slowly, and found it exceedingly pleasant to travel along the roads shaded with the spreading branches of fruit-bearing trees, bending under their luscious burthens of bananas, mangoes, and tamarinds. Beneath the trees, were many cool springs and wells of the finest water in the universe, with which the whole country of Indostan abounds: a striking instance of the wisdom of Providence, that tempers 'the bleak wind to the shorn lamb,' and the scorching heat of the torrid zone to the way-worn traveller.

The former natives of this part of the world, whose purity of manners is still perpetuated by several tribes of their posterity, having foreseen the absolute necessity of such refreshment, and that in the region they inhabited, none could be more seasonable than founts of water for the use of succeeding generations, contrived those inexhaustible sources of relief in situations most frequented; and to prevent any thoughtless vagrant from polluting them, took care to inspire the people with a sacred piety in favour of their wells, and a religious dread of disturbing them. For this reason, they remain pure and undefiled, through every age, and are held in the most profound veneration. Wherever we found them, on the march, our Besties stopped to afford the men some time to recruit themselves, and take in a fresh supply of water, which was carried by bullocks, in leathern hanpacallies or bags made of dried hides, some of which were borne by the Besties on their shoulders.

*Letter VII*

Dear Sir,

In about fifteen days after we left Fulwherea, we arrived at Chrimnasa, and encamped on the banks of the Ganges: the Morattoes fled on our arrival. Chrimnasa is an open plain, near which is a small river that flows into the Ganges. We remained here in a state of tranquility, occasionally enjoying all the rural pleasures of the delightful country around us. After a stay of a few months, we received orders from Colonels Morgan and Goddard, to march hence to Monghere [Monghyr]; and Messieurs Baker, Scott, Besnard and the Artillery Quarter Master, set out before the army, between one and two o'clock in the morning, with the baggage and military stores, in the middle of the year 1771. We continued on the march near a month, and when we came within thirty miles of Monghere, a small antique house, built on a rock in the middle of an island, in the Ganges, attracted our notice: we halted towards the close of the evening, at some distance from it: the next day, Mr Baker, Mr Besnard, and the other Gentlemen, made a hunting match: I accompanied them: and about noon, after the diversion was over, we turned our horses towards the water side, and taking a nearer view of this solitary little mansion, resolved on crossing the river.

We gave our horses in charge to the sahies or servants, who have always the care of them, and passed over to the island in one of the fishing boats that ply here. When we advanced towards the hermitage, which, as an object of curiosity, is much frequented by travellers, the Faquir or Hermit, who held his residence here for many years, came out to meet us: he wore a long robe of saffron colour muslin down to his ancles, with long loose sleeves, and on his head a small mitre of white muslin, his appearance was venerable from a beard that descended to his breast; and though the hand of time conferred some snowy honours on his head, that negligently flowed down his shoulders a considerable length, yet in his countenance you might read, that health and cheerfulness were his companions: he approached us with a look of inconceivable complacency tempered with an apparent serenity of mind, and assured us that whatever his little habitation could afford, he was ready to supply us with. While he was thus speaking, he seemed to turn his thoughts a little higher; for with eyes now and then raised towards Heaven, he continued to count a long bead that was suspended from his wrist; and he had another girt about his waist. We went with him into his dwelling, which was one of the neatest I have ever seen; it was quite square, and measured from one angle to the other, not more than five yards: it rose to a great height, like a steeple, and the top was flat, encompassed with battlements, to which he sometimes ascended by a long ladder. At certain hours in the day, he stretched in a listless manner on the skin of some wild animal, not unlike a lion's, enjoying the pleasure of reading some favourite author. In one corner of the house, he kept a continual fire, made on a small space between three bricks, on which he dressed his food that consisted mostly of rice, and the fruits of his garden; but whatever was intended for his guests, was laid on a larger fire outside the door. When we spent a little time in observing every thing curious inside his residence, he presented us some mangoes and other agreeable fruit, which we accepted; and parted our kind host, having made him some small acknowledgment for his friendly reception, and passed encomiums on the neatness of his abode and the rural beauty of his garden.

We passed over to the continent in a boat, belonging to the Faquir, that conveyed provisions from the island to the people passing up and down the river, who left him in return such commodities as he most wanted; and joined the army, which arrived early the following day at Monghere.

The European brigade marched into a fine spacious barrack: and the Seapoys into the chaumnies inside the fort, which is near two miles in circumference, and built on the Ganges in a square form, with the sides and front rising out of the water, and overlooking all the country seats along the coast.

The Officers' apartments in the front, were laid out with the greatest elegance; the soldiers', quite compact; and nothing could be handsome than the exterior appearance of the building, which was of glittering hewn stone. The old palace of Cossim Alli Cawn [Mir Kasim Ali Khan], inside the ramparts, still uninjured by the waste of time, was put in order for the residence of Colonel Grant. The entrance into the fort was by four wide gates, constructed in a masterly manner; one at each side, opening into the barrack yard. It was originally built by some of the Nabobs; but since it came into the possession of the Company, it has served as a proper place for our cantonments. There are no other structures of any figure here. About a mile hence is a long row of low, obscure huts (such as the common natives inhabit in several parts of India) occupied by a class of people who prepare raw silk; and, at a little distance from them, reside the manufacturers. The people, in general, here, are remarkably ingenious, at making all kinds of kitchen furniture, which they carry to such an extent, as to be enabled to supply the markets in the most opulent cities around them; and are in such esteem, that they even send for them from Calcutta, and other parts of Bengal. There is a description of inhabitants in this country, who supply the markets, and have continued in this employment through many succeeding generations, always dwelling in one place; and others who follow the army under the denomination of bazars.

*Letter VIII*

Dear Sir,
     There are some very fine seats and villas round Monghere, built by European Gentlemen in the Company's service, who retire to the country in the warm months of the year: among others, is the house of Mr Grove, an elegant building finished in the English style, and standing in the centre of every rural improvement; a mile hence is the residence of Mr Bateman, a very handsome structure, where we spent a few pleasant days in the most polite circles: amid such scenes, the riches and luxury of the East, are displayed with fascinating charms. Our host was that elevated kind of character, in which public and private virtues were happily blended; he united the Statesman with the private Gentleman; the deep Politician with the social Companion; and though of the mildest manners, he was brave in an eminent degree having led

the way to victory in many campaigns. Twelve miles from Monghere, is a famous monument erected on a hill called Peepaharea [Pirpahar], which the love of antiquity induced us to visit: it is a square building, with an arch of hewn stone rising over a marble slab, supported by small round pillars of the same, without any inscription: and what is very remarkable, a large tiger, seemingly divested of the ferocity of his nature, comes from his den at the foot of the hill, every Monday and Wednesday, to this very monument, without molesting any person he meets on the way, (even children are not afraid to approach him) and sweeps with his tail, the dust from the lower part of the tomb, in which, it is supposed, are enshrined the remains of some pious character, who had been there interred at a remote period of time. The people have a profound veneration for it, which has not been a little increased by the sudden and untimely fate of a Lieutenant of Artillery, who came hither to indulge an idle curiosity, and ridicule those who paid such respect to the memory of their supposed holy man, who had been deposited here. He imputed their zeal to the force of prejudice and superstition, and turned it into such contempt, that he made water on the very tomb that was by them held sacred: but shortly after, as if he had been arrested by some invisible hand, for his presumption, having rode but a few paces from the tomb, he was thrown from his horse to the ground, where he lay some time speechless; and being conveyed to Monghere on a litter, soon after his arrival expired. Here is an awful lesson to those who, through a narrowness of judgment and confined speculation, are too apt to profane the piety of their fellow-creatures, merely for a difference in their modes of worship. At a little distance from Peepaharea was the bangaloe of Gen. Barker, constructed by him on the most elegant plan. Here he retired to spend some part of the summer, and entertain his friends: it was resorted by the distinguished Officers of his corps, and particularly by Colonels Grant, Morgan, Goddard, Tottingham, and Majors Morrison and Pearce, of the Artillery. At other times, he resided in a stately edifice in the fort, newly built, with exquisite taste and grandeur. Having received orders from Colonel Grant, to proceed to Calcutta, we made the necessary preparations for marching, and set out from Monghere in the beginning of the year 1772. The first day, we reached Sitakund (where we halted three days) to collect our market people, &c. It is a small village, about twelve miles from Monghere, and in its environs are seven baths or wells, two of which are committed to the care of Bramins, who attend them, and will not suffer any person out of their order, to touch the waters, but such as come with a steadfast faith in their virtues (which they generally possess) to be relieved from various disorders by their application. The other five are common to all who travel this way. The two first are near each other, though very different in their qualities: the water of the one which is of a whitish colour, having an agreeable cool taste, while that of the adjacent well being of a darker hue, is continually boiling up. The people of the country make the most frequent use of them, and the Bramins, who dispatch their orders to all quarters round them in earthen jars filled at their hallowed founts, considerably benefit by their pious credulity. They even send it to the north of the Ganges; and it is held in holy veneration by the Hindoos in Calcutta, and the other districts of Bengal.

As we were advancing on our march, we met a number of Hindoo pilgrims proceeding on their journey to Sitakund, and reached Bohogolpore [Bhagalpur], in about fifteen days after we left Monghere. We encamped outside the town, which is, by no means, inconsiderable for its manufactures. It has a mud fort thrown round it, and contains a regiment of militia, to protect it's trade, consisting of a famous manufactory of fine napkins, table cloths, turbans and soucy, a kind of texture composed of silk and cotton, some of which is beautifully variegated with stripes, and some of a nankin colour, used mostly by the Ladies of the country for summer wear. Governor Pelham, who commanded here, entertained our Officers in a very splendid manner. We halted four or five days to refresh our army, and during the time, the Cooleys were employed to clear and level the rugged narrow road, from Bohogolpore through Skilligurree [Siclygully]. Before we set out, we perceived that Captain Brook [Brooke], a very active Officer, at the head of five companies of Seapoys, stationed in the different parts of the neighbouring country, had been, some time, engaged in the pursuit of the Pahareas, a savage clan that inhabit the mountains between Bohogolpore and Rajamoul [Rajmahal], and annoy the peaceable resident and unwary traveller: numbers, happily! were taken, through the indefatigable zeal of the above Gentlemen, and justly received exemplary punishment; some being severely whipped in a public manner; and others, who were found to be more daring and flagitious, suspended on a kind of gibbets, ignominiously exposed along the mountain's conspicuous brow, in order to strike terror into the hearts of their accomplices.

### Letter IX

Dear Sir,

Hence as we proceeded on our march, we beheld the lifeless bodies of these nefarious wretches elevated along the way for a considerable distance, about half a mile from each other; and having passed through the lofty arches or gateways of Sikilligurree and Tellicgurree [Tiliagarhi] planted with cannon, and erected by former Nabobs, as a kind of battery against the hostile invasions of those Mountaineers, we reached Rajamoul, where we remained a few days.

Our army being very numerous, the market people in the rere were attacked by another party of the Pahareas, who plundered them, and wounded many with their bows and arrows: the picquet guard closely pursued them, killed several, and apprehended thirty or forty, who were brought to the camp. Next morning, as our hotteewallies, grass cutters, and bazar people, went to the mountains about their usual business of procuring provender for the elephants, grass for the horses, and fuel for the camp; a gang of those licentious savages, rushed with violence on them, inhumanly butchered seven or eight of our people, and carried off three elephants, and as many camels, with several horses and bullocks. Such of our hotteewallies, &c. as were fortunate enough to escape with their lives from those unfeeling barbarians, made the best of their way to the camp, and related the story of their sufferings to the Commanding Officer, who kindled into resentment at the recital, instantly resolved to send the three Quarter Masters with two companies of Seapoys, in the pursuit of the lawless aggressors, some of whom, they luckily found ploughing in a field, to which they were directed by two of the men whom Providence rescued from their cruelty; and observed numbers flocking from the hills to their assistance: our men, arranged in military order, fired on them; some of the savages fell on the plain, others were wounded; and the greater part of them, after a feeble resistance with their bows, arrows, and swords, giving way to our superior courage and discipline, fled to the mountains for shelter, and raised a thick cloudy smoke, issuing from smothered fires, in order to intercept our view, and incommode us. Our gallant soldiers, swift as the lightning's flash, pursued, overtook, and made two hundred of them prisoners, who were escorted to Head Quarters, and by order of Colonel Grant, severely punished for their crimes; some having their ears and noses cut off, and others hung in gibbets. Their bows and arrows, and ponderous broad swords that weighed at least, fifteen pounds each, of which they were deprived, were borne in triumph as trophies of the little victory. Two of our hotteewallies, supposed to be massacred by them before this expedition, were found in a miserable state from their unmerciful treatment: they were endeavouring to crawl to the camp, disabled, and almost bleeding afresh from their recent wounds. The elephants, camels, &c. which those useful people took with them, for the purpose of bringing certain supplies to the army, were left behind in the hurry of the sanguinary and rapacious enemy's flight, cruelly mangled and weltering in their blood: our very horses and bullocks had iron spikes driven up in their hoofs, from which they must have suffered extreme torture. They were all, with some difficulty, brought back to the camp, and though taken every possible care of, a few only of the animals were restored, and the rest died in the anguish of exquisite pain.

We continued our march towards Calcutta; and on our way thither, encamped at Gouagochi [Godagarhi], which takes its name from a large black fort built on the banks of the Ganges, three miles from the place of our encampment, where we remained about two months. Our situation was extremely pleasant; the tents being almost covered with the spreading branches of mangoe and tamarind trees, which under the rigours of a torrid sun, afforded a cool shade, and brightened the face of the surrounding country; whilst the Ganges, to heighten the beauty of the varied landscape, rolled its majestic flood behind us. Hence we went to Dumdumma [Dumdum], where we had a general review. Governor Cottier [Cartier] came from Bengal in order to see it, with his Aid-du-Camps, and a numerous train of attendants: his entry into Dumdumma was very magnificent: he was accompanied by our Colonel and some of the principal Officers, who met him on the way: all the army were drawn up, and received him with a general salute.

The entire night was spent in preparations for our appearance next day: every individual was employed; and at four o'clock, on the coming morn, we were all on the plain in military array, with twenty field pieces, attended by two companies of Artillery: not a man, through the whole of the business, in which we took up several acres of ground, but displayed uncommon abilities; and was rewarded for his exertions, by the unanimous consent of the Officers, with an extra allowance of pay and refreshment. The natives, who flocked from all quarters, for many miles around, were delighted and astonished at the sight——

'Of martial men in glitt'ring arms display'd,
'And all the shining pomp of war array'd;
'Determin'd soldiers, and a gallant host,
'As e'er Britannia in her pride cou'd boast.'

The General received the Governor's compliments on the occasion, who declared that such brave fellows never before adorned the plains of Asia. The review was over at twelve o'clock, when all the Gentlemen were invited to breakfast with the General. The men, overjoyed with the approbation of their Officers, retired to their tents to talk over their military achievements, and form, by the creative power of fancy, a second grand review round their copious bowls of *Arrack*, a generous, exhilarating liquor, distilled from the fruit of the tree that bears the same name. The Governor remained a few days here, and was entertained in a style of elegant hospitality, by the military Gentlemen and the most distinguished Personages of the country. The scene of their convivial festivity, was the former habitation of a grand Nabob of this place, constructed on an ancient plan, and containing a number of spacious apartments; but from the change it received from the hand of recent improvement, it had more the appearance of a modern European mansion, than an uncouth pile of building, that reared its gothic head in remoter time.

*Letter X*

Dear Sir,
    Shortly after the review was over, we marched from Dumdumma to Calcutta, where we arrived in the year 1772. The first

brigade that lay in Fort William, and thence proceeded to Dena-pore, was relieved by a part of our army (which formed the third brigade) consisting of one battalion of Europeans that marched into the fort, and three regiments of Seapoys that occupied the chaumnies at Cheitpore; the other battalion of Europeans, to which Mr Baker belonged, and three regiments of Seapoys, were ordered to Barahampore [Baharampur], after some short stay here.

Calcutta is a very flourishing city, and the presidency of the English Company in Bengal. It is situate on the most westerly branch of the less Ganges in 87 deg. east lon. and 22, 45 north lat.; 130 miles north east of Balisore, and 40 south of Huegley [Hoogly]. It contains a number of regular and spacious streets, public buildings, gardens, walks, and fish ponds, and from the best accounts, its population has advanced to upwards of six hundred thousand souls. The principal streets are the Chouk, where an endless variety of all sorts of goods are sold; the China Bazar, where every kind of china is exposed to sale; the Lalbazar, Thurumthulla [Dharamtala], Chouringee [Chowringhee], Bightaconna [Baitakkhana], Mochoabazar [Machuabazar], and Chaunpolgot [Chandpal Ghat], where the European Gentlemen, of every description, mostly reside. The greatest concourse of English, French, Dutch, Armenians, Abyssinians, and Jews, as-semble here; besides merchants, manufacturers, and tradesmen, from the most remote parts of India.

Near Chaunpolgot is the old fort, which contains the Com-pany's stores garrisoned by the invalids and militia, and inhabited by Collectors, Commissaries, Clerks, and in my time by a Mr Paxon, the Director or Superintendent of the people employed in the mint, to coin goulmores, rupees, and paissays. Fort William is a mile from the town, and the most extensive in India. The plan of it was an irregular tetragon, built with brick and mortar made of brick dust, lime, molasses, and hemp, a composition that forms a cement as hard and durable as stone. The different batteries surrounding it, are planted with about six hundred cannon: and its inner entrance is by six gates, four of which are generally left open: outside these are fourteen gate-ways leading through different avenues, to the inner gates severally situate in opposite directions to the river, the Hospital, Kidderpore, and Calcutta. Near each gate is a well, from which water is easily raised for the use of the army by engines happily contrived for that purpose. The Commander in Chief resides in an elegant edifice within the fort, where there is also a bazar constantly held to supply the army with every necessary: and the Officers of rank next to him, dwell on the very arches of the gates, in beautifully constructed buildings, that, in such elevated situations, have a very fine effect on the delighted beholder. Inside the fort there are eight barracks, for the other Officers and privates; stores for the ammunition and accoutrements; magazines, armories, and a cannon and ball foundry, almost continually at work, for the general use of the Company's troops throughout India. In short, Fort William is an astonishing piece of human workmanship, and large enough to contain, at least, ten thousand inhabitants.

The other principal public buildings, are the Court-Houses, Prisons, and Churches. There are three Court-Houses; one fronting Loldigee, one near the Governor's mansion, and the other in Chaunpolgot: two prisons; one in Lalbazar, and another in Chouringee: and several Churches, besides the English, Armenian, and Portuguese, which are the most noted places of worship, in point of magnitude, exterior figure, and decoration. On the opposite side of the river are docks for repairing and careening ships; and outside the town is an hospital, encompassed by a sheltering grove; some pleasant villas, the summer retreats of the European Gentlemen, delightful improvements, aromatic flower gardens, winding walks planted with embowering trees on each side, and fish ponds reflecting, like an extended mirror, their blooming verdure on each margin, and Heaven's clear azure in the vaulted canopy above. There is also a very fine canal formed at the expense of Mr Tolly, which is navigable for boats passing up and down: it was cut through the country, and extended from Kidderpore to Culman [Kalna], a distance of five or six miles, connecting the Ganges with the river Sunderbun [Sunderbans]. Mr Tolly benefited considerably by this mode of conveyance; as it was deemed more convenient than that of land carriage, and became the principal channel of conveying goods to different parts of Bengal.

*Letter XI*

Dear Sir,
    Our stay in Calcutta was so short, that I have been only able

to give you some account of the town, forts, and environs; and am concerned that I could not contribute more to your entertainment, by a description of the manners of the people, as we received too sudden orders to march to Barahampore, where we arrived in the year 1773, having met with no extraordinary occurrence on the way. The cantonments here are situate on the banks of the river Bohogritee [Bhagirathi], and consist of twenty-two barracks, besides a magazine, stores, and offices. There are two barracks on the south near the river, in which the Colonels and Majors reside: six on the east, and six on the west, occupied by the other Officers: in the northern direction, the privates of the Artillery and Infantry Corps dwell: the Commander in Chief has a superb building, about a mile from the barrack of the privates; and the intermediate space between the different barracks, which form a square, is a spacious plain where the men exercise. Barahampore is very populous, and connects with Muxadabad [Murshidabad] by an irregular chain of building, comprehending Calcapore [Kalkapur] and Casambuzar [Cossimbazar], two famous manufactories of silk and cotton, where merchants can be supplied on better terms than in any other part of India. The city of Muxadabad, to which I had been led by curiosity, is the mart of an extensive trade among the natives, such as the Moguls, Parsees, Mussulmen, and Hindoos; the houses are neat, but not uniform; as every dwelling is constructed according to the peculiar fancy of the proprietor: those of the merchants are, in general, on a good plan, and built of fine brick made in the country; and such as have been erected by the servants of the Company, near the town, are very handsome structures. The city, including the suburbs, is about nine miles in length, reaching as far as Barahampore; and the neighbouring country is interspersed with elegant seats belonging to the Governors, and other Officers; among which, was the Nabob Mamarah Dowlah's [Mubarak al-Daula's] palace, finished in a superior style to the rest, and surrounded with arched pillars of marble, decorated with variegated purdoes—over the arches, native bands of music played on their different instruments, every morning and evening—on one side of the palace flowed the river Bohogritee in winding mazes: on the other, stood the Chouk, where people assembled to sell horses, wild and tame fowl, singing birds, and almost every product and manufacture of India.

Soon after my arrival here, I was dazzled with the glittering appearance of the Nabob, and all his train, amounting to about three thousand attendants, proceeding in solemn state from his palace to the temple. They formed in the splendour and richness of their attire one of the most brilliant processions I ever beheld. The Nabob was carried on a beautiful pavilion, or meanah, by sixteen men, alternately, called by the natives, Baharas, who wore a red uniform: the refulgent canopy covered with tissue, and lined with embroidered scarlet velvet, trimmed with silver fringe, was supported by four pillars of massy silver, and resembled the form of a beautiful elbow chair, constructed in oval elegance; in which he sat cross-legged, leaning his back against a fine cushion, and his elbows on two more covered with scarlet velvet, wrought with flowers of gold. At each side of his magnificent conveyance, two men attended with large whisks in their hands, made of some curious animal's tail, to beat off the flies. The very handles of those whisks were of silver. As to the ornaments of his person—he wore a very small turban of white muslin, containing forty-four yards, which quantity, from its exceeding fineness, would not weight more than a pound and half; a band of the same encompassed his turban, from which hung silver tassels over his right eye: on the front was a star in diamond of the first water: a thin robe of fine muslin covered his body, over which he wore another of cream-coloured satin, and trousers of the same, trimmed with silver edging, and small silver buttons: a valuable shawl of camel's hair, was thrown negligently about his shoulders; and another wrapped round his waist: inside the latter, he placed his dagger, that was in itself a piece of curious workmanship, the hilt being of pure gold, studded with diamonds, and embellished with small chains of gold.

His shoes were of bright crimson velvet, embroidered with silver, and set round the soals and binding with pearls. Two Aid-du-Camps, one at each side, attended him on horseback; from whom he was *little* more distinguished in splendour of habiliment, than by the diamond star in his turban. Their saddles were ornamented with tassels, fringe, and various kinds of embroidery. Before and behind him, moved in the pomp of ceremony, a great number of pages, and near his person slowly advanced his life guard, mounted on horses: all were clad in a stile of unrivalled elegance: the very earth with expanding bosom, poured out her treasures to deck them; and the artisan essayed his utmost skill to furnish their trappings.

His pipe was of a serpentine form, nine cubits in length, and termed hooka: it reached from his lips, though elevated his situation above the gay throng, to the hands of a person who only walked as an attendant in the train, for the purpose of filling the silver bowl with a nice compound of musk, sugar, rose-water, and a little tobacco finely chopped, and worked up together into a kind of dough, which was dissolved into an odoriferous liquid by the heat of a little fire made of burnt rice, and kept in a silver vessel with a cover of the same, called Chilm, from which was conveyed a fragrant cool smoke, through a small tube connecting with another that ascended to his mouth.

The part which the attendant held in his hand, contained at least a quart of water: it was made of glass, ornamented with a number of little golden chains admirably contrived: the snake which comprehends both tubes was tipped with gold at each end, and the intermediate space was made of wire inside a close quilting of satin, silk, and muslin, wrought in a very ingenious manner: the mouth piece was also of gold, and the part next to his lips set with diamonds.

A band of native music played before him, accompanied with a big drum, conveyed on a camel, the sound of which, could be heard at a great distance: and a halcorah or herald advanced onward in the front of the whole company, to proclaim his arrival, and clear the way before him. Crowds of people from every neighbouring quarter, thronged to see him. I waited for some time, to see him enter into the temple with all his retinue, who left their shoes at the door as a mark of veneration for the sacred fanc into which they were entering. The view of this grand procession, gave me infinite pleasure, and induced me to continue a little longer in Muxadabad.

### Letter XII

Dear Sir,

Shortly after the procession, I met with a relation of mine, a Mahometan, who requested my attendance at the circumcision of one of his children. Previous to this ceremony, which I shall describe in the order of succession, it may be necessary to premise, that a child is baptized three times according to the rites of this religion. The first baptism is performed at time of the birth, by a Bramin who, though of different religious principles, is held in the utmost veneration by the Mahometans, for his supposed knowledge in astrology, by which he is said to foretell the future destiny of the child; when he discharges the duties of his sacred function on such an occasion, which consists in nothing more than this prophecy, and calling the child by the most favourable name, the mysteries of his science will permit, he receives some presents from the parents and kindred, and retires.

The second baptism, which takes place when the child is four days old, is performed by the Codgi, or Mulna, the Mahometan Clergyman, in the presence of a number of women, who visit the mother after her delivery; he first reads some prayers in the alcoran, sprinkles the child with consecrated water, and anoints the navel and ears with a kind of oil extracted from mustard seed, which concludes the ceremony. The Priest then quits the womens' apartment, and joins the men in another room. When he has withdrawn, the Hajams' wives enter the chamber, and attend the mother of the child with every apparatus necessary in her situation: one assists to pare her nails, and supplies her with a bason of water to wash her hands in; and others are employed in dressing her in a becoming manner. Several Ladies of distinction come to visit her, presenting her their congratulatory compliments on her happy recovery, and filling her lap, at the same time, with a quantity of fresh fruit, as the emblem of plenty. When this ceremony is over they sit down to an entertainment served up by the Hajams' wives, and prepared by women in more menial offices. Their usual fare is a variety of cakes and sweetmeats. The men, who also congratulate the father, wishing every happiness to his offspring, are regaled much in the same manner. Thus is the second baptism celebrated; from which the third, which is solemnized on the twentieth day after the birth, differs only in point of time.

The Mahometans do not perform the circumcision, or fourth baptism until the child is seven years old, and carefully initiated in such principles of their religion as can be well conceived at such a tender age. For some time before it, the poorer kind of people use much economy in their manner of living, to enable them to defray the expenses of a splendid entertainment, as they are very ambitious of displaying the greatest elegance and hospitality on such occasions. When the period of entering on this sacred business is arrived, they dispatch Hajams or Barbers, who from the nature of their occupation are well acquainted with the city, to all the inhabitants of the Mahometan profession, residing within the walls of Muxadabad, to whom they present nutmegs, which imply the same formality as compliment cards in this country. The guests thus invited assembled in a great square, large enough to contain two thousand persons, under a semiana of muslin supported by handsome poles erected at a certain distance from each other; the sides of it were also made of muslin, and none would be suffered to enter but Mahometans. The arrival of the Mulna was announced by the Music, who had a kind of orchestra within the semiana: attended by one of the Hajams, he approached the child who was decked with jewels and arrayed in scarlet muslin, and sat under a beautiful canopy richly ornamented with silk hangings, on an elegant elbow chair with velvet cushions to the back and sides, from which he was taken and mounted on a horse, accompanied by four men, his nearest relations, each holding a drawn sword in his hand, who also wore a dress of scarlet muslin. People of condition, among the Mahometans, contribute largely to the magnificence of this ceremony; and appear on horseback in the midst of the gay assembly, with their finest camels in rich furniture led after them.

But to return—the child was conducted in this manner to a chapel, at the door of which he alit, assisted by his four relations, who entered with him into the sacred building, where he bowed in adoration to one of the Prophets, repeating with his kindred, some prayers he had been before taught by his parents; after this pious duty is over, he is again mounted on his horse, and led to another chapel, where he goes through the same forms, and so on to them all, praying with the rest of the company, and fervently imploring in the attitude of prostrate humility, the great Alla to protect him from every harm in the act of circumcision.

After they had taken their rounds to the different places of worship, they returned to the square in which the semiana was erected, and placed him under the glittering canopy, upon his accustomed chair. The music that played before him suddenly ceased, when the Mulna appeared in his sacerdotal robes, holding a silver bason of consecrated water, with which he sprinkled him; while the Hajam slowly advancing in order to circumcise him, instantly performed the operation. In this critical moment, every individual in the numerous crowd, stood on one foot, and joined his father and mother in heartfelt petitions to Heaven for his safety. The Music again struck up, and played some cheerful airs: after which, the child was taken home by his parents and put to bed. The company being served with water and napkins by the Hajams, washed their hands and sat down barefooted on a rich carpet, to partake of a favourite dish called by the natives *pelou*, composed of stewed rice and meat highly seasoned, which they are in general fond of. The entire scene was illuminated with torches, which, by a strong reflexion of artificial lustre, seemed to heighten the splendour of their ornaments.

## Letter XIII

Dear Sir,

I shall now proceed to give you some account of the form of marriage among the Mahometans, which is generally solemnized with all the external show of Oriental pageantry. The parents of the young people, first treat on the subject of uniting them in the bands of wedlock, and if they mutually agree on a connection between them, the happy pair, who were never permitted to see each other, nor even consulted about their union, are joined in marriage at a very youthful time in life, the female seldom exceeding the age of twelve, and the lad little more advanced in years: they must always be of the same cast, and trade; for a weaver will not give his daughter to a man of any other occupation: in the higher scenes of life, each of the parties bring a splendid fortune; but among people of the middle class, the woman has seldom more allotted her than her apparel, furniture, and a few ornaments of some value, as the parents of the man provide for both, by giving him a portion of such property as they can afford; in land, merchandize, or implements of trade, according to their situation. When they conclude all matters to their satisfaction, Hajams are sent with nutmegs, in the usual form, to invite their friends and acquaintance to the wedding, and the houses of each party are adorned with green branches and flowers. Outside the doors they erect galleries for the musicians, under which, are rows of seats or benches for the accommodation of the lower class of people, who are forbid any closer communication. Allured by invitation and the love of pleasure, the welcome guests arrive, and discover the houses by the green branches and flowers with which they are gayly dressed, to distinguish them from others. The entire week is spent in the utmost mirth and convivial enjoyment. The finest scarlet muslin is procured for the young people and their relations, by their parents on both sides: those of the youth supply the dresses of the young woman and her kindred; and her's furnish him and his relatives with suitable apparel.

Thus arrayed, the bridegroom is carried on a palanquin, with lighted torches in his train, attended by a number of people, to the house of the bride, whose friends meet him on the way. At his arrival, the ceremony is performed, if the mansion be large enough to contain the cheerful throng that assemble on this festive occasion; if not, which is generally the case, a semiana is erected in a spacious square, in the centre of which is a canopy about seven feet high, covered on the top with the finest snow-white muslin, and decorated inside with diversified figures representing the sun, moon, and stars. Beneath this temporary dome, the coy maid reclines on a soft cushion, in an easy posture, while the raptured youth, scouring through fancy's lawn, on the wings of expectation, and already anticipating the joys of connubial felicity, leans opposite his sable Dulcinea in a similar attitude. The breathing instruments now wake their trembling strings to announce the coming of the Mulna, who enters the scene with an air of characteristic solemnity: the music gradually ceases, till it's expiring voice is lulled into a profound silence; and the Priest opens the alcoran, which is held according to custom by four persons, one at each corner, and reads, in grave accents, the ceremony. The bride and bridegroom interchange rings, which they put on their fingers; and one of the bridesmaids, supposed to be her relation, comes behind both, who are veiled, and ties, in a close knot, the ends of their shawls together, to signify their firm union. The Mulna, finally, consecrates a glass of water and sugar, which he presents to them: they alternately taste it, but the man gives it round to a few select friends of the company, who, in turn, put it to their lips, wishing happiness to the married couple. They now sit down to an elegant supper, after which the dancing girls are introduced, who make a splendid appearance, clothed in embroidered silks and muslins, and moving in a variety of loose attitudes that allure admiration and excite the passions.

When the entertainment is over, a silver plate not unlike a salver, is carried about, into which almost every individual drops some pecuniary gratuity to reward the trouble of the Hajams, and the guests retire in company with the newly wedded pair, who are conveyed on separate palanquins to the house of his father, while bands of music in cheerful mood are playing before them, numerous torches flaming round them, that seem with their blaze to disperse the gloom of night, and fireworks, exhibiting in the ambient air, a variety of dazzling figures. When they arrive, the Mulna gives them his benediction, and sprinkles the people about them, with perfumed water coloured with saffron: a second entertainment is then prepared for their friends and acquaintance, which concludes the hymeneal festivity. Among people of rank, merchants, and tradesmen, who have made any acquisitions, in life, the Lady never goes outside the doors after marriage, except when she is carried on a palanquin, which is so well covered that she cannot be seen by any body. A man of any consequence in India, does not stir out for a week after his nuptials, and would deem it dishonourable to suffer his wife to appear in public: the indigence of the poorer kind of people precludes them from the observance of this punctilio. The husband's entire property after his decease, comes into the possession of his wife. It may be here observed, that the Hindoo, as well as the Mahometan, shudders at the idea of exposing women to the public eye: they are held so sacred in India, that even the soldier in the rage of slaughter will not only spare, but even protect them. The Haram is a sanctuary against the horrors of wasting war, and ruffians covered with the blood of a husband, shrink back with confusion at the apartment of his wife.

## Letter XIV

Dear Sir,

The Mahometans are, in general, a very healthful people: refraining from the use of strong liquors, and accustomed to a temperate diet, they have but few diseases, for which their own experience commonly finds some simple yet effectual remedy. When they are visited by sickness, they bear it with much composure of mind, partly through an expectation of removing their disorder, by their own manner of treating it: but when they perceive their malady grows too violent, to submit even to the utmost exertions of their skill, they send for a Mulna, who comes to the bedside of the sick person, and putting his hand over him, feels that part of his body most affected, and repeats, with a degree of fervency, some pious prayers, by the efficacy of which, it is supposed the patient will speedily recover. The Mahometans meet death with uncommon resignation and fortitude, considering it only as the means of enlarging them from a state of mortal captivity, and opening to them a free and glorious passage to the mansions of bliss. Those ideas console them on the bed of sickness; and even amid the pangs of dissolution, the parting soul struggling to leave its earthly prison, and panting for the joys of immortality, changes, at bright intervals, the terrors of the grim Monarch into the smiles of a Cherub, who invites it to a happier region.

When a person dies among them, the neighbours of the same religious principles, bring the family of the deceased to their houses, and use every means to comfort them in their affliction. The corpse is stretched on the death bed, which is covered with white muslin, and adorned with flowers: wax tapers are lit about it, and the room hung round with white cotton. Numbers assemble together to pray for the departed spirit, and twenty-four hours after the decease of the person, on account of the excessive heat of the climate, the body is wrapped up in muslin, and carried towards the grave, near which it is laid down, before it is interred: all the people who attend the funeral kneel in a direct line beside it, imploring the great Alla to give the soul eternal rest: it is then consigned to the silent scene of interment, and the relations throw a little clay on it, after which it is covered. The Mulna consecrates a quantity of thin cakes, which he distributes in broken pieces among the people, who share them with each other, and join in prayer, while the eldest son of the deceased sprinkles the grave with holy water, and spreads a large white sheet over it. Four days after the funeral, the relatives entertain their neighbours and a multitude of poor people with unlimited hospitality, who, in gratitude for their munificence, offer up their united petitions to Heaven for the kinsman of their benefactors.

People of condition have grand monuments erected to their memory, and lamps lighting at their tombs throughout the year: their houses also, on certain festivals, are magnificently illuminated in remembrance of them. The poorer natives perform this ceremony at the grave and their own habitations, but once in the year, for a short space of time. After the death of a husband, his wife puts on no mourning, and disrobing herself of all the ornaments of dress and jewels, wears only plain white muslin. In the middle walk of life, the widow enjoys the sole property, which, making some reserve for herself, she generally divides in a very equitable manner, among her children: in more elevated situations, the son succeeds his father in rank or employment.

The Mahometans are strict adherents to the tenets of their religion, which does not, by any means, consist in that enthusiastic veneration for Mahomet so generally conceived: it considers much more, as its primary object, the unity of the supreme Being, under the name of Alla: Mahomet is only regarded in a secondary point of view, as the missionary of that unity, merely for destroying the idol worship, to which Arabia had continued so long under bondage: and so far from addressing him as a deity, that in their orisons, they do not pray to him, but for him recommending him to the divine mercy: it is a mistaken, though a generally received opinion, that pilgrimages were made to his tomb, which, in a religious sense, were only directed to what is called the cahabah or holy-house at Mecca, an idol temple dedicated by him to the unity of God. His tomb is at Medina, visited by the Mahometans, purely out of curiosity and reverence to his memory. Most of his followers carry their veneration for the supreme Being so far, as not only, never to mention the word Alla or God, on any common occasion, but think it in some degree blasphemous to praise or define a Being, whom they consider as so infinitely transcendent to all praise, definition or comprehension. Thus, they carry their scrupulosity to such a length, as not even to approve of calling him good, righteous, or merciful, from their thinking such epithets superfluous and impertinent; as if one were emphatically to say of a man that he had a head, or any other member necessary to the human form: for they conceive it to be a profanation of the name of God, to accompany it with human attributes; and that no idea can be so acceptable to that Being, as the name itself, a substantive infinitely superior and independent of the connexion of any adjective to give it the least degree of additional emphasis.

## *Letter XV*

Dear Sir,

I shall now change the subject from *grave* to *gay*, and endeavour to entertain you with some account of the dancing girls of this country. At a very youthful time of life, they are regularly trained in all the arts of pleasing, by a hackneyed matron, worn in the campaigns of Venus, whose past experience renders her perfectly adequate to the task of instruction, for which she receives from her pupils a share of the pecuniary favours conferred on them by their gallants, and also procures them every article of dress that can set them off to advantage. They have different places of abode, sometimes occupying the handsomest houses in towns or cities; and in the fine season of the year, they retire to the country, where their villas, gardens, bowers, and every other rural improvement, are laid out in such a manner, as to allure the most unconcerned observer. Hither, some of the principal Nabobs and European Gentlemen of the first distinction, are drawn by the love of pleasure, and lavish immense sums on these creatures, who are generally recruited out of the people of all casts and denominations, though not without a peculiar attention to beauty or agreeableness; yet, even the knowledge of their being so common, is with many totally forgotten in the ravishing display of their natural and acquired charms. They dance to the music of cymbals, fifes, and drums, they term tum-tums, and often represent in pantomime such scenes, as a lover courting his mistress; a procuress, endeavouring to seduce a woman from one gallant to another; and a girl, timorous and afraid of being caught in an intrigue. All these love-scenes, they perform, in gestures, air, and steps, with well-adapted expression. In some of their dances, even in public, modesty is not much respected in the motions of their limbs, the quivering of their hips, and other lascivious attitudes, into which they throw themselves, without exposing any nudity. But in private parties, they introduce other dances, in which, though they never offend delicacy, by discovering any part of their bodies, they betray such fascinating looks and postures, as are probably more dangerous. In short, there is no attraction, of which they are not capable, and by these unfailing arts, they frequently arrive at the temple of fortune. In many parts of India, there are several fine Mahometan chapels built by them, and rich factories established, where various artisans and tradesmen find the greatest encouragement.

The dress of these women, which differs according to the custom of the country, is in all, however, the most splendid conceivable. Their persons glitter with jewels from head to toe, since even on their toes they wear rings. Carcanets adorn their necks, bracelets their arms, and chains of gold and silver, enriched with precious stones, their very ankles. They also wear nose-jewels, to which the familiar eye is soon reconciled. Their breasts are covered with thin muslin, embellished with gems, and the swell of the tempting bosom displayed to such advantage, warms even frigid insensibility with a glow of soft sensations. Their necklaces are composed of flowers strung together, which they call mogrees, resembling Spanish double jessamy, but of a more agreeable odor, and preferable to any perfumes, delighting at once the sight and smell. Their dress consists of a long white muslin gown, extremely clear and fine, with a short body and long sleeves, and the skirt which contains near twenty yards, is ornamented in its train, with silver fringe; a long trousers made of fancy silk, exactly fitted to their shapes, and a large shawl, that covers the head and shoulders, embroidered with a deep silver fringe. On the head they wear jewels and flowers; and their long black hair is generally braided. Many of them, especially those in commerce with the Moguls and Moors, follow the old Eastern custom, of forming a black circle round their eye borders, by drawing a bodkin between them, with their eyelids shut, that both sides may receive the tint of the stibium, or powder of antimony that sticks to the bodkin. The powder is called by them surma; which they imagine refreshes and cools the eye, besides exciting its lustre, by the ambient blackness. They avoid every degree of affectation in their manners, and copy nature, as their grand original, in the imitation and refinement of which, their art chiefly consists. Besides, they have nothing of that gross impudence which characterises the European prostitutes; their style of seduction being all softness and gentleness· their caresses are not only well managed, but well timed in the cloying minutes of satiety. There are some of them, even amidst their vices and depravity, whose minds are finely impressed with generous sentiments. The following authentic account is a striking proof of it:

One of them lived, some years ago, at a pleasant seat a few miles from Cossumbuzar, where she had been visited by some of the principal men of the country, among whom was a rich factor, whose attachments to her diverted his attention from business, in such a manner, that he became a bankrupt. This misfortune preyed so much on his mind, that his melancholy could not well escape the observation of his mistress, from whom he endeavoured to conceal it as much as possible, dreading to be forsaken by her in his poverty. After repeated entreaties on her part, he, at length, made her acquainted with his situation: she suddenly left him, and to his great astonishment, shortly returned with money and effects, to such an amount as enabled him to conduct his business with more spirit and application than ever.

Here is an instance, that even the human heart plunged in crimes and immorality, may sometimes be roused from its torpor by the voice of humanity.

### Letter XVI

Dear Sir,

That part of our army which we left in Calcutta, arrived at Barahampore, before our departure; and shortly after, the entire brigade received orders to march to Denapore, where we arrived in the year 1775. On the Bengal establishment, there are three brigades, who all wear the usual scarlet uniform: that of the first is faced with blue—of the second with black—and the third with yellow. Each brigade contains one regiment of Europeans, six regiments or twelve battalions of Seapoys, three companies of European Artillery, five companies of native Artillery, called Gullendas, and two companies of native Cavalry. A regiment of Seapoys on the present establishment, consists of two battalions, each battalion 500 men or five companies, with a Captain, two Lieutenants, three Ensigns, one Serjeant-Major, Europeans; besides one Commedan, five Subidars, ten Jemidars, thirty Howaldars, thirty Homaldars, five Tombourwallas, five Basleewallas, and five Troohewallas, Natives.

As you may not understand those terms, I shall thus explain them to you.

| | |
|---|---|
| Comedan signifies | *a Captain* |
| Subidar | *a Lieutenant* |
| Jemidar | *an Ensign* |
| Howaldar | *a Serjeant* |
| Homaldar | *a Corporal* |
| Seapoy | *a private Soldier* |
| Tombourwalla | *a Drummer* |
| Basleewalla | *a Fife* |
| Trooheewalla | *a Trumpeter* |

The Seapoys are composed of Mahometans and Hindoos, who make no other distinction in their exterior appearance, than that the Hindoos colour each side of the face and forehead with a kind of red paint, produced from the timber of the sandal tree. The dress of both, is a thin muslin shirt, a red coat in uniform, a turban, sash, and short trousers. The turban, which is of muslin, is mostly blue as well as the sash: it is quite small, fitted very closely to the head, and not unlike a Scotch bonnet in form, except that the front is more flat, to which they affix a cockade of white muslin puffed and trimmed with silver lace, with a star in the middle. It is also ornamented with curious narrow festoons made of thin wire. Round the neck are worn two or three rows of wooden beads, and a shield on the left shoulder. An Officer wears silver or glass beads, a coat of scarlet cloth, in uniform with the brigade to which he belongs, a blue sash and turban, containing twenty yards each, a pair of long trousers, half boots, and a shield on the left shoulder.

The Seapoys, who are in general well disciplined in the use of arms, serve as a strong reinforcement to a much less number of Europeans, and on many occasions, display great firmness and resolution.

As a sequel to this letter, I beg leave to subjoin an alphabetical explanation of Persian and Indian terms, not commonly understood in this country.

EXPLANATION of PERSIAN and INDIAN TERMS

| | |
|---|---|
| Amdanny | *Imports* |
| Argee | *a Petition* |

| | |
|---|---|
| Assammees | *Dealers in different branches of trade* |
| Bang | *an intoxicating juice of a vegetable* |
| Bazar | *a Market* |
| Baudshaw | *a King* |
| Baudshawjoddi | *a Queen* |
| Begum | *a Princess* |
| Betel | *a leaf growing on a vine, and chewed by all ranks of people* |
| Bramin | *a Priest* |
| Buckserrias | *Foot Soldiers, with only sword and target* |
| Buxey | *Treasurer to the Mogul, or Paymaster of troops* |
| Bundar | *a Custom-house* |
| Cawn | *a title of dignity* |
| Codgi | *a Bishop* |
| Chop | *a small seal, on which is engraved the name of the Mogul* |
| Choultry | *an open house for all travellers* |
| Chout | *a fourth part: or a tribute exacted by the Morattoes* |
| Chowkeys | *Turnpikes; or guards at landing places* |
| Caffres | *Negroes from Africa, trained up as soldiers by the Europeans* |
| Cooley | *a Porter, or Labourer of any kind* |
| Coss | *a distance of two miles and more* |
| Cossid | *a foot Messenger or Post* |
| Cowle | *a protection* |
| Crore of Rupees | *a hundred lack or near 1,250,000l. sterling* |
| Dawgahs | *Custom-house Officers, or Collectors* |
| Decoyt | *a Robber* |
| Dewan | *King's Treasurer* |
| Dewanny | *Superintendency over the royal revenues* |
| Dooley | *a woman's chair, like a sedan* |
| Dummadah | *a river* |
| Durbar | *the Court or Council of a Mogul Prince* |
| Dustuk | *an order* |
| Firman | *a royal mandate, or grant* |

| | |
|---|---|
| Fouzdar | *a Governor, military Officer, or Renter* |
| Gentoo | *a native Indian, in a state of idolatry* |
| Gomastah | *a Broker, Factor, or Agent* |
| Gunge | *Grain Market* |
| Gwallers | *Carriers of palanquins* |
| Hackeries | *Carts or coaches drawn by oxen* |
| Harkarahs | *Spies* |
| Jaghire | *a district granted as a mark of honour, or allotted as a pension* |
| Jaggernaut | *the Gentoo pagoda* |
| Jemidar | *an Ensign* |
| Killedar | *the Governor of a Fort* |
| Kistbundee | *Times of the payment of the country Revenues* |
| Lack of Rupees | *about 12,500l. sterling* |
| Maund | *between 70 and 80 pounds, at Surat only 37 pounds* |
| Moonshee | *a Persian Secretary* |
| Mulna | *a Mahometan Priest* |
| Moories | *Writers* |
| Muchulcas | *Bonds of obligation* |
| Musnud | *the throne of an Indian Prince* |
| Muxadabad | *the capital of Bengal* |
| Nabob | *a Governor of a Province, appointed by the Soubah* |
| Naib | *a Deputy to the Governor of a place* |
| Omrahs | *Privy Counsellors to the Mogul, and men of the first rank in the Empire* |
| Paddy | *Rice in the husk* |
| Paddy-grounds | *Rice fields* |
| Pagoda | *an Indian temple* |
| Pagoda | *an Indian coin worth 7s. 8d. sterling* |

| | |
|---|---|
| Palinquin | *a kind of canopy bed for travelling* |
| Parsees | *Worshipers of fire* |
| Patamar | *a Messenger or Post* |
| Peons | *Foot soldiers armed with a broad sword* |
| Pergannahs | *Villages* |
| Perwannah | *a letter, order, or command* |
| Pettah | *the town surrounding an Indian fort* |
| Podor | *a Money Changer* |
| Polygar | *the Lord of a District* |
| Ponsways | *Guard-boats* |
| Pettahs | *Grants* |
| | |
| Raja | *the highest title claimed by the Gentoo Princes* |
| Royran | *the King's Officer for receiving the revenue* |
| Rafftanny | *Exports* |
| Rupee | *a silver coin worth about 2s. 5d. sterl.* |
| | |
| Saneds | *commissions from the Mogul, Soubahs, or Nabobs* |
| Sardar | *an Officer of Horse* |
| Seapoys | *Indian foot soldiers, hired and disciplined by Europeans* |
| Shroff | *a Banker* |
| Sircar | *a general name for the Government, or those concerned in it* |
| Sirpah | *a rich dress of the country, worn by way of distinction* |
| Soubah | *the Viceroy of the Deckan, or of Bengal* |
| | |
| Tank | *a pond, or pool of water* |
| Tanka | *the Revenue appropriated by the Mogul, for maintaining a fleet at Surat* |
| Tanksal | *a mint for coinage* |
| Telinga | *the Carnatic country* |
| Telingas | *Soldiers raised in the Carnatic* |
| Tum tums | *Drums* |
| Topasses | *a tawney race of foot soldiers, descended from the Portuguese marrying natives, and called Topasses, because they wear hats* |

| | |
|---|---|
| Tunkahs | *Assignments upon lands, or rents assigned to the Company* |
| Tursaconna | *Wardrobe* |
| Ginanah | *Seraglio* |
| Vakeel | *an English Agent, or resident at the Nabob's court* |
| Vizerut | *the grant for the Viziership* |
| Zemin | *Ground* |
| Zemindary | *an Officer who takes care of the rents arising from the public lands.* |

*Letter XVII*

Dear Sir,

On our march from Denapore to Belgram [Bilgram], we halted some days at Benaras, a rich and populous city on the north side of the Ganges, and celebrated for it's learning in past time. There was once a very fine Observatory here; and a few years ago, some European Gentlemen, led hither by the love of science and antiquity, discovered a great many astronomical instruments, of a large size, admirably well contrived, though injured by the hand of time. It was supposed they might have been constructed some centuries ago, under the direction of the great Akbar, the fond votary of science, and the distinguished patron of the Bramins who applied, with unwearied assiduity, to the study of astronomy.

The country about Benaras, is considered as the Paradise of India, remarkable for its salubrious air, fascinating landscapes, and innocence of its inhabitants, whose simple manners had a happy influence on all who lived near them. While wasteful war spread her horrors over other parts of India, this blissful country often escaped her ravages, perhaps secured by it's distance from the ocean, or more probably by the sacred character ascribed to the scene, which had, through many ages, been considered as the repository of the religion and learning of the Bramins, and the prevailing idea of the simplicity of the native Hindoos, a people unaccustomed to the sanguinary measures of, what they term, civilized nations.

But to return—the city of Benaras is built on the banks of the Ganges, and extends along the river from Rahajgaut, at one end, to Raja Cheyt Sing's [Chait Singh's] palace, at the other, which makes a distance of, at least, four miles. About the centre of the city, stands an ancient and lofty pile of building, called Mawdodasthrohur [Madho Das Dharahara], which strikes the eye, at first view, with a kind of sublime astonishment, and appears like a collection of rising towers that seem to survey in majestic pride the subject town and surrounding country. It is the temporary residence of the Hindoo pilgrims, who occasionally occupy it as they journey through this peaceful region. At some distance from it, is the elegant edifice of Bene, an extensive dealer in diamonds: this mansion is built at a slip, or gaut, called, by being united with the proprietor's name, Benegaut [Beni Madho Rai Ghat]; as if we said, Sullivan's-quay, or French's-slip. There are also other wharfs, or slips, ascending from the river, by many stone steps, termed from the names of the owners, who have built fine houses thereon, Ramgaut [Ram Ghat], Ranagaut [Rana Ghat], Pilleegaut [Pilai Ghat], Chowkgaut [Chawki Ghat], and Marattagaut [Maratha Ghat], &c.

At the east end of the town, there is a large square of building, called Serai, encompassed by walls, and laid out for the reception of travellers of every description; the better sort of people pay for their accommodation: but the poor are entertained free of expense: this laudable institution is supported by the voluntary contributions of the merchants of the city.

There are many other handsome dwellings belonging to the different traders and manufacturers, and several pagodas, or temples, of Hindoo worship.

The streets in Benaras, are rather confined and narrow; and the houses, which are crowded together, are in general very high and flat at the top, where the inhabitants, in the cool hours of the day, enjoy the benefit of the air. In different parts of the town, there are tanks, or wells, for the use of the citizens and the refreshment of passing strangers, who if in indigence, are also humanely supplied with food by persons employed to attend at the tanks for this very purpose. This city is well peopled, and persons of consequence, when they appear abroad, either on horseback or in their palanquins, are attended in great pomp, by numerous retinues. Manufactures of silk are carried on here to a great degree of perfection, and few places in India can surpass this market in such a varied assortment of sattins, keemcaus, and gooldbudthen, an elegant kind of silk, beautifully wrought with flowers of gold, besides muslin shawls, embroidered with gold and silver at each border. It is also remarkable for it's fine carpets, saltpetre, sugar, musk, and perfumes; and trades largely with the Morattoes, and other dealers of India, with whom its commodities are bartered for their diamonds, and other articles of value.

About three miles north of the city, stands the Raja's palace, a superb mansion, where he usually spends the summer season, amidst the delightful scenery of groves, lawns, umbrageous walks, ponds, and cascades.

## *Letter XVIII*

Dear Sir,

You will now expect from me, an account of the Hindoos, the natives of this country; who are classed into four tribes, namely, Bramins, Sittri, Bice, and Sudder. The Bramins, or first class, which are esteemed the most ancient and honourable, are the Priests, the Instructors and Philosophers: the Sittri, or second class, are the military, who are entrusted with the defence and government of the state; in war, the soldiers who fight it's battles; in peace, the magistrates and rulers who direct it's councils: the Bice, or third class, are the merchants and husbandmen, who provide the necessaries and comforts of life by trade and agriculture, and thereby circulate through various channels the wealth of the nation: the Sudder, or fourth class, are the artisans, labourers, and servants. There is another class, which is the meanest of all, composed of cherwallees or gold-finders, chemars or shoe-makers, and domerah, or basket-makers, who are held in such sovereign detestation, that the very mention of their names conveys to the mind of a Hindoo, every idea of meanness and servility. No person, unless he be excommunicated, can quit his cast, or tribe; nor will he, on any account, be admitted into any other. This distinction of the people into different classes, seems to be an institution of some antiquity, and probably will continue unaltered till the end of time, so steady and persevering is every individual in his attachment to his respective cast.

The Bramins are again divided into five orders: first, into those that eat no flesh: second, into those that eat some kind of flesh; third, those that marry; fourth, those that vow celibacy; and fifth, the Bramins that forbear walking at all, for fear of destroying some living creatures; these wear a piece of silk or muslin before their mouths, lest the smallest fly should be drawn in by their breath. They are so exceedingly scrupulous in this respect, that they will not burn wood, through an apprehension of destroying any insect by it; and they always carry a brush in their hands to sweep the place they design to sit on, lest they should dislodge the soul of some animal. Their scrupulosity arises from a belief in the transmigration of souls, and their followers are so firmly persuaded that departed souls enter the bodies of animals, that they no sooner observe any of them frequent their houses, than they immediately conclude, their deceased friends, under this new disguise, come to visit them. They cannot, without horror, think of depriving any thing of life, and do not less respect it in the smallest insect, than in the huge elephant.

They hold there is but one God infinitely perfect, who has existed from all eternity; but that there are three subordinate Deities, namely, Brama [Brahma], whom he vested with the power of creation; Whistnow [Vishnu], the preserver; and Routeren [Rudra], the enemy and destroyer of mankind. The supreme Divinity is often typified under the form of a Being, with a number of eyes and hands, to impress the minds of the people with a strong idea of his penetration and power, and induce them to be very exact in the performance of moral duties. The Bramins advise their followers to go in pilgrimage to certain places, esteemed holy, and especially to the pagodas near the mouth of the Ganges: washing in that river alone, will, in their opinion, cleanse them from a multitude of sins. Their women rise early in the morning to bathe, carrying pieces of dough on silver salvers, adorned with flowers, to the river side, and lighted lamps in their hands: after bathing, they form the dough into images, which they worship with much adoration, at the same time ringing bells and burning incense, and afterwards commit their images to the bosom of the Ganges, with some formality. However strange their doctrine may appear to Europeans, yet they are much to be commended for the exercise of the moral virtues they inculcate, namely, temperance, justice, and humanity. Amidst a variety of extravagant customs, strange ceremonies, and prejudices, we may discover the traces of sublime morality, deep philosophy, and refined policy; but when we attempt to trace the religious and civil institutions to their source, we find that it is lost in the maze of antiquity. The native Indians, or Hindoos, are men of strong natural genius, and are, by no means, unacquainted with literature and science, as the translation of the Ayeen Akberry [Ain-i Akbari] into English, has fully evinced. We may trace the origin of most of the sciences, in their ancient manuscripts. Even before the age of Pythagoras, the Greeks travelled to India for instruction: the trade carried on by them with the oldest commercial nations, in exchange for their cloth, is a proof of their great progress in the arts of industry.

The women in general, except in the higher scenes of life, prepare the food for their husbands and families; as no Hindoo would make use of any but what his wife dresses for him: it consists chiefly of rice, fish, and vegetables, well seasoned with pepper and other spices, to which they add pickles of various sorts. The men, who always eat together, unaccompanied by the women, previously take off their turbans, shoes, and outside garments, and wash before and after meals. They afterwards withdraw to another apartment, where they enjoy themselves with smoking tobacco and chewing betel. They use no spirits or other liquors, but are particularly nice in the taste of different waters, and consider their choice of them a great luxury.

As to the funerals of these people—some bury the bodies of the deceased, which they place in the grave in a sitting posture, with rice and water near them: their dead are generally decked with jewels and other ornaments, of which they are disrobed by their kindred, before the grave is filled up. The usual way, however, is to burn the corpse on a funeral pile erected for that purpose near the water side; the nearest relation in tattered apparel, which is, in their opinion, the expressive garb of sorrow, sets fire to it, and shews every symptom of frantic grief on the occasion: the body being soon consumed, the ashes are collected and thrown into the river. The ashes of the great are placed in an urn, which is carried with some degree of ceremony by a Bramin, and cast into the Ganges, to whose waters they attribute a peculiar sanctity.

*Letter XIX*

Dear Sir,

After halting some days at Benaras, in order to refresh the army, we proceeded on our march towards Belgram, delighted, as we passed along, with a continued view of the finest country on earth, diversified with fields of rice, plantations of sugar, and gardens abounding with a variety of fruits and flowers; and encamped at Duci [Joosi], opposite Alahabad [Allahabad], a large fort, about 412 miles to the south of Delhi, 540 from Calcutta, and 850 from the mouth of the Ganges. It is pleasantly situated between that river and Jemina [Jamuna]. Inside the fort is a royal palace, in which are apartments for the Mogul, a Durbar, and Zenanah, with a number of houses occupied by the Officers of the court, and their families. Each house is built like two dwellings joined together, and walled round, for the purpose not only of concealing their women from their neighbours, but even from their own male domestics; and contains very spacious and lofty rooms, opening towards the river, with smaller apartments adjoining them, which are extremely dark, without the least aperture to admit either light or air. To these they retire in the heat of the day, to enjoy the calm refreshment of sleep; for the natives find by experience, that in order to render a situation cool, in this sultry region, they must totally exclude every ray of light, and breath of air, till the fervid sun descends into the lap of Thetis. To the tops of their houses, which are flat, they ascend by narrow, steep, staircases, and inhale the evening breeze after Sol's friendly departure.

The palace of Alahabad was entirely built of stone, hewn out of the rocks, at some distance from the banks of the Ganges, and brought hither at a vast expense. It is not unlike the Portland stone, but of a coarser kind, and infinitely more porous. Not only the walls, but the roofs, floors, and pillars of the palace, were formed of it; and even the vary squares and passages were paved with it. Neither glass, iron, brick, or other materials for building, were introduced here, until the fort came into the possession of the English. The slightest walls of this great pile are, at least, five feet thick. There are some good houses about it, built in the Indian style, that make a handsome appearance. Nothing can be more striking, nothing can display a more sublime air of grandeur, than the lofty gateways here, which resemble in some manner, the old triumphal arches of the Romans.

The country and climate of Alahabad, are very delightful; when the rains are over, not a cloud is to be seen in the azure Heavens, and the heat of torrid suns is frequently tempered by the breath of fanning gales, which Providence occasionally permits to pant, on the bosom of the sultry air. Vegetation is so rapid, that it seems almost perceptible to the eye; and the naked plains, which appeared, but a week before, to be only a broad surface of sand, are instantly clothed by the benignity of those tears shed from above, with the verdant robes of blooming nature. The face of the country is entirely changed; even the marshy grounds that had been covered with water, produce their golden harvests; and the luxuriant earth, under the genial influence of the clime, pours forth her various plenty. Rice, wheat, peas, and beans, grow here in abundance; and a sort of grain called jow, something like the oats of Europe. The indigo shrub thrives exceedingly in this soil; it is not higher than a rose tree; and it's leaves, when stripped off, are steeped in tubs of water, which extracts the blue from them; the sediment, after the water has been drained off, is exposed to the sun, which occasions the moisture to evaporate, and the indigo to remain at the bottom of the vessels. The gardens are painted with a variety of beautiful flowers, that feast the sight, without gratifying the smell: to the rose, and a white flower resembling jessamine, we are only indebted for their fragrance. The fruits are mangoes, guavas, pomegranates, ananas or pine apples, musk and water melons, limes, lemons, and oranges, all which spring up spontaneously, and grow to a great degree of perfection. Ginger, and tumeric, which has much the same qualities of ginger, are produced in this fertile soil, in their highest state of excellence.

*Letter XX*

Dear Sir,

Our march from Alahabad was extremely pleasant, until we came to Mendegaut on the river of Ganges, when a violent storm arose, accompanied with hail, lightning, and thunder, which continued for three days, and greatly annoyed both men and cattle. We remained here a week, to repair some damages suffered by the weather, and then crossed over to the plains of Belgram, on the opposite side of the river, where we encamped in the year 1776. These plains take their name from the village of Belgram, situate about two miles farther up the country. In a few months after our arrival, the Nabob Aspa-doulah [Asaf al-Daula], in consequence of a difference with the Fouzdars Maboub and Cossi-bussant [Faujdars Mahbub Ali Khan and Khwaja Basant Ali Khan], arising from their non-compliance to pay the usual annual tribute, due for some time, collected his troops together, in order to march against them, having first dispatched an express to General Stibbert, who commanded our army, acquainting him of his intended expedition, and requesting his immediate assistance. At the instance of Aspah-doulah, two regiments of Seapoys, under the direction of Colonel Parker, were ordered to a place called Coragh [Kora], about eighty miles from Belgram, in order to reinforce the Nabob's troops, which they met on the way, advancing with a few pieces of cannon. Maboub apprized by his scouts, of the route of our detachment, sent Deputies to Col. Parker, to request a personal interview with him. The Colonel wishing to accommodate matters if possible, without resorting to the horrors of war, agreed on it; and the result of their meeting, was apparently amicable, on both sides. On the next day, our Officers were invited by Maboub, to dine with him: he, in the mean time, prepared his men for a secret attack, and previously poisoned the provisions intended for their entertainment. The Gentlemen, by no means, suspecting his dark design, were actually on the way to their perfidious host, and must have met with an untimely fate at his inhospitable table, had not one of his servants providentially disclosed the secret before their arrival, and informed them that there was a plan concerted to surprise the main body, in their absence. The Colonel, Capt. Gravely, and the rest of the Officers, alarmed at this intelligence, instantly returned to the camp, and perceived at some distance, numbers of Maboub's men, advancing in regular order, to give them battle. Our soldiers, at a moment's notice, were prepared to oppose their force, and made so vigorous a charge on them, at the first onset, when they came up, that their ranks were broken, and the greater part of them discouraged from disappointment, and deserted by the hope of an easy conquest, fled, in the utmost confusion and disorder, after an engagement in which, though soon over, many of the enemy fell. Cossi-bussant escaped with those who made off, at the commencement of hostilities; and Maboub was pursued, taken, and sent prisoner, under a strong guard to Aspah-doulah at Lecknow, where he received that punishment, which his perfidy deserved.

A few of our Seapoys were killed; and the gallant Captain Gravely, no less distinguished for his prowess in the field, than his conduct in private life, received an ill fated wound, of which he died, in a few months after Col. Parker, and the two regiments under his command, returned to Belgram. He was sincerely regretted by his brother Officers; by whom and his weeping Soldiers, his funeral was processionally attended to the grave, and he was interred with due military honours. His afflicted widow erected a very handsome monument to his memory, near the ground where his own regiment usually paraded.

Lecknow [Lucknow], the town, to which Maboub was sent, is a place of considerable trade, and one of the principal factories in the Mogul's dominions. The inhabitants are opulent and industrious; and the Nabob Aspa-doulah, with other Noblemen, occasionally reside here, living in all the ease and splendor of eastern luxury, and frequently indulging themselves with their dancing girls. There are some good houses in Lecknow, occupied by merchants and factors; nor is it less remarkable for it's cotton manufactories, than for a beautiful kind of porcelain and earthen ware.

The Nabob keeps a kind of a military force here, called Burkendaws, who are not so uniform in dress as the Seapoys. Their arms are match fire-locks, bows and arrows, spears, daggers, swords, and shields.

## Contents of Volume the Second

*Letter XXVI*

Of Bombay, it's fine harbour, castle and out-forts: situation of the English church and houses of the inhabitants: description of the cocoa-nut and palm tree.

*Letter XXVII*

Practice of chewing betel, considered a polite custom: of arek, chunam, cachoonda, and catchoo: of tobacco and sugar plantations.

*Letter XXVIII*

Of gambling; managers licenced, give security for their conduct, and amass great riches: anecdote of a Seapoy who receives bad coin in exchange for good, from a sharper: of jugglers, their deceptions: incantation of snakes: dancing snakes: method of curing the sting of one.

*Letter XXIX*

Description of the elephant: manner of taking it: anecdote of the sagacity of one, similar to gratitude in the human species: of the rhinoceros, and animal next in bulk and figure to the elephant: of the camel, considered as a beast of burden, or for dispatch.

*Letter XXX*

March from Fort-william to Barahampore: arrival there: particular description of the fort of Ganlin [Gwalior], which is stormed by the English, and though deemed impregnable, surrenders to them: Colonel William A. Baillie is attacked by Hyder's son, and repulses him.

*Letter XXXI*

Capt. Baker is appointed to the command of the Seapoys' battalion: march to Barahampore: halt at Denapore: the Author, now market-master, is dispatched with two Seapoys to Goolden-gunge [Golding's Ganj], to purchase corn: one of the Seapoys is

killed in a fray with some of the peasantry: the other makes off:
the Author narrowly escapes with his life, and proceeds to Gooldengunge, from whence he forwards the supplies for the army:
he is afterwards appointed Jemidar, and goes with the army to
Caulpee [Kalpi]: detachments are sent from the main body to
disperse the Morattoes: the entire brigade arrive at Caunpore
[Cawnpur]: Governor Hastings orders the Raja Cheyt-sing to be
arrested: he is rescued by a body of his own troops, who massacre
the guard about him; and escapes to Lutteefgur [Latifgarh].

*Letter XXXII*

Ramjaum, Cheyt-sing's General pursues Governor Hastings: attacks a strong force of the English at Ramnagur: several killed
and wounded: Captain Blair effects a good retreat: Ramjaum
proceeds to the fort of Pateetah [Patita]: Lieut. Pohill defeats a
party of the enemy at Seekur: Major Popham and Capt. Blair
attack a large body of the enemy within a mile of Pateetah: and
conquer them after a dreadful carnage on both sides: Col. Morgan
with his entire force marches from Caunpore to Chunar, by order
of Governor Hastings, and joins Major Popham in that garrison:
detachments proceed to Lutteefgur, Seckroot [Sacrut] and Lora:
two companies under the direction of Capt. Baker, march to
Pateetah, which after three days siege is taken: Captain Baker
distinguishes himself in this action: Major Crabb attacks Ramjaum on his way to Lutteefgur, and puts him to flight—Cheyt-
sing escapes from Bidgegur [Bijigarh], and seeks a refuge among
the Morattoes.

*Letter XXXIII*

Captain Baker proceeds to Ramnagur, and from thence to Gochipour [Ghazipur]: Major Popham marches to Bidgegur, attacks it,
and after a month's siege, obliges the Raja's mother to surrender
the fort by capitulation: the property taken at Bidgegur is divided
among the captors: extracts from the Raja's letters to Governor
Hastings, expressive of his humility and sufferings: his manifesto
to the native Princes.

*Letter XXXIV*

A disturbance arises at Gochipour between the natives and Fouzdar: Capt. Baker attacks them at a little village called Bellua, and brings them under subjugation: Ramjaum's cattle is taken and divided as a booty among the men: march to Jouanpour [Jaunpur]: another skirmish with the natives, who, after an obstinate defence, escape in the night: a few thoughts on war: short description of a cavern near Jouanpour: restoration of peace: return to Chunargar.

*Letter XXXV*

Captain Baker discloses his intentions of going to Europe, the Author resigns his commission, in order to accompany him: passage from Chunargar to Dacca: pleasant seats and improvements on each side of the river: Dacca the first manufactory in India for embroideries, muslin and filligrane work wrought only by men: provisions cheap: descriptions of a large cannon: of the grand Nabob's entertainment on the water, on his accession to the throne: his elegant samsundars, or barges described.

*Letter XXXVI*

Celebration of the festival of Hassan, Hussen: description of the most inimitable paper edifice, called Gouwarrah, carried in grand procession through the town, to the burial ground of Hassan, Hussen: account of the Mohametan lent, their strict observance of it: real anecdote of a Banyan merchant, who almost perished through excessive thirst, for the sake of his religion.

*Letter XXXVII*

Voyage to Calcutta: description of the river Sunderbun; the woods on each side of the river infested with wild beasts: the tygers most dangerous: several villages along the banks: the cottages simply constructed, are easily removed when the floods come on: the natives very simple in their manners: a few huts between the villages, built by European adventurers: arrival at Calcutta: people of rank appear with more eclat there than their equals in Europe: every private gentleman is attended by twenty servants, at least:

first rate characters attended by a greater number: description of a gentleman's derawan or door-keeper: of certain punishments, and the crimes for which they are inflicted.

*Letter XXXVIII*

The author's departure from Calcutta: he proceeds to Belcoor, and embarks in a Danish Indiaman bound for Europe: arrival at Madapallam: description of Madras or Fort St George: its strength, situation, public and private buildings, Governor's guard and attendants when he appears abroad: return to Madapallam: pass the Cape of Good Hope: sketch of a storm: touch at St Helena: arrival at Darmouth [Dartmouth] in England.

## Reproduction of the letters of Vol. II

*Letter XXI*

Dear Sir,

At some distance from Lecknow [Lucknow], is the town of Oude; and it will ever be a place of constant resort while it holds the remains of Sujah-doulah [Shuja al-Daula], which are deposited here in a magnificent tomb, illumined every night with a number of glittering lamps, and covered with ornamented muslin. It is sheltered by a grand dome supported by pillars, and on each side is placed a large silver jar of water, from an opinion that he may rise in the night to bathe, which the Mahometans look upon as a purification necessary to prepare them for their admission into the regions of happiness. This town is much indebted to him for the great improvements it received during his reign; and the surrounding country also, which appears like one extensive garden. His palace in Oude is an ancient but spacious mansion, and still retains the striking appearance of pristine grandeur.

In the environs of the town, there are lofty groves and wide extending parks, called by the natives, circarga, where he had often passed some of his leisure hours in the pleasures of the chase and riding. His ponds were stored with a variety of curious fishes, both exotic and domestic, with their fins and tails adorned with small golden rings. He frequently made it the amusement of his evenings to feed them with rice, and observe them leap above water to receive it from his hand. He was so extremely fond of curiosities, that he kept a menage constantly supplied with a number of strange animals wild and tame, which he collected from different parts of the world, and confined in iron cages. His great revenues were scarcely sufficient to support his extravagance, and gratify his unbounded love of pleasure.

Some time before Sujah-doulah's death, he repeatedly sent to Mulnahoffis [Maulana Hafiz Rahmat Khan], Nabob of the Rohellas [Rohillas], for the customary tribute, which the latter, on consulting his Officers, not only refused to pay, but even threatened, *vi et armis*, to oppose him. Sujah-doulah, without delay, having acquainted General Champion of his conduct, was reinforced by him, and marched with his brave auxiliaries to the Rohellas, where he met the numerous troops of the enemy on the field of battle, and warmly engaged them, until victory inclining to our side, conferred on us her unfading laurels, as the meed of military virtue. Col. William Ann. Bailie, then Major of artillery, distinguished himself by his intrepid zeal and gallantry in this expedition.

A great part of the enemy's army were killed; the rest fled, and some of them were pursued and taken. General Champion returned with his men to head quarters, at Belgram; and Sujah-doulah directed his course to the very palace of Mulnahoffis, who was also in the number of the slain, and compelled his daughter, a beautiful young woman, whom he found in one of the grand apartments to come along with him to Oude. Having placed this unfortunate Lady in his seraglio, where nine hundred pining beauties, with their attendants, were already immured, he forced her to yield to his licentious desires, but purchased his enjoyment at a dear rate, as his life was the forfeit of it. The violated female, with a soul, the shrine of purity, like that of the divine Lucretia, whose chastity will ever adorn the historic page, fired with indignation at such unmanly treatment, grew frantic with rage, and disdaining life after the loss of honour, stabbed her brutal ravisher with a lancet, which she afterwards plunged into her own bosom, and expired. Notwithstanding the dangerous wound he received, by the appointment of Heaven, from the avenging hand of injured innocence, he might have lingered some time longer in life, had he kept within the bounds of moderation, by restraining the impetuosity of his unruly passions. But his career was pleasure, to which he gave such a loose, that his recent wound opened, and bleeding afresh, reduced him to a state of debility that terminated in his death. On account of his elevated rank in human life, his obsequies were conducted with great pomp and ceremony; and his funeral formed a pageant procession, in which his officers and soldiers walked in solemn pace, to the sounds of pensive music. After his interment, the women who composed his seraglio, laid aside their jewels and ornaments, to denote, at least, in appearance, their sorrow on this mournful occasion.

## Letter XXII

Dear Sir,

I shall now give you some account of the city of Delhi, which is the capital of the province, and situate in the centre of the empire: it lies in 78 degrees, east longitude from London, and 26 degrees north latitude. It's form is something like a crescent standing on the river Jemma, which runs through it. At present it is divided into three spacious towns, about 130 miles to the northward of Agra, in a very pleasant country, and pure, wholesome climate.

The first town of Delhi, is supposed to have contained nine castles and fifty-two gates; and at some distance from it, is a handsome stone bridge. The second town, which had been taken from the Indians, a long time since, by one of the former Mogul's, has a very fine appearance, and fills the mind with ideas of the true sublime, from the ruins of the many grand monuments of their ancient heroes who fell in war, and other magnificent buildings, nearly demolished by Shah Johan [Shah Jahan], the father of Aurengzebe [Aurangzeb]. The third town, which lies close to the second and almost built on its ruins, was called Johan Abad [Shahjahanabad], but the Moguls have given it the name of Delhi. It is imagined, from the frequent wars that desolated a great part of the country of Indostan, at the time of the accession of the Patan Princes, that Shah Johan had laid the foundation of this city in blood, the better (he observed) to cement the stones. This city receives no small embellishment from the delightful gardens that surround it; and forms it's principal entrance by a very wide street of a prodigious length, with arches on each side, for the purpose of stores and ware-rooms, to which the merchants and tradesmen bring whatever is valuable or curious from all parts of India. This street leads to the royal palace, at the outer gate of which, stand the figures of two huge elephants, with images mounted on them, representing two Rajas, famous in the history of Indostan, for their uncommon valour. They were brothers, who lost their lives in their gallant defence of some possessions, against a powerful army headed by Ekbar [Akbar].

Around the palace, which is two miles in circumference, is a great wall built of hewn stone, and defended with battlements, and a vast number of strong towers, at a little distance from each other. It consists of several courts, and the first of these belongs to the chief nobility, who frequently parade here, on their elephants, in all the pride of Oriental grandeur.

Within this court, is a square adorned with handsome porticos, from which you descend to convenient apartments occupied by the guards: On the east, are the courts of justice; on the west, the apartments of the ladies; and in the middle, an elegant canal formed with vast judgment and art, into basins. From the first court is a grand avenue leading to the second where the Omrahs or Nobles mount guard in person, and deem it a particular honour to wait on the present Mogul, Ahamut Shaw Baudshaw [Ahmad Shah Badshah].

The next object that presents itself to the view, is the Divan, which is held in the third court, where the Emperor gives public audience. It is a superb edifice, open at both sides and covered with a spacious dome, supported by thirty marble pillars of masterly workmanship, ornamented with painted flowers. It contains a grand hall, the ascent to which, is by a flight of marble steps, and in the centre is an alcove magnificently embellished, where the grand Mogul is proudly seated on a brilliant throne, glittering with diamonds, and a profusion of costly jewels.

The history of the revolutions of his court is fraught with so much fiction, that it would be impossible to reconcile it to reason or reflection; yet if we believe the records and traditions of the natives, it's sovereigns were the greatest and most arbitrary Monarchs in the world. Their orders, though ever so extravagant, were submissively obeyed; and their mandates observed by the remotest nations. Their very names struck terror into the hearts of their enemies; but so rapid has been the decline of their power, that the race of the great Tamerlane is now little respected since the days of Nizam Almoulud [Nizam al-Mulk]. The royal tenure of the throne, is grown so insecure, that the Mogul has been, of late years, deposed at pleasure, to make way for such of his servants as could gain over the people, that great engine of power! to their cause. His authority, which prevailed, in former ages, over most of the Kings of the earth, now reaches little farther than his seraglio, where he dreams away life, drowned in the enjoyment of dissolute pleasures. His Viziers, who transact the affairs of the state, study rather to promote their own views than advance his interest; and often abridge his power in order to increase their consequence. They make peace or declare war, without his knowledge; and his Viceroys, on the other hand, who were, some years ago, appointed, or dismissed from office by him, have, of late, shaken off their dependence, and even nominated their own successors. They also, like so many independent Sovereigns, grant leases and other privileges to the Europeans, or those whom they wish to serve. His Omrahs are extremely tyrannical, and must, sooner or later by their impolicy, precipitate the ruin of the entire empire. From their oppression it's great metropolis has but few manufacters, who are obliged to work for any price those tyrants please to pay them for their labour, which is always considerably less than the value. This ungenerous treatment has not only compelled the ingenious artisan to seek encouragement elsewhere, and proved the certain means of supplying the English factories with skilful workmen, but reduced the people of Delhi to the necessity of purchasing the goods of other places, at a much dearer rate, than they need pay at home, had they given sufficient support to their own manufacturers.

## Letter XXIII

Dear Sir,

The principal rural sports of the people of Indostan, are hunting and hawking: they purchase hawks and other birds of prey from Persia, which are taught to fly at all manner of game.

The Soubahs and other great characters of the country, find much amusement in the combats of wild beasts. The elephant often encounters the elephant, with a rider mounted on each, to manage them, on a larger space of ground paled in with bamboes to keep off the crowd of spectators: they attack each other with great fury, for several hours, till one of them with it's rider, is either killed or disabled. The buffalo commonly engages with the tyger, and, though ferocious the latter, frequently worsts his quadruped antagonist. It would be endless to enumerate the many diversions of this kind, which consist of various animals attacking each other or combated by men who risque their lives in such dangerous enterprizes.

Among the joyous inhabitants of this country, there are some content to live on what is just sufficient to supply human necessity: which is strictly pursuing the idea of Goldsmith, that elegant writer, who observes in his Edwin and Angelina,

> Man wants but little here below,
> Nor wants that little, long.

They acquire a support, by administering to travellers as they journey along the roads and highways, a chilm, or pipe of tobacco, for which they receive a small gratuity. The rich and poor, sometimes, promiscuously mingle together, and often partake of the same refreshment.

At Muckenpore [Manikpur], a small village sixty miles from Belgram, is the resort of a number of Faquirs, from Delhi, Oude, and the neighbouring provinces. Hither the pious natives flock, to bestow their charity on these holy men, and think it a kind of religious humanity, highly acceptable to their God, to confer their benefactions on his faithful servants.

From the prayers of the Faquirs, great blessings are expected, and many calamities thought to be averted, as they obtain the reputation of sainted martyrs, by torturing their bodies, and suffering a variety of punishments, by way of penance, during this earthly pilgrimage. Some pierce their flesh with spears, and drive daggers through their hands: others carry on their palms, for a length of time, burning vessels full of fire, which they shift from hand to hand: many walk, with bare feet on sharp iron spikes fixed in a kind of sandal: several of their order turn their faces over one shoulder, and keep them in that situation till they fix for ever, their heads looking backward: another sect clinch their fists very hard, till the nails of the fingers grow into the palms, and appear through the back of their hands, and numbers, who never speak, turn their eyes to the point of the nose, losing the power of looking in any other direction. These last pretend to see what they call the sacred fire. Strange as this austerity may seem, if accompanied with purity of intention, it must be considered by the unprejudiced, as less offensive to the Deity, than the indulgence of the passions: though man be not forbid to enjoy the good things of this life, yet an abuse of that enjoyment, which evinces his ingratitude to Heaven, is punished even here below, by wasting the ungenerous being to an untimely grave— but he who foregoes the pleasures of a fleeting period, through an expectation of permanent happiness, and suffers temporary torture in order to obtain endless bliss, with a mind all directed to that great Power who gave him existence, must, notwithstanding the ridicule of the world, meet with a more favourable sentence at his awful tribunal.

Not long before our departure from Belgram, we were honoured with a visit from the Nabob Aspa-doulah, accompanied by General Stibbert, his Aid-du-Camps, and other Officers of distinction, who met him on the way, in his usual style of grandeur, mounted with his Nobles, on an elephant richly caparisoned, and attended by his numerous train of Burkendaws, Chopdars, pages, &c. and a native band of music to enliven the procession, of which the annexed plate will give you a more perfect idea, than this description.

His entry through Belgram was announced by the beating of drums, firing of cannon, and other marks of military honour. After a repast at the General's, he retired to a large decorated tent erected for him, which covered almost an acre of ground; adjacent to his, others were pitched for his attendants.

The day after his arrival, our Commander in Chief issued his orders to prepare for a review. Early next morning, one regiment of Europeans, six of Seapoys, two companies of artillery, and one troop of cavalry, amounting in all to about seven thousand, were in perfect readiness on the wide plain. The Nabob on his elephant, in company with the General, passed the lines. Shortly after, the former descended from the back of the unwieldy animal, and mounted a beautiful Arabian horse, on which he received the salute of the Officers. Colonel Ironside ranged the troops in the following order: the cavalry were placed on the right and left wing;

three regiments of Seapoys on each side next to them; and the European infantry in the centre. At first, they were all reviewed in one body, and afterwards formed different corps, observing the most exact discipline and regularity in their various evolutions, which gave much satisfaction to the General, Officers, and numerous spectators. Aspa-doulah, in particular, was exceeding pleased with the beauty and order of our tactics, and expressed his approbation in the terms of that lively kind of gratitude arising from a high sense of received pleasure. After the review, a breakfast was prepared for him, during which, the artillery continued to salute him with their cannon. His fare was served up by his own servants, as he could not touch any thing from the hands of a Christian, consistent with the duties of his religion: however, to shew his politeness, he ate at the same table, with our Officers of rank, and having remained a few days in the camp, returned to his own territories.

*Letter XXIV*

Dear Sir,

Having received orders to march to Calcutta, we quitted Belgram; and finding it unnecessary to keep a force any longer there, on account of the good understanding that prevails, at present, between the Court of Delhi and the East India Company, the chaumnies were entirely demolished, and every vestige of a house or building razed to the ground.

On our way, we passed by some small factories belonging to the Dutch, Danes, French, and others, that were once in the hands of the Portuguese, but being since reduced, have come into the possession of the English. Our brigade, at length, arrived at Fort William in the year 1778, and replaced the other, which marched to Denapore.

About fifteen miles from Fort William, on the opposite side of the river, is a Danish settlement, called Serampour [Serampore]. It's manufactures consist of cotton, baffety, calico, chintz, table cloths, and napkins.

The houses of the inhabitants are very neat, and on the river side is a small battery, with the Governor's castle in the centre, and the Danish flag flying a'top.

In Chinsura, a Dutch settlement, much the same kind of trade is conducted, as at Serampour.

A little farther on, is Chandernagore, or Frasdanga, the scene of many disputes between the French and English; the latter of whom are now the proprietors of it; on the west, it lies exposed to an enemy, though encompassed by a wall, and, in other situations, pretty well fortified. It drives a brisk trade, and carries on, to some extent, the manufacture of handkerchiefs and striped muslins.

Near Frasdanga, and in the same direction, is Gretti, then belonging to the French, under the government of Monsieur Chevalier, but now in possession of the English. The Governor's house, which takes it's name from the place about it, was a superb mansion, rising in all the pride of architecture, over the margin of the Ganges, and decorated inside in a style of unrivalled elegance: part of the furniture was covered with a rich embroidered sattin, and the very purdoes of the windows were of scarlet quilted sattin. The avenue to this grand edifice was shaded on both sides, with rows of embowering trees; and the beauty, the fragrance of his gardens, which perfumed the wanton air, ravished the senses: his fish-ponds, cascades, and groves, heightened the imagery of the varied scene; and his expanding lawns were adorned with figures of snow-white marble, that almost started under the artist's hand, from the rude material into life. On the domain was an Opera-house for his amusement. At the outside entrance to the palace, stood the Governor's guard.

Fifty miles from Calcutta lies the town of Hugley, defended by a strong fortress, and surrounded by a deep ditch: it is a place of considerable traffic, particularly in the article of opium, which is brought chiefly from Patna. Notwithstanding the fatal effects of this plant, the irresistible avarice of the Dutch, induces them to raise it wherever they possess a spot of ground in India; but the Chinese, from its destructive qualities, forbid, under the penalty of death, the cultivation of it, and demolish any house, in which it is exposed for sale.

It is used by the people of every class, among the Hindoos and Mahometans: the lower order take it, when they enter on any arduous enterprise, to render them insensible of the danger; and the gentry, who are fond of every thing that tends to a gratification of the passions, consider it as a great luxury. It's effects, however, are various, according to the manner of preparing it. Opium in it's original state, is the produce of a species of poppy, the root of which is about the thickness of a man's finger, full of a bitter juice that runs through the whole plant. The flower resembles a rose, and the stem which is commonly pliable, grows to the height of two cubits, and produces a kind of leaves (not unlike those of the lettuce) oblong, indented, curled, and of a sea-green colour. When it is full of sap, a slight incision is made on the outside, from which flow some drops of a milky nature. These drops soon congeal; and when moistened and kneaded with warm water and honey, become more consistent and viscous like pitch; after this process, the glutinous matter is made into small cakes fit for immediate use. The good kind is that, which is soft and yielding to the touch. Patna is allowed to send the best to market: it is there purchased at a cheap rate, though extremely dear in some parts of India. It has nearly opposite qualities, stupefying, at one time, and raising exhilarating ideas at another; it occasions drowsiness, and vigilance; and taken to an excess, brings on a madness that ceases only in death.

*Letter XXV*

Dear Sir,

As an instance of the wealth and consequence that aggrandize any situation, where trade is introduced, I shall give you some account of Surat, which lies in twenty-one degrees, thirty minutes, north latitude; and seventy-two degrees east longitude from the meridian of London.

About the middle of last century this place was only the resort of a few merchants, who by extending their commerce, invited numbers to settle among them; and thus, by the introduction of arts, population, and industry, Surat became in a few years, one of the most considerable towns in the world. It is defended by a wall and towers, and has a square castle with a tower at each angle on the S.W. part of it, which commands both the river, and the avenues to the town by land. It is said to contain above two hundred thousand inhabitants: while the Mogul government was in vigour, merchants of all religions and denominations were induced to take shelter under it; and such was the honesty of the traders, that bags of money ticketed and sealed, would circulate for years without being weighed. The Gentoos are very numerous here, particularly the tribe of the Banyans, who are the fairest dealers in the world, and remarkable for plain integrity, and an admirable command of temper, in the course of their transactions. It is impossible to rouse them into passion, and when others are subdued by that temporary frenzy of the mind, they wait with patience till it subsides, and by these means, enjoy a superior advantage over the rest of mankind.

The Governor of Surat keeps his seat of administration at the Durbar or Court, where all actions criminal and civil are brought before him, and summarily dispatched in the Eastern manner. The buildings are in the Gentoo and Morisque style; and the houses of the great are so contrived that their gateways are defensible against any sudden irruption of a few armed men. The private apartments are backwards for the greater security of the women, of whom the Moors, especially, are extremely jealous. They have always, at least, one room, in each dwelling, where a fountain is kept playing in the middle of it, by the murmurs of which they are lulled to sleep, and refreshed by the coolness it diffuses through the apartment. Their saloons, which they call diwans, entirely open on one side to their gardens, where fountains, cascades, meandering rills, and variegated flower beds, form the most delightful assemblage of rural beauty and prospect. In summer, they often go in parties, to country recesses, a little way out of town, in order to enjoy themselves in their frescades, by the side of the waters with which they are furnished. The English have a very pleasant garden here, for the use and recreation of the Gentlemen of the factory.

The streets of Surat are irregularly laid out; and the stories of the houses are carried up projecting over one another, in such a manner, that the uppermost apartments on each side, are so close, as to darken the streets below, without excluding a free circulation of air. As to provisions I cannot imagine that there is in the universe a better place. The great plenty of every article, which an unbounded influx throws into the market, renders all kinds of eatables extremely cheap: wild fowl and game can be had at an easy rate; and nothing can exceed their sallads and roots. Among the articles of luxury, which they have in common with other parts of the East, there are public hummums for bathing, cupping, rubbing and sweating, but the practice of champing, which is derived from the Chinese, appears to have been known to the ancients, from the following quotations.

*Percurrit agili corpus arte tractatrix*
*Manumque doctam spargit omnibus membris.*

[The female masseuse/shampooer, with her agile art, runs over his body and spreads her skilled hands over all his limbs]
MART. Lib. iii. Epig. 82.

Seneca, at the end of his sixty-sixth letter, inveighs against it as a point of luxury introduced among the Romans, thus—*An potius optem ut malacissandos articulos exoletis meis porrigam? ut muliercula, aut aliquis in mulierculam ex viro versus digitulos meos ducat?* [Should I desire to be allowed to stretch out my limbs for my slaves to massage/shampoo: or to have a female masseuse/ shampooer pull my finger-joints?] The person who undergoes this operation, lies, at full length, on a couch or sopha, on which the operator chafes or rubs his limbs, and cracks the joints of the wrist and fingers. All this, they pretend, not only supples the joints, but procures a brisker circulation to the fluids apt to stagnate, or loiter through the veins, from the heat of the climate, which is, perhaps, the best recommendation of such a practice.

*Letter XXVI*

Dear Sir,
At a small distance from Surat lies Bombay, an island so situate as to form one of the most commodious bays perhaps in the world; from which distinction it received the denomination of Bombay, by corruption from the Portuguese Buon bahia. The harbour is spacious enough to contain any number of ships; has excellent anchoring ground; and by it's circular position, can afford them a land-locked shelter against any winds, to which the mouth of it is exposed. The castle is a regular quadrangle, well built of strong hard stone; and round the island there are several little out-forts and redoubts. The English Church at Bombay, is a neat, airy building, standing on the Green, a large space of ground, and pleasantly laid out in walks planted with trees, round which are

mostly the houses of the English inhabitants. These consist only of ground-floors, after the Roman fashion, with a court-yard before and behind, offices, and outhouses. They are substantially built with stone and lime, and whitewashed on the outside, which has a decent appearance, but very offensive to the eyes from the glare of the sun. Few of them have glass windows to any apartment, the sashes being generally panned with a kind of transparent square-cut oyster-shells, transmitting sufficient light, and excluding, at the same time, the violence of it's glare.

At some distance farther on the continent, there are fairs held, that last generally nine or ten days. Hither the Banyans resort, and such dealers as are sometimes disappointed by the Factors or Agents of the Company, (who bespeak their commodities) to expose their goods for sale on banks of earth raised for that purpose, under small sheds. The soil of this country is chiefly employed in cocoa-nut groves, palm-trees, &c.

As to the cocoa-nut tree itself, not all the minute descriptions I have heard of it, seem to me to come up to the reality of it's wonderful properties and use. Nothing is so unpromising as the aspect of this tree; nor does any yield a produce more profitable, or more variously beneficial to mankind: it has some resemblance to the palm-tree; perhaps one of it's species. The leaves of it serve for thatching; the husk of the fruit for making cordage, and even the largest cables for ships. The kernel of it is dried, and yields an oil much wanted for several uses, and forms a considerable branch of traffic under the name of copra. Arrack, a coarse sort of sugar, called jagree, and vinegar are also extracted from it, besides many other particulars too tedious to enumerate. The cultivation of it is extremely easy, by means of channels conveying water to the roots, and a manure laid round them, consisting of the small fry of fish, known by the name of buckshaw.

There are also here and there interspersed a few brab-trees, or rather wild palm trees (the word brab being derived from Brabo, which in Portuguese signifies wild) that bear an insipid kind of fruit, about the size of a common pear, and produce from incisions at the top, the toddy or liquor drawn from them, of which the arrack that is made, is esteemed much better than that from the cocoa-nut tree. They are generally cultivated near the sea-side, as they thrive best in a sandy soil. It is on this tree that the toddy birds, so called from their attachment to it, build their exquisitely curious nests, wrought out of the thinnest reeds and filaments of branches, with inimitable mechanism. The birds themselves are about the bigness of a partridge, but of no consideration either for plumage, song, or the table.

The banian tree, which is a species of fig, grows here to an enormous height. Some of it's branches shoot forth horizontally from the trunk; and from them proceed a number of less boughs, that fall in a perpendicular direction, downwards, taking root from other bodies, which, like pillars, serve to support the arms they sprung from. Thus, one tree multiplies into twenty or thirty bodies, and spreads over a great space of ground, sufficient to shelter, at least, five hundred persons. Neither is this, nor any other of the Indian trees, without leaves all the year. Under the branches of the banian, the Gentoos frequently place their images, and celebrate their festivals; and the Faquirs inflict on themselves, different kinds of punishment. Milton, in his Paradise Lost, gives a very natural description of it in the following terms:

> The fig-tree, not that kind for fruit renown'd;
> But such as at this day to Indians known
> In Malabar, or Decan, spreads her arms,
> Branching so broad and long, that in the ground
> The bending twigs take root; and daughters grow
> About the mother-tree, a pillar'd shade!
> High over-arch'd, and echoing walks between.

### Letter XXVII

Dear Sir,

As the practice of chewing betel is universal throughout India, the description of it may not prove unentertaining. It is a creeping plant cultivated in the same manner as the vine, with leaves full of large fibres like those of the citron, but longer and narrower at the extremity. It is mixed with the arek and chunam before it is used. The arek-nut is exactly in form and bigness like a nutmeg, only harder: it is marbled in the inside with white and reddish streaks, and wrapped up in the leaf. Chunam is nothing more than burnt lime made of the finest shells. To these three articles is often added for luxury, what they call cachoonda, a japan earth, which from perfumes and other mixtures, receives a high improvement. The taste of it is, at first, little better than that of common chalk, but soon turns to a flavour that dwells agreeably on the palate.

Another addition they use, termed catchoo, is a blackish, granulated, perfumed substance; and a great provocative, when taken alone, which is not a small consideration with the Asiatics in general.

So prevalent is the custom of chewing betel, that it is used by persons of every description; but it is better prepared for people of condition, who consider it a breach of politeness to take leave of their friends, without making presents of it. No one attempts to address his superior, unless his mouth is perfumed with it; and to neglect this ceremony even with an equal, would be deemed an unpardonable rudeness.

The dancing girls are eternally scented with it, as being a powerful incentive to love, and a composition that gives fragrance to the breath and lips. It is taken after meals, during a visit, and on the meeting and parting of friends or acquaintance; and most people here are confirmed in the opinion that it also strengthens the stomach, and preserves the teeth and gums. It is only used in smoking, with a mixture of tobacco and refined sugar, by the Nabobs and other great men, to whom this species of luxury is confined.

In several parts of the country, the soil and climate are very favourable to these latter productions. Tobacco of the finest quality, grows in rich moist grounds, in which it is generally planted, and brought by cultivation to great perfection. The sugar plantations employ thousands of the natives, who alone, inured to the excessive heat of vertical suns, are adequate to the fatigue of this laborious business. The cane commonly shoots up to the height of five or six feet, and is about half an inch in diameter: the stem or stock is divided by knots, above the space of a foot from each other: at the top, it puts forth a number of green leaves, from which springs a white flower. The canes, when ripe, are found quite full of a pithy juice (of which the sugar is made), and being then carried to the mill in bundles, are cut up into small pieces, and thrown into a large vessel much in the form of a mortar, in which they are ground by wooden rollers plated with steel, and turned either by the help of oxen, or manual labour; during this process, a liquor issues from them, which is conveyed through a pipe in the vessel above described into another in the sugar-house, and thence passes into a copper, that is heated by a slow fire, so as to make it simmer; it is then mixed with ashes and quick lime, in order to separate the unctuous parts, which float upon the surface in a thick scum, that is constantly taken off with the skimmer. After this, it passes through a second, third, fourth, and fifth boiler, which last brings it to the consistence of a thick syrup. In the sixth boiler, it is mixed with a certain quantity of milk, lime-water and alum, and receives it's full coition, which reduces it to almost one-third of it's first quantity. It is finally put into small baskets, where it remains some time to cool, and, afterwards, becomes fit for immediate use.

This is the manner of preparing the East Indian loaf sugar, so much esteemed in London, and confessedly allowed to be the best made in any part of the world.

## *Letter XXVIII*

Dear Sir,

The practice of gambling so dangerous in it's effects to many of it's votaries, is pursued in India with much eagerness, and even sanctioned by the laws of the country. It is, however, regulated under certain restrictions, and permitted only for a limited time. During the term, which in the Indian dialect, is called dewalli, and continues but a fortnight, the gaming table is frequented by persons of every description. Those who conduct this amusement, are under a heavy license, and give ample security for their observance of peace and good order. On such occasions, they generally keep police guards at their houses, to prevent disputes among the adventurers. Before they enter on this business, every manager, or keeper of a gambling house, is supplied with a large sum of money, for the accommodation of the gamesters, to whom he lends it out, on very advantageous conditions. The winner pays him in proportion to his gain, and the loser secures him in the principal borrowed, with interest. Thus, by a rapid increase of growing profits, he accumulates, in a little time, vast riches.

Notwithstanding the passions of men, and the quick circulation of cash, amid such bustling scenes, it seldom happens that base coin is ever found among the gains of the fortunate. The following is the only instance, within my recollection, of it's being passed in the country.

A Seapoy, possessed of fifty rupees, his sole treasure, was going from Calcutta to Patna; on the way, he met a man of genteel appearance, to whom, in the course of a free conversation, he unbosomed himself, and discovered the bulk of his fortune. His fellow traveller, who proved to be a coiner, observed, that as his (the Seapoy's) rupees were the currency of Calcutta, it would be his interest to change them for those of Patna, whither he was going, as he would benefit considerably by the exchange; and that he could oblige him with the coin of that city. The poor soldier, thankfully accepting the offer, counted down his fifty good pieces of silver, for fifty glittering base ones of the sharper, and parting him with a mutual shake of the hands, proceeded on his journey. Not until his arrival at Muxadabad, where he was about purchasing some necessary, did he discover the shining specimens of his friend's ingenuity, and making some very dismal, though pertinent reflections on the occasion, with a countenance, on which you could read in legible characters, A BLANK he exclaims—*I was a stranger, and he humanely took me in.*

After perambulating every street and alley of the large town of Muxadabad, and pervading every corner of it's precincts, he, at length, found his quondam companion at a gaming table, and in a paroxysm of gratitude not to be expressed by my unequal pen, seized him by the collar, bestowing on him, at the same time, such violent caresses of rude friendship, as greatly disfigured his person and apparel. When the first transports were over, he requested his money, which after some pressing solicitations, he obtained, and went his way, but not without leaving his worthy acquaintance some visible signs and tokens of lasting remembrance.

Though few the individuals in India, who impose on the unwary by the arts of swindling and fraud, the jugglers, or slight-of-hand men, are numerous, and greatly excel in their tricks and deceptions, any thing of the kind exhibited in Europe.

I have seen one of this astonishing class of men, place in the centre of a bazar, a little shrub or branch of a tree, with only a few leaves on it, over which he has thrown a cloth, and after playing for about half an hour, on a baslee, a sort of instrument consisting of a tube made of the shell of a pumpkin, and connected with two small reeds, through which the sounds pass from the tube applied to the mouth, he has desired some person in the crowd to take off the cloth, and the same branch, to the surprise of every beholder, appeared laden with fruit and blossoms. It would be endless to describe their other deceptions, which are equally unaccountable as wonderful. Their incantation of snakes, in particular, has been attributed by many of your countrymen, to magic and the power of the devil. Their hooded snakes, as they call them, are brought from place to place in close baskets, which are uncovered at the time of exhibition; and these reptiles, when the jugglers begin to play on their instruments, raise up their heads and dance while this strange music continues; but if it should stop, they also cease from dancing, and instantly hiss at each other. The dreadful infection raging in the human blood from the sting of a snake, is effectually cured by a juggler, who, if sent for in time, by playing on his baslee, as usual, calls forth the venomous reptile from it's hole, and compels it to bite the person already affected, till it's poison is exhausted, after which, it expires, and the patient recovers. Some of these men will sometimes present themselves to public view with two snakes writhing round the neck, without receiving the least injury. There is another species of the serpent, which is very large and long, with a head as big as an infant's, and a beautiful face resembling the human: it has been remarked by several, that this kind is supposed to be the same as that which tempted our first mamma, Eve.

### Letter XXIX

Dear Sir,

Of all the animals in the East or elsewhere, none can equal the elephant in magnitude. To excite your wonder, and, at the same time, afford you some entertainment, I shall here give you a particular description of this quadruped, which is (nem. con.) the largest in the universe. It is from twelve to fifteen feet high, and seven broad: it's skin about the belly is so tough, that a sword cannot penetrate it: the eyes of it are exceeding small, the ears large, the body round and full, and the back rises to an arch: it is of a darkish colour and very much seamed: on each side of it's jaws, within the mouth are four teeth or grinders; and two teeth which project outwards: in the male, they are stronger and thicker;

in the female, they are sharper and smaller: both male and female use one, which is sharp as a defensive weapon, and the other, which is blunted to grub up trees and plants for food. The teeth of the male sometimes grow to the length of ten feet, and have been known to weigh three hundred pounds each; the teeth of the female, though less, are the most valuable ivory. They naturally shed their teeth once in ten years, and bury them carefully in the earth, to prevent, as it is imagined, their being found by man. The elephant's tongue is small, but broad; the feet round and ample, and the legs have joints, which are flexible: the forehead is large and rising; the tail resembles that of a hog; and the blood of this creature is colder than that of any other; but the organ which most peculiarly distinguishes it, is the trunk. This singular member is crooked, grisly, and plaint, about seven feet in length, three in circumference, and gradually diminishing to the extremity. At the root, near the nose, are two passages, the one into the head, the other to the mouth; through the first, it breathes; and by the latter, it receives it's provisions, the trunk serving the purposes of a hand to feed it, and a weapon to defend it. So strong is this powerful animal, that it can lift a prodigious weight; and so delicate in the sensation of feeling, that it can take the smallest piece of coin from the ground. It delights much in water, and will swim a great way.

They are taken by stratagem in different parts of India, as they descend from the mountains, where they feed, to the lakes or rivers, to water. The hotteewallies, or people employed to take them, dig deep trenches in their direction, which they conceal with reeds covered over with earth and grass; the elephants, on their way to the watering places, unacquainted with the danger before them, fall into the pit contrived by these artful men who often risque their lives in the execution of such hazardous projects. The old animals, by some means, extricate themselves, and escape to the woods, but the young ones, who thus become an easy prey to their pursuers, are suffered to remain in this situation, for some days without food, till they are almost spent, and unable to make any resistance: an easy descent is then opened into the pits or trenches, and collars thrown round their necks, after which they are mounted, and following a tame elephant as their leader, conducted with great facility to the next town or village. When a considerable number of them, is collected in this manner, they are regularly trained by the hotteewallies, for the use of the Nabobs and other great men; and when rendered by age unfit for their amusements, they serve to carry the equipage of camps and other burdens. Under the management of their tutors, they are taught to do any thing, and, in a short time, become as tractable as the horses of the most famous riders in Europe.

It is related of one of them, that when the child of it's keeper, lay some time in a cradle, crying for want of nourishment, in the absence of the parents, this huge but generous animal took it up gently, gave it suck, and afterwards laid it down in the cradle with the utmost solicitude. This tenderness, which is not unlike gratitude in our species, proceeded from the kind treatment of it's keeper.

An elephant is commonly sold by measurement; and some of those animals, which are young and well trained, are purchased at the rate of 150 rupees per cubit: they are measured from the head to the tail, which is about seven cubits long, and at this calculation will amount to above one hundred pounds sterling each.

Next to the elephant in bulk and figure, is the rhinoceros, called by the modern Indians, abadu; it is not unlike the wild boar, but much larger, having thicker feet, and a more unwieldy body. It is covered with large hard scales of a blackish colour, which are divided into small squares, raised a little above the skin, and nearly resembling those of the crocodile. It's head, which is large, is wrapped up behind in a kind of capuchin; it's mouth is little; but its snout extends to a great length, and is armed with a long thick horn, which makes him terrible to other animals, it's tongue is as rough as a file, and a sort of wings like those of the bat, cover the belly.

In the Eastern territories, there is no beast more useful than the camel, either for burden or dispatch: some of them will carry a thousand weight, and travel, at least, seven or eight miles an hour: they have no teeth, except in the lower jaw, and one bunch on the back: none of the brute creation, of such a bulk, less voracious than this creature. They lie down on their bellies to receive their loads, and are always governed by the voice of the driver, who could never mend their pace, by beating them. They are naturally fearful, and extremely patient under fatigue.

*Letter XXX*

Dear Sir,

In the year of 1779, we marched from Fort William to Bara-hampore, and in some time after our arrival, the strong fortress of Ganlin was taken by our troops; the particular account of which, is as follows:

The Morattoes, whose depredations in every quarter, had given a general alarm, were making constant sallies from the different posts they fortified in many parts of the country. Their strongest hold, however, was the fort of Ganlin [Gwalior], in which they centred all their hopes of security, as it was always considered to be impregnable. It stands on a rock about two coss in length, and in many places above four hundred feet high, in some three hundred, but in no situation less than one hundred and fifty feet in height. The table is entirely surrounded by a rampart of stone, rising immediately from the edge of the rock, which in most parts, is rendered perpendicular. Within the rampart are many fine buildings, large tanks, innumerable wells, and cultivated land.

The only access to the fort, is by a flight of steps, defended by the rock on the one side, and a large stone wall on the other, flanked with bastions; and on the summit, is a passage through seven gateways. The craggy rock frightfully lofty, into which are hewn many caves, at whose entrances are gigantic figures of men and animals; the rampart seeming almost a continuation of this awful precipice; and the rising edifices, whose solemn domes, battlements, and balconies, are suspended, as it were, over the dreadful steep, forming all together, the most sublime view I ever beheld, strike the imagination with a kind of horrible aston-ishment far beyond simple admiration. A tribe of Morattoes, who lived by robbery, about this place, informed the Rana, that they ascended the fort in the night, and found the Chokeedars asleep; and offered, if encouraged by a sufficiently pecuniary recompense, to lead his troops to the very spot from whence they climbed up, promising also their assistance, by fixing ladders to help them to mount; but the Rana, through want of confidence in his troops, declined the enterprise.

Captain Popham, one of the English Officers, having procured some intelligence of the proposal made to the Rana, requested of him to send those men to him: they accordingly came, through the hope of reward, and went to the appointed place, with some of his own spies, who were particularly directed to watch their actions. The accounts brought back were so satisfactory, that he made instant preparations for a surprise, which he conducted with secrecy and dispatch.

In a month's time, during which he obtained some knowledge of this important situation, he was in perfect readiness for the intended attack, and on the third of August, about eleven o'clock, at night, Captain William Bruce, at the head of his British grenadiers, was ordered to march in front, attended by Lieut. Cameron, engineer, with his apparatus for scaling; Captain Popham, with two battalions, followed soon after, to support the assailants, and direct the entire expedition. Captain M'Clary was ordered with his battalion to march round towards the town, and intercept Ambassee [Ambaji Inglia], a Morattoe Chief, who had cantoned in it with four hundred horse; and Captain Clode was left in charge of the camp, at Raypore [Raipur], near four coss from Ganlin. In this disposition, the party advanced by private roads, and arrived at the foot of the rock, an hour before day-break. Captain Bruce's people were provided with sacks of coarse cloth, stuffed with cotton, to prevent the noise of their feet in mounting, and just as they arrived, the guards of the fort were going their rounds (as is the custom with the Chokeedars), their lights were seen, and the men distinctly heard. This seemed to portend the ruin of the plan, but firmness and resolution conquered every apprehension of danger. The spies observing the utmost silence, mounted the rock, and ascended the wall, from whence they brought intelligence that all was quiet: Lieut. Cameron then fixed the wooden ladders by which he mounted, and gave those of rope to the spies, who fastened them by a noose round the battlements of the wall.

Every thing in readiness, Capt. Bruce ascended with twelve men, and when he had got within the fort, he ordered them to sit down as closely as possible under the wall, till the others would come up. Near the place where they concealed themselves, three Chokeedars lay asleep, and three Seapoys rashly fired, which had almost defeated the success of the enterprize, and sacrificed the lives of the little party, which was soon surrounded by alarmed numbers of the garrison. Before they had recovered from their astonishment, of seeing our gallant soldiers within their walls, thirty Seapoys had ascended, and the rest followed very fast: a few shots and rockets were exchanged, and their principal Officer being wounded, the enemy dismayed and confounded at the boldness of the undertaking, took shelter in the inner buildings of the fort, from which they escaped in the utmost confusion.

Their Officers collected within one house, with their women, and hung out a white flag: a detachment of the English was sent to receive their arms, and give them quarters.

Thus fell, in less than two hours, the great and, as it was deemed, impregnable fortress of Ganlin, without the loss of a man; and twenty only were wounded. The place where the assault was made, from the foot of the rock to the wall is above two hundred feet high; to behold it even, must astonish you, beyond description, and you would have considered the execution of such a project all together impracticable, and not within the compass of human courage or abilities.

The enemy hitherto regarding any intention of disturbing them, as the greatest presumption, attributed our success to the divine interposition: such an attempt was indeed above common conception, and it had never succeeded, but for the terror, with which the boldness of the enterprise, had struck the unwary dupes of heedless security. The greatness of the undertaking, reflects the highest honour on the Officers and men employed in it; and proves the general opinion that there is no difficulty so arduous which may not be subdued, by the resolution and perseverance of a British soldier.

The Morattoe parties in this country, having heard with aston-ishment of the surrender of Ganlin, began to dread, and venerate the very names of the conquerors; and shortly after it was sur-prised, they evacuated eight forts, which they had formerly taken from the Raja of Ghoad [Gohad]. From one of the apartments of the Imperial palace, built by Akbar, within the fort, I looked down, and beheld, as it were from the clouds, the town, four hundred feet below me: such an awful scene forms a subject for the pencil of the most sublime artist.

About this time, Col. William A. Baillie, who was marching with a detachment of two hundred Europeans, and a battalion and half of Seapoys, from one of the provinces to join the main army, which was going to the relief of Arcot, was attacked by Hyder's son, with a large force, and repulsed him with slaughter.

The Colonel as usual, distinguished himself on this occasion with great firmness and intrepidity.

## Letter XXXI

Dear Sir,

In the year of 1781, Captain Baker, after his appointment to the command of the Seapoys' battalion, in the second brigade, with Lieutenants Simpson and Williamson, two companies of Europeans, and two companies of Seapoys, marched from Barahampore, in order to join the second brigade in Caunpore [Cawnpur]: on his promotion, he appointed me market-master to supply the bazar. We halted at Denapore to refresh the party, and draw their pay; and as they proceeded on their march, I was dispatched, with an escort of two Seapoys to Gooldengunge [Golding's Ganj], which was considered the cheapest market, to purchase corn for the army, and had in my possession for that purpose, four hundred goolmores, with bills on the Commissary there, amounting in all to fifteen hundred pounds sterl. As we journeyed onwards, one of the Seapoys happened to trample some melons in passing through a plantation near the river side, and on being observed by the proprietor, who desired him to be more cautious in his career, he returned him some impertinent answer, which roused the peasant's resentment, and discord expanding her gloomy wings, a battle ensued; the neighbouring cottagers thus alarmed, flocked to their friend's assistance, and cruelly stabbed his adversary, who fell a breathless corpse beneath their murderous weapons. The other Seapoy made off through the country, but I was dismounted from my horse, which I was obliged to leave behind, and having plunged into the Ganges, on whose verge I stood trembling for my fate, with the utmost difficulty I gained the opposite shore, fainting under the fatigue of my exertions in crossing the wide river, with my clothes on, and such a weight of gold about me. A few of the peasantry, who beheld me thus struggling for life, ran to my assistance, and after supporting me to the next cottage, kindly ministered what relief was in their power. As the night approached, I sunk to rest, and forgot the dangers of my late journey in the sweet oblivion of sleep.

Next morning, finding myself tolerably restored, I made my acknowledgements to these humane people, whose footsteps, an all-ruling Providence must, in that crisis, have directed, to save me from impending dissolution; and having gone forthwith to the Fouzdar of Gooldengunge, and given him up my money and bills, I related the story of my adventures: he seemed much affected at the recital, and detained me till the supplies for the use of the troops were purchased; a part was sent by water to Caunpore; and the rest by land, consisting of several loads of corn drawn by bullocks, with which I travelled, and joined the army at Buxar. From the early intelligence of the Seapoy, who escaped before me, the greatest surprize, and even doubt of the reality of my existence at my arrival, was almost graven on every countenance, as the prevailing opinion unanimously agreed on by all parties, was, that I had fallen a sacrifice with the other Seapoy to the rage and resentment of the country people.

From Buxar we marched for Caunpore, where we arrived in the latter end of February. On the first of March, Capt. Baker took the command of the battalion of Seapoys in Major Roberts' regiment, to which he had been recently promoted, and by his recommendation, I was appointed Jemidar in the same battalion.

Having received an account of the insurrections of the Morattoes in the vicinage of Caulpee [Kalpi], on the banks of the river Jemina, the entire brigade, by order of Colonel Morgan, proceeded to that town, and a part of the main army in different detachments, scoured the neighbouring country, in order to disperse those disturbers of the public tranquility, who, after some slight skirmishes, entirely fled, overawed by the terror of our arms.

We remained a few weeks in Caulpee, and then returned to Caunpore, where our stay was of no long continuance.

About this time Governor Hastings having required of Cheytsing his stipulated subsidies, towards defraying the expenses of the late war with Hyder Ally; and finding him either unwilling or unable to pay them, sent a guard consisting of two companies of Seapoys to arrest him: the alarming news of his being made a prisoner, soon spread through the country, and roused the indignation of his troops, who were seen in a large body, crossing the river from Ramnagur to the palace, in which he was confined. The two companies of our Seapoys, who formed the guard in an inclosed square outside the palace, were mostly massacred by this powerful force which rushed onward, like an irresistible torrent, that sweeps all away before it.

Ramjaum [Ramjiwan], one of the Raja's Generals, after killing a serjeant of the Seapoys, who opposed his entrance, broke into the royal mansion, and made way for the soldiery, who escorted their Prince through a garden which led to the river. As the banks were high above the surface, they let him down by turbans tied together, into a boat that conveyed him to the other side, whence he escaped under the friendly shade of night, to Lutteefgur [Latifgarh], one of his strongest fortresses, with a chosen band of men to protect him.

*Letter XXXII*

Dear Sir,

The day following, a large party of the Raja's, with Ramjaum at their head, went in pursuit of Governor Hastings, who proceeded to Chunargar; and having fought him in vain, they returned to Ramnagur, where they attacked a strong body of the English under the command of Capt. Mayaffre, of the artillery, who was hemmed in on every side by the narrow streets and winding alleys of the town, with which he was unacquainted. Being thus exposed to the fire of the enemy from all quarters, and particularly to that of a covered party that greatly annoyed him, he fell in the scene of battle, with upwards of one hundred and fifty of his men, among whom were Captain Doxat, and Lieutenants Stalker, Symes, and Scott, besides eighty wounded. After many brave struggles, Captain Blair, at last, effected a regular and steady retreat, which gained him much honour. He prevented the eager pursuit of the enemy, who followed him till he came within a few miles of Chunar, from having any bad effect.

This success gave fresh ardour to the Raja's friends, and plunged Governor Hastings into new difficulties.

Ramjaum having put Ramnagur into a state of defence, conducted his principal troops to a fort called Pateetah, to which a detachment under the command of Major Popham was directed, composed of what men could be spared from the garrison of Chunar. In mean time Captain Blair was dispatched with his battalion and two companies of grenadiers to surprise the fort;

and Lieutenant Polhill, who just arrived from Allahabad, with six companies of Seapoys from the Nabob Aspah-doulah's life guards, was ordered to encamp on the opposite shore, in order to keep the communication at that side open. In two days after his arrival, this spirited Officer defeated a considerable body of the enemy at a small fort called Seekur [Sacrut], where he found a vast quantity of grain, which proved an acceptable prize, as it was much wanted.

Major Popham and Captain Blair having arrived within about a mile of Pateetah [Patita], nearly at the same time found a party of the enemy in seeming readiness to oppose them. They fought on both sides, with great ardor and intrepidity, till victory perplexed with doubt, waited the arrival of Lieutenants Fallow [Fallon] and Berrille [Birrell], whose gallant conduct with the united bravery of their countrymen, preponderating in the scale of her unbiased judgment, induced the Goddess to bestow on them, her unfading laurels, as the reward of their exertions. After a dreadful carnage of killed and wounded on each part, the conquered fled for refuge to their fort, and the victors advanced to Chunar to recruit their losses. At the commencement of these commotions, Governor Hastings dispatched a courier to Colonel Morgan, at Caunpore, with instructions directing him to send an immediate reinforcement to Chunar: three regiments were accordingly sent with the utmost expedition; two of which were under the command of Majors Crabb and Crawford [Crawfurd] with one company of artillery, and two of European infantry; and the other under Major Roberts, which marched by the route of Lecknow. Early on the tenth of September, Majors Crabb and Crawford, at the head of their respective corps, appeared within view of Chunar on the opposite shore: the following day, the Nabob Aspa-doulah arrived, and encamped at the same side of the river; and shortly after Major Roberts came from Lecknow, with his troops. The English crossed the river, and joined Major Popham, who had now the command of four complete regiments, one battalion of Colonel Blair, another of the Nabob's life guards, two companies of Europeans, one of artillery, and one of French rangers. From this main body, Major Crabb, with one detachment, proceeded against Lutteefgur, Major Crawford with another, crossed the mountains to Seckroot and Lora; and two companies under the direction of Captain Baker, and Lieutenant Simpson, advanced towards Pateetah with a twelve pounder, which they played on the north side of the fort, for, at least, an hour, with good effect, till an halcarah, who just arrived, informed them that there was a large tank on the eastern situation with a great heap of earth thrown up about it, which might answer the purpose of a temporary battery. When the tank was discovered, and found adequate to the description given of it, an additional supply of cannon and ammunition was directly sent for. We now began the siege with the most lively ardor, and continued it for three days without intermission: on the fourth morning, at three o'clock, Captain Baker and Gardner kept up a brisk cannonading, and threw the enemy into the utmost confusion, amidst which, Captain Lane, Lieutenants Simpson and Williams, with whom I adventured and three companies of determined Seapoy grenadiers, stormed the fort and rushed on the disordered enemy with manly resolution. After some opposition, they evacuated their strong hold, with Ramjaum at their head, and made off towards Lutteefgur, leaving their military equipage, elephants, camels, bullocks, &c. behind them.

Captain Baker distinguished himself in this action, as in many others, by the greatest exertions, and displayed the courage of the active soldier united with the experience of the hoary veteran.

> Whilst memory dwells on virtues only thine,
> Fame o'er thy relics breathes a strain divine.

Major Crabb having met Ramjaum on his way to Lutteefgur, gave him battle, and obliged him with his vanquished forces to fly for shelter to Lora, and from thence to Bidgegur [Bijigarh], whither Cheyt-sing had escaped. The Raja, however, not finding himself safe in Bidgegur, fled for refuge to the mountains among the Morattoes, taking with him what diamonds and other valuable effects he could possibly convey on his camels.

## Letter XXXIII

Dear Sir,

Captain Baker with the detachment under his command, marched to Ramnagur, where he remained till further orders; and Major Popham advanced with his troops, in pursuit of the enemy, to Bidgegur, which lies about fifty miles to the south east of

Chunar: the fort is erected on the summit of a lofty rock, and rises to the great height of seven hundred feet above the surface of the country. It was considered next to Ganlin, among the strongest in India, being deemed, like that fortress, impregnable. The Raja, however, not judging the strength of Bidgegur a sufficient security against the conqueror of Ganlin, abandoned it, leaving behind him a part of those treasures, which were the cause of his misfortunes; and resigning that honour in the persons of his women, which he had so highly estimated, himself a wretched fugitive flying for protection to the uncertain asylum of those who were only in a state of precarious security.

The Ranee, his mother, besides his women, and such of the descendants of Bulevant-sing [Balwant Singh], as still adhered to him, continued in the fort, with a certain military force, as guardians of the remainder of his treasure, which, in diamonds and specie amounted to a very considerable value.

Major Popham, who behaved with great spirit and firmness, spent an entire month in subduing the utmost difficulties, and, at length, as he was on the point of springing a mine, the Ranee, who seemed to have the sole direction of affairs after the departure of her son, surrendered the fort by capitulation, in the terms of which, she was to be allowed fifteen per cent on all the effects given up by her, and to have her choice of residing unmolested, either with her son, or elsewhere in the country. In the one case, she was to be escorted by a proper guard to the frontiers; in the other to meet with the greatest protection.

A principal part of the property taken at Bidgegur, became a prize to the captors, as a reward for their services. A letter written by the Governor to Major Popham, during the siege, was understood as giving a sanction to such a distribution of the spoil. The Officers acted with so much expedition in the business, that their dividend, with that of the privates, was apportioned in two days after the place was taken, and the residue went to the Company. Scenes of joy and conviviality now succeeded the toils of war; and the private soldier, as well as the Officer, forgot his dangers in the indulgence of his pleasures.

Such was the issue of the war with the unhappy Raja Cheytsing, whose humility and sufferings cannot be better described than in his own words; thus, expressing himself in a letter to the Governor, when he was arrested by his order, he says,

'Pity me, I pray you, in remembrance of the services done by my father, and in consideration of my youth and inexperience: whatever may be your pleasure, do it with your own hands—and as I am your slave, what occasion can there be for a guard?—It depends on you alone to deprive me, or not, of the country of my ancestors—what necessity is there to deal in this way with me, who am ready to devote my life and property to your service.'

—Many other letters followed this, and all were equally pathetic.

His manifesto, addressed to the native Princes, abounds with many sublime sentiments, free from that sounding phraseology too frequently used in India; and expressive of the most lively sensibility for the fate of a country, which he thus finely contrasts with the other territories surrounding it.

In vindication of his government, he says,

'Look to my country; look to others—Do not the different pictures they present to you, mark the limits of them more, than the boundaries which nature itself has drawn out. My fields are cultivated; my villages full of inhabitants; my territory a garden; and my subjects happy. From the security I have given to property, my capital is the resort of the first traders of India; and the treasures of the Morattoes, the Jairs [Jains], and the Saiks [Sikhs], are deposited here, as well as those brought hither from the remotest borders of the eastern world. Hither the widow and the orphan convey their property, without dread from the violence of rapacity, or the gripe of avarice. The way-worn traveller, within the bourne of my country, lays down his burden unmolested, and sleeps in security.

Look to other provinces, there famine and misery stalk hand in hand, through neglected plains and deserted villages: there you meet with aged men drooping under the weight of years, and unable to transport themselves from the grasp of the prowling ruffian, watching to waylay their helplessness.

Here every passing stranger has been used with kindness, his hardships alleviated, and even his weary Cooleys have had their loads taken off their shoulders, and carried for them, through the humanity of my peasantry, from village to village.

To men of condition, who have travelled here, I have sent my Officers to enquire their wants, and supplied them with provisions and carriages at my own expense: their interior testimony will evince the truth of these assertions, and enable them to form a discriminative comparison between mine and the neighbouring districts.'

Such was the happy situation of the Prince, and the philanthropy of the man, who shortly after became the sport of fortune, amidst the vicissitudes of life, and the trials of adversity.

## Letter XXXIV

Dear Sir,

This commotion had scarcely subsided, when a fresh disturbance arose at Gochipour [Ghazipur], a place famous for distilling rose water, between the natives and the Fouzdar of that quarter, who enjoyed the same post which he held under Raja Cheyt-sing. As he availed himself of a general pardon granted by the Governor, he was permitted to continue in his employment. The people dissatisfied with the fate of their late Raja, could, by no means, be reconciled to the sovereignty of the English; and when the Fouzdar, consistent with his duty, attempted to collect the customary revenues, he was every where opposed, and with the greatest difficulty escaped the fury of the natives.

On the first rise of the male-contents, he wrote to the Governor for a reinforcement of troops to assist his own, which were quite insufficient to quell the insurrection. Captain Baker was therefore sent to his relief from Ramnagur, with his battalion. The day after our arrival at Gochipour, we marched onward to a little village called Bellua, where the motley crew were assembled within a small mud fort, seemingly determined to maintain an obstinate defence.

After withstanding the fire of our musquetry with a degree of courage not to be expected in an undisciplined rabble, on the approach of our cannon, some fled, were pursued and taken, and the rest, who were still very numerous, sent Deputies to the Captain, requesting a cessation of hostilities, which he granted on receiving the most solemn assurances, that they would peaceably return to their respective employments, and disturb, no more, the public tranquility.

One of the captives, before he obtained his liberty, having informed us that there were some cattle belonging to Ramjaum in a neighbouring plain, to which he offered to direct us, I was ordered to accompany him with an escort of Seapoys to the very place he described, where I found two elephants, two camels, and twelve Arabian horses, under the care of a few peasants, who made off on the appearance of our arms. I seized the cattle as the property of an enemy, and drove them to Gochipour, where the party waited my return.

Captain Baker reserving only one horse for his own use, generously divided the spoil among the soldiers as the well earned meed of their military labours.

After a month's stay here, we were relieved by Captain Lane, and marched hence to Jouanpour [Jaunpur], which has little to recommend it but a good fort and a few tolerable buildings: it is however equally remarkable, as our last cantonments, for its rose water and rose oil, which are peculiarly esteemed throughout Asia for their odoriferous excellence.

We were again involved in new broils, and obliged to penetrate farther into the country, in order to disperse the unruly natives who assembled in a hostile manner within a fort, which they put into some state of defence. They were armed with bows and arrows, and long barreled guns of their own construction, generally known by the name of match-locks. They held out so obstinately, that they kept possession of the fort for nine or ten days, and then escaped under the favouring gloom of night, leaving a number of their dead behind them.

After this commotion, the country became quiet, and no future disturbances were heard of, at least, in this quarter.

The refractory were awed into submission by the terror of our arms; yet humanity must lament the loss of those whom wasting war had suddenly swept away.

> Alas! destructive war, with ruthless hand,
> Unbinds each fond connection, tender tie,
> And tears from friendship's bosom all that's dear,
> Spreading dire carnage thro' the peopled globe;
> Whilst fearless innocence, and trembling guilt,
> In one wide waste, are suddenly involv'd.
> War wake's the lover's, friend's and orphan's sigh,
> And on empurpled wings bears death along,
> With haggard terror, and with wild dismay,
> And desolation in the savage train:
> From slow-consuming time, his lazy scythe,
> With ruffian violence is torn away,
> To sweep, at once, whole Empires to the grave.

Near Jouanpour is a spacious chapel much frequented by the Mahometans, under which is a subterraneous cavern extending a considerable length of way. It is a fort or arsenal, and serves as an asylum for the natives in time of war, as the entrance to it, is only known to themselves. When peace was restored to this distracted country, we returned to Chunargur.

*Letter XXXV*

Dear Sir,

A few months after our arrival at Chunargur, Captain Baker disclosed his intentions of going to Europe: having a desire of seeing that part of the world, and convinced that I should suffer much uneasiness of mind, in the absence of my best friend, I resigned my commission of Subidar, in order to accompany him. We took boat at Chunargur, and proceeded to Calcutta, by the way of Dacca, sailing along the Ganges a distance of three hundred miles. Our passage was very agreeable, as the season was fine, and the farmers were just returning from the fields with the fruits of the harvest. It was not uncommon to see two thousand bullocks carrying corn, the property of one yeoman, to the granaries. There are many fine seats on each side of the river, with a continued variety of beautiful improvements, striking landscapes, and sublime scenes of rural imagery, which, at once astonish and delight the enraptured view.

Having completed the most pleasant voyage imaginable, we, at length, arrived at Dacca, one of the most extensive cities in the province of Bengal, which lies in twenty-four degrees north latitude, on an eastern branch of the Ganges. It is near five miles in length, but very narrow, and winding with the river.

Dacca is considered the first manufactory in India, and produces the richest embroideries in gold, silver, and silk. It also receives considerable advantages from its cottons, of which the finest striped and worked muslins, calicoes, and dimities, are made, much superior to those finished in other parts of the country. The best kind manufactured for the immediate use of the Great Mogul, and his Zannanahs, are of exquisite workmanship, and greater value than any permitted to be sold either to the natives or foreigners.

The filligrane, in particular, is admirable, the workmanship being more costly than the metal itself. It is not perforated, as with us, but cut in shreds, and joined with such inimitable art, that the nicest eye cannot perceive the juncture. The embroidery and needlework, for elegance, surpass all description, and greatly exceed any thing of the kind done in Europe: but it is remarkable that there are no female embroiderers or sempstresses here; the men do all the work in these branches, and their patience is astonishing, as their slowness is singular. Provisions of all sorts are exceeding cheap and plentiful in Dacca: the fertility of its soil, and the advantages of its situation have, long since, made it the centre of an extensive commerce; it has still the remains of a very strong fortress, in which, a few years back, was planted a cannon of such extraordinary weight and dimensions, that it fell into the river, with the entire bank on which it rested; the length of the tube was fourteen feet, ten and a half inches, and the diameter of the bore one foot, three and one eighth inches: it contained two hundred and thirty-four thousand four hundred and thirteen cubic inches of wrought iron, weighed sixty-four thousand four hundred and eighteen pounds avoirdupois, and carried a shot of four hundred and sixty-five pounds weight.

Here is also the residence of a grand Nabob, who, at his accession to the throne, conformable to an old custom, something similar to that of the Doge of Venice on the Adriatic, enjoys a day's pleasure on the river, in one of the most curious barges in the world, called a samsundar. It is sheathed with silver, and in the centre is a grand eminence of the same, on which his crown is placed on the day of coronation: nearer the stern is a brilliant seat encompassed with silver rails, and covered with a rich canopy embroidered with gold, under which he reclines in easy majesty. This boat and another of considerable value, that conveys his attendants, are estimated at a lack of rupees. He is accompanied by a number of the most distinguished personages, and there are no bounds to the lavish waste of money expended on this occasion, in order to aggrandize the pomp of this ancient ceremony. Travellers of every description, who pass this way, are led by a prevailing curiosity to see these elegant boats.

*Letter XXXVI*

Dear Sir,

Before we left Dacca, the celebration of the festival of two supposed saints, whom the Mahometans call Hassan, Hussen, was commenced on the first day of the new moon, and continued, with great solemnity, for ten days. The first day, several parties forming in different quarters of the town, assembled together in one spacious square appointed for the general meeting, where they raised an extensive canopy on eight poles, in the centre of which were three others composed of finer materials of various colours, and under the smallest canopy was a silver salver filled with clay, to represent the remains of these saints. The Mahometans, during this ceremony, cease from the pursuits of business, and spend the time in repeating their prayers, singing canticles, and other pious exercises, to which they add many exterior marks of devotion, emphatically expressed by thwacking the bosom, extending the arms, upturning the eyes, muttering ejaculations, fetching deep sighs, and emitting hollow groans on a tremendous key. The Gentoos and other dissenters are excluded from their society, by a railing of bamboes, which in the night time is hung with glittering branches that illuminate the entire scene, while a number of colours are flying from the poles. There are four other colours of a particular kind, trimmed with a beautiful gold fringe, within the small canopy: under this the salver is placed, to which the entire Mahometan assembly kneel in adoration, whilst bands of music swell the strain of religious enthusiasm.

On the ninth day, they exhibit a kind of edifice made of stained paper, which is perhaps one of the most curious specimens of filligrane work ever attempted by human ingenuity. It consists of many spires, rising above each other, and gradually diminishing towards the top; the variety of ornaments about it is admirable, and the taste with which it is executed, inconceivable: you can form but an imperfect idea of such a masterly piece of workmanship, and I am therefore unhappy that my abilities will not permit me to pursue such a combination of inimitable art and elegance, through all the complicated minutiae of an adequate description.—It is carried in grand procession through the town, during the night, with the salver and two turbans placed on the battlements of the fourth spire:

before which, were thousands in the attitude of prostrate humility, paying their adoration and distributing alms to their indigent fellow creatures around them, whilst numbers followed, with flames and torches lighting, colours flying, and various instruments of music, on which they played the most solemn airs. The tenth day this paper structure, which in the Indian dialect, is termed Gouwarrah, is carried to the burial ground of their supposed saints or holy men, and thrown into a large tank, which concludes the ceremony.

The Mahometans keep a strict lent once in the year, in the month Ramzaun, for a space of thirty two days: during this time, they never sleep on a bed, nor cohabit with their wives, and live only on rice and vegetables: they also abstain from their usual enjoyments of chewing betel, and smoking tobacco, avoiding every kind of amusement, and spending the time in prayer, and the performance of charitable offices. They are so extremely tenacious of their principles that even under the painful longing of excessive thirst, they will not taste a drop of water, each day, till seven in the evening. As an instance of their severity in the observance of their religious tenets, I shall introduce the following real anecdote. An considerable Banyan merchant was on his passage from Bombay to Surat, in an English ship, and having made such a provision of water in vessels under his own seal, as might serve for that short voyage, which was commonly completed in two or three days; it happened however that, through retardment by calms and contrary winds, his liquid store was expended, and he reduced to a condition of perishing with thirst, though there was plenty of water on board: but, no entreaties could prevail on him to use it, as his religion forbade it, which to him was more dear than life itself. He felt all the torments occasioned by the fever of thirst, and would have actually sunk under them, had not a favourable breeze springing up, brought him to Gundavee [Gandevi], near Surat; but he was so faint on his arrival, that his soul was almost panting between his lips.

*Letter XXXVII*

Dear Sir,

Having remained some time in Dacca, we proceeded on our voyage to Calcutta, and, in about two days reached the river

Sunderbun, which is extremely narrow, and winds into many branches, that feast the delighted eye with a variety of new scenery: the land on each side is low, and covered with great trees, close to the water's edge: the water was smooth and transparent when we passed through, and appeared like an extended mirror reflecting the tall trees that grew upon each border. Creation seemed to be at rest, and no noise disturbed the silence which reigned around; save, now and them, the roaring of wild beasts in the adjacent woods: the scene was truly great, and raised into unaffected grandeur, without the assistance of art.

The most remarkable trees that grow on each margin of the river, are the sandal, aumnooze, and ceesoe. The woods are infested with ferocious animals of different kinds, which frequently destroy the unwary traveller; and the tigers in particular are daring enough to approach the river side, and dart on the very passengers in the boats going up and down, of whom they make an instant prey. Along the banks are many villages, at about ten or twelve miles distance from each other, where we sometimes laid in a fresh supply of provisions. There is no display of art in the construction of the cottages, which are only composed of broad green flags fastened together, and supported by frames of bamboes. When the floods begin to overflow the country, the natives, with much ease, remove their dwellings from one place to another, first taking them asunder, then rolling up the partitions and roofs, and finally carry them in bundles, wherever convenience of situation, out of the reach of danger, might allure them to fix their moveable abodes. The inhabitants live in a state of nature, sequestered from the tumult of bustling crowds: their wants, which are few, are easily satisfied; and their manners are rendered simple, from the unvarying tenor of their lives, and their remote distance from great towns and cities, where vice finds an asylum amidst luxury and dissipation, and guilty greatness lords it over the trembling wretch who crouches at her feet. Between the villages, we observed a few scattered huts, built by some European adventurers, as a temporary residence, while they are employed in cutting down timber which they sent to different parts of Bengal for shipbuilding, and other uses.

In January 1783, we arrived at Calcutta, that great emporium of wealth and commerce, where people of rank appear in a style of grandeur far superior to the fashionable eclat displayed in the brilliant circles of Europe. Every private gentleman is attended by twenty servants, at least, eight of whom called bahareas, are alternately employed in carrying his palanquin: and two footmen termed halcarahs, walk before this travelling vehicle: he also keeps three or four domestic servants, namely, a consumma or butler, a bowberchee or cook, and a kizmutgaur or valet: to these may be added seven or eight others under the following appellations, viz. a hookeburdar or person whose chief business is to prepare his master's tobacco pipe, and attend him when smoking, an offdaur to cool the water for his drinking, two or three sahees who have the care of the horses, a gusseara or grass cutter, and three or four mussalchees or torch bearers.

Great characters still increase the number of attendants, by adding to the train already described, nakeeves or criers, to clear the way before them, chowkdars or pages, who carry large silver rods in their hands, sotiburdars the bearers of small silver rods, and piadas or letter carriers.

Those elevated personages, who bask in the sunshine of exalted life, look down, as from a lofty eminence, on your second-rate people of quality, with as much supercilious disdain, as the second-rates survey all, without distinction, in the humbler walks of life, in which are some sentimental souls whose wounded sensibility gives rapture to enjoyment, when they behold *them* held in such sovereign detestation and sneering contempt by their distant superiors.

I have frequently seen a circar or writing clerk, attended in the day time, by a servant holding an umbrella over his head to shade him from the sun, and one or two torch bearers illuming the way before him by night.

Every man of rank has a derawan or door-keeper at his gate, to announce the arrival of a visitant, whose name he cries out in a vociferous tone, which is heard in the gentleman's mansion, and repeated by a servant at the foot of the grand staircase leading to his apartment: pages posted in different situations on the stairs, usher the sound to each other, till, at last, it reaches the jemidar or principal page, at the drawing-room door, who conveys it, with great formality, to his master, in order to prepare him for the reception of the visitant.

In passing through some parts of the town, I have observed several men employed in repairing the streets, who had logs chained to their feet, as a punishment, which the law inflicts for the commission of small crimes. Women guilty of petty offences, appear abroad quite bald, their heads being close shaved, in order to expose them to public scorn. Persons in the matrimonial state, detected in criminal conversation, are mounted on a large jackass, with two spears or bayonets fastened round the brows of each, to denote their shame, and render them more conspicuous to the populace. These examples are indeed like black swans, and very seldom seen in Asia, where a breach of conjugal fidelity is considered an odium that must doom the parties to eternal solitude, for ever precluding them from the benefit of society.

## Letter XXXVIII

Dear Sir,

Having passed through a variety of scenes in India, we left Calcutta in January 1784, and went by water to Belcoor, a little village about twelve miles down the river, where a Danish East-Indiaman, commanded by a Captain Duck [Doack], bound for Copenhagen, lay at anchor waiting for the passengers, who embarked with us, and proceeded on our voyage for Europe. The weather being fine, and the wind favourable, we reached Madapallam in seven days, and came to an anchor. The Captain and passengers went ashore, some remaining here, and others, whom I accompanied, being led by curiosity to visit Madras about eight miles hence, while the ship, which was to continue here a fortnight, was taking in some bales of chintz and callico.

Madras or Fort St George is a regular square about a hundred yards at each side, with four bastions, built with what they call iron stone, being of the colour of unwrought iron, and very rough, on the outside like honeycomb. There is no ditch about the fort, and the walls are arched and hollow within, and are therefore not cannon proof. It has two gates, one to the east, and the other to the west.

The western gate which looks towards the land, is pretty large, and here the main guard is kept, the soldiers of the guard lying on the right and left of it, under the wall, which being hollow, serves them instead of a guard house. The east gate towards the sea, is but small, and protected only by a file of musqueteers. In the middle of the fort stands the Governor's house, in which are apartments for the Company's servants: it is a handsome, lofty, square, stone building; the first rooms are ascended by ten or twelve steps, and from thence another pair of stairs leads to the council chamber and the Governor's lodgings.

The fort stands near the centre of the white town where the Europeans inhabit. This is an oblong square, about a quarter of a mile in length, but not half so much in breadth. To the northward of the fort are three handsome streets, and as many to the south: the buildings are of brick; and several of the houses have one floor above the ground floor. Their roofs are flat, and covered with a plaster made of seashells, which no rain can penetrate. Opposite the west gate of the fort is a long room where the soldiers lodge when they are off the guard, and adjoining to it, on the north, is a commodious hospital; at the other end is a mint, where the Company coin gold and silver. On the north side of the fort is the Portuguese church, and to the southward the English church, which is a neat elegant building, and moderately large: it is floored with black and white marble, the seats regular and convenient, and all together, the most airy lightsome temple any where to be found, for the windows are large and unglazed to admit the cooling breezes in the warm season.

Here is also a free school, where children are educated in reading and writing; besides which there is a library. On the west part of the town a river runs close to the buildings, which are protected by a large battery of guns commanding the plain beyond them. On the east there is a slight stone wall, built on an eminence, that appears something grand to the shipping in the road; but here is very little occasion for any fortification, the sea coming up close to the town, and no large vessels can ride within two miles of the place, the sea is so very shallow; nor is there any landing but in the country boats, the surf runs so high, and breaks so far from the shore. The north and south ends of the town, are each of them defended by a stone wall, which is hollow within, like the fort walls, and would hardly hold out one day's battery. To the southward is a little suburb, inhabited only by black fishermen; it consists of low thatched cottages, which hardly deserve the name of buildings. Beyond this is an outguard of Blacks, who serve to give intelligence to the fort; but there is no other fortification on this side.

The black town, situate to the northward, adjoins the white town, and is considerably larger. Here Portuguese, Indians, Armenians, and others dwell. It is build in the form of a square, and more than a mile and a half in circumference; being surrounded with a brick wall seventeen feet thick, with bastions at proper distances, after the modern way of fortification: it has also a river on the west, and the sea on the east; and to the northward a canal is cut from the river to the sea, which serves for a moat on that side. The streets of the black town are wide, and trees planted in some of them; and having the sea on one side and a river on the other, there are few towns so pleasantly situated or better supplied; but except some few brick houses, the rest are cottages built with clay and thatched. The houses of the better sort of Indians, are of the same materials, and built usually in one form, with a little square in the middle from whence they receive all their light. A stranger seldom comes farther than the door, before which is erected a little shed supported by pillars, where they sit cross-legged morning and evening, to receive their friends or transact their business. The great streets and the bazar, or market place, are thronged with people, for notwithstanding the houses are low and small, they are well filled; and the people from the highest to the lowest are exceedingly cleanly, washing themselves several times a day. In this black town, there is an Armenian church and several little pagodas or Indian temples, to which belong great numbers of female choristers, who spend half the time in singing to the idols, and the rest in intriguing or chanting in companies before the great men as they pass along the streets. The Governor of Madras makes a splendid appearance, and his usual guard is upwards of an hundred black men: when he goes abroad on any public occasion, he is attended by trumpets, fifes, and drums, with streamers flying, and accompanied by his principal Officers on horseback, and their ladies in palanquins.

Having returned to Madapallam at the appointed time, we continued our voyage till we came within view of the Cape of Good Hope, and met with no extraordinary occurrence on the passage. We saw several kinds of the finny inhabitants of the liquid element, a description of which I must here omit, as uninteresting to a gentleman of your information. A speck now observed in the mariner's horizon, was to him an evident sign of the impending storm, which collected with rapid increase, and bursting with resistless impetuosity over our heads, incessantly raged for three days. The howling of the tempest, the roaring of the sea, the dismal gloom of night, the lightning's forked flash, and thunder's awful roll, conspired to make this the most terrifying scene I ever experienced.

Fair weather providentially succeeding this violent tornado, we reached St Helena in a week, and met with the Fox English Indianman, which received some damage by touching on a rock at some distance from the shore. There were also lying here at anchor, three more Indiamen, in one of which was Governor Hastings' Lady on her return to Europe, and in another the remains of that great and gallant Officer, Sir Eyre Coote. Having laid in a supply of fresh provisions and water, and proceeded on our voyage, we arrived at Darmouth [Dartmouth] in England in September 1784.

1. Dean Mahomet an East Indian (frontispiece in Travels).

2. A Native Officer (1.);
   A Seapoy or private Soldier (2.), in the Company's Service,
   on the Bengal Establishment (Letter XVI in Travels).

3. View of the Grand Nabob Aspahdoulah of Lechnough and his Retinue (Letter XXIII in Travels).

(1) The Camel of the Bandar and the Neoarra;
(2) The Bullock and Bestie carrying Water;
(3) The Music and Colours;
(4) The Subadars or Principal Officers;
(5) The Chopdars and Sortipardars with Silver Rods;
(6) The Petit Nabob's Elephant;
(7) The Great Nabob's Elephant;
(8) The Nabob and his Aid-du-camp;
(9) The men with Whisks;
(10) The Raja's Elephant;
(11) The Birkandazes;
(12) The Duffedar's Horse;
(13) The Nakive Camel;
(14) A Nobleman;
(15) A Hukabardar;
(16) Hottewallas.

4. The Benares skyline with Madho Das Dharahara, 'The Towers of Madho Das' (Etching by E. Therond, mid-eighteenth century).

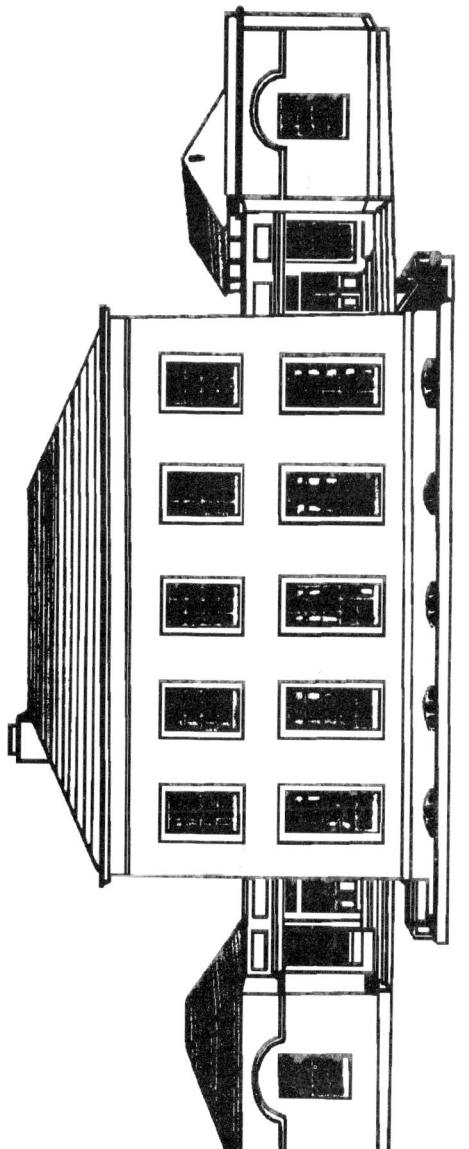

Fortwilliam

5. Fort William (Courtesy Fitzpatrick Silver Springs Hotel, Tivoli, Cork.)

6. Figure of Vapourizer (Cochrane, Improvement [1809], fig. 4).

7. Figure of patient in vapour bath (Cochrane, Improvement [1809], fig. 2).

A Patient receiving the vapour topically.
(a) The flannel bath, drawn round the patient's loins at (b). In this figure the vapour is supposed to be medicated: passing from the boiler through the medicating vessel, the conducting tube enters the vapour receiver at (c); emerges on the opposite side at (d); and is introduced into the flannel bath at (e).

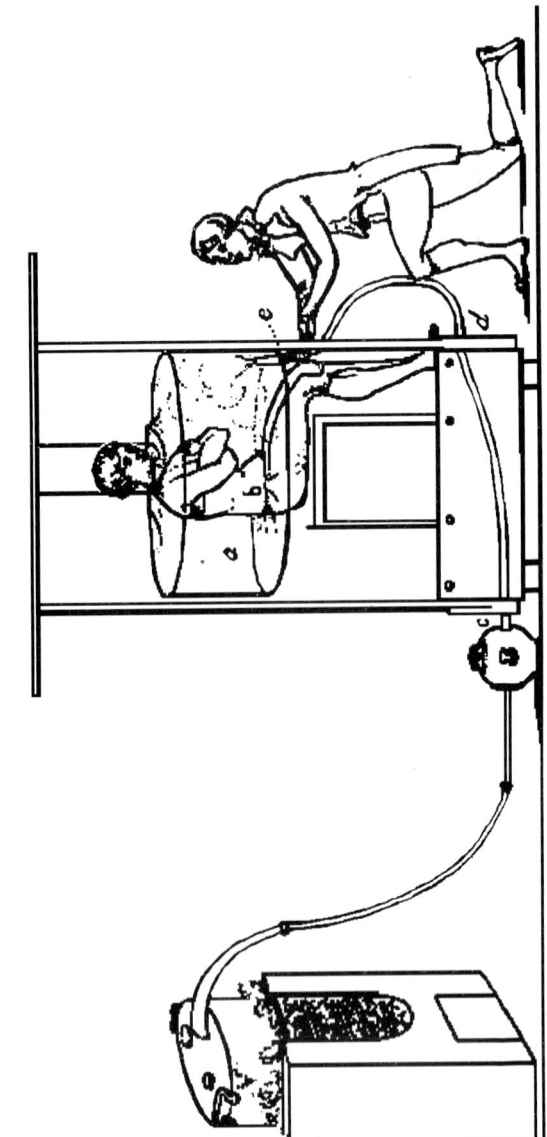

8. Figure of patient and attendant in vapour bath (Cochrane, Improvement [1809], fig. 1).

9. Front of the Brighton Marine Pavilion (Etching by John Nash, 1826).

10. Rear of the Brighton Marine Pavilion (Horsfield, History [1835], vol. 1, p. 148).

Mrs MAHOMED

*Wife of Mr Mahomed Shampooing Surgeon*

BRIGHTON

11. Mrs Mahomed, Wife of Mr Mahomed, Shampooing Surgeon, Brighton
(Courtesy East Sussex County Library).

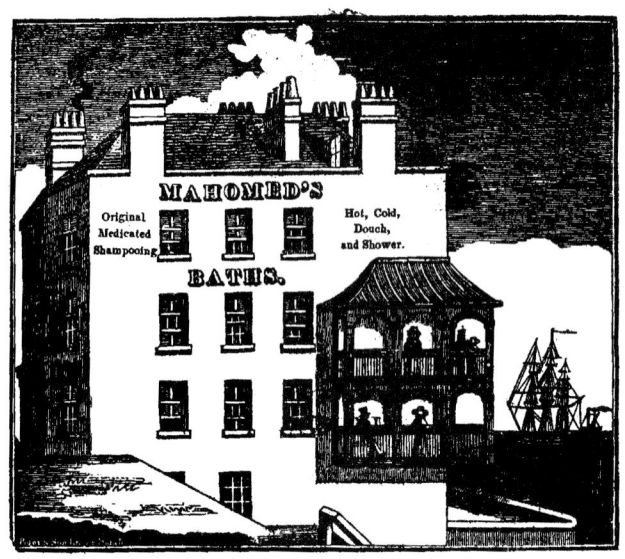

# SAKE DEEN MAHOMED,
## Shampooing Surgeon,

INVENTOR OF THE

### *Indian Medicated Vapour and Shampooing*
# BATHS;

### No. 39, EAST-CLIFF, BRIGHTON.

THE soothing efficacy of the application of steam to the human body, has been long known in the eastern parts of the world. Medicated with fragrant herbs of peculiar virtue, the vapour is rendered more beneficial, whilst the addition of Shampooing the various parts of the body enveloped in steam, augments its sanative energies throughout the whole animal system. In Rheumatism, Parylitic, Gouty Affections, Asthma, Roughness and Diseases of the Skin, Stiff Joints, and Old Sprains, it is a safe and certain remedy; and in all cases of corporeal weakness, or where the circulation is languid, or the nervous energy debilitated, its effects have excited astonishment. Scarcely any disease, to which the human frame is liable, but may be relieved by the use of these Baths. They have been sanctioned by the first medical men in the united kingdom; and have been patronized by many of the nobility, both of England, France, and other places on the Continent, who have received relief from them in many hopeless cases, and whose written testimony of approval may be seen at the Baths.

The art of Shampooing first introduced into England, by S. D. Mahomed, in 1784.

☞ *Cupping performed by D. MAHOMED, Jun. late pupil of Mr. Mapleson Cupper to his Majesty.*

12. Sake Deen Mahomed, Shampooing Surgeon (Pigot's National Directory [1826], Advertisements).

Fig. 1 (A) The machinery, in miniature; the situation is the kitchen.

  (b) A vessel for receiving condensed vapour.

  (c) The conductor of the condensing vapour.

  (d) A boiler of water, heated by the stove (e), for the common use of the patients, and other purposes of cleanliness.

  (f) The steam and hot air pipes that pass through the floor at (g).

Fig. 2 The consultation-room, into which the steam and hot air pipes, in Fig. 1, enter at (h), and extend to (i), heating the apparatus in their passage.

Fig. 3 The hot air and steam pipes here branch off; the former passing under the floor, and heating the rooms by means of the pataras, (j), (j), (j), (j), (j), (j); and the steam pipe entering at (k) proceeds along the wall, at (l), through the partition, (m), and terminates at (n).

(o), (o) Two steam-receivers, with their stools and foot-stools.

(p), (p) Two baths with their cane-work.

(q), (q) Branches of the steam pipe, with their cocks.

The points marked 1 and 3 form into a close apartment and the point 2 is a partition that divides it into two distinct rooms. The one contains the bath for general and topical uses, the other partakes of the Russian method; the vapour being admitted at (s) soon fills the room, and the patients receive it sitting, or lying on the benches, (t), (u), going from one to the other as the heat becomes too violent, or as it decreases.

(v) 1. The cold shower-bath, and (Dd) the cold shoot, supplied from the cistern, (x).

(v) 2. A cistern supplied with heat from a pipe, (w), for the hot shoots.

(y) A dressing-room, heated by its patara, (j).

(z) A water-closet.

(Aa) A pipe to clean the water-closet.

(Bb) Lights to the closet and dressing-room. (Cc) Beds.

13. Diagram of a Bath House (Cochrane, Improvement [1809], plate 5).

14. S.D. Mahomed, Shampooing Surgeon, Brighton
(frontispiece in Shampooing).

15. Sake Dean Mahomed in court robes
(Erredge, History of Brighthelmston [1862], vol. 4).

16. Mahomed's Baths (Computer altered form of Berthou and Georges, Album de Brighton [Brighton: The Authors, 1838], plate 5).

# Chapter Three

# The World of
# Eighteenth-Century India

## The Mughal Empire and Regional States

Over the generations preceding Dean Mahomed's birth, his family—and many similar families—had to make fundamental choices about their loyalties. None of these choices proved clear or easy since the eighteenth century comprised a time of transition for Indian society and politics at all levels. The Mughal Empire, which for two centuries had provided political and cultural leadership, fragmented, although it continued as sovereign in name. From the early decades of the eighteenth century onward, a variety of regionally-based rulers seized power. They continued to clash with the Emperor, with each other, and with local landholders and villagers long after Dean Mahomed left India. Little sense of a single unified Indian nation existed; rather, ethnic, regional, communal, and class identities cut across each other, each demanding a different set of conflicting commitments. The expanding presence of rival European trading companies inserted further levels of discord into this contentious world.

During the Mughal imperial dynasty's centuries of political domination, it had—to some degree—woven together immigrants and members of India's regionally distinct local populations into a relatively centralized empire, something never before accomplished. The Mughals, who had invaded India from Afghanistan in 1526, were Sunni Muslims from central Asia. They descended from world-conquerors: Changiz Khan and Timur (Tamerlane). The Mughal Emperors drew their initial support from a band of central Asian and Iranian adventurers. Over time, they had managed to command the submission or service of most people in India. Further, the great wealth and prestige of the Mughal imperial court continued to attract ambitious warriors, scholars, and merchants from west and central Asia well into the eighteenth century. Dean Mahomed asserted that he was descended from a marriage between two Shi'ite immigrant families—respectively Afshar Turk and Arab in ethnic origin—drawn to India from Iran by the richness of the Mughal imperial court. While the Mughals never fully unified India, they did create an overarching structure and ideology that appealed to elite groups across most of India.

At the Mughal Empire's peak in the sixteenth and seventeenth centuries, its extensive land-revenue collection system drew from the Indian countryside sufficient wealth to support its elaborate superstructure. The ornate Mughal imperial court and household, and the nearly as grand households of its upper officials, lavishly expended these vast resources. In turn, these households provided employment to cascades of subordinate families (including that of Dean Mahomed), providing as well cultural models for them to imitate in consumption patterns and norms of comportment.[1] The arts and architecture of the Mughal imperial court inspired imitation in a range of elite households of both Muslims and Hindus across the subcontinent. The Mughal Empire offered honourable and lucrative employment for large numbers of both immigrants and indigenous Indians. It thus created an expansive service elite of administrators and military who continued to dominate Indian life for centuries.

Most officials in the Mughal Empire, whatever their other duties, held military responsibilities as well. The top two thousand or so officials each had two numerical ranks: one was personal to himself (zat) and the other was military (sowar, literally the number of horsemen whom he had to raise, support, and lead in the Emperor's service). The Mughal imperial armies provided regular or occasional employment for millions of people. One authoritative Mughal account from the sixteenth century listed 343,696 cavalry and 4,039,097 infantry as the Mughal military manpower base.[2] These Mughal armies, in turn, comprised vast markets for a variety of clothing, weapons, foodstuffs, and other necessities and luxury goods. They thus employed many times their number of provisioners, artisans, entertainers, and other camp-followers. Mughal armies remained almost constantly deployed in extending the Empire, in enforcing Mughal rule over resisting peoples within it, and in succession struggles among contending Mughal princes. Thus, their consumption of people and other resources continued to be insatiable. Indeed, one major factor in the eventual decline of the Mughal Empire from the end of the seventeenth century onward stemmed from its over-expenditure on the imperial court and army, given its declining income from an over-taxed agricultural and manufacturing base (XXII). Nevertheless, the Mughal Empire continued to provide India with cultural and political models long after the Emperors themselves had lost control over their provinces, their armies, their courts, and their own personal safety.

During the first half of the eighteenth century, each province in the Mughal Empire broke away from the effective control of, if not nominal submission to, the Emperor. A number of imperial governors entrenched themselves in their provinces, transforming their appointments into hereditary possessions. One such dynasty was the Shi'ite family ruling Awadh (see Map). Dean Mahomed himself claimed kinship with another, the Nawabs ruling Bengal and Bihar. This dynasty's founder, Alivardi Khan, secured a Mughal imperial appointment as Governor of Bengal around 1740 and then established a virtually autonomous regime. Later, Alivardi Khan further forcibly seized the neighbouring province of Bihar, in whose capital, Patna, Dean Mahomed grew up.

During Alivardi's regime, Patna endured several bloody assaults from the Nawab of Awadh (in 1742–3), Alivardi's own mutinous army (in 1745), and his rebellious heir (in 1752). While the Nawabs of Bengal and other regional states could not match the scale and wealth of the Mughal Empire at its height, for a time they nevertheless provided opportunities for advancement and fortune to families such as Dean Mahomed's. His extended family expanded through the administration of both Bihar and Bengal; in 1773, Dean Mahomed encountered his relatives at the Nawab of Bengal's court at Murshidabad (XII).[3] To support Dean Mahomed's family's hereditary service, the Nawab of Bengal assigned it revenues from specified lands in Bihar.

## Dean Mahomed's Family Traditions

Unlike many Hindu and Muslim landholding clans rooted within a particular region, Dean Mahomed's family identified less with the villages that generated their income and more with the Nawab's administration they served and that protected them.[4] While such assignments of land revenue remained nominally subject to resumption on the death (or disgrace) of the holder, by the eighteenth century most had become virtually hereditary. Thus, Dean Mahomed's father continued to enjoy the grant from the Nawab, although he served the East India Company. Following his death, his widow retained it and also received a stipend from one of the late Nawab's wives (II). For an urban-centred family like his to draw an income from its assigned lands in the countryside meant a continual struggle to enforce payments from recalcitrant villagers and to fend off armed incursions by avaricious neighbours. In his descriptions of the countryside, Dean Mahomed revealed the distance between his urban-based elite and the landholders and villagers who comprised the great majority of the population (I, VI). A contemporary of Dean Mahomed in Patna explained (to the British) this urban elite view:

> It is deemed an undeniable truth amongst the men of sense of this land, and it was a standing rule amongst the Princes of these kingdoms, that no trust is to be reposed in the words of a Zemindar [landholder], not even in his most solemn promises and treaties, as they are, to a man, a refractory, short-sighted, faithless set of people . . . and require always a strict hand. Our [Nawab's] Government took care, therefore, that they should not get an opportunity of resisting or disobeying, . . . as they are evildoers by profession, and at all times ready to invest the highways, to plunder and kill the travellers and the unwary; ever ready to torment the subjects, and even the Nobles, to destroy the country, to ruin the revenue, and to distress and injure Government. All these are the accustomed performances of that malevolent race . . . [5]

Thus, men of Dean Mahomed's class sought to distance themselves from, and to control, landholders and villagers.

While the most prestigious Muslim noble households in the Mughal Empire identified themselves with west Asian ancestry, in fact most had indigenous Indian progenitors, particularly in the female line. The Mughal dynasty itself had predominantly Indian Hindu ancestors on the maternal side, since Emperors had often taken wives from the ruling Hindu families of the regions they conquered. Dean Mahomed's family apparently likewise had at least some indigenous Indian ancestors. His physical appearance in all his portraits suggests an indigenous Indian inheritance (see Illustrations 1, 14, and 15). Further, his rich descriptions of his family's birth, baptism, circumcision, and death ceremonies revealed strong links to the indigenous Brahmanic-Hindu culture of the Ganges plain (XII–XIV). When a Hindu family converted to Islam, such domestic rituals often remained unchanged for generations.

In addition, Dean Mahomed highlighted the dowager Begum in Murshidabad as foremost among those particularly favouring his family. This lady, Mani Begum (d. 1813), began life as a professional dancer who had charmed a Nawab of Bengal, Mir Jafar, into marriage, albeit as a lower-ranked wife.[6] After his death, she, by force of personality, took charge over the household of her young step-son, Nawab Mubarak al-Daula (r. 1770–93), a man about Dean Mahomed's age. Such dancers often descended from Hindus or from converts to Islam. Had Dean Mahomed been of a family of distinguished and impeccable west Asian origin, he might not have been so proud of her patronage.

Further, Dean Mahomed in his *Travels* did not use for himself any honorific or patronymic which boasted of family origin in west Asia or Arabia, as many immigrant (or putative immigrant) Muslim families did. When, much later in life, he finally adopted the honorific Sake ('Shaikh'), he chose a title usually associated with Indian families who had converted to Islam.

Finally, there is some slight evidence that Dean Mahomed wrote in the Bengali language. His grandson reported seeing a book in Dean Mahomed's library with his name inscribed on the flyleaf in a language which the grandson guessed was 'Sanscrit—a thing of dots, crescents, three sides of a square, etc'.[7] By this, the grandson probably meant the Sanskrit-derived script of Bengali. All this evidence points strongly to his family having at least some ancestors indigenous to India.

## Bengal, Bihar, and Other Regional States

As the Mughal Empire had expansively conquered India over the sixteenth and seventeenth centuries, it had coerced or enticed many local rulers into subordinating themselves to the Emperor. Their states often became Mughal administrative units. Many factors held each individual region together as a political, but also a cultural and commercial, entity.[8] The majority of the people in each region had a distinctive language or dialect, although Persian had become the language of court and high art linking the elites of each region to the Mughal Empire.

As the imperial centre weakened, indigenous peoples in several regions produced leaders who fought to re-establish their autonomy. Such regional peoples (who appeared in *Travels*, usually in a threatening way) included Marathas, Sikhs, Hindu Jats, and Rohilla Afghans (see Map). Unlike the Nawabs of Bengal, these other rulers of regional states held strong cultural bonds to the dominant people of their home region. Nevertheless, these regional rulers generally continued to submit symbolic and monetary offerings and promises of revenues to the Mughal court in order to legitimate their rule with imperial sanction. Especially in the eighteenth century, these regional rulers fought to extend their rule over their neighbours, with varying degrees of success. Conquered people often regarded their rulers as outsiders. For example, largely Eastern Hindi-speaking people of Bihar were subordinated to the Bengali-speaking province of Bengal, under a Persian-speaking Nawab, who boasted family origins from outside of India, but defended the province from Marathi-speaking conquerors from the south-west. In short, political identity proved highly complex and many loyalties remained divided.

The countryside, where the vast majority of India's peoples lived, generated the agricultural products supporting all the superstructures described above and also formed yet another arena for conflict. Even in regions where indigenous people ruled, there were vast gaps between the social and economic classes. Some landholders and villagers proved able to assert their relative autonomy from weaker regional rulers, while many more tried occasionally to do so. Most villagers, however, paid their revenues to one or another local functionary or grant-holder, often facing disruptive or insupportable demands for grain, cash, and manpower. In this context, grant-holders like Dean Mahomed's family found continued service to the regional ruler useful in securing not only support for their revenue collection rights but also supplementary income, prestige, and opportunities for further advancement. During Dean Mahomed's youth, service to one of the European companies seemed an attractive opportunity for families such as his.

## The European Companies

The English East India Company was never the only European body in India. European travellers and merchants had been coming overland to India, or via the established Indian Ocean trading networks, for centuries. The Portuguese had discovered a direct sea-route to India in 1497 (three decades before the Mughal Empire established itself). As the cosmopolitan Mughal Empire grew, at first it simply accommodated the burgeoning European presence without radical dislocations: in Mughal eyes Europeans were just another set of peoples, having different values and strengths, but people with whom they could deal.

During the seventeenth century, major northern European states had established one or more national trading companies including England (founded 1600), Holland (1602), Denmark (1616), and France (1664). Even after these European companies began to send ships directly by sea to India on a more regular basis, they arrived at a time when many peoples and levels of authority and power competed within the Mughal Empire. Each European company built warehouse-bases (called 'factories') on the Indian coast with satellites inland. In Patna, the English (c. 1650), Dutch (c. 1650), and French (c. 1720) had each erected such a satellite factory.

To Dean Mahomed's family and others like it, the various European companies may not have seemed at first threatening to their order. Patna's particular commercial attractions for these European companies came from its production of saltpetre (essential for manufacturing gun-power), indigo (a powerful dye for cloth), and opium (vital for European trade with China) (XVII, XIX, XVIV). By the mid-eighteenth century, however, the expanding presence and aggressive policies of the various European trading companies had began to dislocate and reorient trade and culture at all levels.

The European companies vied with each other and with private European merchants for control over both trade and production. Reflecting military alignments in Europe, the French East India Company appeared to the British as their greatest commercial and political rival throughout Dean Mahomed's years in India. In 1770, for example, the English Company's Council in Calcutta warned London that

> . . . our natural enemies the French are so prevalent. These crafty people have, we are persuaded, some hostile designs on our possessions in India, but in what part they will first throw off the mask is yet a matter of speculation. As Bengal is the most considerable of all your possessions so it may not improbably be their first object.[9]

Much of the English strategy in India revolved around frustrating this French object.

The English felt threatened by French operations in Europe, west Asia, and north Africa, and by the French diplomatic and military presence in the courts of many of the Indian states. They dreaded a French invasion from the Bay of Bengal or Indian Ocean. Napoleon's invasion of Egypt in 1798 intended to threaten the British in India. Although the British had driven the French Company out of its factory in Patna just before Dean Mahomed's birth, French officers continued to provide military advice to many of the regional rulers who fought against the English in Bihar and elsewhere well into the nineteenth century. The Bengal Army to which Dean Mahomed attached himself spent much of its time and energy preparing to repel a French assault on Calcutta. Thus, the French and the British continued hostilities in India virtually throughout Dean Mahomed's years there, and would remain at war in Europe until 1815, when Dean Mahomed was fifty-six years old. Nevertheless, Dean Mahomed wrote about the French without hostility. Rather he admired their arts and architecture as found in the former French factories—both satisfyingly captured by the English at the time he wrote about them (XXIV).

While the other European companies in India at times proved annoying to the English, they did not present the same military threat as did the French. The English fought one brief war with the Dutch Company in 1759, the year of Dean Mahomed's birth, and subsequently reduced the Dutch Company to a limited role in India. The Danish East India Company, with a factory in Serampore near Calcutta, also remained an irritating commercial rival, but not a substantial danger to the English. Indeed, the Danes in India stood in an uneasy state of dependence on the English, relying on purchases of cotton cloth and other goods controlled by the English, like saltpetre. Nevertheless, the Danes resisted English control. They provided an alternative channel for Britons trying to repatriate their private capital from India, outside of the English Company's jurisdiction and tariffs. Dean Mahomed's own journey to Europe in 1784 was in a Danish ship. In addition, many private European merchants spread across the face of India. In 1762, for example, the Nawab of Bengal complained to the English that nearly 400 new factories had been opened in Bihar alone by the various European companies and by private European merchants, creating severe dislocations to the local and regional economies and also fundamental threats to his authority.[10] Thus, in eighteenth-century India, a variety of European companies and private merchants interacted in competitive—and often in hostile—ways.

From the mid-eighteenth century on, the English East India Company sought to continue and expand its own special exemptions from the judicial and tax authority of the Nawab of Bengal. The English Company first involved itself with various Indian polities as an antidote to French involvement and also to secure commercial advantages (especially low tariffs on its trade) and protection against intervention by local, regional, or imperial administrators. Over Dean Mahomed's lifetime, the English Company expanded its commercial and political control over virtually all of India.

In Patna and elsewhere in north India, many families succumbed to these trying circumstances and their own infelicitous choices of allegiance and commitment. Other families managed to take advantage of the problematic situation and thereby to establish themselves in one of the reconstituted elites. Over time, the most successful families of their social class emerged from those who oriented themselves toward commercial, administrative, or military service to the English East India Company, as did Dean Mahomed's own family.[11] Since Dean Mahomed and his family chose to serve the Bengal Army, it will be useful to examine this Army's origins and early development.

## An Overview of the Diverse Origins of the Bengal Army

The complex entity known as the Bengal Army arose directly out of the conflicts between the English Company and the Nawabs of Bengal. During the first half of the eighteenth century, the English Company had only a limited military component: a few European officers (drawn either from the Royal Army or from the Company's merchants) serving to supervise the usually non-British but European or Anglo-Indian 'sentinels' and Indian 'peons' who had guarded the Company's factories.[12] By the 1750s in Bengal, the Company had only some 500 soldiers (including Europeans, Anglo-Indians, and Indians) and 10–20 British officers.[13]

In June 1756, Alivardi's grandson and heir as Nawab of Bengal and Bihar, Siraj al-Daula (r. 1756–7), ended this first attempt by the East India Company to maintain a military force in Bengal. He expelled the English from their base in Calcutta in retaliation for English repudiation of his authority and to seize the Company's reputedly large treasury. Many of the Company's higher ranking British officials and officers took to ignominious flight, abandoning most of the Company's Indian employees and soldiers to his mercy. On receiving word in Madras of this disaster for the Company, it rushed by sea what forces could be spared from the Company's Madras army: some European, telinga, and topasi soldiers (the last two traditional military types are discussed below).

This hurried expedition under Robert Clive's command rapidly recaptured Calcutta (January 1757). Clive soon began local recruitment of 300–400 Indian soldiers and officers, mostly professional and semi-professional soldiers, originally from Bihar or Orissa.[14] Given the velocity of this and subsequent recruitment drives, Clive must have hired from the extant military labour market, inducting groups of soldiers under their designated contractor (jemadar, *jam'dar*, 'leader of a body of men'), as well as individual Indian soldiers and officers seeking employment in one or another army in India. For most of these recruits, therefore, military service to the English Company would have been a job opportunity, rather than a career or a ideological cause. Only gradually did the Company shift the model of military employment from more traditional and indigenous forms to a new pattern developed through the compounding of European military traditions into those of India.

During the eighteenth century in India, there were a number of traditional military models, each in contrast to that which the English Company developed as its own specialty, the sepoy. Each traditional Indian military type had a distinguishing set of weapons, clothing, and general deportment and had associations with a particular ethnic group, jati (caste), and/or a definite region of India.[15] For example, Mughals, who classed themselves as gentleman-immigrants, harked back to the traditions of the Mongols and Turkmans from whom they were descended, particularly serving as heavy cavalry with a distinctive dress and manner.[16]

A type might provide the template which various men emulated, even if they had not been born into that jati or region. Individual semi-professional soldiers and also bands of men under a jemadar both tended to pattern themselves on one or another military type based on their personal skills and/or place of recruitment. One traditional type dominant on the Gangetic plain, the bukhserria (or buxaria), took its name from the town of Buxar on the western boundary of Bihar (XVI). Buxar remained historically a major recruiting centre for Rajputs and Bhumihar Brahmins in particular. Because many men patterned themselves on that model, it proved an abundant type during Dean Mahomed's youth. Another north Indian military type was the burkendaws (*barq-andaz*, 'lightning thrower') (XX). The predominant type originating from east-central India was the telinga, armed with a fire- or flintlock musket and with a partially European-style military uniform (XVI). As a type, telingas included not only the eponymous Telegu-speaking people from the region of Andhra (particularly the Naik jati), but also (from further south on the peninsula) Muslims from the Carnatic, and Tamil-speakers with traditions of military service as well.

A different military type bore the name topasi, which signified a soldier evoking both Indian and European (usually Portuguese) traditions. This type included men who boasted at least one Portuguese or other European ancestor and also Indian converts

to Roman Catholic Christianity. The most widely accepted ety-
mologies for topasi all reflect characteristics associated with this
military type.[17] One etymology suggests a Turkish origin: from
*top-chi*, 'cannoneer.' For centuries, Indians generally associated
expertise in gunnery with the west: both Ottoman Turks and
Europeans. A second pair of derivations stem from either the
Hindi *topi* ('hat') or the Portuguese *topo* ('top'). Both allude to
those wearing hats of a style associated with Europeans, as opposed
to turbans or caps in the style of one or another Indian or Asian
community (XVI). The third etymology locates the origin of this
term in *do-bhashiya*, 'someone of two-languages', usually an agent
working for Europeans. In each case, the dual identity of the topasi
as having both European (or Ottoman Turkish) and Indian elements stands out clearly.


## The New Model: the Sepoy

Under Clive, the English Company started to homogenize some
of this diversity by beginning to prepare Indian recruits uniformly
along the lines of an innovative and distinctive category: the sepoy.
This Persian term (*sipahi*) had long been current in India to mean
a cavalryman. From the mid-eighteenth century onward, however,
the French and English East India Companies adapted it into
their prime model for an Indian infantryman, trained, dressed,
and armed in a semi-European manner.[18] While Dean Mahomed's father and elder brother apparently only partially went
through this transformation into a sepoy type, Dean Mahomed
himself took up the sepoy military drill, uniform, and discipline
from age twelve (IV).

The military science of Europe, which had developed over
decades of costly war on that continent, brought to India a pattern
of military discipline and supply that would prove decisive in the
English Company's conquest of India. The quality of European
weaponry was not then superior to the best that India could
produce. Nevertheless, England's system of mass manufacture
meant that large numbers of identical weapons of reasonable
quality could be supplied at a relatively low cost. The European
models of 'rational-bureaucratic' organization of the army, the
regular training of units in disciplined field manoeuvers, and the

supply of uniform weapons made the difference in India (and elsewhere in the European colonies).[19] In Europe, military scientists had discovered empirically that rigorous close-order drill of a standing, professional army enabled trained officers to reposition orderly bodies of troops even while under heavy fire or cavalry attack. In India, this meant that companies of sepoys with European or European-trained officers could stand up to—and manoeuver while under attack by—the heavy cavalry that formed the core of many Indian armies. Further, the larger groups of less drilled foot-soldiers that filled out the forces of Indian rulers, landholders, and others had to give way before the sometimes smaller but frequently more disciplined and uniformly armed units of Company sepoys. As a contemporary of Dean Mahomed recognized in his Persian language commentary: so long as the British-commanded soldiers 'maintain their formations, which they call "lines", they are like an immovable volcano spewing artillery and rifle fire like unrelenting hail on the enemy, and they are seldom defeated.'[20] The category sepoy thus formed the dominant model for soldiers within the Company's new model armies.

When Clive began to re-create the Bengal Army after recapturing Calcutta, he depended heavily not only on remnants of the pre-1756 Bengal forces who survived the loss of Calcutta, but also on veterans of previous military training and experience in other armies. Since the 300–400 bukhserria, burkendaws, and other Indian soldiers whom Clive recruited in Bengal fought as part of the contingent of 2200 Indian soldiers at the decisive battle of Plassey (June 1757), these recruits would have had only a few months for retraining and reformation into the sepoy pattern.[21] The battle of Plassey proved, indeed, to follow more in the traditional pattern of battles between Indian regional rulers than in that of a formal, European-style battle between well-disciplined and drilled professional armies. Clive's troops stood firm, but his victory came mostly through his successful inducement of the various commanders of Nawab Siraj al-Daula's army to abandon their ruler and either support Clive or hold their troops out of the battle. Indeed, the history of the East India Company's conquest of Bengal and Bihar has been told by Persian language histories in terms of internal factionalism and moral decline among the ruling Indian families of the region, more than in terms of English military superiority.[22] Following Plassey, the Company installed Mir Jafar (r. 1757–60, 1763–65), brother-in-law to the late Nawab Alivardi Khan, in Siraj al-Daula's place as Nawab of Bengal and sent troops to garrison Patna in the name of its client. Thereafter, the Company gradually shifted the financial and man-power resources of Bengal and Bihar into the service of its own burgeoning army and administration.[23]

In the subsequent years of the rapid expansion of the Bengal army, the Company continued to recruit individuals and entire units of bukhserria, burkendaws, and other types of soldiers and officers from the army of the Nawab of Bengal and others. The men—mostly originating from Bihar and Orissa rather than Bengal—gradually retrained as sepoys. The telingas and topasis whom Clive had brought with him to Bengal largely either returned to the Madras Army or left the Company's service.[24] Soon, sepoys provided the mass of the fighting component of the Company's Bengal Army.

As European officers and sepoy infantry units became increas-ingly a factor in war during the second half of the eighteenth century, Indian regional rulers began to seek to add such elements to their own armies. Such units proved relatively expensive. In-dividual European officers demanded large salaries and (often) autonomy. The weapons, uniforms, training, and salaries of Euro-pean-model sepoy units became a constant drain on the treasury of the regional rulers who employed them. In the long run, only the English East India Company managed to sustain the fiscal burden of such European-pattern Indian armies. It did so through a com-bination of an extensive and effective revenue collection admini-stration (particularly over the productive provinces of Bengal and Bihar), unprecedented financial support and subsidies from the English Government, and unsurpassed borrowing credit in India and England. The Directors and the Parliament in London pro-tested regularly about this cost but recognized that only the military could make the Company's trade and rule in India possible. The army enforced the revenue collection and defended the Company's holdings against its neighbours. The rival European companies and the regional rulers of India could not command such a range and scale of resources and thus could not support the continuous employment of the tens of thousands of European-trained Indian officers and men—like Dean Mahomed's family—who composed the English Company's armies.[25]

For many regional rulers, alliance with the Company, and hence access to the service of its sepoy armies, proved an attractive but ultimately even more costly strategy. The Company subsidized large portions of its army by effectively renting troops to its Indian allies; these troops went over to the payroll of the Indian ruler, but remained under the command of the English. Dean Mahomed described how the Awadh ruler paid Company troops to fight for him during the Rohilla War (1774) but also revealed the discomfort felt by the Bengal Army at this kind of service (XXI). Military dependency on the Company in the end meant the loss by these rulers of their treasuries, sources of revenue, and finally independence. Over the course of the period described in *Travels*, for example, we can see the ruler of Awadh slip from command over the most powerful military force in north India to almost complete military dependence on the Company's Bengal Army and therefore on the Company's will. By the mid-nineteenth century all Indian regional rulers had succumbed either to annexation or to indirect control at the hands of the Company.[26]

Throughout the period of Dean Mahomed's *Travels*, the boundaries of the Bengal Army remained ill-defined. Sepoys and Indian officers moved relatively easily from one army to another, including into or out of the Company's army and that of its opponents of the day. For example, Clive raised his third battalion of sepoys (*c.* 800–1,000 men) at Patna in April 1758, mainly out of men from near Buxar who had probably seen military service in other armies. Dean Mahomed's father most probably entered the Company's army in this recruitment drive, between the births of his first and second sons. We cannot know if he, like so many other of its recruits, brought with him prior experience of service in another army, perhaps even experience of fighting against the Company. During the years of Dean Mahomed's youth in Patna, the Company's sepoys saw action against, or in support of, congeries of rival powers in north India.

## The Patna of Dean Mahomed's Youth (1759–69)

As Dean Mahomed grew up in Patna, that city lay at the intersection of a variety of contending powers. From Patna eastward stretched the territories of the Nawab of Bengal, in which the

English East India Company struggled for supremacy over not only the Nawab but also rival European companies. To the west lay the would-be resurgent Mughal Emperor and the expansive regional powers of north and west-central India—Awadh and the Marathas in particular—who regarded Patna as the first major prize in their invasions of Bihar and Bengal. Within the countryside surrounding Patna raged local conflicts between, on the one hand, the Nawab's and English Company's administrators demanding revenues and, on the other, landholders and villagers resisting these demands. As a consequence of its strategic yet vulnerable position in many of these conflicts, Patna endured a series of often violent struggles for political control among a variety of antagonistic peoples and polities. The relentless series of assaults on Patna during Dean Mahomed's youth reflect a measure of the uncertainties and opportunities faced by his family and others like it. Such conflicting forces required them to continue to reconsider their values and traditions and make choices that could literally determine life or death. Each of these conflicts had an impact on Dean Mahomed.

Some of the conflicts which repeatedly threatened Patna had their origins in Europe. Throughout Dean Mahomed's youth and through his middle-age, England remained almost continually at war against shifting combinations of continental European, as well as Asian, powers. In 1759, even as he was born, the ongoing Seven Years' War in Europe (1756–63) reflected itself in India through a brief conflict between the English and the Dutch companies. Since both companies had factories in Patna, fighting also broke out within that city. In these battles, the Dutch Company suffered defeat and subsequently held a much reduced position in India. In July 1781, Britain and Holland again went to war, so the Court of Directors ordered the Company to seize the Dutch ships and factories present in India.

Dean Mahomed wrote critically about the Dutch. He blamed the remaining Dutch Company's factory in Bengal (at Chinsura) for the extensive and immoral trade in opium from India to China (XXIV). Dean Mahomed did not explain that opium regulation, collection, and sale was actually an English East India Company monopoly and that the importation of opium into China remained far more in British, than in any other, hands. Even the Company's Directors in London recognized the immorality of this trade, writing in 1781: 'Under any circumstances it is beneath the Company to be engaged in such a clandestine trade; we therefore, hereby positively prohibit any more opium being sent to China on the Company's account.'[27] The Company in India, however, responded that, given the economics of the tea trade, this 'was not a matter of choice but necessity' since they had little else the Chinese would buy.[28] The Company's solution was to auction its opium in India to other merchants, including the Dutch and private English traders, who then imported it into China.

The Mughal Emperor also punctuated the years of Dean Mahomed's youth in Patna with his numerous efforts to regain control over Bengal and Bihar by force. Prime among the imperial governors supporting—and even directing—the Mughal Emperor's attacks on Patna stood Shuja al-Daula (r. 1754–75), the ruler of Awadh. This ruler not only hereditarily controlled that province but also, for much of this period, held the title of Wazir: 'Chief Minister' to the Mughal Emperor. Awadh armies had captured and occupied Patna on earlier occasions as well (most recently in 1742–3). Perhaps as a result of these assaults, Dean Mahomed's attitude toward Shuja al-Daula remained quite critical (despite the fact that this ruler had become a subordinate ally of the English when Dean Mahomed was only five years old).

The Mughal Emperor's opponent in these several campaigns against Patna was whichever Nawab of Bengal the English East India Company currently backed. In April 1759 (weeks prior to Dean Mahomed's birth), the heir to the Mughal throne (soon to be Emperor Shah Alam II, r. 1759–1806) proclaimed that he would be taking an imperial 'tour' of Bihar and ordered the Nawab of Bengal and the English Company to submit to him.[29] The Nawab and the Company, although legal subordinates of the Emperor, regarding this more as an invasion than a royal procession, opposed it diplomatically and militarily. The Nawab's administration in Patna followed a delicate line of submitting to the Emperor in diplomatic statements but resisting actually obeying his orders. Later in 1759, the Emperor's army—some 30,000 soldiers belonging to the Awadh ruler—besieged but narrowly failed to capture Patna from the forces of his nominal subordinates, and had to withdraw temporarily. In December 1759 and into early 1760, the Emperor once more drove toward Patna with the imperial army, but again barely missed taking the city. That April, he returned to attack Patna a third time, with the addition of French support to his other forces. In this campaign as well, he only just failed to capture the city after a bloody assault.

The Emperor, having proved unable to dislodge the Bengal Nawab and the English Company from Patna, placed himself in their hands. They negotiated a diplomatic settlement under which the Emperor received the formal obeisance from these subordinates, an expense allowance of Rupees 1000 (later 1800) per day, and the promise of Rupees 2,400,000 (later Rupees 2,600,000, about £325,000) annually from the revenues of Bihar and Bengal. In exchange, the Emperor graciously authorized the Nawab to continue as Governor of Bengal and Bihar. After a ceremonial entry into Patna, the Emperor received the escort of the Company's troops out of Bihar.[30]

The Company's next political manoeuver in Bengal produced yet another threat to Patna. In 1760, the Company, dissatisfied with Mir Jafar as their choice of Nawab, deposed him. In his place they installed his son-in-law, Mir Kasim Ali Khan (r. 1760–63). After Mir Kasim himself rejected the Company's control three years later, it deposed him and reinstalled his predecessor, Mir Jafar. Defiant, Mir Kasim retreated to Patna, fortifying it as his base of resistance to the Company. Mir Kasim also encouraged European and Indian soldiers to desert from the Company's armies into his own. In June 1763, a Company expedition seized Patna from Mir Kasim, only to have troops loyal to him retake the city within hours—and with it capture a quarter of the Bengal Army. In all, about 300 Europeans and 2500 sepoys fell into the hands of Mir Kasim. Those Company soldiers who were not subsequently massacred by his forces either joined Mir Kasim's army or looked elsewhere for employment.[31]

Even as the English Company continued its campaign against Mir Kasim, it hurriedly sought to rebuild its army. The Company, following each of the succeeding series of military victories over his forces, recruited whole units from his defeated army into its own.[32] Not until October 1763 did the Company's Bengal Army prove able to seize Patna again. Mir Kasim then fled but soon returned with an army of the Awadh ruler, again led by the Mughal Emperor.

The Emperor, at the head of this imperial force, re-entered

Bihar in May 1764. Battles raged around Patna until October, culminating in a devastating defeat for the imperial allies at Buxar.[33] Thereafter, the Mughal Emperor turned again to the Company as his main prop, his source both for military and financial resources.

In 1765, the Emperor officially offered the post of Diwan of Bengal and Bihar to the East India Company. This office held authority over the collection of the land and other revenues of those provinces. The Company interpreted this authority to mean that it could keep all the revenues which it collected, beyond its obligations to the Mughal Emperor; in 1772 the Company formally accepted this appointment within the Mughal Empire. The Company also ceded to the Emperor the districts of Kora and Allahabad which it had won in battle but felt unable to defend or administer by itself. For about six years, the Emperor remained in Allahabad, under British protection. Thus, in 1769, when Dean Mahomed attached himself to the Bengal Army, about a third of its forces remained encamped around Allahabad or in Awadh, in nominal service to the Emperor and Awadh ruler.

The English Company continued sporadically to pay substantial amounts of the tribute from Bengal and Bihar which it owed the Emperor by treaty.[34] In 1771, however, the Emperor grew frustrated at the unfulfilled promises of the English to restore his power. He then placed himself under the protection of one of the Company's enemies, the Marathas, who escorted him back to his imperial palace in Delhi. The English Company thereafter ceased its submission of tribute to the Emperor, although it did not repudiate its *de jure* recognition of his sovereignty until 1857.

The Emperor, indeed, hired Major Morrison (III, VIII) to quit the Bengal Army in December 1771 and enter the Mughal imperial service. Morrison first proposed creating under his command an army for the Emperor of 8000 sepoys on the Company's model and 2000 cavalry. When the Company vetoed this, the Emperor appointed Morrison to represent his cause as ambassador in London in 1773, which the English Company called 'little short of treason' on Morrison's part but could not prevent.[35]

Dean Mahomed's attitude toward the Mughal Emperor remained one of respect, yet he also described with sympathy the ruler's tragic decline into powerlessness and lamentable condition as a palace prisoner in Delhi (XXII). After Dean Mahomed left

India, the British subsequently resumed its protection over this Emperor (in 1803, when they captured Delhi and granted the imperial family a pension of Rupees 1,130,000 annually) and remained the guardian over succeeding Emperors until 1857. As a consequence of the anti-British insurrection of that year, which the incumbent Mughal Emperor nominally led, the British executed much of his family, tried and convicted him of treason against them, and exiled him to Burma. Thus, the Mughal Emperors remained a powerful, albeit problematic, symbol in India throughout Dean Mahomed's lifetime.

Other regional powers also threatened Patna during Dean Mahomed's youth there. The alliance of Maratha rulers remained a particularly powerful contender for military and political control over much of India until the early nineteenth century. Either in support of Mughal efforts or on their own, they repeatedly invaded or threatened to invade Bihar and Bengal. While Patna itself never fell to a Maratha force, the city frequently had to take defensive measures in preparation for such an assault, particularly between 1740 and 1751. Throughout Dean Mahomed's service with the Company's army, the Marathas remained the most dangerous enemy of the English across India. Dean Mahomed repeatedly portrayed the Marathas as brigands and enemies of public order (V, VII, XXXI–XXXII). Not until 1818 did the British finally crush the Maratha military threat to their rule over India. Thus, coming of age in Patna during this period meant surviving many sieges and several sackings of the city, as well as enduring the dread of many others. When the Emperor, a Nawab, or a European company could threaten as a dangerous enemy in one campaign but turn guardian in the next, a family's political loyalties had to be flexible for it to survive.

### Joint Nawabi and English Rule over Bihar

Over time, the English Company proved the most consistent patron for Dean Mahomed's family and many others like it. Nevertheless, he grew up in a context where the English Company increasingly forced and precipitated changes in virtually all aspects of life in India. In terms of the Patna administration over Bihar, these were years when the Company began to assert ever broader authority. By installing a series of their clients as Nawabs of Bengal, the English Company had gained political supremacy over the incumbent officials in Bihar as well. From 1757 to 1765, the English Company largely attempted to use the Nawab of Bengal's existing administration to extract revenues from the Bihar countryside. Dissatisfied with the results, the Company thereafter created an ever more British-run administration. In particular, the Company appointed Thomas Rumbold in 1766 to head the Patna Revenue Council, supervising the Nawab of Bengal's deputy Governor for Bihar, Shitab Rai.[36]

To remain in this position, Shitab Rai had to please the English Company. In addition to entertaining British officers and officials (II), he collected ever-increasing land revenues from Bihar. Under his direction, the Patna authorities themselves used force (in the form of Company troops, including those under the command of Dean Mahomed's father) to enforce its land revenue demands on the surrounding countryside. Both landholders and villagers frequently engaged in armed resistance to such revenue exaction by the state. Only when hard pressed would they negotiate payment of that year's revenue.

In a particularly relevant instance of this, Dean Mahomed's father died in 1769 while enforcing the revenue payments of Rajas Boudmal (Budhmal) and Corexin (Kora Singh)—probably Bhumihar Brahmins from Saran District (I). This was the last year that Shitab Rai had direct charge; the Patna Revenue Council took over direction of such punitive expeditions as of October 1770.[37] Despite the resistance of these Rajas which killed Dean Mahomed's father, they subsequently paid that season's revenue and thus soon obtained their release from prison.[38] Thus, in the annual conflict between landholders and Shitab Rai over revenue collection, the tragic death of Dean Mahomed's father was only an unfortunate but minor incident, minor except to his family.

Concomitant with the English Company's influence over the Nawab and his administration came tariff privileges which it insisted upon for its trade—and for the trade of its European employees. This led eventually to a reorientation of much of the commerce in Bengal and Bihar at the cost of established Indian merchants. In particular, the English Company reshaped the region's extensive hand-weaving industry around its demands and requirements.

Over these years as well, cultural expressions and values also shifted as local elites and the English negotiated common ground. The social intercourse between Indian officials, like Shitab Rai, and the Europeans in Patna reveals an asymmetry that would continue to grow. Shitab Rai tried to use such social occasions to bolster his status. A contemporary of Dean Mahomed wrote in a Persian history: 'Magnificent and generous in his household, [Shitab Rai] strove as much as his finances could afford, to live up to the grandeur, and hospitality of a middling Omrah [noble] of Hindostan . . . In the entertainments and feasts which he used often to give, he always imitated the splendidness and the customs of the Moghuls; and when at table, he used to invite his guests with the utmost politeness and courtesy to taste of such and such particular delicacies.'[39] Nevertheless, Shitab Rai served at the pleasure of the English. In 1772, he himself endured an arrest and trial by the Company which, although he received exoneration, led to his despondency and then death the next year.[40]

Europeans worked to transform the Indian countryside as well as the army, administration, and economy. Dean Mahomed noted with respect the many striking mansions, garden-houses, and military cantonments erected by the British officials, officers, and merchants throughout Bihar and Bengal (especially III–IV, VII–VIII). Yet the architectural styles which the English chose reflected their efforts to incorporate Indian patterns as well as European ones. Thus, over the years of Dean Mahomed's youth, the English Company used its military, political, and economic forces to continue to assert an increasing control over India, but they had to do so through compromise with the Indians who both resisted and served them.

## Sepoy Battalions in the Bengal Army

Muslims families like that of Dean Mahomed comprised an important component of the Company's army and administration (particularly in the upper ranks), far in excess of their minority proportion of the general population. In the Bengal Army over the period that Dean Mahomed chronicles, Muslims consistently provided nearly half of the higher Indian officer corps, about two-fifths of the lower Indian officers, and about one-third of the sepoys.[41] As the power of the Nawab of Bengal (and the other mainly Muslim-ruled states of north India) declined, many members of the Muslim service elite decided to attach themselves to the rapidly expanding English East India Company's armies or administration. Additionally, Clive and others in the Company sought to retain an even balance between Hindus and Muslims in the Bengal Army. Clive wanted 'each Battalion composed of an equal number of Gentoos and Mussulmen, and to encourage a rivalship of disc[ipline] between them' thus preventing 'their holding Cabals'.[42] Many Europeans in the Company sought to implement their stereotyped preconceptions about the racial and religious characteristics of different communities of Indians. The Company throughout this period devalued Bengalis as soldiers. It preferred to recruit for its army men from outside of Bengal, whom it referred to as 'the fighting Tribes of the Hindoos and Musselmen', seeking 'as many of the latter as can be procured'.[43]

Not until 1764 did the Bengal Army formally start to institutionalize its European-type organization and sepoy model discipline. In that year, Major Sir Hector Munro of the Royal Army (recently appointed Commander-in-Chief of the Bengal Army), found that the existing relatively informal organization and discipline of the army had led to mutinies variously by its European officers, European soldiers, and sepoys. Following his suppression of a mutiny by sepoys near Patna in 1764, Munro established a regularized body of discipline and systematic set of manoeuvers, based on the Royal Army's code of standing orders.[44] This code of standing orders sought to bring further uniformity to the military conduct of the Bengal Army, both to its Indian and European members.

Traditionally, the military labour contractor bargained for the best deal for himself and his peasant-soldiers or mercenaries from any one of a number of possible military employers. These units had felt free to shift from army to army as opportunities offered. Despite the English Company's objections to such a labour contract system, under the pressures of war it continued to recruit bodies of men under labour contractors as late as 1781.[45]

Munro's plan was to reorient the sepoys until they saw themselves as individuals bound professionally to the Company's army, or at least to their unit within that army. Nevertheless, many sepoys continued to regard service with the Company's army as a temporary situation, to be entered into or left at their pleasure. The Company periodically complained that whenever a sepoy battalion relocated to a different region, locally-recruited sepoys regularly deserted it and re-enlisted in the new battalion transferring into that region, rather than accept relocation.[46] The idea of 'honour' binding a sepoy to his regiment, which Mason presents as the soul of the Company's Army, was clearly not operative at this point, despite British efforts to inculcate it.[47]

Under Munro and his successors, such a homogenizing model strove to minimize individuality and visible ethnic or community differences by standardizing appearance and deportment through a semi-European uniform and drill. On his part, Dean Mahomed particularly noted as a distinctive feature of the Bengal Army that Hindus and Muslims, indeed that Indians from all religions and regions, had to dress and act uniformly, at least while on duty (XVI). Thus, the Company sought to make sepoys into a new, standardized military type with mixed Indian and European accoutrements.

The sepoy uniform reflected European elements mixed with British interpretations of Indian traditions. The standard-issue military coat and 'Tower musket' (a musket stamped as tested at the Tower of London) were purely European in pattern. The necklace of beads—the varying quality of the glass, conch-shell, or precious metal beads denoting different ranks—was apparently a British adaptation of the gorget used in European uniforms to denote rank of what they saw as an Indian tradition.[48] The Company's official specifications for a sepoy's uniform required specified patterns: '1 turban, 1 cummerbund and caross [waist-shawl and crossed bands], 1 linen jacket, 1 pair of junghiers [military shorts], 1 coxcomb or turah [turban ornament], 1 silver regimental device for ditto.'[49] In addition, Dean Mahomed described an iconic target (round shield) suspended at the back of the left shoulder of both sepoys and Indian officers (Illustration 2), a clear connection to the traditional bukhserria type.

For the Company, profit remained an intrinsic organizational principle in its army as well as civil administration. Each sepoy had to purchase his own uniform for six rupees, allowing a generous profit to his commanding officer who arranged to supply it. In addition, each sepoy had a fixed sum withheld from his monthly salary to pay for the one uniform coat he received each

December. Yet the sepoy did not own the coat he so purchased; a discharged or promoted soldier had to give his used coat to his replacement. The quality of the cloth in this coat reflected the rank of the wearer: the 'Subadar's coat [must be] of Superfine Cloth, laced with gold or silver; the Jemmautdars of 2nd ditto, laced with silk lace, the non-warrant officers of aurora, and the Sepoys of Sacca.'[50] Each of the three brigades further distinguished itself with a specific colour for the facings and trim on its coat.

Dean Mahomed (and many other Indians) clearly found the uniform appearance and discipline of the Company's sepoys striking. He frequently commented on the remarkable discipline, uniform appearance, and periodic drill and practiced field man-oeuvres of the Bengal Army units to which he was attached, contrasting them with the motley armies of the Company's allies and enemies. Thus, the Indians inducted into the Company's Bengal Army increasingly found a vocation with professionalized characteristics growing ever more distinct from earlier military service patterns.

The Company continued to recruit heavily for its Bengal Army from the 1760s on. The Bengal Army rose in numbers from its initial 300–400 men in 1757 to 8289 men by 1762. In addition, by 1762 the Madras and Bombay armies contained about 9000 and 2500 Indian soldiers respectively.[51] By 1765, Clive had expanded the Bengal Army and reorganized it into three equally sized, symmetrically composed, and autonomous brigades (each consisting of 7 battalions of sepoys plus 1 regiment of European troops, 1 company of European artillery, and 1 troop of cavalry), totalling some 14,000–15,000 Indian soldiers and some 3000 European officers and men.[52] Each year from 1766 to 1768, the Bengal Army expanded on average by about 5000 Indians until, in 1770 as Dean Mahomed was attaching himself to it, the Bengal Army totaled 27,277 active Indian officers and men (in addition to about 522 European officers and 2722 European soldiers).[53] By the time Dean Mahomed resigned from the army (1782), some 52,500 Indians were currently serving in the Bengal Army, and over 115,000 in the Company's three Presidency armies combined. Like him, many more Indians entered and then left it over the years (through resignation, death, or disability).[54] Thus, large numbers of Indians chose to enter the Company's military structure; their contribution to it should not be overshadowed by the largely British accounts that have survived from this period.

During the 1760s and early 1770s, the Army's brigades rotated among the three major theatres: the Calcutta area (including Fort William and Barahampur); the centre (Monghyr, Denapur, and Bankipur); and the west (the frontier moving progressively westward during Dean Mahomed's career, including Buxar on the Karamnasa River, Allahabad, Chunar, and Bilgram) (see Map). Threats from the west (from Awadh, the Marathas, or the Rohillas at different times) or east (particularly from the French) led to movements by the three brigades. Since supplemental pay allowances (*batta*) and chances for booty and glory increased while on the western frontier, each brigade expected its turn there on a two year rotation.[55] In addition to opposing external threats to the Company's administration, sepoy battalions frequently enforced the Company's rule over the people within its territories, particularly coercing villagers and landholders into obedience to the Company's land revenue demands.

For the Company, as for the Mughals, strong class distinctions separated high Indian 'warrant officers' from lower officers and sepoys. It was particularly difficult in these early days for an ordinary Indian soldier to rise through the ranks of the Bengal Army to an officer's status. The elite background of Dean Mahomed's father apparently led the Company to appoint him an officer. His father may, indeed, have brought with him into the Bengal Army a body of soldiers who had served with him in the past. The role of military labour contractor, jemadar, had for a long time been a well-established one in north India.[56] Dean Mahomed tells us that by 1769, his father commanded a company (under the direction of a British Captain) with the rank of 'subadar', the second highest—after 'commandant'—that an Indian could attain at that time in the Company's army. Perhaps because of earlier service, Dean Mahomed's father served in the part of the Bengal Army closest to the pre-sepoy pattern.

## Pargana Sepoy Battalions

Dean Mahomed's father served at least part of his career in the 'pargana' [district] sepoy battalions. These battalions were the more paramilitary part of the army, particularly designated to subdue the Bihar and Bengal countryside and enforce land revenue demands by seizing revenue defaulters. The pargana sepoy force originated as a branch of the Bengal Army, but one which developed a distinctive status, and patterns more in keeping with traditional Indian military service.

As the English Company began to engage in land revenue collection activities, it found increasing need to enforce these revenue demands through the use of military force. At first, the Company assigned companies or battalions of sepoys from the three regular brigades to undertake this work. The nature of this kind of service, however, proved quite different from that of the rest of the Army and, as the Company saw it, detrimental to military discipline. Regular service with one of the brigades consisted mainly of practising close-order drill, building a sense of unity with the remainder of the Army, and occasionally marching and fighting against other armies. In contrast, the sepoys who engaged in revenue collection had to serve in small, detached units (usually at the company level or below), rarely in contact with their home brigade, and often under the direction of the Nawab of Bengal's officials. Pargana battalions had proportionately fewer European officers so Indian officers and sepoys enjoyed more autonomy. They interacted mainly in an adversarial role against villagers, landholders, and insurgents in the countryside, enforcing the unwelcome revenue demands of the state.

Since Clive found this type of revenue collection service so derogatory to the military discipline which the Company sought to instill in its sepoys, he determined to separate off special pargana battalions from the rest of the Army. He and other Britons felt that sepoys were tempted by relatively unsupervised opportunities to use their coercive power in their own interests. In 1765, Clive removed one battalion from each of the three brigades and designated these three battalions for extended service in this line.[57] These three full-time pargana sepoy battalions came under the command of civilian officials rather than the Army's brigade officers. They specialized in revenue-enforcement service, while the remainder of the battalions remained protected from what the Company saw as such degrading duties.

During the remainder of the 1760s, the British officials of the Company increasingly assumed authority over revenue collection hitherto exercised by the Nawab's officials. These British officials felt the constant need for enhanced coercive power and demanded more pargana sepoy battalions. Instead of diverting further battalions from the regular Brigades, the Company raised a total of nine new battalions specifically for such pargana service. For a number of years, these pargana sepoy units worked under the joint (and often conflicting) direction of the Nawab's and the Company's revenue supervisors and other officials. Such dual government continued to confuse lines of authority in all branches of the administration and army.

The theoretical distinctions between regular sepoy and pargana sepoy battalions did not always remain in effect. To extract revenues from a reluctant countryside, European and Indian officials continued occasionally to demand in addition the use of one or more battalions from whatever units of regular brigade sepoys were present in the region. For particularly large-scale assaults on the forts of unsubmissive zamindars they required artillery as well as regular brigade sepoy units, in addition to their pargana sepoy forces. The Calcutta Council, however, made repeated (but usually vain) attempts to prevent this diversion of regular brigade units into such work.[58] Conversely, at other times the distinction between pargana and brigade sepoy units became blurred because pargana battalions joined large-scale expeditions alongside brigade battalions. In the English Company's 1767 invasion of Nepal against the Gurkas, for example, about a third of that ill-conceived expedition consisted of pargana companies.[59]

In 1767, the Company increased the number of pargana battalions stationed in Bihar to four, by raising the 31st Battalion under Captain Thomas Goddard. Dean Mahomed's father, as an experienced officer, apparently transferred into this new battalion, taking command of one of its ten companies.[60] At first, conditions in the new battalion were inadequate: '[This] Battalion not yet having received any clothing, and numbers of them being armed only with bamboos, have not much the appearance of sepoys, but they are good looking men, well recruited and when furnished with firelocks (which I am just informed are arrived) they will make a very different figure to what they do at present.'[61] In fact, this battalion improved rapidly until it held the reputation as the best—although it was the newest—of all the pargana battalions.[62] In 1769, one company of the 31st Pargana Battalion—apparently the one under the command of Dean Mahomed's father—held station in Tajpur in Bihar's Saran District (I).[63]

Overall, the pargana sepoy battalions had a mixed record. On the one hand, they extracted land revenues that the Company would otherwise have been unable to collect. On the other, the Company believed them less disciplined and more abusive of villagers and landholders. Warren Hastings called this force 'a rascally corps . . . our own plunderers . . . without discipline, without control and employ'd in the most unsoldierly of all services'.[64] Nor did the Army like 'this motley system . . . [t]his blending of Civil and Military Authority together'.[65] After a particularly embarrassing and costly series of defeats by a band of armed sannyasis (religious ascetics) in 1772, the pargana sepoy units were all demobilized or integrated by the Company into the regular sepoy battalions. In 1773, the Company created units of invalid European and Indian officers and sepoys, organized at the company, not battalion, level to carry out the land revenue enforcement duties formerly done by pargana sepoys. In 1783, the Company replaced this invalid establishment with a separate corps of 'sibandis' (revenue police). In addition, to deal with particularly hostile situations, the Company raised special corps of light infantry (VIII). The Bengal Army, both its sepoy and its pargana components, extended the power of the English Company over the various Indian states and into the countryside.

## The Famine of 1769

In 1769, a severe and extended drought cut drastically into the production of food grains in Bihar and western Bengal. This disastrous famine revealed the inadequacies of the Company's administration. While the Company desired to profit from its power over Bengal and Bihar, it did not yet conceive of itself as responsible for their government. The Company considered one of its first responsibilities to feed its army, at the least cost to itself. The army consumed 240,000 maunds (8280 tons) of rice annually, a vast quantity to extract from a drought-struck countryside.[66] One relief measure would be to move one brigade out of the most severely affected area (so as to relieve the pressure on supplies there) but the Company decided not to do this because the march might risk the health of its European soldiers.[67]

The Company did undertake some modest ameliorative meas-ures. Some Company officials tried to reduce the price of rice by importing cheaper grain from still productive areas to the west, particularly from Awadh, and selling it for only modest profit in the famine areas. The Company reduced the revenue demand in the worst hit areas, hoping 'the distressed natives, who by ex-periencing such a timely act of Lenity, may be impressed with a favourable opinion of the Government, may be induced to exert their industrious labours to promote its welfare, and may be enabled to pay their rents more regularly in future'.[68] Some British and Indian officials of the Company, and private merchants as well, responded to the growing human disaster through small acts of charity: distributing rice to the starving people who surrounded them.[69] Other Britons and Indians evidently hoarded rice until they could maximize their profits since prices rose over 2200 per cent.[70] With the Company's approval, the Awadh ruler aided a few destitute families by purchasing their sons and daughters as his domestic slaves, thus preventing either the parents or the children from starving, but at the cost of a lifetime of bondage for the children.[71]

Even though the famine occurred when Dean Mahomed was only eleven years old, he was impressed enough to write movingly and sympathetically about this disaster twenty-five years later. While Dean Mahomed presented the Company's viewpoint of the landholder's resistance to revenue demands, he also recorded the human cost of this famine, during which as many as ten million people died of starvation in Bihar and western Bengal (I, III). His words suggest the contrast between the horrors of 150 people dying of starvation per day in Patna and the simultaneous lavish life style enjoyed by both the Europeans of that city and also those Indians who worked with or for them.[72] While some other Indian and European commentators wrote with empathy about this tragedy, others did not.[73] For example, in his diary Colonel Alexander Champion only remarked on how the multi-tude of exposed corpses disturbed his travels: 'This day's journey was very disagreeable from the great number of carcasses lying both sides of the road and by the river side.'[74]

For families like Dean Mahomed's, the late eighteenth century proved a time of difficult choices and conflicting loyalties. The Mughal Emperor and the regional rulers whom their ancestors had followed no longer could offer the same opportunities for employment and advancement. In many ways, service to the English Company during this early period continued some of the same traditional military and administrative patterns. Nevertheless, over time, the English colonial administration altered the political, social, and economic worlds of India. The Bengal Army imposed the new English colonial order on Indian society. Tensions increased among the expanding English Company, Indians within the Company's service, and other Indian villagers, townsmen, and rulers. By attaching himself to the Bengal Army, Dean Mahomed thus entered a complex world during a formative phase of English colonial rule.

## Notes

1. See J.F. Richards, 'Norms', in Barbara Daly Metcalf, *Moral Conduct* (1984), pp. 255–89.
2. Abul Fazl Allami, *Ain-i Akbari*, translated by H.S. Jarrett (1988 reprint), 2: 141–368. These figures are compiled by Dirk H.A. Kolff, *Naukar* (1990), p. 3.
3. In 1703 Nawab Murshid Quli Khan changed the name of Bengal's capital from Muxadabad (or Makhsudabad) to Murshidabad. Dean Mahomed, like many others, continued to use the older name.
4. C.f. Richard G. Fox, *Kin, Clan, Raja, Rule* (1971).
5. Khan, *Seir* 3: 204–5.
6. Khan, *Seir* 3: 41–2, 147.
7. George Mahomed, 'Sake Deen Mahomed', *Sussex County Magazine* 14 (1940), p. 42.
8. Joseph Schwartzberg quantified this dimension in 'chorochronic units', *Historical Atlas* (1978), pp. 254–62.
9. Select Committee to CoD 18/3/1770, FTWM 6: 197.
10. Nawab Mir Jafar's letter 2/5/1762 cited in N.N. Raye, *Annals* (1927), p. 269.
11. C.f. Shubhra Chakrabarti, 'Collaboration and Resistance', *Studies in History* 10, 1 n.s. (1994), pp. 105–29.
12. Henry Dodwell traces the origins of sepoys from peons employed by the European companies from the 1720s. *Sepoy Recruitment* (1922), pp. 1–12.
13. P.J. Marshall, *East Indian Fortunes* (1976), p. 15.

14.  Arthur Broome, *History* (1850) 1: 92–3; Williams, *Historical Account*, p. 4.
15.  For further discussion of these types of soldiers, see Kolff, *Nauker*, pp. 169–81.
16.  Indeed, the Bengal Army employed troops of such 'Mughal Horse' as its irregular cavalry well into the nineteenth century. For discussion of three troops (some 1200 men) of such cavalry see: From CoD 25/3/1772, FTWM 6: 159. See also Provincial CinC 10/6/1782 BPbC 9/7/1782 and Seema Alavi, 'The Makings of Company Power', *Indian Economic and Social History Review*, 30, 4 (October 1993), pp. 437–59.
17.  See *Hobson-Jobson*, s.v. 'Topaz'.
18.  See *Hobson-Jobson*, s.v. 'Sepoy'.
19.  There is much debate over the significance of any technological advantage that European military science may have had over indigenous Asian armies. The Calcutta Council believed that European small arms and other weapons must be kept under their monopolistic control. Letter to Court 3/9/1766 in J. Long, *Selections* (1869), 1: 427. For somewhat differing assessments of this issue see Bruce P. Lenman, 'Weapons', *Journal of the Society for Army Historical Research* 36 (1968): 33–43 and Gayl D. Ness and William Stahl, 'Western Imperialist Armies in Asia', *Comparative Studies in Society and History*, 19 (1977): 2–29.
20.  Mir 'Abdul-Latif Khan Shustari, *Tuhfat al-'alam va zayl al-tuhfah*, translated by Juan R.I. Cole, 'Invisible Occidentalism: Eighteenth-Century Indo-Persian Constructions of the West', *Iranian Studies* 25, 3–4 (1992): 3–16.
21.  At Plassey, Clive had 613 Europeans, 48 Bengal and 43 Bombay Topasees; 171 artillery [including 50 sailors, 7 midshipmen]; 2100 sepoys, including some from Madras, some from Bengal, and a company of Bombay sepoys (via Madras). George William Forest, *Life of Lord Clive* (1918) 1: 437.
22.  E.g. Khan, *Seir*, passim.
23.  In addition, the high officials of the Company extracted vast personal fortunes (totaling some £2,600,000) as gifts from successive Nawabs of Bengal in the 1757–65 period. Marshall, *East*, pp. 163–6, 179.
24.  See Bruce Lenman, 'Transition' in John Lynn, ed. *Tools of War* (1990), p. 121.
25.  See C.A. Bayly, *Indian Society* (1988); Douglas M. Peers, 'War and Public Finance' in *The International History Review*, 11, 4 (November 1989): 628–47.
26.  See Michael H. Fisher, *Politics of the British Annexation* (1993), Introduction.
27.  From CoD 12/7/1782, FTWM 9: 61.
28.  To CoD 5/4/1783, FTWM 9: 378.
29.  Ali Gauhar to Clive 10/1/1759, recd 17/2/1759, FTWM 2: 420–1; see Kalikinkar Datta, *Shah Alam II* (1965), Chapter 1. Dean Mahomed celebrated his birthday as May 1759.

30. To King, 10/7/1761, CPC 1: 112.
31. Only Dr Fullarton and 4 European sergeants escaped back to rejoin the Company's army. Bengal Select Committee 16/6/1763 cited in Broome, *History* 1: 362–9. See Nandlal Chatterji, *Mir Qasim* (1935), especially pp. 260–76.
32. For example, the 12th N.I. consisted of men recruited from Mir Kasim's defeated army in October 1763. After the surrender of Chunar by Awadh, many of the garrison enlisted in the Company's army (February 1765). Broome, *History* 1: 390, 506. The Company also took hundreds of men from the Nawab of Bengal's remaining army. From Prov CinC 24/1/1781, BPbC 25/1/1781. The British continued to recruit from their former enemies as well. Indeed, the two pillars of the Bengal Army during and after the conflict of 1857 were its two recent opponents: Punjabi Sikhs and Nepali Gurkas.
33. For a detailed and personal account of the defence of Patna in May 1764 and then the battle of Buxar in October that year, see Diary of Champion, HMS 198. Lenman, 'Transition', p. 119.
34. On the accession of the Nawab of Bengal in 1770, the Mughal Emperor requested and received Rupees 300,000 as the Nawab's succession offering to him. The Company's last payments were Rupees 475,000 in 1770 and Rupees 600,000 in 1772. Select Committee to CoD 31/10/1770, FTWM 6: 238. To King 14/2/1772, CPC 3, p. 271.
35. Memorial of John Morrison and Order 6/12/1771, BSMC 6/12/1771, 12/12/1772; Secret Letter to CoD 10/12/1772, FTWM 6: 455–6.
36. Sir Thomas Rumbold stood as the highest civil official in Patna: Chief of the Patna Factory and Supervisor of Bihar Collections (1766–69). He was simultaneously a member of the Governor General's Council in Calcutta (but often in absentia). In December 1769, Rumbold resigned and then left India, thereafter elected to Parliament (for New Shoreham, near Brighton where Dean Mahomed eventually settled). He returned to India as Governor of Madras (February 1778–April 1780) and died in 1791. Letter from Chapman 25/6/1769, BSC 6/7/1769. Marshall, *East*, p. 198. Khan, *Seir* 2: 266–8, 419 20; 3: 13ff, 49.
37. Copy Book of Letters issued by the Controlling Council of Revenue at Patna 13/11/1770 to 28/5/1771, ff. 1–2, IOL.
38. Circumstances of the People who are now in Confinement in the Nizamut Cutcherry at Patna on account of Balances of the Revenues in the Bahar Province in Letter of Alexander to Governor and Secret Committee 16/3/1770, BSMC 29/3/1770. The specific names which Dean Mahomed used to describe this conflict (Captain Adams and Rajas Boudmal and Corexin) do not appear in surviving Company records. Possibly Dean Mahomed conflated the name of the officer under whom his father served with Major Adams, who had led an expedition in the Patna region in August–November 1763, but had died by 1769. Nevertheless, the scenario he recounted of crude conflict in the negotiations over revenue payments proved quite common.

39. Khan, *Seir* 3: 49.

40. Khan, *Seir* 3: 47ff. His son inherited his office.

41. I calculated the above figures for sepoy infantry battalions from BMC 1778–84, Infantry Native Officers and Sepoys examined by a Committee of Surgeons as to their fitness for further service. The Madras Army had similar proportions, Dodwell, *Sepoy*, pp. 11, 40–9. There were no perceptibly single religion regiments; each had a substantial number from each community within each rank.

42. From CoD 16/3/1768, FTWM 5: 100.

43. Minutes of Council 22/4/1782, BMCG 29/4/1782; GOCC 11/5/1782.

44. Broome, *History* 1: 455–8 citing this document in Caraccioli, *Clive* 2: 46–7.

45. The larger the body of recruits, the higher the military rank their contractor received. See Dodwell, *Sepoy*, p. 19. Madras Military Consultation 15/3/1781 ff. 668–9: Military Consultation 22/11/1768 f. 1716; 13/11/1798 ff. 6853–5; 19/2/1799 ff. 1018–19; G.O.G No. 44 10/4/1799. For the cavalry, such block recruitment continued far later. Provincial CinC 10/6/1782, BPbC 9/7/1782; Major Fletcher to Futteh Aly Cawn, Persian Department No. 46 (1765) in Long, *Selections* 1: 415.

46. From CoD 11/4/1781, FTWM 8: 295; BSMC 6/8/1781.

47. Philip Mason, *Matter of Honour* (1974). C.f. Douglas M. Peers, 'Habitual Nobility', *Modern Asian Studies* 25, 3 (1991): 545–69, Dodwell, *Sepoy*, pp. 29–30; David Arnold, *Police Power and Colonial Rule* (1986); Francis Gordon Cardew, *Sketch of the Services of the Bengal Native Army* (1903); T.A. Heathcote, *Military in British India* (1995); David Omissi, *Sepoy and the Raj . . . 1860–1940* (1994).

48. The uniform—including the 'Kuntah', or necklace of 30–40 conch beads worn around the necks of sepoys—is described in Williamson, *East Indian* 1: 426.

49. Minutes of Council 7/5/1781, BMCG 11/5/1781.

50. Minutes of Council 7/5/1781, BMCG 11/5/1781.

51. Broome, *History*, appendices P–W; Raymond Callahan, *East India Company* (1972), p. 6.

52. Broome, *History*, appendices; Williams, *Historical Account*, p. 3.

53. GRT 31/7/1770. See also Statement of the Army, BPbC 16/12/1769; this roughly accords with less recent figures in From CoD 16/3/1768, FTWM 5: 99–100. The figures in Return of the Company's Troops in India, in the Eighth Report of the Committee of Secrecy, however, give a far less rapid rise in the number of sepoys. I have accepted the consensus of the reports from India rather than from London.

54. Broome, *History*, Appendices P–W; Callahan, *East*, p. 6. See Seema Alavi, 'The Company Army', *Modern Asian Studies* 27, 1 (1993): 147–78.

55. Batta first began in the 1750s, later Mir Jafar doubled the officers' batta. In 1766 Clive tried to abolish double batta which led to a mass resignation of British officers. Callahan, *East*, pp. 28–9.

56. See Kolff, *Naukar*.

57. Minute of the President, BSMC 20/7/1768. See also Gerald Bryant, 'Pacification in the Early British Raj, 1755–85', *Journal of Imperial and Commonwealth History* 14 (1985): 3–19.
58. BSMC 3/8/1768, 17/8/1768, 6/3/1769.
59. See George Kinlock, 'Journal', MS Eur F.128/40, IOL; Rumbold to Verelst 19/12/1767, BSMC 12/1/1768.
60. A less probable possibility is that Dean Mahomed's father served in a brigade battalion seconded to revenue collection duties. Until mid-1769, the 2nd Brigade held post in Bihar, so Dean Mahomed's father would have to have been from this Brigade. In June 1769, however, the 2nd Brigade shifted to Monghyr and then Barahampur. Dean Mahomed says explicitly that his elder brother (only 16 at the time) took his father's place (I). If we take this literally, the brother would have been in the same battalion as the father. Yet, the brother visited Dean Mahomed in Bankipur, long after the 2nd Brigade had left Bihar. Thus, the predominant weight of evidence indicates that his father was in the 31st Battalion of pargana sepoys.
61. Rumbold to Verelst 19/12/1767, BSC 12/1/1768.
62. In 1768, its fine reputation prevented it from being 'reformed' (i.e. broken up with its sepoys and officers reassigned as replacements to other units) in a budgetary retrenchment. From CoD 16/3/1768, FTWM 5: 89–101.
63. Rumbold to Council 22/9/1769, BSMC 19/10/1769. Broome, *History* 1: 618–19.
64. President's Minute, HPC 10/10/1772; Hastings to Josias Dupre, 9/3/1773 in Hastings, *Memoirs* 1: 303.
65. Minute of Barker, 27/1/1772, BPbC 17/2/1772.
66. Minute of Board, BPOC 23/10/1769, No. 1.
67. To CoD 9/5/1770, FTWM 6: 203–4.
68. Select Committee, BSMC 6/3/1769.
69. Letter of James Alexander, Supervisor of Bihar 14/3/1770, BSMC 29/4/1770.
70. From CoD 10/4/1771, 28/8/1771, and To CoD 9/3/1772, FTWM 6: 107–8, 119–20, 368–9. Marshall, *East*, pp. 144–5.
71. Harper to Alexander 25/3/1770, BSMC 15/4/1770.
72. Letter of James Alexander, Supervisor of Bihar to Gov. and Select Committee 14/3/1770, BSMC 29/4/1770.
73. See also Khan, *Seir* 3: 25–6, 56–7.
74. Colonel Champion's journal, 10/2/1770, in Macpherson, *Soldiering*, p. 30.

## Chapter Four

# Dean Mahomed and the
# Bengal Army (1769–84)

### Dean Mahomed Chooses the Company of the English
### (1769–70)

As the second son of a distinguished (but deceased) officer,
Dean Mahomed had to establish a career for himself. In
earlier generations, he might have drawn on the traditional ties between his family and their relatives and patrons, the
Nawabs of Bengal, for a military or administrative career. By 1769,
however, the Nawab had himself fallen on difficult days as a dependent of the Company. The Company reduced each succeeding
Nawab's pension, constantly pressuring them to reduce expenses
by cutting off retainers like Dean Mahomed's family.[1] In particular,
the Company regarded the Nawab's army as both a waste of money
and a threat to public order. In its place, the Company determined
to substitute the Bengal Army. For Dean Mahomed, therefore,
entering the Nawab's service was virtually precluded just as a career
with the Company became especially attractive.

In Patna during Dean Mahomed's youth, social intercourse
flourished between Europeans and Indian elites, albeit asymmetri-
cally and within prescribed limits. An Indian contemporary of
Dean Mahomed described in Persian such intercourse in Patna
and its objectives:

> [T]he English of some rank spent their time merrily and in pleasures,
> and lived upon terms of much friendship and intimacy with the
> noblemen and other persons of distinction, natives of this country.
> They were endeavouring to engage them in conversation, especially
> upon the politics of the country; and so soon as an Englishman could
> pick up any thing relative to the laws or business of this land, he

would immediately set it down in writing, and lay it up in store for the use of another Englishman; nor had they any other view in taking notice of a Moghul or a native, or in courting an acquaintance with him.[2]

Indians, as well as the British, however, turned these social inter-actions to their own advantage. Both the above account about the habits of the British and also Dean Mahomed's own book, *Travels*, demonstrated that Indians could also record and learn from their observation of the British. Further, both Raja Shitab Rai and Dean Mahomed used these social occasions to their own advantage by developing relationships with the British.

Due to his family's status, Dean Mahomed gained access to parties hosted by Shitab Ray for European officers of the Company's army. Raja Shitab Ray devoted much of his energy to pleasing the officials and officers of the Company, even at the cost of squeezing the Indian landholders, villagers, and nobility for funds to do so, even during a period of mass starvation in Bihar at this time (II).[3]

On occasion, the English played host to Indian guests. A major fire in 1768 had destroyed not only the Company's factory but much of Patna city as well. As a result, the British shifted much of their activities to the garden of their long-time agent in Patna (until 1754), Mir Afzal. Indeed, it was at a tennis court built by Colonel Alexander Champion in Mir Afzal's Garden that eleven year old Dean Mahomed recalled catching the eye of his future patron, Godfrey Evan Baker, a newly appointed cadet at the beginning of his military career (II).[4]

## Godfrey Evan Baker as a Cadet (1769)

When the Company created the entry level position of cadet (as distinct from the civilian position of 'writer'), it added a professional military career track for its British employees and marked its recognition of its permanent military engagement in Indian politics. Earlier, the Company had simply appointed military officers on an ad hoc basis, drawing men from either the Royal Army or its civilian ranks.[5] In 1768, when Baker obtained his nomination as cadet, it could not have been clear to him or the Company exactly what this career choice entailed.

For young Anglo-Irishmen, Englishmen, and Scotsmen, employment by the East India Company seemed to promise a lucrative future. The Company's military victories of Plassey (1757) and Buxar (1764), and the millions of pounds sterling acquired by its prominent officials during these years, astounded the British public. In 1764, Horace Walpole, an English man of letters, coined the term 'Nabob' to describe the fabulously rich, India-returned men who stunned society with their wealth—if not their breeding.[6] The year Baker obtained his appointment as cadet, Robert Clive had just returned to Britain as only one of the richer 'Nabobs'. Indeed, the newspapers of Baker's native Cork and the other cities of Britain continued for years to publish lists of 'Nabobs', giving the details of their reputed fortunes.[7] Thus, when Baker decided to seek a cadetship, he probably sought wealth, and perhaps military glory as well.

In background, Baker largely reflected the social norm for a cadet joining the Bengal Army at this time. His fellow Anglo-Irishmen formed a large component among the Company's military and civilian employees. Like him, over 70 per cent (20 out of 28) of the cadets of his cohort came from the middle classes (merchants and professionals); while only 25 per cent came from the landed aristocracy.[8] Thus, Baker entered into a society of officers containing men much like himself, separated by racial lines from their Indian subordinates and by class lines from their European soldiers.

Entry into the ranks of the cadets took influence or money. The year of Baker's appointment, his father, a rising merchant, won election as the Mayor of Cork, the second largest city in Ireland after Dublin. Appointments as cadet came by nomination by one of the Company's Directors or by the British Government.[9] If the possessor of such patronage would not give such an appointment, he might sell it. Indeed, men who themselves had received a cadetship on occasion resold it. Although sales of cadetships were not legal, they were common, and openly advertised in newspapers.

To qualify for appointment as a cadet, there were few requirements. Baker's fellow Anglo-Irishman, William Hickey, described the pro-forma interview he underwent in 1768, completely unprepared as he was, before obtaining the cadetship which his despairing father had purchased for him as the last resort for a wayward son.[10] Until 1772, the Company set no minimum age requirement for cadets.[11] While we cannot know Baker's actual age, it is likely he was only in his mid-teens when he arrived in India and received his formal appointment as a cadet (dated 21 March 1769).

No special training programme existed for newly-arrived cadets like Baker. Rather, each cadet received an assignment to one of the three European regiments where he would be socialized into his new profession.[12] The Bengal Army, like the Royal Army, believed that (except for specialists like engineers and artillery-officers) a gentleman could learn all he needed to know about his profession from his superior officers. As one Bengal Army Colonel—only partly facetiously—described the lessons a cadet received:

> To be a gentleman [officer] you must learn to drink by all means—a man is honoured in proportion to the number of bottles he can drink; keep a dozen dogs, but in particular if you have not the least use for them and hate hunting and shooting. Four horses may barely suffice; but if you have eight, and seven of them are too vicious for the syce [groom] to feed, it will be much better.
>
> By no means let the horses be paid for; and have a palanquin covered with silver trappings—get 10,000 rupees in debt, but 20,000 would make you an honest man, especially if you are convinced that you will never have the power to pay. Endeavour to forget whatever you have learnt—ridicule learning of all sorts—despise all military knowledge—call duty a bore—encourage your men to laugh at orders—obey such as you like—make a joke of your commanding officer for giving those orders you do not like, and, if you obey them, let it be seen that it is merely to serve yourself.[13]

Despite the obvious deficiencies of such training, it did produce a band of young men whose common experience bonded them to each other over and against the rest of the world.

For people of Baker's social status and above, the Company's army remained a second-rate, mercenary career. Of the three Company armies, the Bengal Army in which Baker obtained his appointment rated more highly than those of Madras or Bombay at that time.[14] Nevertheless, a Company army commission carried less prestige—and sense of honour to King and country—than a commission in the Royal Army might. Since the concept of a national army had not yet developed in England, however, officers joining the Royal Army had some of the same egoistic motivations as Company cadets. Further, at that time a mercenary officer could still be a gentleman. Nevertheless, throughout Baker's military career, Royal Army officers serving in India continued to consider themselves superior to, and to demand precedence over, Company officers of the same military rank.[15] Eventually, the growing identification of the English Company with the English state and also the increasing professionalization of the Company's armies began to allow Company officers 'to mask their private interest under the guise of the national interest'.[16]

Baker had chosen what would prove a particularly perilous career. Among the cohort of 108 cadets of 1769–70 (Baker's year and the next), within about five years nearly 20 per cent had died, 10 per cent had resigned, one had gone insane and returned to Europe, and only two-thirds were still on the army list.[17] Of the 256 cadets who joined the Bengal Army in the years 1760–83, over 65 per cent ultimately died in service in India, mostly of disease.[18]

Even compared to a civil appointment in the Company's service, a cadetship was second-best. Although mortality rates were comparable between the two cadres, the opportunities for enrichment had become more limited for army officers than for civilian officials.[19] This relative valuation reflected itself in the disparate prices paid for appointments as cadet versus writer. For example, London newspapers in 1783 advertised cadetships for 50 guineas while appointments as a writer went for 1000 guineas (down from £2000–3000 a decade earlier, but well above the £150 paid two decades later).[20]

During Baker's career, private trade carried out by a European employee of the Company could prove a major source of wealth, since the Company and its employees enjoyed tariff exemptions and a range of monopolies. For civil officials of the Company, this trade (plus lucrative perquisites from offices they held) put many on the road to riches. For military officers, however, private trade was more difficult to sustain: the routine two year rotation of brigades among cantonments, in addition to occasional campaigns in the field, tended to disrupt trading arrangements. Booty seized from a captured Indian city, town, or village and gifts from Indian allies were a more likely source of rapid wealth for officers. By 1769, however, such opportunities had become less frequent and more regulated by the Company (Baker himself would be charged with extorting money from villagers and recalled in disgrace at the end of his career).

Once in command of a sepoy battalion or European regiment, a Company officer might tap into other sources of income. Officers of field rank (Majors and above) divided a share of the land revenue of Bengal that could run to Rupees 45,000 annually for a Brigadier General and Rupees 15,000 for a Colonel.[21] In addition, commanding officers personally profited from equipping and provisioning their troops. Such commanding officers divided the 'Off Reckoning', the sum deducted from the pay of Indian sepoys and officers for uniforms. These and other 'stoppages' were a substantial proportion of an Indian's pay. A subadar, for instance, received Rupees 60 monthly in pay but had Rupees 6 out of that stopped; stoppages comprised about 5 per cent of a sepoy's basic salary of Rupees 6.[22] This amount handsomely supplemented the income of their European commanders. In 1780, for example, the amount deducted from the Bengal Army totalled Rupees 431,616 but the cost of the clothing supplied was less than two-thirds of that amount: the European officers divided Rupees 155,064 among themselves according to their rank.[23]

British commanders also supplemented their income from provisioning their troops. Commanders and field officers established bazars, from which their sepoys had to purchase their food, other necessities, opium, and arrack. Even today, many market towns have the name 'Colonel-gunj' (Colonel's market) or are called by the surname of the European officer who established them. Despite orders from the Company's Directors prohibiting the practice—on the grounds of the high prices and low quality of the goods which the sepoys had available to them—most commanding officers seem to have continued these monopolistic and profitable practices.[24] Further, several British officers defrauded the Company or the Europeans or Indians under their command.[25]

In short, while Baker's appointment as a cadet in the Bengal Army held some promise of honour and fortune, it also held shortcomings and risks. Nonetheless, Baker's youngest brother, William Massey Baker, returned to Ireland in 1796 with a considerable fortune while only a junior Captain, and Baker himself may have been equally enterprising during his fifteen years in India.

## Dean Mahomed and Baker in Patna (1769–70)

As the newly-arrived Baker made his first journey up the Ganges from Calcutta to Patna during the summer of 1769, his anticipated fortune remained far off. While still a cadet, Baker received no salary and an inadequate living allowance (Rupees 31 monthly in cantonment, more while in the field). He had to wait until August 1769 before his regiment managed to return to Patna and he received his promotion to Ensign.[26] Even after that, however, he would have had to supplement his monthly income of Rupees 96.5 with funds from his family or by borrowing from money-lenders.[27] Thus, Baker's gift of Rupees 400 to Dean Mahomed's mother (IV) meant a substantial sum of money for him.

When Baker first reached Patna, his assigned unit, the Third European Regiment in the Third Brigade, remained stranded upstream. This regiment had been stationed at Allahabad, in support of the Company's manoeuverings with the Mughal Emperor, the Nawab of Awadh, the Marathas, and the Sikhs to the west. Since the end of the cool-weather campaigning season of 1769, the Company had been trying in vain to withdraw this regiment to Patna. Its advanced position in Allahabad threatened to involve the Company in wars beyond its desired frontier.

The Company's Board of Directors disapproved of such costly and dangerous involvements. While the Third Brigade remained so far advanced to the west, it was particularly expensive for the Company; the officers and troops (both Indian and British) received additional pay while they served beyond Buxar on the Karamnasa River—which traditionally marked the western border of Bihar. By May 1769, the Company judged that an invasion from the west was no longer likely that year. Additionally, the French factory at Chandernagore had begun to strengthen its fortifications and the English feared that this signalled preparation for a French assault on Calcutta from the sea.[28] For all these reasons, the Calcutta government ordered the Third Brigade to withdraw to Patna and simultaneously ordered the Second Brigade to shift east from Patna to Monghyr.[29]

This simultaneous movement of two brigades proved beyond the logistical capacity of the Army's primitive quartermaster service. As the hot season intensified, the commanding officers of both brigades sought to protect their European soldiers against the debilitating effects of the climate. The Second Brigade's European Regiment at first tried to march out of Patna but the first day's march of less than 10 miles, even undertaken as it was before dawn, led to the death (from heat) of 10 European soldiers and the hospitalization of 23 more. Distraught at such losses at the very outset of his march, the Brigade's commander demanded the Chief of the Company's Factory at Patna, Thomas Rumbold, supply 100 large boats (of 14–17 tons burden each) for transport. Only by forcefully seizing all the boats in the Bihar region of the Ganges (that were not required for the Company's own trade) did Rumbold eventually assemble enough shipping to move the Second Brigade down river. This empressment of boats did severe damage to the other merchants in Patna since their cargoes were off-loaded and delayed, even from vessels they themselves owned.

Further upstream at Allahabad, the Third Brigade, which had orders to go by river, remained stranded by a lack of vessels. Its press-gangs of sepoys managed to seize a score of boats but thereby provoked at least one riot as villagers and boatmen defended their property and livelihood.[30] As the number of sick and dead among the European soldiers of the Third Regiment increased with the heat, their officers became increasingly frustrated. At the same time, the Company found its strategies against the French stymied since its troops were left literally high and dry, far from Calcutta. Finally, in August 1769, after the monsoons had cooled the land but also made marching more cumbersome due to thick mud, the Third Regiment gave up on water transport and marched the more than 200 miles from Allahabad to Patna. There, the regiment divided between two newly built cantonments: the first battalion of the regiment going to Denapur cantonment on the Ganges River and the second battalion, to which Baker was posted, to Bankipur near Patna also on the bank of the Ganges.[31] The waiting Baker was finally able to join his post and Dean Mahomed joined him. Resentment against Rumbold for having failed to provide boats apparently persisted within the regiment since Dean Mahomed remembered him as 'Mr Rumble, a Gentleman who received the Contracts of the Company, for the supply of Boats and other small craft' (III) when Rumbold was actually the Chief of the Company's entire administration at Patna.

During the following campaiging season, the same tense strategic scenario persisted. The Company tried to deploy its military so as to balance defense against a French invasion from the sea with protection against any combination of Marathas, Sikhs, Jats, Rohilla Afghans, the Mughal Emperor, and/or the Nawab of Awadh from the west. Baker's Third Regiment remained on alert from February 1770 onward, ready to march instantly westward should any one of these invaders make a decisive threatening move.[32] In June 1770, the brigade prepared to move by reuniting at Denapur cantonment. The Company, however, restrained the brigade from any premature commitment to the west that might leave Calcutta vulnerable to the French. Further, considerations of cost and the recent experiences of transportation difficulties made the Company hesitate to order the Third Regiment into the field before it was absolutely necessary.

As a temporizing measure, the Company deployed a number of sepoy units to the west of Bihar: two battalions serving in Awadh, two with the Mughal Emperor, and a garrison in the Allahabad fort. The Company proved able to charge most of the cost of these sepoy battalions to the Mughal Emperor and the Nawab of Awadh. Further, the Company considered sepoy battalions easier to replace than its European regiments and therefore more suitable for risky and wearing marches beyond the territories under the Company's administration.

Leaving his family and joining Baker at the cantonment at Bankipur and then Denapur, Dean Mahomed lived as a camp follower, part of Baker's entourage. Dean Mahomed wrote movingly about how personally traumatic he found leaving his mother behind and going off with Baker and the Bengal Army (IV). By so completely entrusting himself to young Baker, Dean Mahomed (who had just turned twelve) undertook a very real risk.

Strong but asymmetrical personal or business relationships between Indians and Britons occurred frequently. Many Britons took Indian wives or mistresses, although few of these Indian women or their children found a comfortable place in either British or Indian society. Most European officers, officials, and private merchants had Indian junior partners, as well as Indian managers, clerks, and servants working for them. While these economic relationships could prove mutually profitable, they also reflected the developing colonial situation in which white Europeans held the overt power and Indians—while by no means powerless—largely held subordinate positions. Dean Mahomed remained dependent on Baker's patronage throughout their sixteen years together (until Baker's marriage and death soon after); even as a subaltern officer, Baker had considerable patronage to dispense.

A continuing theme in the Bengal Army, and the Company as a whole, remained the inherent conflict between a 'rational-bureaucratic' orientation toward one's position and a 'personalistic' one. While the Bengal Army gradually bureaucratized, personal links and patronage nevertheless stayed strong.[33] Throughout his career, Dean Mahomed received appointments and promotions due to the patronage of Baker. Neither Dean Mahomed (nor later Indian military autobiographers, like Sita Ram) conventionally referred to their regiments by their numbers, but rather by the names of their European officers. Such personalistic bonds continued to remain powerful in the Company, in the British Army, and in British society generally throughout Dean Mahomed's life.

In particular, the identification of an officer with the military unit he commanded also reflected the sense at the time that an army appointment was the property right of the incumbent. As in the British Army, within the Bengal Army, officers occasionally 'bought out' their superiors: paying a superior to retire so as to obtain promotion to his post. For example, Alexander Champion recorded how he arranged with his own two subordinates to pool their money and buy out his immediate superior, Colonel Chapman, for Rupees 80,000. Chapman took the money and retired to England. Each of the three officers who contributed then rose one rank.[34] Indeed, British society itself only gradually moved away from such a patronage system. Some members of the British Parliament openly purchased their seats, particularly prior to the Reform Bill of 1832 which abolished some of the more 'rotten boroughs'. The Company's Directors exercised their patronage in the appointment of cadets and writers until 1856. Royalty and the British Government granted sinecures throughout—and beyond—Dean Mahomed's life in England. British Royal Army officers legally purchased commissions until 1871. Thus, a post in the army remained property that could be bought or sold.

At the same time, however, the Company continued to institutionalize more bureaucratic features into the Bengal Army. The very military type of sepoy required uniformity in the rules and conditions of service. Promotions among the British officers in the Bengal Army began to occur more by seniority than by influence or purchase. Throughout the period described in *Travels*, therefore, we can see two overarching but incomplete shifts in the Bengal Army: from Indian to European patterns of military types and also from personalistic to bureaucratic models of military service.[35]

## European Regiments in the Bengal Army

As Ensign and then, from 1772, as Lieutenant, Baker served in a European regiment (containing only European soldiers). Officers, like Baker, who served with such regiments often had a very different experience from those serving with sepoys. While the Company's Directors exercised their patronage so extensively that they often produced a surplus of cadets, they had more difficulty recruiting European soldiers.

While European troops continued to be in short supply, of brief service in India, and of great cost, the Company believed them the heart of its army. This was at the height of the long English wars in Europe, so able-bodied European males were hard to recruit (even for the Royal Army which, by law, had precedence in recruiting over the Company). Consequently, the Company engaged contractors ('crimps') to supply Europeans (of any nationality, including French, German, and Swiss prisoners of war) at the rate of 1–5 guineas per man.[36] Indeed, London newspapers reported that the Court of Directors had arranged for European men to be kidnapped and illegally impressed into its armies, a charge the Company vehemently denied.[37] Only after 1778 did the British Government allow the Company to recruit in Ireland. Irish recruits quickly rose to about half those entering the Company's armies.[38]

During this period, Company officers in India constantly complained, and London regularly made excuses, about the low quality and inadequate quantity of its European recruits. Mortality rates on the voyage to India sometimes reached 50 per cent. In addition, the high rates of deaths in India from disease, and occasionally from wounds, meant a constant, and largely unmet, demand for European soldiers. In 1770, for example, the Bengal Army had only half the European soldiers active that it wanted. Further, in 1770 only 452 European soldiers survived to reach India or could be recruited there. This number of replacements fell ten men short of the total of casualties and desertions that year.[39] On an average over the decade 1762–72, about 70 per cent of troops that the Company sent each year to India went to replace soldiers who had died, deserted, or retired from the army, making any expansion in the number of European troops extremely slow.[40] Despite nominal requirements of age, size, and health, many of the recruits who actually reached India proved unfit for duty.[41] The Commander-in-Chief of the Bengal Army, on viewing the latest crop of European recruits wrote in 1768: ' . . . they are exceedingly bad . . . the refuse of our metropolis . . . The Company are at a great expense to send abroad annually a number of soldiers when in fact, instead of recruiting our army, they only serve to increase our Hospitals . . . [A]t present our European Regiments compared to a Battalion of Sepoys appear like a Regiment of Dwarfs.'[42]

Despite the difficulties in recruiting such European soldiers, and the relatively abundant supply of Indian soldiers, the Company saw these European infantry regiments (which comprised only 12–15 per cent of the Company's army in India) as its moral core. While at this time European officers and European troops 'mutinied' about as frequently as Indian troops, this reliance on European troops remained central to the Company's ideology. In 1766, the Calcutta Government wrote to London: ' . . . we cannot avoid being alarmed at the extraordinary disproportion of numbers between your European and Black Infantry. The very signal instance of fidelity and attachment exhibited by the Sepoys during the late Mutiny of the [British] Officers, might indeed be sufficient to quiet our apprehensions and remove all suspicion of their conduct, if experience the preceding year of their dangerous insolence and turbulent spirit had not evinced the necessity of keeping the Black troops in awe and subjection.'[43] Many Britons in the Company believed that sepoys would only stand firm in battle if European regiments provided 'stiffening'. (An explanation in many British minds for the bloody 1857 'mutiny' was the inadequate ratio of European to Indian troops in the Bengal army.)

The Company made great efforts, and went to much expense, not only to recruit but to further guard these European regiments from unnecessary danger. On an average over the decade 1762–72, each of the 17,082 (mostly unsatisfactory) European soldiers sent out cost the Company £7.4 to recruit and £13.8 to transport to India (whether they arrived alive or not).[44] Further, once in India, each European soldier demanded pay and generated expenses many times that of a sepoy. Thus, a European regiment proved a costly investment. In order to protect that investment, the Company tended to reserve its European troops for the most crucial operations. At the same time, the attitude and treatment by Company officers toward these European soldiers remained far from humane by today's standards.

The Company placed its greatest faith in its European artillery. London believed European artillery to be virtually a secret weapon, giving its army a vital advantage over its Indian enemies. The Directors demanded that its artillery, and its technological secrets, be kept a secure monopoly. Even European Catholics (who might have pro-French sympathies) were officially barred by the Company from the artillery.[45] The Directors repeatedly enjoined the Artillery to exclude Indians, except as manual labourers (lascars): 'As it is very essential that the natives should be kept as ignorant as possible both of the theory and practice of the artillery branch of the art of war, we esteem it a very pernicious practice to employ the people of the country in working the guns, and therefore direct that in future . . . no native be trusted with any part of this important service, unless necessity should require it.'[46] In fact, given the conditions in India, this exclusion of Indians proved unfeasible. Despite the repeated wishes of the Directors, in 1778, there were still three battalions of 'native artillery' (*gol-andaz*, 'ball throwers') totalling some 2962 Indian officers and men plus 35 Europeans.[47]

The cavalry remained one of the weakest arms of the Company's armies. The supply and maintenance of horses has always been costly in India. As a result, the Company often relied on irregular cavalry, or contingents from its Indian allies, for this arm of its forces.[48]

## The Brigade on the March to the Bihar Frontier (1771)

Since Baker served in a European regiment and because of Dean Mahomed's youth, no place existed for him except as unofficial camp follower. Although Dean Mahomed dressed and drilled in the regimental style, he nevertheless remained attached to the Bengal Army only as a member of Baker's entourage. Over Baker's years in India, his entourage would grow significantly. A Captain (the rank at which Baker retired) ordinarily maintained 35–40 servants and attendants, and often more.[49] As Dean Mahomed matured, he probably took charge of Baker's household as major domo. We know that Baker eventually entrusted him with procuring supplies for Baker's encampment (XXI).

For the first dozen years of Baker's military service, he chose the career track as a quartermaster (provisioning the army), rather than as a line officer with a regular infantry company. From Baker's initial promotion to Ensign until his final promotion to Captain, he held the posts first of Deputy Quartermaster (1770–2) and then Quartermaster (1772–82) of the Third Regiment. In these posts, Baker commanded some of the regiment's 700 lascars and other official, uniformed camp servants (IV). This type of service also meant that Baker had far more contact with Indian society than most British officers. Further, he had continual opportunities to profit from provisioning his regiment, as well as to conduct his own personal trade. This intersection of a commercial and military life—profiting from the commercial component of war—reflected Baker's own family tradition. It would also account for his and his younger brother's apparent financial success while in India, a financial success not ordinarily available to junior officers such as themselves. Indeed, a number of the Britons whom Dean Mahomed named while describing his life in the Army were clearly men who associated professionally and socially with Baker either as quartermasters (Landeg and Mayaffre), commissaries (Berry), or brigade paymasters (Herbert and Hollingberry).[50]

The Bengal Army, like any army, meant big business. It consumed a high percentage of the Company's budget: in 1770, about 60 per cent of the Company's expenditures in Bengal went to its military.[51] Over the decade prior to 1770, the Company spent about £8,000,000 directly on the Bengal army (in addition to the costs of building and maintaining the army's cantonments), over

50 per cent more than it spent on the purchase of trade goods.[52] In the eyes of some Company Directors and shareholders, the army was a largely unproductive expense; indeed, the army's activities seemed only to generate further costly entanglements in India. Nevertheless, the Company recognized the growing necessity for an army for the defence and subjugation of the territories under its control.

Early in 1771, a threatening advance by the Marathas toward Company territory finally determined the Calcutta Government to dispatch the Third Brigade westward to Buxar.[53] A brigade's movement entailed massive dislocations and a vast procession through the countryside of approximately 7000 soldiers as well as many times that many servants and camp followers. Quartermasters like Baker had to pack up or sell off existing stores in the Denapur cantonment—including tents, clothing, weapons, ammunition, and a panoply of other goods—and purchase new stocks for the expedition.[54] Quartermasters had to requisition a thousand or more bullocks from reluctant villagers for the transport of the brigade's stores. The families of soldiers, servants, and camp followers all had to pack up and march along or be left behind. Everyone had to wind up his financial arrangements with local businessmen or moneylenders.

A variety of official servants and informal camp followers enveloped the European and Indian officers and soldiers. Camp servants formally employed by the Company worked under the command of quartermasters to set up and move the camp, transport its baggage and equipment, and handle the distribution of its supplies. They wore uniforms similar to sepoys: cocked turbans, cummerbunds, shorts, waistcoats, linen jackets, and shoes (not boots), all coloured and decorated according to the Brigade they served.[55] Further, individual soldiers, officers, and units had a variety of personal servants and camp followers, according to their rank and purse. The Indian mistresses or families of soldiers or officers, both European and Indian, often accompanied the army even in the field but stood outside of the formal authority of the British commander. A contemporary put it: 'The Camp followers are a very independent set of people; and only remain with the army to which they attach themselves as long as it suits their convenience.'[56] A vast number of Indians did so.

The ratio of official Bazar Department workers and unofficial camp followers to soldiers varied but generally averaged two or three of each per soldier: some 35,000 per brigade. To illustrate, in 1778 Colonel Thomas Goddard (probably Dean Mahomed's father's old commander) led a detachment from the Bengal Army on a long and dangerous expedition to Bombay. In this detachment, the ratio of soldiers to supporters came in at over one to five: 103 Europeans (only .2 per cent of the expedition) and 6624 sepoys (17 per cent), attended by 19,779 official camp servants (51 per cent) and followed by some 12,000 bazar people and unofficial servants (31 per cent). Similarly, General Eyre Coote in south India had approximately 6000 sepoys and 15,000 followers in one expedition; later he had 12,000 fighting men plus 30,000–40,000 followers.[57] Feeding, clothing, and defending such a large concourse of people proved a continual logistical problem of vast proportions. Arthur Wellesley (later famous as the Duke of Wellington) maintained that his experience of organizing the logistics of his campaigns in India (1799–1804) prepared him for his successful contest with Napoleon in the Iberian Peninsula. Dean Mahomed would himself number among the unofficial camp followers until he was twenty-three years old.

The world of a brigade's encampment was neither well-bounded nor a total community. Markets attached to each unit provided links to less visible but extensive supply networks extending out in ever more diffuse ways into the countryside. Quartermasters contracted with grain dealers, either individual merchants or else *banjaras*—groups of cattle herders who transported grain on their bullocks (each bullock could carry 180 pounds of grain on its back). Quartermasters also drew upon the Company's civil administration for food and transport animals. The presence of a brigade affected the price of food, fuel, and cattle for miles around.[58] While the brigade offered villagers opportunities for the sale of food, goods, and services, its interactions with the rural populace also caused discord and disorder (XXXI).

Foraging soldiers and their servants disrupted life in all the villages they passed, proving a source of friction for the countryside. Until the Company eventually made provision for regular supplies of transport cattle, a brigade simply foraged the boats and bullocks it needed.[59] Villagers who encountered this march of the Third Brigade to the Karamnasa River in 1771 equated the damage from the brigade with that of a hailstorm.[60] One British civil official typically lamented:

> the inconvenience which this Province [Bihar] is exposed to by the Demand for Carriage Bullocks upon the march of a Brigade. Application is made to us by the Commanding Officer of the Brigade to furnish about a thousand [bullocks] with all possible expedition . . . A General Alarm spreads itself among the petty Merchants who gain their livelihood by the Inland Trade. They put a stop to their Business and endeavour to conceal their Cattle till the press is over. And the bringing in of the Company's Cloth and Salt Petre meets with the same interruption . . . [A]ll which can be found are seized and sent to us and delivered to the Commanding Officer . . . [N]o compensation is made to the owners for the time which may have elapsed since the seizure of them. After some days the Commanding Officer judges that the Service requires his immediate marching but still finds himself unprovided with a sufficiency of Bullocks and . . . he send[s] parties of Brigade Seapoys in search of more into the Suburbs of the City and the neighbouring Purgannahs. But to furnish a thousand it is necessary that more than twice that number should be pressed, many are rejected as unfit for Service. Many make their escape from the People who guard them, and many are released in consideration of two or three Rupees . . . [W]ithout Force we should not be able to procure a single one.[61]

Other British and Indian civil officials echoed this lament, describing the way sepoys plundered villages with the pretext of searching for hidden bullocks and drove away the revenue payers along their line of march.[62]

Managing logistics of such an undertaking comprised Baker's first command (V–VII). In addition, this journey to the edge of Bihar apparently took Dean Mahomed on his first trip outside the Patna area and into territory alien to him, territory not reconciled to English rule. The Third Brigade progressed south-west from its Denapur base on the Ganges, then via Pulwari to cross the Son River at Turwherea[63] and finally to where the Karamnasa and Ganges Rivers met, near the famous battlefield at Buxar. There, the brigade poised ready to advance further against the Marathas. Yet the Company restrained it from crossing over this boundary of Bihar. Such a crossing would garner for the army an extra 'batta', at the expense of the Company. Such a crossing could also involve the Army in war with the Marathas that might bring glory (and/or death) to the British officers, but costs and complications for the Company.

## The Brigade's March down the Ganges (1771–2)

In May 1771, as the Maratha threat receded and the hot season advanced, the Company ordered the Third Brigade to withdraw down the Ganges to Monghyr. In the usual two year rotation among the Company's three brigades, another brigade simultaneously transferred into its place guarding the western approaches to Bihar. In February 1772, after a nine-month posting in the cantonment at Monghyr, Baker and Dean Mahomed marched with the regiment down to Calcutta in order to repulse a perceived French threat.[64]

These passages through the countryside brought Dean Mahomed into the presence of a series of Indian holymen and shrines at Jangerah, Pirpihar, and Sitakund.[65] In his description of this variety of religious men and sites, Dean Mahomed expressed his admiration and reverence for each of them. Unconcerned with a classification of them into Hindu or Muslim, he presented the people of India as possessing a diffuse religiosity. He contrasted this undifferentiated faith with the skepticism of Europeans (VIII).

Leaving Monghyr, at the start of their long journey from western Bihar down the Ganges River, the brigade passed through countryside particularly resistant to Company rule. The narrow passes through the hills between Bihar and Bengal had long been a much contested route. People living in those hills, Paharis ('hill-people', probably Santals and other tribes people), fought off outside control. Part of the Bengal Army's assignment was to suppress such resistance. The Company even raised a special sepoy force of some 500 light infantry under Captain Brooke to secure these particular passes: Siclygully and Tiliagarhi.[66] Dean Mahomed remarked about the gruesome results of such clashes between the Bengal Army and the local populace (VIII–IX).

Wherever the Army passed, it looted. One of the towns that Dean Mahomed's brigade passed through (near Rajmahal, just beyond the passes described above) suffered greatly from being on the regular route of march for Company troops. A British official described the devastating effects of a brigade's arrival in 1770:

> Sepoys, Lascars, and Camp followers innumerable were pillaging and plundering in all Quarters of this town. The tops as well as the sides of Houses and Boutiques were carried away in heaps to form Hutts in Camp or to serve instead of firewood, nor were the Insides of the poor Inhabitants' houses more secure, but women and goods were purloined with as little ceremony.
>
> By these frequent outrages it is that this once large and populous city is now reduced to a poor small thinly inhabited village and every other town in the Province being equally liable to and often experiencing the same Evil . . . [67]

Leaving such a trail behind it, Baker and Dean Mahomed's brigade moved slowly across Bengal, camping a month at Qara Garhi (April 1772), then down the Hoogly to Calcutta, where they arrived on 18 May 1772.[68] For Dean Mahomed, the next two years would acquaint him with life in the British capital, Calcutta, and the Nawab's capital, Murshidabad.

### Dean Mahomed Explores Calcutta and Murshidabad (1772–4)

As someone who grew up in provincial Patna, Dean Mahomed found both Calcutta and the Nawab of Bengal's court at Murshidabad far more impressive than anything he had previously encountered (X, XI). By 1772, fifteen years after its recovery by the English, Calcutta had burgeoned into a prosperous commercial and administrative centre, growing into the second city of the Empire (after London). Its reputation as the city of palaces had already begun.

Since Fort William in Calcutta itself proved quite crowded, the Company constructed for its troops a large cantonment at Baharampur, adjacent to the Nawab's capital of Murshidabad. At the time of Dean Mahomed's arrival there, this cantonment was just being completed at a prodigious expense, amidst many complaints by the Company about 'neglect or dishonesty' by the contractors.[69] The Third Brigade and Dean Mahomed remained quartered in Baharampur for the next two years (1773–4). While his depiction of Calcutta and Baharampur tended toward the professional soldier, his account of Murshidabad became highly personal.

Murshidabad, in contrast to Calcutta, continued as a city in decline from its former glory. The Company's periodic cuts in its pension to the Nawab, its reductions in his army, and its diversion of the administration into its own hands all meant that Murshidabad had lost its sources of income. Even the main channel of the river had shifted away, making Murshidabad a literal backwater.

Dean Mahomed's highly personal remarks here perhaps reflected his projection of himself onto the role of a courtier, as might have been intended by his family tradition. He may also have been highlighting for his elite European audience his own putative aristocratic credentials. Nevertheless, in Dean Mahomed's self-location with respect to Nawab Mubarak al-Daula (r. 1770–93, a man about Dean Mahomed's own age), he also expressed his distance from that world. By regretfully placing himself in his description among the onlookers, rather than inside that culture, Dean Mahomed admitted his marginality to it.

Following closely on the above experience, Dean Mahomed narrated other examples of his continuing links to his past. As his entrée into a series of auto-ethnographic descriptions of Muslim culture, he explained how his relatives in Murshidabad welcomed him into their domestic world. Dean Mahomed then recounted, from the perspective of an invited and honoured relative, the circumcision, wedding, death, and other religious and cultural ceremonies of his community (XII–XV). Some of these rich descriptions depicted customs in ways which differ significantly from both ethnographic accounts by Europeans (at the time or later) and also from accounts from other 'native informants'.[70]

Here as well, Dean Mahomed distanced himself somewhat from these relatives. He identified his father and other relatives as Muslims, but never himself as one. By 1794, at the time of writing Travels, he had converted to Protestant Christianity; he may have been projecting this distance from Islam back onto his earlier condition. Thus, Dean Mahomed never fully relinquished his links to his culture of origin, although he described them as an observer, rather than a principal.

At the conclusion of Dean Mahomed's section on Baharampur cantonment, he inserted an extensive and technical categorization of the world with which he had identified himself: the Bengal Army. Here as well, Dean Mahomed provided us with evidence about this army otherwise largely inaccessible.[71] In this way, Dean

Mahomed repeated, in the course of his *Travels*, his own transitions from Nawabi and Muslim worlds to those of the English Company and its army.

## Up the Ganges River into Awadh (1775–7)

In February 1775, the Third Brigade completed its two year posting at Barahampur and received orders to march up the Ganges to Denapur.[72] There it remained until November, when the high command ordered it to march west into Awadh to deal with a political crisis there.[73] This journey brought Dean Mahomed into contact with the world of the central Gangetic plain— further west than he had ever been before. His fresh description of the countryside and cities through which he passed reminds us of the cultural and ecological variety of the Indian subcontinent which made them so new and striking to him.

The city of Benares (a.k.a. Varanasi) particularly excited Dean Mahomed's interest and pride for its antiquity, accomplishments, and sanctity. Dean Mahomed wrote *Travels* at the end of the eighteenth century, even as European 'orientalism' had begun to change the European image of India. As European scholars collected and translated into European languages the classical Sanskrit and Persian texts of India, a new appreciation of India's venerable past arose both in Europe and in India. In the context of the ongoing British conquest of India, this appreciation of India's past accomplishments led Europeans to make a valuation of India as once glorious but currently decadent.

Many Europeans and also many educated Indians of Dean Mahomed's time shared this valuation. Dean Mahomed revealed his personal pride in the scientific attainments of the ancient people of India and the positive impression these had on European men of science. This assessment further implied, however, the decline of Indian civilization: India's past may have been glorious but its present relative poverty and subjugation by Europe only accentuated its descent. Thus, Dean Mahomed represented Benares to his European audience as embodying India's past achievements 'though injured by the hand of time' (XVII).

At the time of his arrival in Benares, the peace and prosperity of the city and its surrounding countryside contrasted strikingly with the war-torn regions of Bihar to the east and Awadh to the northwest. It also contrasted with its later violated condition following the conflict of 1781 between its ruler, Chayt Singh, and the Bengal Army—in which Dean Mahomed participated, to his sorrow. Thus, his first visit to Benares remained in his memory as an entry into 'the Paradise of India' (XVII), a paradise all too soon lost.

Benares also impressed Dean Mahomed by its 'sacred character' (XVII). While much of this character stemmed from Hindu traditions, Dean Mahomed displayed no evidence of the antipathy between Hindus and Muslims which later commentators, both European and Indian, would stress. As a particularly conspicuous example, some Hindu nationalist politicians of the late twentieth century have recently tried to portray the imposing mosque at Panch Ganga Ghat as a instance of Mughal oppression. In their rhetoric, the Mughal Emperor Aurangzeb erected this fortress-like mosque as a mark of Muslim domination (see Illustration 4). In Dean Mahomed's eyes, however, this mosque, while imposing, retained an amalgamated Hindu and Muslim character. He called it by a Hindu's name: Mawdodasthrohur (*Madho Das Dharahara*, 'The Towers/Minarets of Madho Das'). Further, Dean Mahomed linked it with a Hindu pilgrimage rest-house (*dharmshala*), which retains the name of Madho Das's Garden even today.[74] Thus, for Dean Mahomed, Benares stood as a city sacred to Indians generally, although to Hindus in particular.

His description of Benares led Dean Mahomed smoothly into his ethnographic account of Hindus (XVIII). Dean Mahomed drew his earlier account of Muslim customs from his personal experience among his relatives, but he clearly based his ethnography of Hindus on more general impressions. He conflated the four *varna*s ('colours', which he called tribes) from traditional Brahmanic sociological texts with the multitude of *jati*s ('birth groups', which he called classes) of everyday life. This conflation reflected the term 'caste' (which he spelled 'cast') that Portuguese and later European commentators applied promiscuously to both *varna*s and *jati*s. Indeed, 'caste' has come into common parlance in Europe and India today, referring to both these social groups. Dean Mahomed's somewhat vague account of the religious and social practices of Hindus also revealed his perspective as a relative outsider.

Overall, the synthesis of Hindu and Muslim cultures remains clearly evident in Dean Mahomed's account. As one example of this synthesis, he ascribed to 'The native Indians or Hindoos' the book *Ayeen Akberry* (*Ain-i Akbari*) which was actually the product of the Mughal Emperor Akbar's court. From his reference (XVIII), it is clear that Dean Mahomed knew about but had not read this book (either in its original Persian or in its first English translation published by Francis Gladwin in 1783). Dean Mahomed thus took pride in Benares, but as an Indian not born in that region.

Nearly as glowing was Dean Mahomed's description of Allahabad city, which he entered in early December 1775.[75] This city resonated for Dean Mahomed with the Mughal traditions of his own family. Here the homes, the Mughal imperial palace, and the economy all found praise in his words (some of which he borrowed from an Englishwoman, Jemima Kindersley). His several allusions to Greek and Roman civilization, used to relate the scale and standards of Allahabad, however, again reflected his sense of India's glorious past, but somewhat archaic present.

In his account of the Mughal imperial capital, Delhi (a.k.a. Shahjehanabad), Dean Mahomed continued in this same vein (XXII). We cannot tell if he personally visited Delhi (some 225 miles from Bilgram where he spent nearly two years). He may have taken elements of his account from an earlier visitor to Delhi, since he anachronistically referred to Emperor Ahmed Shah (r. 1748–54) instead of his cousin and (eventual) successor, Emperor Shah Alam II (r. 1759–1806). Dean Mahomed's detailed description of the Mughal capital and court displayed his respect for past Mughal glories, and also a melancholic awareness of its current decrepit condition. For instance, Dean Mahomed perceptively pointed to the fissiparous policies of the Mughal imperial governors as a cause of the susceptibility of the Empire to its current weaknesses. He also noted that regional rulers and Mughal courtiers had so exploited the Indian producers and merchants that the Indian economy lay open to penetration by the English Company. Dean Mahomed's appreciation of the internal causes of Mughal decline may help explain to us his pragmatic decision to seek his fortune with the English Company.

The expedition of the Third Brigade to Bilgram in Awadh proved to be an instance of the English Company's mistaken policies. The Third Brigade reached Bilgram by the end of 1775.

and set up a cantonment there.[76] This had the apparent advantage to the Company of shifting the cost of the brigade to the Awadh ruler, but the brigade's exposed position left it vulnerable to involvement beyond its control. The English Company's alliance with the Awadh ruler had led it to commit elements of its Bengal Army to a number of engagements which it found distasteful.

Winning succession dispute as ruler of Awadh, Asaf al-Daula (r. 1775–97) had ousted his half-brother (Saadat Ali Khan) but not won over that rival's supporters. In April 1776, units within the Awadh army sympathetic to his ousted brother refused to obey the new ruler. The eunuch Mahbub Ali Khan, who was local Faujdar (military and police commandant), led one such uprising against Asaf al-Daula. At Asaf al-Daula's request, the Third Brigade sent two sepoy battalions from its camp at Bilgram to suppress this alleged mutiny.[77] Since Baker served in the European regiment, which the brigade's commander, General Stibbert, refused to put at risk in such adventures, neither he nor Dean Mahomed personally took part in the fighting that ensued. Nevertheless, Dean Mahomed knew some of the brigade's 127 casualties in this controversial action.

Dean Mahomed's description of the conflict stressed the perfidy of the Awadh troops and the bravery and self-sacrifice of the Bengal Army, particularly its British officers (XX). The situation, however, was more complicated than he implied. The Governor General remained sympathetic to the cause of the ousted pretender, Saadat Ali Khan (whom the Company gave refuge and a pension, and later installed as ruler in Awadh in 1798). The Army's high command condemned—for excessive use of force and disobedience of orders—the very officers whom Dean Mahomed praised: General Stibbert and Colonel Parker. The Company considered Asaf al-Daula's motivations suspect and lamented the Third Brigade's 'unnecessary effusion of so much Blood on that occasion and the discredit which has been thrown upon our arms by employing them against those whom the World will still consider as the servants and soldiers of our Ally . . . '[78] Nor did Mahbub receive much punishment following his defeat; he quickly regained Nawab Asaf al-Daula's favour.[79] This episode proved another instance of the Bengal Army's unsatisfactory involvement in north Indian politics.

Dean Mahomed's account of this conflict, the nearest he had

yet come to battle, led him to describe the major cities of Awadh: Lucknow and Oude (a.k.a. Ayodhya or Fyzabad). While we know that Dean Mahomed personally visited Lucknow in 1781, it is possible that he travelled to both cities during the two years that the Third Brigade remained posted at Bilgram. In his account of both cities, however, Dean Mahomed emphasized his critique of the immorality of the Awadh rulers, both Asaf al-Daula and his predecessor, Shuja al-Daula (r. 1754–75).

As a demonstration of how these rulers embodied the very excess of sensual 'luxury and dissipation' which he decried, Dean Mahomed detailed their vast seraglios and opulent pleasure gardens, and also recalled the Rohilla War of 1774. Dean Mahomed apparently based his narrative of this war on the recollections of others in the Bengal Army. He also interpreted it as a morality play in which the Awadh ruler violated the innocence of a young princess and died because of his unrestrained lust.

## The Rohilla War (1774)

The Rohilla War, like the Company's actions near Bilgram described above, arose out of its commitment to support the Awadh ruler with its Bengal Army. The Awadh ruler used the Bengal Army, part of which he rented from the Company, to impose his will on his rivals and enemies. Here as well, the officers and men of the Bengal Army found themselves carrying out policies neither to their taste nor to their perceived advantage. To explain the context for the Rohilla War, we must briefly refer to earlier conflicts among north Indian regional states.

The Rohilla Afghans comprised one of the ethnic groups threatened by the frequent Maratha incursions into north India in the 1770s. Their Regent, Hafiz Rahmat Khan, entered into an agreement in 1772 with Shuja al-Daula, the incumbent Awadh ruler, to pay Rupees 4,000,000 in exchange for the defence of their territories. When the Marathas subsequently retreated in 1773, in part due to the movement of Company and Awadh troops against them, the Awadh ruler demanded the stipulated payment from the Rohillas. Since no battles had actually occurred, the Rohillas refused to pay this immense sum. Thereupon, the Awadh ruler invoked his treaty-right to deploy Company troops on his behalf in enforcing this payment.[80] In 1774, Awadh invaded the Rohilla territories, supported by a British brigade—for which Awadh paid the Company Rupees 210,000 per month. After the defeat of the Rohillas, Awadh annexed their territory (except for a small enclave around Rampur).[81]

Following the Rohilla War, the Awadh ruler and Company officers made accusations of misconduct against each other. The Awadh ruler asserted that the Company's troops had looted property belonging not only to the Rohillas, but also to his own troops and state.[82] Nevertheless, this ruler paid the full subsidy to the Company and also made a gratuitous donation of Rupees 700,000 to the Company's troops and Rupees 300,000 to their commander, Colonel Alexander Champion.[83]

While Dean Mahomed's brigade took no part in this war, he reported what the general attitude was within the Company's armies toward it. Although they defeated the Rohillas, the Company's armies resented their own situation, subordinate to the Nawab of Awadh. In particular, the British commander, Colonel Champion, indignantly wrote: 'the British . . . are the modern Romans: their Senate could never overlook the prostitution of the national honour in subjecting a British general to the command of an infidel Prince.'[84] Further, the Bengal Army believed that the loot and booty legitimately theirs had been appropriated by the Awadh ruler and his troops. These resentments emerged through a series of accusations about the ungentlemanly behaviour of the Awadh ruler toward the defeated Rohillas, especially toward their noblewomen.

Both Dean Mahomed and many contemporary British commentators made the honour of the Rohilla princesses a measure by which to judge the Awadh ruler. Champion accused the Awadh ruler of violating that honour by exposing the captured Rohilla princesses to public display. Warren Hastings largely accepted these accusations: 'English manners are abhorrent of every species of inhumanity and oppression, and enjoin the gentlest treatment of a vanquished enemy.'[85] Nevertheless Hastings, while ordering the Company's resident agent in Awadh 'to make the strongest representations on this subject', precluded intervention that might provide the Awadh ruler with an excuse to withhold payment of the subsidy owed for the services of the Company's troops.[86] On his part, the Awadh ruler denied all the charges, asserting that a freak windstorm had simply blown down the *pardas* (cloth partitions) sheltering the family of Hafiz Rahmat, exposing the ladies to public view.[87] Dean Mahomed presented a more elaborate and graphic account of the denouement of this issue (XXI). His lurid account of the Awadh ruler's death due to sexual misconduct apparently emanated from the women of Shuja al-Daula's harem and was widespread at the time.[88] While most British sources agreed that Shuja al-Daula died as a result of illness originating in the Rohilla War, there was no consensus about the precise cause, ranging from acute blood poisoning to sexual excesses.[89] Nevertheless, his highly valourized explanation revealed that he shared with many Europeans of his day a view of some Indian rulers as immoral and sensually unlicensed. Further, Dean Mahomed and others in the Bengal Army resented their part in supporting such immorality, particularly with so little benefit to themselves.

At the end of October 1777, the Third Brigade finally took their leave of Bilgram and Asaf al-Daula's territories. This movement marked the Company's effort to withdraw from such deep involvement in the policies of the Awadh ruler. As the brigade prepared to depart from its Bilgram cantonment, Asaf al-Daula sought to improve his image in the Bengal Army. He paid a visit in all the panoply of state (XXIV, Illustration 3). Asaf al-Daula further donated a thousand rupees to the brigade's European officers and another thousand to its Indian officers and sepoys. On its part, the Company wished to cut off such ties; it forbade the brigade to receive this donation and chastized Stibbert for allowing it to occur.[90] Further, the brigade burned its Bilgram cantonment to the ground rather than allow Asaf al-Daula to use it. The incoming brigade which took station on the Company's western front went no further than Allahabad, much to Asaf al-Daula's dismay.[91]

The Third Brigade itself marched over the next three months down the Ganges, passing Manikpur (10 November 1777), to Fort William in Calcutta, which it reached on 22 January 1778: a 78 day march, averaging about 10 miles per day, punctuated with only 16 days of rest.[92] Thereupon, the Third Brigade and Dean Mahomed remained in barracks for nearly three years: in Calcutta (January 1778–September 1779), then in Barahampur (September 1779 to November 1780).

## Dean Mahomed in Bengal (1778–81)

While Dean Mahomed remained in cantonment in Bengal, other elements of the Company's armies won and lost against its enemies elsewhere in India. In 1778, a substantial detachment from the Bengal Army (including Edward Heard, a close friend of Baker and a patron of Dean Mahomed) marched across north India to Surat and then Bombay to reinforce the English Company's Bombay Army in the First Anglo-Maratha War (1775–82). While Dean Mahomed himself never visited Surat or Bombay, he inserted descriptions of them into his narrative (XXV–XXVI).[93] Further, both cities had long histories of commercial importance that Dean Mahomed wished his readers to understand. The highpoint of this war for the Bengal Army was its daring capture from the Marathas of the supposedly impregnable fortress of Gwalior (3 August 1780, XXX).[94] Although Dean Mahomed remained in garrison in Baharampur at the time of this capture, he either quoted or paraphrased a first-hand account by an unnamed participant.

*Travels* also mentions the Company's Second Anglo-Mysore War (1780–4) in south India. The Company fought against Haydar Ali, a military entrepreneur who had subordinated the Hindu dynasty of Mysore state and then challenged the Company for control over all of peninsular India. The final defeat of this Mysore dynasty did not come until 1798, long after Dean Mahomed had left India. Since the Madras Army, rather than the Bengal Army, largely carried out this war, its events would have been less involving for Dean Mahomed. In fact, Dean Mahomed highlighted only one battle, which he presented as a great victory for Colonel Baillie. Here either Dean Mahomed was being disingenuous or he was simply confused. Contrary to Dean Mahomed's account, the Mysore army defeated Colonel Baillie. This defeat would have been known all too well to his readers, even those without experience in the Indian army, since it featured as a 'remarkable event' in the Cork press.[95]

Dean Mahomed also included a range of illustrative stories about Indian culture. Among these many accounts, three in particular would have major significance later in his life. First, he detailed the practice of shampooing (from *champi*, meaning to knead the flesh in therapeutic massage, XXV), which he made the speciality of his later distinguished medical career in England. Second, he remarked on distinctive Indian flora and fauna (XXVI), which he would use to adorn the walls of his lavish bathhouse in Brighton. Third, he noted the art of preparing smoking tobacco for the hooka (XXVII), which would be one of his featured attractions at the coffee house he would start in London. His presentation of each of these three features would change substantially between his inclusion of them in *Travels* and his later use of them in his several careers in Britain.

For the English Company in Bengal, the French Company appeared as the most immediate threat (XXIV). News of the declaration of war between France and England reached Calcutta in July 1778 and led to massive preparations for the defence of that city from the expected French invasion. In the Calcutta area, the Bengal government concentrated two-thirds of its army: two of its three European regiments (including Baker's) and twenty sepoy battalions (some 2095 Europeans and 11,932 sepoys). Further, the Company resolved to raise another three battalions of sepoys through a large bond issue.[96] In 1780, the Company determined to reorganize the Bengal Army as a more efficient force. All these growing military expenses led the Company to pressure its subordinated rulers, including the Nawab of Awadh and the Raja of Benares, to contribute ever more substantially to its coffers.

By 1780, after a dozen years in the lucrative post of Quartermaster, Baker had sufficient seniority to expect promotion to Captain and command of his own battalion during this military expansion. Baker, by secretly appealing to the Commander-in-Chief, Eyre Coote (a fellow Anglo-Irishman), made an initially successful effort to pass on his lucrative post as Quartermaster of the First Battalion in the Third European Regiment to his fourth brother, recently arrived in India and recently promoted to Lieutenant, William Massey Baker.[97] The Brigade commander, Colonel Ironside, on learning of this irregular intervention by the Commander-in-Chief in his Brigade's affairs, immediately arrested the elder Baker, tried, and convicted him under a General Court Martial for 'disobedience of General Orders' and 'unmilitary conduct' (under Article II of Section 15 of the *Articles of War*).[98] Ironside had himself recently just escaped a court martial for embezzling the salaries of dismissed soldiers, appropriating Company equipment and camp servants for his personal use, and forging a subordinate officer's signature to cover all this up. Ironside subsequently killed his chief accuser and second in command in a duel. Indeed, Baker had himself played a small part in the Company's prosecution of Ironside.[99] Then, it is not surprising that no one openly sprang to Baker's defence against Ironside's technically correct charges against him. The sentence levied by the Court Martial called for a reprimand of the senior Baker by the President of the Court Martial in the presence of Colonel Ironside.[100] Thus, Ironside's honour could be satisfied by a brief shaming of Baker before him, an incident which Dean Mahomed proved unwilling to divulge to his readers.

Despite this court martial, Baker's promotion to Captain and appointment to command a sepoy battalion in the Second Brigade (outside of Ironside's command) came routinely on the basis of seniority.[101] Further, the Army high command arranged for the younger Baker brother to receive an appointment in his elder brother's new battalion. The next year, the younger Baker then received an appointment as Quartermaster in the Second European Regiment.[102] Thus, the career of neither brother apparently suffered, whatever the cost to Baker's self-esteem.

## Dean Mahomed as Market Master (1781)

In 1781, the Commander-in-Chief reorganized the Bengal Army. At least part of the reason was the superabundance of European officers for the established number of commands and also the shortage of European soldiers. He created Native Infantry regiments (under a Major), consisting of two sepoy battalions (each under a Captain). This meant that Captains now commanded 500 sepoys instead of 800 but there were far more Captain's commands available. It also meant an immediate demand for 36 new Majors, creating room for the promotion of as many senior Captains. This, plus the new openings for Captains, led to 84 Lieutenants being promoted to Captain, including Baker.[103]

As a direct result of this reorganization, in January 1781 Baker obtained the command of one of the two sepoy battalions in Major William Roberts's Thirtieth Regiment of sepoys in the Second

Brigade, then stationed at Cawnpur.[104] As Baker left the garrison at Baharampur and journeyed to Cawnpur, he took command of a detachment of two companies of sepoys and two companies of Europeans (some 400 men) also going in the same direction. He used his newly acquired patronage to appoint Dean Mahomed as market master to supply his detachment (XXXI).

As Baker's detachment marched up the Ganges during January and February 1781, Dean Mahomed moved out into the countryside to gather the food and necessities required by this substantial body of men. He had been empowered by Baker to work with the local civil authorities to requisition grain on behalf of the Bengal Army. As Dean Mahomed recounted it, on his way with a large sum to obtain provisions at the cheapest possible rate from Gooldengunge (a market named after the District Collector, Golding),[105] he ran into trouble as peasants resisted depredations by his sepoy escort. Despite this set-back, Dean Mahomed described how he completed his mission, reaching the faujdar, arranged for the purchase and transport of supplies, and then rejoined Baker's detachment (XXXI).

This incident reveals much about the role and attitude of Dean Mahomed as market master. The detail that he was on horseback, while his sepoy escort was on foot, indicated his class distinction above them. This one example of interaction among the army (in the form of three Indian soldiers), the local administration (an Indian faujdar), and the countryside (local Indian peasants) suggests the constant and extensive negotiations and transactions by the colonial administration outside of British hands. Finally, Dean Mahomed's moral scale of values appears as well. That he blamed one of his sepoys for provoking the incident by careless destruction of the peasant's property and then for his arrogant rejoinder indicates an awareness by Dean Mahomed of the culpability of the army; it, too, could disturb the public order.

## Dean Mahomed in Battle (1781)

Baker, after taking command of his new battalion at Cawnpur (1 March 1781), exercised his patronage by arranging to have Dean Mahomed appointed Jemadar in one of its elite grenadier companies under his command. This appointment of Dean

Mahomed, however, violated the principles which the Bengal Army was currently attempting to implement for such appointments. A fixed procedure would specify how sepoys and their Indian officers were to be promoted: 'That when a Vacancy happens for a Jemautdar in either of the Battalions of a Regiment, the Captain shall report it to the Major Commandant, who shall recommend by letter (through the channel of the commanding officer of the Sepoy Corps) the most deserving Havildar in that Battalion, describing his length of service and particular pretensions to the Colonel or Commanding Officer of the Brigade to fill it; who if he approves of such recommendation shall order a Warrant to be made out for him and published in Brigade orders.'[106] Obviously, this did not describe the way that Baker had Dean Mahomed appointed Jemadar, since he had no seniority as a Havildar in the Regiment.

The irregularity of his appointment may have made Dean Mahomed feel out of place in command of this grenadier company. Further, he was much shorter (about five feet) than the men he commanded, who were selected for their imposing height. Nonetheless, Dean Mahomed took command (although he never mentioned any of his men or other Indian officers in *Travels*). As was customary, Dean Mahomed had personally to pay half a month's salary to Major Roberts, commanding the regiment, for confirmation of his appointment. As officers in a sepoy regiment, Dean Mahomed and Baker participated in much more personal interaction with the countryside and combat than when they were in a more protected European regiment.

By 1781, the Company's financial situation had become particularly precarious. The military expansion and extremely costly wars against the Marathas and Mysore had drained its treasury. Governor General Hastings believed that the Company's enemies and allies should both be forced to pay these expenses and thus placate the British Parliament and Company's Directors. Dean Mahomed thus first fought to seize land from the Company's enemies and then marched to extract wealth from its subordinated allies.

From Cawnpur, Baker and Dean Mahomed's Thirtieth Regiment joined the expedition under Colonel Morgan to drive the Marathas out of the Kalpi region and collect the region's revenues for the Company.[107] In April 1781, Morgan attacked the fort overlooking Kalpi and drove out the slight Maratha garrison. He then 'requisitioned' the local administration to pay the Company whatever revenues or tribute they had previously submitted to the Marathas. When the Maratha local agent sought to prevaricate until that season's harvest could be fully collected, Morgan launched a preemptive strike that expelled the Maratha army. Although the Maratha force consisted of some 2000 cavalry, they withdrew in the face of Morgan's sepoys (including Dean Mahomed's company) with no loss on either side. Thus, while Dean Mahomed echoed the Company's line that the Marathas were engaged in an insurrection (XXXI–XXXIII), in fact this was an instance of the Company using military force for fiscal and territorial gain at the expense of its enemies.

Governor-General Hastings sought to extract financial subsidies from the Company's allies as well as its enemies. Hastings had been demanding that Raja Chayt Singh of Benares (r. 1770–81, d. 1810) provide both money and troops to assist the Company in its wars. The Raja of Benares had been contesting these fiscal and military demands for some time. Until 1775, Benares had been a semi-autonomous state, subordinate to the Awadh ruler. That year, the English Company took Benares under its indirect rule, but left the internal administration to the Raja. In return, the Raja promised to pay Rupees 2,340,249 annually to the Company, and to maintain troops ready to assist its army. In 1778–9, the Company increased its demands on the Raja. Hastings argued that Chayt Singh, as a 'feudal vassal' of the Company, was obliged to provide whatever cash and military support to his overlord that it needed. Indeed, the Bengal Army still continued to rely on its subordinate allies for cavalry and other bodies of soldiers. Chayt Singh argued these demands exceeded what the extant treaties required of him, and that he could not afford to meet them in any case.

In the fall of 1781, Hastings undertook a personal visit to Benares to exert further pressure on the Raja, to be followed by a trip to Lucknow for similar negotiations with the Awadh ruler. After a brief time back in Cawnpur, Dean Mahomed's battalion marched to Lucknow to form the honour guard and escort for Hastings when he arrived. Immediately after having reached Lucknow, however, they received a desperate message from Hastings ordering them to rush to Benares and rescue him.

After his arrival in Benares in August, Hastings had upped the pressure on Chayt Singh by ordering two companies of sepoys to arrest him. Chayt Singh's loyal troops assembled to release him and slaughtered the Company's sepoys. By an oversight on the part of their British officers, these sepoys had not been issued ammunition; 171 sepoys were killed or severely wounded and their British officers (Lieutenants Stalker, Symes, and Scott) also died.[108] When open warfare broke out, Hastings himself nearly fell into Chayt Singh's hands and had to retreat while issuing frantic orders for all the Company's troops in the region to assemble for his rescue. Another ill-conceived Company attack led to another massacre of sepoys, French 'rangers' in the Company's service, and their officers: Captains Mayaffre and Doxat. This second defeat forced Hastings to flee for his life. Dean Mahomed's battalion marched rapidly from Lucknow, while other Company troops escorted from Lucknow Rupees 50,000 (borrowed from the Awadh ruler) in order to pay the Company's troops their overdue salaries.

After Dean Mahomed's company arrived at Benares on 13 September, he took a leading part in the attack on Patita fort. Hastings described this fort as: 'much stronger, and the approach more hazardous, than he had expected . . . a small square house of stone, itself fortified with four round towers, and enclosed with a high rampart, and a ditch, which is in most parts broad and deep. Its greatest advantage against an enemy to whom delay was defeat, was that it was invisible to its assailants.'[109] Grenadier companies of the Thirty-fifth and Thirtieth Regiments—including Dean Mahomed's company—assembled into a shock force which successfully stormed the fortress, with a loss of 11 killed and 10 wounded.[110] In his report, Hastings especially commended the grenadiers and their commander, Captain Lane—who received a field promotion to brevet Major. Dean Mahomed modestly highlighted Baker's service in this battle rather than his own.

Following this action, Dean Mahomed and Baker's units took on the task of gathering much needed supplies from the hostile countryside and escorting them to the forces pursuing Chayt Singh's remaining army. After Major Popham drove Chayt Singh into exile, he negotiated a surrender of the virtually impregnable fortress of Bijigarh in November. When this fortress fell, Popham interpreted a private letter from Hastings to mean that he could divide Chayt Singh's vast treasure among his troops 'on the drum-head' (i.e. immediately, on the spot). Since this treasure amounted to some Rupees 4,000,000 (£400,000) cash plus much jewellery, and since the whole purpose of Hastings' journey was to extract funds from Chayt Singh for the Company's official use, this summary distribution led to considerable acrimony within the Company. Popham himself took Rupees 294,000 while each captain received Rupees 22,478 and even sepoys received Rupees 50 each.[111] While Dean Mahomed recorded the 'Scenes of joy and conviviality' among those troops (XXXIII), neither he nor Baker received anything since their units were not present at the time Bijigarh surrendered. Baker and dozens of the other officers in the region submitted their petitions for a share, recounting their contributions to the campaign.[112] The Company, on its part, demanded all the prize money be returned, and instituted court martial proceedings and civil suits against those officers who refused to comply.[113] Dean Mahomed did not explain this sordid outcome to his readers.

While Dean Mahomed's narrative largely accorded with those of Hastings and other European commentators in terms of dates, names, and general events, it provided some otherwise unknown details about his unit's actions. Further, his inter-pretation of these events stood in strong contrast to these other accounts. Most striking in Dean Mahomed's memoir is his advocacy of Chayt Singh. Most accounts by European witnesses to this conflict tended to demonize Chayt Singh, picturing him as a traitorous outlaw whose troops murdered members of the Bengal Army.[114] On his part, Dean Mahomed sympathetically narrated Chayt Singh's actions and presented Chayt Singh's letters defending himself against Hastings' demands and attacks on him (XXXIII).[115] Dean Mahomed's clear sympathy for Chayt Singh indicated that he saw Warren Hastings as the one violating law and order. Thus, in this instance, he evidently felt that the Bengal Army, while nobly carrying out its duty, had displaced a virtuous ruler. Significantly, years later the English House of Commons concurred with Dean Mahomed's position and made Hastings' treatment of Chayt Singh a major accusation against him in his impeachment and seven year trial before the House of Lords.

## Suppressing Insurgency in the Benares Countryside (1782)

The final series of operations of the Bengal Army that Dean
Mahomed recorded concern the suppression of opposition to
Company rule within the Benares countryside. After expelling
Raja Chayt Singh, the Company installed his infant nephew in
his place (under the guidance of a Regent), but with the reduced
status of *zamindar* (landholder) rather than ruler. The Company
also raised its financial demand from Benares to Rupees 4,000,000
annually. It further placed the civil and judicial administration
under the supervision of its Resident.[116] This divided authority
led to tension and mutual recriminations. Baker and Dean Mahomed's battalion had orders to impose this new government's
authority on the villagers in the region, who resisted it.

In particular, Baker and Dean Mahomed's battalion undertook
punitive expeditions into the countryside around Ghazipur.[117]
Once, after they crushed some villagers from Bellua (perhaps
Belluagaon), Dean Mahomed's own detachment seized valuable
booty (XXXIV).[118] Another time, near Jaunpur, Baker and Dean
Mahomed attacked villagers in a small fort, killing some of them
(XXXIV).[119] Such suppression of Indian people, however, apparently took its toll on Dean Mahomed and inspired him to
elegiac poetry about the tragic waste of war (XXXIV).

Subsequently, Dean Mahomed abruptly recorded that Baker
decided to resign his commission and return to Ireland. Dean
Mahomed also resigned as subedar in order to accompany him
there (XXXV). Behind these cryptic statements about their resignations lies much that illuminates both Dean Mahomed's own
possible divided loyalties and also the relationship between the
Bengal Army and the Indian countryside. Although Dean Mahomed did not mention this, Baker's resignation eventuated from
accusations against him by villagers that he had extorted money
from them. The Benares Regent complained to Governor-General
Hastings that he had ordered Baker to arrest three alleged mur-
derers of a Brahmin named Dharma Dube, early in 1782. As the
Governor-General wrote:

> [I]nstead of attempting to apprehend such only of the kosacks [or
> Konuhs] as were guilty of the offence, [Baker] first made a general
> attack upon all who resided in the village of Burragong [perhaps

Belluagaon]; and when he had subdued them, with as little discrimination, and as it is alleged for his private emolument, set them
all at liberty, and again restored them to their possessions.

Remembering the conduct of Captain Baker upon a former occasion of this kind, I flattered myself that he would never be again employed on any service that might give him a possible pretence for
interfering in the affairs of the zemindarry [of Benares]. If he is not
yet recalled, I request that he may be without a moment's delay . . . [120]

Governor-General Hastings thus ordered Baker recalled from active duty in disgrace in July 1782.

In this light, Dean Mahomed's oblique reference (given above)
to Baker retaining only a limited part of the booty taken from
rebellious villagers at Belluagaon might be Dean Mahomed's effort
to put the best possible light on Baker's actions. Although the
Company's Resident in Benares investigated and declared Baker
not guilty of these accusations, Baker resigned from his command
of a battalion in the Thirtieth Regiment in October 1782. He
may also have given notice that he intended formally to resign
from the Army; a year's advance notice being required by the rules
of service.

While it is difficult to know today whether Baker did coerce
money from Indian villagers, the weight of evidence suggests that
he did not, although other British officers did so at various
times.[121] Governor-General Hastings later admitted that he had
confused the sequence of events: what he had believed to be a
repeated pattern of offenses by Baker was really only a single
accusation. By August 1782, the Resident's investigation convinced Hastings that even that 'charge against Captain Baker
[wa]s utterly false'.[122] The Regent who accused Baker was himself
accused by the Company of corruption, including extortion of
money from peasants in the Benares area; that September, Hastings ordered his arrest and resignation.[123] That August, the
Company's Directors had ordered the Resident himself dismissed
from his post.[124] Further, Hastings himself resigned and left India
in February 1785 under opprobrium from the Directors and was
impeached and tried by Parliament. Baker received an honoured
welcome from the Anglo-Irish society, marrying into a noble
household soon after his return to Cork. Finally, we have Dean
Mahomed's attitude of support for Baker. Dean Mahomed uniformly showed sympathy with those who supported the moral

order of society, even when that meant Chayt Singh or Indian villagers who opposed the Bengal Army. Dean Mahomed determined to accompany Baker, leaving the Army and emigrating to Ireland with him. Thus, evidence suggests Baker had been caught in a power struggle between the Regent, the Resident, and the Governor-General.

Dean Mahomed recorded that, to accompany Baker, he resigned his appointment as Subedar. Ordinarily, promotion to Subedar came only after many years service, going by regulation to the most senior Jemadar in the battalion. Yet Dean Mahomed served less than two years as an officer. Since records for such appointments or resignations as Subedar no longer exist, we have no independent way of proving or disproving his assertion that he had in fact reached that rank. Nevertheless, some of Dean Mahomed's readers knew his status in India, so it is unlikely that he would have claimed this rank unjustly. Therefore we must conclude he enjoyed remarkably rapid promotion due to Baker's powerful patronage.

We can never fully know all the factors motivating Dean Mahomed to resign. He stated only that he decided to accompany Baker, implying that his friendship with Baker overrode his commitment to a career in the Bengal Army. Since Baker intended to leave India for Ireland, Dean Mahomed had made a momentous decision to begin a new life in an unknown land. This echoed his decision at age eleven to leave his mother and join Baker. Dean Mahomed would later make two equally decisive redirections in his life (moving to London in his mid-forties and moving to Brighton at age fifty-five). Thus, such bold undertakings were part of his character. While Dean Mahomed could not have known what lay ahead of him in Ireland, he and Baker followed their decisions to resign with a leisurely exploration of eastern and southern Bengal, either for pleasure or for commerce.

## Dhaka, the Sunderbans, and Calcutta (1782–3)

Following Baker's dishonourable recall and Dean Mahomed's resignation, they took time to visit Dhaka and explore the Sunderbans jungle on their way to Calcutta. Even for ordinary transfers between postings, the Bengal Army allowed British officers a generous amount of time: six weeks for the trip from Chunar to Calcutta.[125] If he followed the usual practice, Baker used his generous travel stipend to hire at least three boats: a twelve-oared budgerow for comfortable travel during the day and for sleeping at night, an attendant baggage boat for luggage and servants, and a separate cookboat. Dhaka, which neither Baker nor Dean Mahomed had visited before, remained famous at that time for the court of its Nawab, its urbane culture, and the quality of its fine muslin cloth and other products. Thus, Baker and Dean Mahomed may have been attracted to Dhaka to indulge in tourism and/or in private trade, purchasing goods for later sale in Calcutta or Ireland. Dean Mahomed's description of Dhaka and its culture, particularly the Nawab's coronation and the Shi'ite commemoration on the tenth day of Muharram (1197 Hijri, 16 December 1782), contained ethnographic detail otherwise largely lost to us.[126]

Dean Mahomed and Baker's subsequent voyage through the deltaic Sunderbans brought them into a striking world. Such trips through the densely jungled maze of low islands would have taken at least ten days travelling. British officers customarily took with them an escort of sepoys, since gang-robbers lurked in fast boats among the islands of the Sunderbans. The trip took them through an environmentally rich jungle which contrasted sharply with the urban life of Calcutta where they subsequently lived. Clearly Dean Mahomed romanticized the local inhabitants and was impressed by the diverse flora of the Sunderbans. The metropolis of Calcutta, particularly since they arrived under the cloud of Baker's removal from his command, evidently struck them in stark contrast.

The year that Baker and Dean Mahomed spent in Calcutta (January 1783–January 1784) must have been somewhat painful for them both. Dean Mahomed, having resigned from his prestigious appointment as Subedar, apparently returned to the status of major domo or dependent companion in Baker's household. Much of his account of Calcutta at this time consisted of a description of the score or more servants in a European gentleman's household.[127] Baker, also having effectively terminated his career in the Army, marked time as a supernumerary officer with no specific assigned command. After Baker's removal from the Thirtieth Regiment, the Army first placed him on the books of the Second European Regiment of the Second Brigade and then, some six months later, of the First European Regiment of the First Brigade, stationed in Calcutta. Both these appointments, however, remained nominal since he apparently never actually joined these units.[128] While in Calcutta, Baker may also have been winding up his business affairs, or passing them on to his younger brother, William Massey Baker, before leaving India permanently. Dean Mahomed stressed in his account the wealth of Calcutta but noted the 'supercilious disdain' of the urban elite: both European and Indian (XXXVII). Also revealing of Dean Mahomed's bitterness about life in Calcutta, he made pointed references to that city's public punishments and ostracism. All this seems to reflect Baker's sense of unjust failure in his career, and his rejection by the English Company.

While in Calcutta, Baker remained off the regular list of officers of the brigades to which he was ostensibly assigned. Instead, Baker appeared on the Town Major's list of such unattached officers, serving at odd jobs around Calcutta, such as taking charge in rotation of the sentries at Fort William's main gate. He also presided over courts martial of European soldiers. Indeed, on one day alone, he sentenced seven men to a total of 2700 lashes, all charged under the same Article of War that he himself had been found guilty of violating three years earlier.[129]

Baker officially resigned on 27 November 1783, citing pressing family responsibilities.[130] In deciding to end his career after some fifteen years in India, Baker was not unusual. In the more prestigious Civil Service, less than half the inductees of his age set still remained in service (43 per cent had died and about 8 per cent returned to Britain).[131] Further, prospects for promotion in the Army's officer corps (even for someone without Baker's tainted record of service) were in decline. The onset of peace meant reductions in the Bengal Army and diminished opportunities for promotion at all levels. Baker had risen to just under half-way up the Captains list, with 49 men senior to him before promotion to Major.[132] In July and August 1783, the Company halted the recruitment and promotion of Indians, annulled some appointments of European officers, and then reduced the size of sepoy battalions from 1000 to 700 rank and file.[133]

As peace loomed, a particularly large number of the Company's military officers resigned or took leave to return to Europe. Six officers (five Captains and a cadet) resigned the same day Baker did; twenty-five officers (including a Colonel and thirteen Captains) resigned during the three month period around that day. Of all the officers named by Dean Mahomed in *Travels*, only twenty remained in active service at the time he and Baker left India.[134]

Further, resignation did not necessarily mean the final end of a British officer's military career with the Company. The Company effectively treated resignation as an extended leave of absence. While in Europe, the seniority of even those officers who had resigned continued to mount. Indeed, a relatively frequent strategy for officers was to resign or take sick leave, wait in Europe until their seniority qualified them for a promotion or command, and then return with the same seniority as if they had remained in India on active duty. Officers who remained in India throughout their careers resented being superseded by officers thus returning so conveniently and comfortably from Europe. Just a few years earlier, the Company had tried to tighten its rules so as to allow only genuine medical reasons for sick leave to Europe, and to allow a maximum of two years accumulation of seniority for those who resigned or remained on leave.[135] Nevertheless, a number of officers (including William Massey Baker and William Popham) stayed far longer than that in Europe without any detriment to their careers. Indeed, William Massey Baker returned to Ireland as a junior Captain, delayed his return through various pleas and excuses of health for four years while his seniority and promotions continued, and went back to India to take up his appointment as a Major.[136] At times of peak demand for officers, the Company pragmatically accepted back such former officers with experience in its Army. Since it to some extent regarded years of seniority as a property right, it usually proved reluctant to deprive an officer of his claim to them.

As part of his pro forma resignation letter, Baker wrote, as was customary: ' . . . it is my firm intention to return to my Duty [with the Bengal Army] . . . '[137] While many other retired officers kept themselves actively on the Company's books by annually petitioning for an extension of their absence, however, Baker never did so. Either his wealthy and distinguished marriage a year after his return or a change in his attitude toward India caused him to give no evidence of wanting to return prior to his death in 1786.[138]

## Departure from Bengal (January 1784)

Behind Dean Mahomed's simple description of his and Baker's departure from Calcutta lies much about the larger economic and political situation. Particularly relevant was the tension between the English and the Danish East India Companies. One of the constant problems for European merchants was acquiring capital in India for the financing of purchases there. Since European goods (such as woollens and other cloth) had limited markets in India, the trade could not be reciprocal. At first, the European companies imported silver specie into India, but that proved too costly for them and led to inflation in India. For the English Company, land revenues generated some of the capital it needed for its investment in Indian goods, the payment of its officials and officers, and the repayment of its debts in Britain, and dividends to its stockholders. Such export of capital from India to Britain became notorious as the 'drain'.[139] During the years prior to Baker and Dean Mahomed's departure from India, the costs of wars and the military establishment had led to heavy deficits in the Company's balance sheets. Calcutta in 1783–4 remained rife with speculation as to whether the Company in London would actually pay the £3,384,611 in outstanding bills of exchange (as of September 1784).[140] Thus, the English East India Company wished to harness the savings of its retiring officials and officers to help finance its purchases of goods in India. Parliament therefore forbade remittances from India except through its hands; the Company then charged a heavy discount (some 20 per cent below par) on such remittances.[141]

From the perspective of men like Baker and Dean Mahomed, other means of sending money to Europe would have appeared more attractive, if risky. Many people speculated in diamonds, purchasing them in major markets like Benares—where Baker and Dean Mahomed had recently lived—and selling them in Europe. The English Company, however, levied a 5 per cent ad valorem duty on diamonds shipped on its vessels. Nevertheless, in the 1783–93 period, some £455,000 worth of diamonds went to England this way.[142] Another means used by many was to purchase either respondentia bonds (loans on the cargo of a vessel, repaid only if the cargo arrived safely) or else bills of exchange based on the China part of the Company operations. These also carried risk and remained subject to controls by the Company. Many people like Baker and Dean Mahomed would have looked for other, less regulated channels for remitting their savings to Europe. They, like many others, found it via a nominally Danish ship.

At this time, the other European companies and many private merchants also—like the English Company—tapped such remittances to finance their own trade. Of particular relevance to us is that Danish ships consistently found it difficult to finance their purchases in India. The English Company's monopoly on saltpetre (the main component in gunpowder, embargoed by the Company during the war) and other goods, its command over the production of higher quality cloth, and its duties on exports, all led to further incentives for Danes and others to avoid the English Company's control. Thus, Danes paid far better rates of exchange to those Europeans willing to make remittances through them rather than through the English Company. The English Company made frequent, but vain, remonstrances against such deals.[143]

Nevertheless, the Danes regularly bought cargoes in India with money from bills of exchange and respondentia bonds, payable in London after the sale of the cargoes in Copenhagen. Danish bills of exchange payable in London and sold in Madras or Bengal totalled £858,216 during this decade (1783–93).[144] The Danes also paid out an estimated £2,000,000 in London on respondentia bonds during the decade leading up to Baker and Dean Mahomed's departure. Danish respondentia bonds were, however, an uncertain mode of remittance since the price the goods would bring could not be known in advance and the British holder was vulnerable to unscrupulous manipulations in Copenhagen. Nevertheless, thus funded, no less than 20 Danish ships sailed for Europe the same season as did Dean Mahomed and Baker.

On a more personal level, Dean Mahomed and Baker also had reasons to avoid travelling on an English Company ship. The English Company had long worked to prevent the creation of an indigent community of Indians in London—generally dismissed or run-away sailors and servants. By law, the Company was ultimately responsible for their passage back to India. Thus, from 1769, the Company required all Europeans bringing an Indian servant with them to post a bond of £50 as surety for the return passage of that Indian.[145] The English Company also repeatedly warned the Danish Company to respect this requirement.[146] We do not know what Dean Mahomed's legal status was (since he was not a simple servant), but sailing on a nominally Danish ship, and boarding it outside of Calcutta, might have avoided the necessity for Baker to post such a bond, one he never would have recovered since Dean Mahomed never returned to India. Although the Danish Company assured the English that they would comply with this request, reinforced by orders of the Danish King as well, it is quite likely that the Danes circumvented this, as they did other English restrictions on them.[147]

The very ship on which Baker and Dean Mahomed sailed added to the tension between the English and Danish Companies. This ship (originally named *Fortitude*), some 700 tons, had been part of the fleet built for the English East India Company. On its previous voyage into Calcutta, *Fortitude* had barely managed to escape capture by the French—receiving a dangerous cannon-shot below the water line. *Fortitude* did not prove so fortunate on its return voyage. In June 1782, the *Fortitude* sailed from Calcutta to Madras with a cargo of rice. Off the Madras coast, *Fortitude* fell victim to a French frigate, *La Fine* (36 guns).[148] The French then sold the captured ship to Portuguese merchants in Calcutta. These Portuguese merchants, however, failed to raise sufficient capital to fill *Fortitude* for a return voyage to Europe.

In the summer of 1783, as peace in Europe between the English and French approached, a particularly large number of Europeans determined to commit their capital to purchase goods for the about-to-be-opened European market, long closed by British blockades. They expected that the first ships to reach Europe with Indian goods would reap a huge profit. One Anglo-Indian consortium in Calcutta, led by the rich merchant firm of Fergusson, bought *Fortitude* for such a voyage. To avoid English Company control, they reflagged and renamed the ship as a Danish vessel, *Christiansborg*, with Ole Bie (head of the Danish factory at Serampore) as the pro forma ship owner and Captain Adam Doack in command (XXXVIII).[149] In so doing, the owners (and passengers, including Baker and Dean Mahomed) accepted the risk that the English Company would choose to make an issue of *Christiansborg*'s real status and seize it, as they did other Danish vessels at this time.

We can presume that Baker and Dean Mahomed took advantage of the opportunity to gain a premium on their savings by entrusting it to the owners of this 'Danish' ship, for repayment in Europe. The ship they chose had been built with all the comforts for its quality passengers demanded by the East India Company. *Christiansborg* carried 96 crewmen and defended itself with 20 cannon. Bookings that season on English Company ships were hard to come by for former officers such as Baker, without special influence with the English Company.[150] The shortage of space in English Company ships proved particularly acute that season since the Company assigned one of its ships to carry the coffin and widow of its late Commander-in-Chief (and Baker's former patron) Eyre Coote back to England, while another ship of that season carried Governor-General Hastings' notorious wife.[151] We can only speculate as to Baker's further desire to avoid travelling with his former colleagues in the English Company.

The ship, along with two other similarly renamed and reflagged 'Danish' ships sailed for Copenhagen partially loaded with cargoes of saltpetre (purchased openly from the English East India Company under a special dispensation from its monopoly).[152] As Baker and Dean Mahomed boarded the newly renamed *Christiansborg* down the river from Calcutta, the ship was also waiting for a more secret cargo. Bie sent a load of cloth from the Danish factory at Serampore, officially consigned for other ships, seeking to evade English Company duties. In fact, the Company's revenue agents briefly seized a Danish sloop, claiming that Bie falsely inventoried its cargo which had been secretly destined for his ship *Christiansborg*. Should a ship miss this monsoon, it might have to wait almost a year until the next favourable sailing season. Even after *Christiansborg* successfully slipped away from Calcutta, this act by Bie led to more conflict between him and the English Company.[153] This voyage by *Christiansborg* proved to be a high point of Danish shipping from India. Baker and Dean Mahomed were sailing with what Bie himself called the 'richest cargo that any Danish ship has ever brought from India to Denmark': its cargo cost 684,375 rix dollars, equivalent to Rupees 1,026,563 or £102,656.[154]

## Dean Mahomed Visits Madras, St Helena, and Dartmouth (1784)

The trip to Madras often took only the week Dean Mahomed mentions; in a less favourable season, this trip could take up to three months. *Christiansborg* touched on the Coromandal Coast near Madras to load more piece goods. As with many other such nominally Danish vessels, it probably loaded cloth diverted from the English Company's stocks by profiteering English Company officials. There is no official record of the arrival of *Christiansborg* in Madras, so it may have stopped further away than Dean Mahomed suggested. Thus, there seems to be some confusion, intended or otherwise, in his description of his arrival in Madras.[155]

During his brief visit to Madras, Dean Mahomed noted both the European and the Indian parts of the city. His military training led him to note the strengths and foibles of Fort St George, at the heart of the European presence. He also remarked upon the pomp of the procession of the Governor of Madras, George Macartney. For someone like Dean Mahomed, the indigenous language, culture, and people of Madras appeared quite different from those of his own Bihar, a thousand miles to the north. He particularly registered the 'female choristers', by which he probably meant *devadasis* (women nominally married to a temple's divinity who were trained in dance and music, XXXVIII). He also recorded that these women spent half of their time 'intriguing' with the great men of the town.

Following a tempestuous voyage, *Christiansborg* finally reached its next port of call, St Helena in the south Atlantic, where it refitted and revictualled for ten days (13–23 June 1784).[156] Dean Mahomed's brief mention of his arrival in England at Dartmouth may also conceal much. This area of the southwest coast remained a centre for smuggling goods into and out of England. It is possible that some of *Christiansborg's* cargo made its way ashore in this small port or was transshipped to a coastal trader bound for Cork where Baker's father was Water Bailiff (Harbour Master). At any rate, disembarking or shifting to another ship at Dartmouth certainly would have been most convenient for Dean Mahomed and Baker in order to reach Cork.

Although thousands of Indians made the trip to Europe over these years, apparently no one else had exactly Dean Mahomed's status. Most were sailors, servants, wives or mistresses of Europeans. A few were travellers or visiting dignitaries. Dean Mahomed clearly fitted into none of these categories. In his decisions to remain in Britain as an immigrant, to create a distinct identity there, and to record his life in his own words, he remained unique during his lifetime.

## Notes

1. E.g. Secret letter to CoD 10/11/1772, FTWM 6: 447.
2. Khan, *Seir* 3: 27.
3. Khan, *Seir* 3: 65–6.
4. Bengal Public Proceedings 22/8/1754, HMS 198, Orme MS O.V. 38.
5. See Gerald Bryant, 'Officers', *Journal of Imperial and Commonwealth History* 4 (1977–78): 203–27.
6. *Oxford English Dictionary*, s.v. 'Nabob'. See James Mayer Holzman, *Nabobs in England* (1926); Lucy S. Sutherland, *East India Company* (1952); Marshall, *East*.
7. E.g. A Cork newspaper published a list of 31 men returned from India with fortunes of over £100,000. HC 15/6/1786.
8. These figures are for 1768. By 1770, over 80 per cent of the cadets were middle class. Suresh Chandra Ghosh, *Social Condition* (1970), p. 31. Razzell claims that over the 1758–74 period, 92.5 per cent of Indian Army Officers were from a middle class origin, versus 1.5 per cent from the aristocracy and 6 per cent from the landed gentry. P.E. Razzell, 'Social Origins', *British Journal of Sociology*, 14, 3 (September 1963): 248–60.
9. Unfortunately, neither the Cadet Papers nor the parish records pertaining to Baker survive so we cannot know Baker's age or patron. Lawrence Sulivan remained a particularly influential Director during much of this period and bestowed his own generous quota of patronage appointments, plus those of his friends and supporters, on many of his fellow Anglo-Irish relatives and friends, perhaps Baker among them.
10. Hickey, *Memoirs* 1: 124–5.
11. Even after 1772, the official age requirement of sixteen was often waived, or bypassed by fraud. Since the Company accepted a sworn certificate of age, many of its underage cadets seem to have raised their declared age to just above that required minimum. At this time, there was no regular registry of births in Britain—each parish following its own procedure— and the Company does not seem to have investigated age anyway.
12. Later, the Bengal Army briefly tried the experiment of placing all the cadets into a separate corps, the Honor Picquet, for training. Not until the nineteenth century did the Company create Addiscombe (near Croyden, outside London) as its 'military seminary', and Haileybury College

for its civil servants. Sons of officers received appointments as 'infant cadets', BMGC 26/3/1783.

13. Extract of letter from Colonel Pearse (1772) in E. Buckle, *Memoir*, ed. J.W. Kaye (1852), p. 34.

14. Hickey tried repeatedly but in vain to get himself transferred from the Madras to the Bengal Army. Hickey, *Memoirs* 2: *passim.*

15. E.g. To CoD 23/10/1783, FTWM 9: 443.

16. Douglas M. Peers, *Between Mars and Mammon* (1995); Lenman, 'Transition', p. 115. See also Lorenzo M. Crowell, 'Military Professionalism', *Modern Asian Studies* 24 (1990): 249–74.

17. BPbC 30/10/1775.

18. Gerald Bryant, 'Officers', p. 224, n. 121.

19. See figures published by Major Scott in *Public Advertizer* 19–21/7/1784 cited in Holzman, *Nabobs*, pp. 29–30.

James Forbes reported that, except for him, all the 19 Bombay cadets of his cohort had died in India. *Oriental Memoirs* (1834 edition) 2: 479–80. By 1767–75, mortality was down to 44 per cent among civil servants (from a high of 74 per cent). Marshall, *East*, 218–19.

20. For negotiations in 1805 over the sale of a cadetship see Edward Blagdon, *Cadetship* (1931). See *Public Advertiser*, 2/6/1773, 14–15/11/1783 cited in Holzman, *Nabobs*, p. 22n.

21. HPC 18/1/1779; GOCC 26/4/1782. See also Marshall, *East*, pp. 209–10.

22. Batta could increase their income above their base pay. BSMC 25/8/1777, BMC 17/3/1779.

23. BMCG 17/11/1781.

24. This practice had been forbidden from 1766; however, the repeated injunctions by the Directors against it indicate that it persisted. E.g. From CoD 10/4/1771, FTWM 6: 100–1.

25. During Dean Mahomed's years with the Bengal Army, Colonel Ironside, Major Grant, and Captains Delafield and Gowan all received convictions for such frauds. Hastings, *Memoirs* 2: 359; To CoD 3/3/1777, 23/4/1778, FTWM 8: 332–3, 339–40; From CoD 28/8/1782, FTWM 9: 69.

26. The Company frequently adjusted the dates on such commissions retroactively in order to determine the relative seniority of officers. The date of commission thus reflected the current political influence of the incumbent, rather than any literal chronology. The Company changed Baker's official date of commission as ensign at least five times during his career, in sequence to: 8/8/1769, 15/1/1770, 9/8/1769, 10/10/1769, and 8/11/1769. Town Major's list of officers appointed from cadets of 1769 and 1770, BPbC 30/10/1775.

27. See Broome, *History* 1: 558.

28. The English Company regarded French fortification of Chandernagore as an act of hostility. BPbC 2/5/1769.

29. Bengal Select Committee Resolution 13/5/1769.

30. General Smith Letter 14/7/1769, BSMC 11/8/1769.
31. Barker Letter 9/10/1769, PBbC 14/11/1769.
32. BSMC 16/2/1770.
33. The Army had no organized compilation of its regulations and standing orders prior to Henry Grace, *Code* (1791).
34. Macpherson, *Soldiering*, pp. 158, 160, 165–6.
35. See Ness and Stahl, 'Western', pp. 26–7.
36. E.g. From CoD 27/5/1779, FTWM 8: 242. See also HMS 24, p. 113; Committee on Shipping Report 3/12/1776, cited in Arthur N. Gilbert, 'Recruitment and Reform', *Journal of British Studies* 15 (1975): 89–111. See also Callahan, *East*, p. 5.
37. Minutes of CoD 16/9/1785.
38. This rate did not remain long at that high level. See Gilbert, 'Recruitment', p. 100n.47. The Company even tried the expensive experiment of recruiting two entire battalions of German troops (some 2000 men) under the auspices of King George III as Elector of Hanover. These 'Electoral Troops' reached Madras but the experiment did not succeed. From CoD 25/1/1782, FTWM 9: 10–15.
39. For the nine months from November 1769 to July 1770, there had been 297 deaths and 50 desertions among the European troops of the Bengal Army. GRT 31/7/1770.
40. The number of European soldiers (including infantry, cavalry, and artillery) sent each year to India for all three Presidencies averaged 1571 for the 1766–71 period. For the 1766–70 period, the number of European troops present in all three Company armies rose only from 7394 to 9947. These figures are calculated from Great Britain, Parliament, 'Account of the Number of Non-Commissioned Officers and Private Men', *Eighth Report of the Committee of Secrecy* (1773).
41. E.g. From CoD 16–17/4/1777, FTWM 8: 85–6, 103–4.
42. Letter from Richard Smith 2/11/1768, BSMC 17/11/1768.
43. Letter to Court 5/12/1766 in Long, *Selections*, p. 467.
44. I have calculated these figures from Great Britain, Parliament, 'Account', *Eighth Report*.
45. The Directors wrote: 'No Foreigner whether in our service or not (except such as hath been admitted into it by the Court of Directors) nor no Indian, black or persons of a mixt breed, or any Roman Catholic of what nation soever, shall on any pretence be admitted to set foot in the Laboratory [of the artillery], or any of the Military Magazines, either out of curiosity, or to be employed in them, or to come near them, so as to see what is doing or sight of any accounts or papers relating to any Military stores whatsoever.' CoD Circular Letter dated 17/6/1748, cited in Broome, *History* 1: 42–3.
46. From CoD 23/3/1770, FTWM 6: 35.
47. The Company periodically disbanded and then reconstituted these battalions. Buckle, *Memoir*, pp. 51–61.
48. See Alavi, 'Makings of Company Power'.

49. Broome, *History* 1: 552–4; Munro, *Narrative*, p. 186.

50. For William Berry (a.k.a. Berrie), the Deputy Contractor who supplied and fed cattle, elephants, and camels for the Army see Macpherson, *Soldiering*, p. 43 and *FTWM* 9: 8. For the careers of George Herbert and John Hollingberry as Paymaster and Deputy Paymaster of the Third Brigade see BPbC 2/8/1770, 28/1/1771, 26/3/1778, 30/11/1778, 31/12/1778; Patna Factory Records 1/1/1771 to 30/7/1771 and 21/9/1771; BMC 25/11/1778.

51. BSMC 1/5/1770.

52. See Great Britain, Parliament, *Eighth*; Lenman, 'Transition', p. 119; Callahan, *East*, p. 6.

53. To CoD 18/3/1770, FTWM 6: 197.

54. For example, a Major in a European Regiment slept in a marquee enclosing 5200 square feet, made of gingham lined with green cloth, and costing about Rupees 250; an ensign like Baker slept in a bell-tent enclosing only 2744 square feet, costing Rupees 70. The tents for a European regiment in the Bengal Army are listed in 'Manuscript Note-book', National Army Museum MS 6709/38, fols. 12, 106. For the cost of camp equipage see Letter of Champion 6/3/1774, BSMC 18/4/1774.

55. GOCC 16/4/1778; see also Macpherson, *Soldiering*, p. 117.

56. Forbes, *Oriental Memoirs* 1: 410.

57. Rennell, *Marches*, p. 99n. and Callahan, *East*, p. 9.

58. To CoD 9/5/1770, FTWM 6: 203–4.

59. In 1779, the Bengal Army carried 6700 bullocks on its regular establishment. GOCC 19/12/1779.

60. One pargana complained of Rupees 15,000 worth of losses. H. Palmer, Superintendent Sircar Rotas 15/6/1771, Patna Factory Records 1/1/1771 to 30/7/1771, ff. 228–30.

61. Letter from Patna Council 19/3/1772, BPbC 31/3/1772.

62. Translation of a letter from Nourul Hussein Cawn 6/3/1772, Patna Factory Records. See also To CoD 31/3/1772, FTWM 6: 391–2; Letter from Richard Becher, Resident at Durbar 13/2/1770.

63. The usual crossing-place on the Son was Koil-war Ghat (a.k.a. Surowdah-Coilure Ghat). See Stibbert 18/11/1777, BMC 5/12/1777.

64. To CoD 26/3/1772, FTWM 6: 390.

65. He later (XXIII) added an account of holy men in Manikpur. This story of a tiger periodically sweeping the floor with its tail persisted at least to the end of the nineteenth century. Edward Lockwood, *Natural History* (1878), pp. 220–1. See also L.S.S. O'Malley, *Bengal District Gazetteers: Monghyr* (1909), p. 249; Khan, *Seir* 2: 443 and n. 238; Williamson, *East* 2: 295–9.

66. Khan, *Seir* 2: 275, n. 150; M.E. Monckton Jones, *Warren Hastings* (1918), pp. 186, 213.

67. William Harwood to Becher 10/2/1770, BSMC 29/3/1770.

68. Spelled variously Godagari, Godacaree, on the left bank of the Ganges/Padma, downstream of its junction with the Mahananda River in

Rajshahi District, Bangladesh. As Dean Mahomed explained it, the name literally means 'Black fort' (from Qara Garhi).

69. From CoD 23/3/1770, 25/3/1772, FTWM 6: 23–7, 145–6.

70. For a European woman's view of her husband's elite Muslim family in the early nineteenth century see Ali, *Observations*. A later Muslim autoethnographer, writing four decades after Dean Mahomed was Shurreef, *Qanoon-e-Islam*.

71. For example, the term *Homaldar* would later be completely replaced by *Naik* as the term for 'Indian corporal' but it appeared in the Military Minutes of the Governor-General's Council for 26/8/1776, NAI.

72. While the army remained in cantonments in Denapur for the next nine months or so, this did not mean that officers and men did not take leave to go out into the countryside. Dean Mahomed recorded none of these tours, but undoubtedly took them. For example, in September 1775 Baker went on a hunting expedition from Denapur to the mouth of the Son River; Dean Mahomed probably went with him. BSC 2/2/1775; Letter from William Elliot 27/9/1775, BPbC 5/12/1775.

73. BSC 20/11/1775.

74. During the conflict between Chayt Singh and the Company described below, Warren Hastings made this garden with high walls in the Kotwali ward his headquarters.

75. BSC 20/12/1775.

76. BSC 20/1/1776.

77. This force consisted of the Fifteenth and Sixteenth Native Infantry and the Second Company of Artillery, probably under Captain Bailie, all part of the Third Brigade. They opposed seven battalions and 17–19 guns. Stubbs' account omits the details about the poisoned dinner invitation and commences with the final confrontation between these two forces. Francis W. Stubbs, *History of the Organization* (1877), pp. 47–9. The Bengal Army had carried out a similar action in 1769. FTWM 5: 592–3.

78. BSC 8/7/1776, 29/7/1776, 12/8/1776, 19/8/1776; BSMC 20/1/1777.

79. Mahbub eventually moved to Delhi around 1780 and later died while on pilgrimage in Mecca. Killed in this conflict, Khwaja Basant Ali Khan, also a eunuch, had risen to command much of the Awadh army under Asaf al-Daula's predecessor. Dean Mahomed indicated that Mahbub died and Basant escaped although the opposite actually occurred. See CPC, 5 (1776–80), nos 143, 211.

80. See Iqbal Husain, *Rise and Decline* (1994) and John Strachey, *Hastings* (1892; 1985 reprint).

81. In 1801, the Company itself annexed half the Awadh ruler's territory, including the Rohilla lands Awadh took in 1774.

82. The King Edward Basement of the British Museum contains some of the loot taken by Britons in this war. Personal observation, 26/10/1994.

83. The Company's Directors did not sanction the disbursal of these funds until twelve years later. Eventually Champion personally received Rupees 105,000 and his officers received amounts proportionate to their ranks,

even Cadets got Rupees 800. 'Distribution Paper', *Calcutta Gazette* 24/5/1787.

84. Champion (14/2/1775) cited in George William Forrest, *Selections* (1910–26) 1: 245.
85. Hastings, *Memoirs* 1: 437–90.
86. BSC 10/7/1776 and Hastings, *Memoirs* 1: 425–7.
87. Shuja al-Daula to Governor of Bengal, 28/11/1774, CPC 4 (1772–75), no. 442.
88. This report circulated in a Persian newsletter. Letter to Patterson, 23/2/1775 in Pearse, 'Memoir', p. 459; Munna Lal gave the same story as Dean Mahomed: "Ibrat Nama', 25b–26b (Aligarh Ms) and 'Waqi'at-i Shah 'Alam', fol. 160, cited in Husain, *Rise*, p. 173, n. 39. Saiyid Ghulam Hossein Khan reported this story as a widely-believed rumour, but discounted its veracity. Haji Mustapha, however, wrote there was much evidence from the women of Shuja al-Daula's harem that this account was true. Khan, *Seir* 4: 60–1 and n. 41.
89. Captain Macpherson called the violation of this princess 'a Report shocking to humanity, and which had some appearance of truth, tho' it cannot absolutely be confirmed.' He says nothing about this incident leading to the death of the Awadh ruler. Macpherson, *Soldiering*, p. 222. Charles Hamilton says Shuja died of a long-standing disorder, *Historical Relation* (1787), p. 271. Major Balfour denied the validity of this story. Strachey, *Hastings*, p. 219. George Foster also reports this rumour about Shuja al-Daula and a Rohilla woman but concluded that it was 'not supported by any substantial authority', *Journey from Bengal* (1790), pp. 175–8. Most historians of today, however, do not concur with Dean Mahomed's account of the death of this Awadh ruler. E.g. Richard B. Barnett, *North India* (1980), pp. 93–5; Strachey, *Hastings*, p. 270, n. 1.
90. Minute by Clavering, BPbC 31/3/1777.
91. BSMC 1/12/1777.
92. Letters of Stibbert 28/10/1777, 18/11/1777, BMC 21/11/1777, 5/12/1777.
93. As we shall see, Dean Mahomed took his descriptions from those of an earlier traveller, John Grose, *Voyage*.
94. This fortress had been captured by the Marathas under Sindhia and the Ruler of Gohad needed the Company's army to recover it. After some ten months in possession, the Company restored this fortress to the ruler of Gohad. Two years later, the Maratha Scindhia recovered it by stratagem from the Gohad Ruler. Hastings, *Memoirs* 2: 378–81.
95. Anthony Edwards, *Cork Remembrancer* (1792), p. 232.
96. BSMC 23/7/1778, 24/7/1778, 27/7/1778, 28/7/1778.
97. Coote pushed a reluctant Military Board and Council to approve the resignation of the post by the senior Baker, the transfer of the younger Baker from the Fifteenth Sepoy Infantry to the Third European Regiment, and the immediate appointment of the latter to the coveted post of Quartermaster. BMCG 22/3/1780. Just three years earlier, Baker

himself had joined a number of other Lieutenants in protesting promotion outside of the strict principles of seniority. Letter from Infantry Officers to Hastings 7/9/1778, BMC 26/9/1778.

98. Minutes of Council, Military Department, 6/10/1780. BPbC 20/3/1780, 13/11/1780, 16/1/1781.

99. Letters of Major Hessman, 2/9/1775, 18/10/1775, Letter from William Elliot 27/9/1775, BPbC 5/12/1775; Letter from Ironside 26/12/1775, Resolution, BPbC 27/12/1775. Other field officers in the Bengal Army repudiated Ironside's actions: Letter from Field Officers 17/1/1776, BPbC 12/8/1776; From General Stibbert, BPbC 1/12/1777.

100. BPbC 23/11/1780.

101. Letter from Stibbert 13/11/1780, BPbC 13/11/1780; From Stibbert to Hastings 29/12/1780, BPbC 1/1/1781.

102. BPbC 28/9/1781.

103. Letter of Hastings 22/10/1781, BSMC 5/11/1781. The Court of Directors in London expressed its displeasure at these wholesale promotions but found it hard to stop their officials in India from making them. From CoD 28/8/1782, To CoD 5/4/1783, FTWM 9: 67, 380. Simultaneously, the Commander-in-Chief reduced the European Regiments from two battalions to one, meaning that their chronically undermanned condition would be more realistically recognized.

104. This Regiment had been raised in 1778 (as the Thirty-seventh Sepoys) and renumbered during the reorganization of 1781. Turnover of officers in this Regiment proved quite rapid. In 1784, after Baker had resigned from the Army, this Regiment was again renumbered, as the Thirty-third Regiment. It was disbanded in 1785.

105. Edward Golding [also spelled Goldin, Goulden], Supervisor of Revenue for Saran and Champaran Districts.

106. Minutes of Council 7/5/1781, BMCG 11/5/1781.

107. Foreign Secret Original Consultations 19/3/1781 No. 8; 14/4/1781 No. 6; 27/4/1781 Nos 16–18; 7/5/1781 Nos 8–9, NAI.

108. Since these events were prior to Dean Mahomed's arrival, his dating the death of these officers one day prematurely is understandable.

109. Warren Hastings, *Narrative* (1782), pp. 180–4.

110. Letter of William Popham 9/10/1781, BSMC 29/10/1781.

111. Hastings, *Memoir* 2: 415–16, 428–9; Hastings, *Narrative*, p. 190n.

112. Baker and Simpson to Blair 9/11/1781, BPbC 17/12/1781.

113. From CoD 28/8/1782, To CoD 14/2/1782, 15/7/1782, 5/4/1783, 17/1/1785, FTWM 9: 70, 318–19, 381, 526.

114. E.g. Hodges, *Travels*, pp. 48–57 and Hastings, *Narrative*.

115. The documents which Dean Mahomed quotes differ somewhat from published British versions. See Hastings' *Narrative*, East India Company records, and the Parliamentary evidence in Hastings' impeachment, e.g. HMS 230, pp. 61–2, Speech of Mr Grey in E.A. Bond, ed. *Speeches of the Managers* (1859) 1: 304.

116. The Company's Resident, William Markham, oversaw both the Regent

(Drigbijai Singh, father of the new Raja, Babu Mahip Narayan) and Ali Ibrahim Khan, the Chief Magistrate of Benares city.

117. Ghazipur (Gochipour) remained long famous for perfume manufacture, especially of rose-water and rose oil.

118. This may be 'Bellia', where Company sepoys and villagers clashed in 1780, leading to a contretemps between Raja Chayt Singh's local faujdar and the Bengal Army high command. BPOC 14/12/1780, Nos 46–8, M.

119. Hastings Letter 13/12/1781, BSC 2/2/1782.

120. Hastings to William Markham, 15/7/1782 in Hastings, *Memoirs* 2: 584–7, modified from Hastings to William Markham, 15/7/1782, BM Addl 29,115. Hastings to Doorbijey Sing 15/7/1782, Persian Correspondence, Translations of Issues, 1781–85, 26, pp. 1–18, No. 38, NAI.

121. E.g. the case of Lt. Thomas Bradley, To CoD 29/3/1779, FTWM 8: 456 and BPbC 8/3/1779.

122. Hastings to Markham, 7/8/1782 in Hastings, *Memoirs* 2: 587–8.

123. Letter from Markham 1/4/1782, BSC 8/4/1782.

124. This Resident (son of the Archbishop of York, Hastings' political ally) resigned from the Company altogether in December 1782. From CoD 28/8/1782 and To CoD 30/12/1782, FTWM 9: 66, 454.

125. Minute of Council 16/6/1786 in Grace, *Code*, p. 11.

126. For example the term gahwara, still used in Dhaka for the more common taziya indicating a model of the tomb of Imam Hussain or Hasan. It may derive from gahwara, 'cradle' (Persian) or else kamra, 'tower' (Persian) or else gumrah, 'Muharram' (Urdu). Dean Mahomed's mention of a thirty-two day Muslim month was clearly an oversight since the Muslim calendar used lunar months, never that long.

127. The Governor of Bengal in Council had attempted to set maximum 'Rates of the hired Servants in Calcutta' working for 'Christian families'. Regulation of 17/5/1774; Walter Kelly Firminger, ed. *Fifth Report* (1969 reprint), p. ccxli.

128. Minutes of Council 20/10/1782; GOCC 1/11/1782, 11/4/1783. See Percival Robert Innes, *History of the Bengal European Regiment* (1885).

129. GOCC 31/10/1783.

130. Letter from Baker 27/11/1783, BPbC 18/12/1783; Minutes of CoD 10/9/1784, IOL.

131. Taking the 107 writers of the years 1768–70 and using figures generated from HMS 79, p. 3.

132. Minutes of Council 14/4/1783, BMCG 17/4/1783.

133. Minutes of Council 24/7/1783, BMCG 26/7/1783; Minutes of Council 29/7/1783, BMCG 2/8/1783.

134. Ten had died and fourteen had resigned (including William Annesley Bailie, Edward Heard, William Lane, William Popham, and William Roberts).

135. BPbC 2/11/1780; From CoD 25/1/1782, FTWM 9: 16–17.

136. Requests of Captain W.M. Baker, Minutes of the CoD 11/7/1798,

18/7/1798, 5/12/1798, 10/4/1799, 26/3/1800, 28/3/1800, IOL. From CoD 11/6/1800, FTWM 21: 178.

137. See also the virtually identical letter of resignation by Heard. Letter of Edward Heard 12/11/1783, Letter from Baker 27/11/1783, BPbC 18/12/1783.

138. Baker's initial resignation and the annual petitions for extensions of their absence by Heard, Bailie, and Gilbert Ironside appear in Minutes of CoD 10/9/1784, Minutes of the Committee of Correspondence 8/2/1785, 26/1/1786, 2/1/1787, 24/1/1787, IOL.

139. See Dadabhai Naoroji, *Poverty and Un-British Rule* (1901). Many scholars have subsequently developed or challenged his assumptions and conclusions about this 'drain'.

140. In 1783–84, British Parliamentary leaders Dundas, Fox, and Pitt were each advancing different bills to deal with this vast Indian debt. Holden Furber, *John Company* (1948), pp. 225–40.

141. Ole Feldbaek, *India Trade* (1969), p. 27 and 'Danish East India trade 1772–1807', *Scandinavian Economic History Review* 26, 2 (1978): 128–44.

142. To CoD 2/1/1778, FTWM 8: 373; Furber, *John Company*, pp. 225–40.

143. To CoD 29/11/1783, FTWM 9: 447. Repeated, CoD Dispatches to Madras 25/1/1782; Feldbaek, *India Trade*, p. 27.

144. For an example of these respondentia bonds totalling £1,450 at 10–12 per cent sent by Captain Peter Grant by Danish ships the same season as Baker and Dean Mahomed sailed, see National Army Museum MS 7410–192 1–7. Furber, *John Company*, pp. 115, 121–2, 130, 135.

145. From CoD 17/3/1769, FTWM 5: 186; To CoD 12/2/1771, From CoD 12/7/1782, FTWM 9: 58–9.

146. To CoD 5/4/1783, FTWM 9: 374; see also CoD to Madras 8/7/1782 warning about 'Black servants' and lascars on Danish ships, HMS 163, pp. 175–86.

147. To Fredricksnagore from GGinC 6/3/1783, BPbC 6/3/1783; from O. Bie, Fredricknagore 18/3/1783, BPbC 24/3/1783.

148. To CoD 15/7/1782, FTWM 9: 314.

149. Earlier in 1783, Adam Doak/Doack had been involved in financial transactions with the ship's real owner, Mr John Ferguson of Calcutta. George Wroughton to James Peter Auriol 21/7/1783, BPbC 7/8/1783.

150. E.g. BPbC 16/9/1783.

151. To CoD 30/12/1782, FTWM 9: 454. See S.C. Wylly, *Life of . . . Coote* (1922). H.E. Busteed, *Echoes* (1908), pp. 137–46; 321–65; 404–10. S.C. Grier [Hilda Gregg], 'Some Fresh Light', *Bengal Past and Present* 5 (1910): 333–4.

152. The other ships were *Christianus Septimus*, formerly *Resolution*, and *Juliana Maria*, formerly *Hornby*. To CoD 10/11/1782, FTWM 15: 158–9.

153. Foreign Letter from Bengal 16/3/1784, To CoD 16/3/1784, FTWM 15: 242–3; To CoD 14/1/1785, FTWM 15: 328–31. HMS 57, pp. 53–86, 227; Foreign Department Consultation 16/12/1783, Nos 28, 31.

154. So great was the inflow of goods beginning with this voyage, that the profitability of such ventures began immediately to decline, as Copenhagen overflowed with Indian goods. The cargo officially sold in Copenhagen for only 836,743 rix dollars, for a gross profit of 22 per cent, less than its owners expected and just adequate to cover commissions, duties, and other costs. Subsequently, a total of 16 Danish ships arrived in Copenhagen in 1785, each making little or no profit on the sales of their cargoes. The owners sold *Christiansborg* in Copenhagen rather than repeat the enterprise; Captain Doack apparently never captained a ship to India again.

155. While Dean Mahomed used the name Madapallam, which was a port further up the coast, it is clear that he described Madras. Madapallam was a thriving port (and English East India Company 'factory') in the southern Godavari River delta, near the current town of Narasapur, Andhra Pradesh. This was, however, some 300 miles from Madras. Often Danish East India Company ships stopped some 150 miles south of Madras, at Tranquebar, the headquarters for the Danish Company in India, but this port does not fit Dean Mahomed's chronology either.

156. St Helena Consultations 14/6/1784. All English Company ships were also required to stop in St Helena. To CoD 23/10/1783, FTWM 9: 415.

Chapter Five

# The World of Colonial Ireland
# (1784–c. 1807)

### Dean Mahomed Enters Cork

When Dean Mahomed disembarked at Cork late in 1784, he must have been overwhelmed with a range of impressions. Since he probably came directly by sea from Dartmouth, Cork would have been the first major European city he encountered. At one level, much would have seemed strangely familiar from his life in Calcutta. Both cities rose out of swampy, low-lying land along a river (although the hills surrounding Cork differed from the flat deltaic lands around Calcutta). Architecturally, Calcutta and Cork shared the same mercantile orientation that favoured a mix of practical commercial warehouses and neo-classical public buildings set among prosperous bourgeois homes. Indeed, both cities contained many of the same families and values characteristic of the burgeoning commercial classes of British empire.

Cork's excellent natural harbour—a few miles away at the mouth of the River Lee, at the entrance to the Irish Sea—made it a convenient entrepot for shipping between Ireland, England, and the rest of the world. In a good year, some 2000 ocean-going merchant ships loaded or unloaded goods in this harbour. Cork flourished in particular as a collection and processing centre for the export of agricultural production from southern Ireland: beef, pork, and dairy products. In addition, Cork prospered from its brewing, distilling, shipbuilding, and textile industries, among others.[1] Locally produced linen cloth was only partially being replaced by Indian hand-woven cotton, itself gradually being displaced by English manufactured cotton cloth. Further,

Protestant Anglo-Irishmen, like the Baker family, formed a large component of the officer corps of the East India Company armies (and the Royal Army and Navy as well) while Irish recruits made up a large portion of their soldiers. Cork thus specialized in drawing resources out of southern Ireland in order to profit by outfitting British and East India Company armies and merchant fleets with stores, manpower, and commercial goods. The many wars of the period meant danger, but also potential profit for such a port city and its people.

The commerce of Cork must have assailed Dean Mahomed's senses in a way quite different from that of Calcutta. The smell of Cork's breweries, which produced nearly six million gallons of porter (ale) annually, would have made a strong impression on him. He probably arrived in the midst of the slaughtering season (September to January), when the butchers of Cork killed and cured some 100,000 head of cattle and filled 100,000 barrels with pork; in this season the streets of the slaughterhouse quarter and the River Lee ran red with the blood of these animals.[2]

Cork city itself expanded dramatically over the score of years that Dean Mahomed lived there. The economy, emerging out of a depression, fostered the city's physical growth. Originally a few islands in the River Lee, Cork created new space for itself as its people gradually filled in the intervening marshes. During his first decade in Cork, Dean Mahomed apparently lived with the Bakers on the prosperous South Mall. This street then fronted on an arm of the river at which merchant vessels tied up. Before Dean Mahomed left, this arm had been filled in to create yet another residential and commercial district.[3]

If the commercial elite of Cork shared features with those of Calcutta, the numerous poor families of Cork must have been shocking to Dean Mahomed. In India, there were few poor White men and virtually no poor White women or children. Even Dean Mahomed's long experience in India with European soldiers (many of whom came from this very Irish poor) would not have prepared him for such extensive and highly visible destitution among White families. Poverty-stricken women and children, as well as men, lined Cork's streets and markets. Most of the poor were indigenous Catholic Irish. Thus, Cork was a colonial city, where the colonizers but not the colonized were somewhat familiar to Dean Mahomed.

The candidly commercial character of Cork struck most visitors. Another Indian, who visited Cork in 1799, remarked on the filth and smell of the streets, concluding 'as this city has been erected for the purposes of commerce, more pains have been taken to facilitate the importation and exportation of goods than to preserve [architectural] uniformity and regularity'.[4] A French traveller to Cork in 1797 named it 'the dullest and dirtiest town which can be imagined . . . [H]ideous troops of beggars, or pigs . . . run in the streets in hundreds, and yet this town is one of the richest and most commercial of Europe . . . The spirit of commerce and self-interest has laid hold of all branches of the administration'.[5] The Bakers embodied this spirit of commerce and civic power.

The population of Cork, while growing rapidly during the years Dean Mahomed lived there, was neither homogeneous nor uniformly thriving. Newspapers from the time assert that the population of the county had risen by 1790 to 375,400, and the city and its environs to 122,000.[6] Many of the people of the city and countryside remained poor, despite the expanding economy—largely controlled by a relatively small elite.

The Anglo-Irish elite—including the Bakers—held economic, administrative, and judicial power in both the city and countryside. Cork served as the base for English rule and culture in southern Ireland. In Cork county, great country houses dotted the landscape, surrounded by tenants and small freeholders. A total of less than 2000 people (.5 per cent of the population), by law all Protestants, held the franchise in the county. Similarly, in the city, only some 1600 (1–2 per cent of the population) were freemen or freeholders with franchise for Parliament.

Civic affairs effectively remained in the hands of an even more limited body. The 'Court D'Oyer Hundred' of voting Freemen established the rules for Cork city; even in a heated election, less than 500 men voted.[7] The Aldermen and Burgesses comprised even more restricted bodies of men who controlled the Cork administration. The annually elected city officials administered the city on a daily basis. Over the course of his career, Baker's father held virtually all the major city offices: Alderman, Burgess, Mayor, Sheriff, and Water Bailiff.

The dominating Anglo-Irish ascendancy that held sway in Ireland, however, did not go unchallenged. Catholics outnumbered

Protestants in Cork city by four to one, and by ten to one in the surrounding countryside. Insurgent groups outside of the city frequently assaulted the ruling class. Raids on the great country houses by people resisting English political domination proved frequent during the period that Dean Mahomed lived in Ireland. Almost daily, the papers of Cork carried accounts of the 'treason' trials of captured insurgents in the city's courts. Further, the Protestant elite (including Baker's family) remained internally divided during this period as to whether they were Protestant Irishmen working for a self-governing Ireland or whether their future lay in union with England.

Economic and political demands by the hard-pressed lower classes, often enforced by violent attacks on the elite, both Protestant and Catholic, led to disorder and lack of confidence on all sides. Catholics called for their rights to full participation in the political process. Protestant elites felt their rising but unfulfilled expectations were being betrayed by England. The French Revolution of 1789 raised fundamental and testing questions about society and government. The vast costs to Britain of the recent wars with continental powers and with the former British colonies in North America all led to increasing political and social disorder that continued through the 1790s. Both Catholics and Protestants increased the level of sectarian agitation through secret societies and rural violence. In 1796—in the middle of Dean Mahomed's life in Cork—Wolfe Tone and 6000–7000 French troops and 17 ships arrived in nearby Bantry Bay. Only adverse weather prevented this long-dreaded invasion force from landing. The shock of this near conquest galvanized Cork into further militarization, with the Baker family among the leaders of this mobilization.[8] The widespread opposition to English colonial rule over Ireland peaked in the risings of 1798 in which various 'rebel' groups totalling many thousands, some led by Catholic clergy, others by Protestant nationalists, rose against the Government, captured towns and villages and fought pitched battles with Government troops. The town of Cashel, near the Baker family estate at Ballymoreen, briefly came under the control of a body of some 400 of these 'rebels'.[9]

The British Government responded to this insurrection through measures designed to reassert its political and military control. The British Government appointed a distinguished officer, Cornwallis (the once and future Governor-General of India, 1786–93, 1805) as Lord Lieutenant and Commander-in-Chief of Ireland (1798–1801). Under the Act of Union (1800–1), the Irish Parliament's nominal independence ended as it merged, despite the opposition of much of the Protestant gentry, into the British Parliament; the Protestant Church of Ireland merged with the Church of England.

Much of Ireland's earlier commercial expansion would falter over the years that Dean Mahomed lived there. In particular, Cork's shortage of iron, coal, and investment capital, as well as innovative entrepreneurs, led to declining industrialization. By the early nineteenth century, the Cork region slipped back in its competition with other industrializing areas of Britain.

## The Bakers in Anglo-Irish Society

Throughout Dean Mahomed's nearly quarter century in Ireland, his most evident ties remained with the Bakers and other India-returned Anglo-Irish elites. Over the generations, the Baker clan had expanded over south-east Ireland as one of the pillars of the Protestant ascendancy. The main branch of the family had extensive landholdings in Tipperary county, next to Cork. The Bakers held land and occasionally entered the professions of Protestant clergymen or lawyers.[10] They reinforced their status through numerous weddings with other powerful Anglo-Irish families.

One branch of the Baker clan prospered in Cork city. In the early 1740s, Godfrey Baker (father of Godfrey Evan Baker) moved as a young man to Cork and soon established himself as a leading merchant, apparently in international trade. As only the seventh son of the family patriarch (William Baker of Lismacue), he had apparently not seen a promising future on the family estates. In 1744, Godfrey married Elizabeth Cossart, daughter of Peter Cossart, a leading burgher of Cork. Godfrey Baker rose quickly in Cork society, voted by the Cork Council into the ranks of 'Freemen' in May 1754.[11] He immediately took a particularly active role in city government: in 1755, the Council selected him to oversee repairs to the City Court House and the Freemen elected him one of the two city Sheriffs. The next year, he became a Burgess of the Cork Corporation. He won elections as Chief Magistrate, then as Mayor. This one-year mayoral term (October 1769–October 1770) brought with it a fine house, a salary of £100 and an allowance for public expenses to match. After his term as Mayor, Godfrey consequently became an Alderman for life. Status as an Alderman also ensured a life pension of £20 annually for Baker's widow.[12] Baker also placed himself among the civic leaders particularly opposed to Irish separatism; for example, when troops were raised in March 1778 to put down unrest, Godfrey Baker's name headed the list of leaders.[13] He also held magisterial powers which he actively used to maintain social order.[14] The Freemen of Cork annually re-elected Godfrey throughout the 1780s to the important office of Water Bailiff: the manager of the harbour and trade, with a handsome salary of £60 annually plus expenses and a silver oar as his badge of office.[15] Further, he kept about £200 annually as his share of the port duties, and deposited the surplus, about £100, in the Corporation treasury, one of the Corporation's major sources of income. Illustrating both the value of this office, and Baker's powerful control over it for nearly a decade, on the day after his death in office (17 September 1788), an immediate electoral and political struggle for possession of this lucrative office broke out; subsequently the Corporation reduced its emoluments.

During his life, Godfrey Baker made careful efforts to retain his family's prominence in the city and region. As was customary, Godfrey arranged for the Cork Corporation to elect his eldest son, Godfrey Evan Baker, as a Freeman of Cork (July 1782).[16] Since Baker was then in Benares, we can only speculate as to whether he intended to abandon his military career and return to Cork even before his dishonourable recall that same month. Correspondence between Ireland and India often took nine months or more, therefore these simultaneous events were not simultaneously known to father and son.

Godfrey Baker also broadened his family's position in Cork society. Besides shifting from landholding to international trade and city government, he located his sons and daughters in other sectors of the elite. Godfrey admired the military; for instance, he helped sponsor a history of the military conquest of Ireland by the English. He also placed three of his four sons in army careers, while seven of his grandsons became military officers.[17] His other son, Peter, obtained the Clerkship in the Permit Office.[18] The Baker family remained prominent civic leaders until the end of the eighteenth century, leading efforts to succor the poor and defend the established elite.[19] Interestingly, none of the Bakers (nor Dean Mahomed) was active in the Cork branch of The Society for the Purpose of Effecting the Abolition of the Slave Trade.[20] In addition, the Bakers also had multiple marriage ties to the titled and landed Protestant aristocracy of Ireland, particularly the powerful Massey clan with extensive estates in several parts of Ireland.[21]

In 1785, within a year of his return from India, Godfrey Evan Baker married the Honorable Margaret, second daughter of Lord Baron Massey (1700–88), Lieutenant General and Commander-in-Chief of Munster.[22] Godfrey Evan Baker's new brother-in-law was the Honorable Hugh Massey, Delegate to the Grand National Congress, Member of Parliament for Limerick, and Knight of the Shire.[23] The elite of southern Ireland thus welcomed Godfrey Evan Baker's return from India as a triumph. Almost certainly, his marriage put him in control of a handsome fortune, in addition to whatever he brought back from India.

Dean Mahomed's own status no doubt benefited from the distinguished reception accorded Baker by the elite of Cork. Less clear would be the effect of Baker's marriage on their close personal relationship. Despite Baker's premature death within a year of his marriage, and his widow's remarriage within a year after that (September 1788), the Massey clan continued for years as patrons of Dean Mahomed.[24]

## The Marriage of Dean Mahomed and Jane Daly (1786)

Soon after his arrival in Cork, Dean Mahomed began to work (under the Bakers' sponsorship) to advance his education, particularly to cultivate his knowledge of English language and literature. As clearly illustrated by the rhetoric and content of *Travels*, Dean Mahomed mastered the classically polished literary forms of the day, complete with poetic interjections and allusions. Occasional poetry remained very much a part of the cultured life of some of the elite of Cork, reflected in the 'Poet's Corner' found in nearly every newspaper. Much of this poetry was published anonymously, some liberally imitative of more established poets. We can never know if Dean Mahomed himself contributed his own verse to the 'Poet's Corner' but the unattributed poetry he included in his *Travels* is typical in style, content, and quality of such work.

In 1786, about a year after Godfrey Evan Baker's marriage and the same year as Baker's death, Dean Mahomed (age 27) eloped with a young woman student, Jane Daly, whom he married nearby.[25] Suggestion of the haste or desire for privacy of this marriage comes from their decision to post a bond with the church where they were married rather than have the banns read for weeks previously from the pulpit. This substantial bond would then indemnify the church should the marriage prove illegal. Any wedding between a Protestant and a Catholic was illegal at this time in Ireland, with the clergyman who performed the wedding held particularly responsible.[26] Although Dean Mahomed must have by this time become a member of the established Protestant Church, we can imagine a lingering doubt in the mind of the clergyman who performed the wedding ceremony of this unusual couple, particularly if Jane's family was not present or approving. The substantial wedding bond also testifies to Dean Mahomed's own comfortable financial position: he either owned considerable capital or he had sufficient credit to borrow it for such a personal undertaking as his elopement.

Given the paucity of information about Jane's natal family, we can only build suppositions. The name Daly was fairly common in Cork and the surrounding region; surviving records do not indicate even her father's first name. If the marriage totally alienated Jane and Dean Mahomed from her family, we should not expect to discover any evidence in their later lives about her family. If they were even partially supportive of their son-in-law, they would presumably have appeared as patrons in *Travels;* no likely Daly does so.[27] Thus, Jane's family does not seem to have supported the young couple. In contrast, many others of the gentry and aristocracy of Cork, particularly those with connections with India, did support them over the years this couple lived in Cork. Nevertheless, Dean Mahomed and Jane lived in a world where a range of generally unflattering images of Indians and Muslims abounded.

## Images in Cork of Indians and Muslims

The people of Cork were not innocent of images of India and Islam before Dean Mahomed appeared in their midst. Many of the Anglo-Irish elite had personal experience of Asia, as officers, officials, or merchants. Some, like William Massey Baker, had an Indian mistress and Anglo-Indian children. Indian sailors and servants passed through or lived in Cork. Additionally, entertainers of all varieties played with images of India and Islam to make a profit. Dean Mahomed had to manoeuver within the limits on his capacity to recreate himself and define India for his neighbours. Further, English attitudes toward non-English people generally were going through a hardening process at this time.[28]

One image of India prevalent in Cork during these years remained that of the exotic. The year after Dean Mahomed arrived, a travelling carnival advertised its display of 'A most Curious Animal, called the Grand Lionphant Tartar, or, Indian Camel'. This creature, allegedly 17 feet long and 8 feet high, could be viewed for the price of 1 shilling admission. Its owners validated its existence by reference to Dr Goldsmith's *History of Animated Nature*.[29] Thus, Dean Mahomed's inclusion in his *Travels* of descriptions of camels, elephants, and rhinoceros (XXIX) might have been a response to the attention he saw paid by the people of Cork to such exotic creatures. Another circus visited Cork exhibiting living human exotica: Indian Chiefs (the north American variety) and 'Happy Africans'.[30] Although Dean Mahomed did not comment in print on such displays, his account of Indians like himself stood in strong contrast to such exploitative images.

The several Cork newspapers did not hold uniform editorial policies with respect to the growing British empire in India (which many inhabitants of Cork had fostered). Some, however, felt that such an imperial enterprise posed dangers to the morality of Britain. The alien religions that Britons encountered in India and the power Britons seized there could both be seductive. As the *Cork Gazette* opined: 'It is to be feared our Soldiers in India will return *Idolaters*—the *golden gods* of Tippoo [Tipu Sultan of Mysore] have great power, and convey a secret influence of corruption to the most *Orthodox* [Christian] hearts.'[31] In another editorial, this paper sarcastically stated: 'The news from Asia is rather *flattering* to the friends of peace and humanity—The last [news] accounts mention the taking of several towns, putting the inhabitants to the sword, ravishing their women, butchering their *criminal* children, and ravishing their unhallowed plains with fire . . . [T]he laurels gained upon such occasions, and from such notions as have caused the war, reflect honour on the humanity and arms of Britons.'[32] For Dean Mahomed the challenge was to present a more 'authentic' account of the religions and wars in India; his words found an eager audience but were in implicit dialogue with such other images.

In some ways, the anecdotes about Indian types in *Travels* paralleled those in the popular press of Cork. Dean Mahomed deployed anecdotes illustrating, for example, the simplicity (but ultimate triumph) of a sepoy confronting a counterfeiter (XXVIII), the tenacity in adherence of an Indian merchant to religious principle (XXXVI), and the (proverbial) generosity of a courtesan saving her lover from bankruptcy (XV). Similarly, Cork newspapers included anecdotes illustrating the extreme pride and sense of honour of Indians: a Rajput servant who, hit unjustly by his master, committed suicide rather than accept the shame of either being struck or betraying his master; Grenadier sepoys who claimed the right to be executed first among 'mutineers', since Grenadiers always had the honour of entering battle first.[33] Indeed, Dean Mahomed or one of his fellow veterans may have been the source of such newspaper stories designed to illustrate the exceptional virtue of Indians.

Most newspaper accounts, however, advanced negative views of Islam, and other non-Britons as well. Political alignments appeared in terms of stereotypes, in which Islam was a standard against which to measure immorality. For example, in 1791, Iberians received negative press: 'The vapouring Spaniard had scarcely begun hostilities, when he pulled in his horns and made friends with the Moors—Such dastardly nations are fit to pay tribute to the Sons of Mahomet.'[34] Catholics and Jews appeared as inferior even to 'the blind and reprobate Sons of the Heathen and Mahomedan worlds'.[35]

Literature also presented images of India and Islam that clashed with those of Dean Mahomed's writings and persona. Cork newspapers extracted and republished 'The Life of Mahomet' from Edward Gibbon's influential *Decline and Fall of the Roman*

*Empire* (1776–86), a work quite dismissive of the Prophet's revelation.[36] During Dean Mahomed's years in Cork, two plays proved particularly popular, staged repeatedly with a professional lead but with townspeople in the other roles. Citizens of Cork staged (1788, 1796) the Reverend Mr Miller's translation of Voltaire's *Mahomet, The Impostor: A Tragedy*. This play presented the Prophet Muhammad as a religious tyrant, using the faith of his followers to advance his corrupt personal agenda.[37] Another popular play was a farce: 'The Sultan; or, a Peep behind the Curtains [or into the Seraglio]' by Isaac Bickerstaff, performed in Cork in 1791, 1804, and 1807.[38] In this play, a plucky English slavewoman resisted the sexually and physically subordinated role specified for her by Islam and the Turkish state, thereby winning over the Sultan, becoming Queen, and freeing the rest of the harem from bondage. This theme of an English Christian woman converting a Muslim to higher principles and then marrying him may have seemed to the people of Cork to be particularly relevant to Jane and Dean Mahomed. Other plays and works of literature also contained similar themes in dialogue with Dean Mahomed's words.[39]

## Dean Mahomed's Conceptualization of His Book (1793)

After Dean Mahomed and Jane returned to Cork from their elopement, they worked to create a place for themselves in society. They took up residence on the prosperous South Mall, probably in Godfrey Baker's house. Unfortunately, Dean Mahomed has left us no record of his life in Cork over the next eight years. In 1793, however, he suddenly publicized his determination to write and publish a book that would explain himself and his understanding of India to the elite of Ireland. Such a decision could not have been easy to make or to carry out.

Up to this point, no Indian had ever written and published a book in English, either in India or in Britain. Some Africans, however, had done so. Indeed, Dean Mahomed may have been encouraged in this undertaking by the work of the most famous Black African author of the age, Olaudah Equiano. Literary commentators of our day have classed Dean Mahomed's *Travels* with such 'Black literature'.[40]

In the late eighteenth century, a number of Africans and people of African descent (both slaves and former slaves, in Britain and the Americas) used the writing of books and other literature in order to demonstrate to Europeans that they and their people had the capacity for intellectual accomplishment. This assertion remained particularly salient, since many White supporters of slavery defended that institution on the basis that Blacks lacked this very capacity. Some White abolitionists as well presupposed that Blacks were unable to write for themselves. Virtually all early Black writers in English therefore explicitly stated in the works that bore their names that they were indeed authors in their own right.[41]

Dean Mahomed almost certainly knew about, and may have met, one of the most influential of such early Black authors. Olaudah Equiano toured Ireland, including Cork, in 1791, publicizing his autobiographical work: *The Interesting Narrative of the Life of Olaudah Equiano, or Gustavus Vassa, The African, Written by Himself.* Nevertheless, comparison between Equiano's work (and other works by African authors at this time) and Dean Mahomed's *Travels* reveals not just parallels in approach and content but fundamental differences as well.

Like many African authors, Dean Mahomed clearly identified himself with his book. He prominently included in his title 'Written by Himself' to dispel any possible doubts about his authorship. The very existence of this book made a statement about his own capacity to produce literature, legitimizing himself by his own work, as did Black authors. This phrase also normatively appeared in the English genre of travel literature to indicate the veracity of the narrative. Thus, he was also asserting that he was eyewitness to the events in the narrative: his identity authenticated the book, as well as the reverse.

Unlike Dean Mahomed's *Travels*, Black literature of that period centred on the author's enslavement and/or emancipation.[42] The Black author often depicted his/her liberation in terms of religious conversion to Christianity, because the two changes seemed morally homologous. They seemed legally homologous as well, because most people believed such conversion precluded further legal slavery: it was popularly believed in Britain that only non-Christians could be slaves.[43] Another major theme in Black literature was the slave-owner's stripping of the old identity and the renaming of the enslaved author. This loss of name often led to an essential questioning of the author's own identity in his/her autobiographical work. In contrast, Dean Mahomed in his *Travels* neither presented himself in terms of slavery nor mentioned his conversion. Further, he retained his original name throughout his life; indeed, his family has borne the name Mahomed into the twentieth century.[44] These central themes in much Black literature were entirely absent in *Travels*. Instead of contributing to the anti-slavery debate as did most Black authors (either explicitly or by implication), Dean Mahomed wrote for an elite, establishment audience to shape their view of India and his place as an Indian in their society.

### Dean Mahomed's Prospectus and Solicitation of Subscribers

In March 1793 (at age thirty-four), Dean Mahomed took out a series of advertisements proposing to publish *Travels*. Since this is his only known self-statement (other than *Travels* itself) during his years in Cork, it is worth reproducing this prospectus in full:

Proposals For publishing by SUBSCRIPTION,
In TWO VOLUMES DUODECIMO, Adorned with Plates
The Travels of DEAN MAHOMET,
Through Several Parts of the Eastern Territory (Being a Native of India.)

In which is more circumstantially related, the Manners, Religion, Manufactures, Productions, etc. of the different Countries through which he passed, than has hitherto been published. With a particular Account of the Solemn Procession of the Grand Nabobs and Rajahs from their Palaces to their Places of Worship; interspersed with many curious Anecdotes of the Inhabitants.

To which is added, an accurate Account of the Wars in India, at which the Author has been present; with a list of the Europeans killed and wounded in the different Engagements.

The Authenticity of this Work can be certified by a great number of Gentlemen of the first distinction in these Kingdoms, who had been in India at the time.

Conditions

I. The Work will be printed in two neat Volumes, Duodecimo, on an elegant Type and fine paper.

II. The Price to Subscribers 5s 5d. Non-Subscribers 6s 6d.

III. The Names of the Subscribers printed as Patrons of the Work.

IV. Each Subscriber to pay on subscribing a British half crown, and another on delivery of the Books.

Subscriptions will be received by Mr T. WHITE, Bookseller, Mr W. FLYN, Printer, Mr J. CONNOR, Bookseller, Mr FIELD, Hair-Dresser, Grand Parade, and the Printer hereof.

N.B. Such Ladies and Gentlemen as honour the Author with their Subscriptions will, he hopes, be particular in inserting their Residence, that no mistake should be made in sending the Books as soon as published.[45]

Dean Mahomed delivered on each of his promises, although the book he finally wrote differed somewhat in emphasis from this initial prospectus. The prospectus first highlighted Dean Mahomed's own background, including his promise of extensive accounts of his relative, the Nawab of Bengal, and of other inhabitants of India. He included such subject matter in his published work, but did not foreground it. Second, the prospectus stressed his eyewitness accounts of the military exploits—and casualties suffered—by British officers in the Bengal Army's several wars. Dean Mahomed scattered such accounts through *Travels*, but he was not himself present at most of the engagements he described. In the prospectus, he next enlisted the prestige of his fellow veterans to authenticate the importance and veracity of his work. For us, one of the values of *Travels* remains Dean Mahomed's voice as an Indian, in contrast with travel narratives by Europeans of the time.

Given the financial uncertainties of publishing at this time, particularly in Ireland, it was quite usual for authors and booksellers to solicit subscribers in advance of the printing, or even the actual writing, of the book. Sometimes the potential author's prospectus would promise only to publish after a specified number of firm commitments to buy had been received. In the case of *Travels*, Dean Mahomed further ensured the commitment to buy by requiring subscribers to pay him half the purchase price in advance.

He could probably not have generated the extensive response he obtained by relying on this newspaper advertisement alone.[46] He may also have followed the common practice of would-be authors in posting broadsheets prominently in the windows of booksellers, publicans, and other shopkeepers. More effective than such impersonal advertisements, however, Dean Mahomed apparently made personal visits to potential subscribers throughout southern Ireland. The extent and quality of the patronage which Dean Mahomed secured testify to his respectable social position, the influence of his friends and connections, and his ability to engender confidence among the elite.

A total of 320 people each entrusted Dean Mahomed with half a crown (2s. 6d.) or more, long in advance of the book's completion and over a year before its delivery. At least some of these hundreds of subscribers were demonstrating their encouragement of Dean Mahomed. Particularly in those many instances where several members of the same family (most frequently a husband and wife) each purchased a copy of *Travels*, the purchasers indicated personal support for Dean Mahomed rather than only seeking knowledge of the content of the book for its own sake. The most sizable block of this type were the 23 members of the Baker clan listed as patrons, who collectively purchased a total of 122 copies of *Travels*. Among the other subscribers, a few clearly had commercial motives. The booksellers Daly and Travers, for example, purchased multiple sets, presumably for resale. For others, particularly those with experience in or connections with India, the content of the book, rather than Dean Mahomed as author, may have been the greatest attraction.

He clearly appealed to the social elite of Ireland, both men and women. Of the 238 males who subscribed, over 85 per cent were gentlemen distinguished by a title, rank, or the epithet 'esquire', while less than 15 per cent bore the mere label 'Mr'. Included among the male subscribers were 17 members of the nobility, 10 military officers (up to the rank of Colonel), 17 clergymen (including 3 Bishops), and 3 medical men. The 82 women, who made up over a quarter of the subscribers, included a Viscountess, 5 Ladies, and several Honourables (i.e. daughters of titled families). In addition to individual women, the Catholic Ursuline Convent purchased a set (which still remains in their library over two centuries later).[47]

The families of a number of Anglo-Irishmen who had served in India and held estates in the Cork region also appeared prominently among Dean Mahomed's patrons. His decision to dedicate his work to Colonel William Annesley Bailie (1740/41– 1821) reveals the importance he must have held in Dean Mahomed's life. Bailie, reaching the rank of Lieutenant-Colonel in 1779, resigned in 1782 and left India for Ireland in 1783 (just before Dean Mahomed's own retirement from the army).[48] Bailie came from a landed Anglo-Irish family of Inishargy and Ringduf-ferin, in county Down. After his return from India, he married the Honourable Elizabeth, second daughter of the First Viscount Doneraile of county Cork, and settled on a sizable estate (416 acres), 14 miles north of Cork city. Bailie, his wife, and his mother-in-law (the Viscountess Doneraile) each subscribed for a set of *Travels*. Five years later, Bailie sold or let his Irish holdings and retired to Bath, England, where he died.[49] Since Bailie was not the highest ranked nor most socially or politically prominent of the subscribers, it would seem to have been a personal relation-ship with Dean Mahomed that induced the latter to dedicate *Travels* to Bailie.

In addition to his personal visitations, Dean Mahomed also made provision for would-be subscribers to deposit their advance at public places in Cork. The listing of printers and booksellers (Thomas White, William Flyn, and John Connor—who even-tually printed *Travels*—plus the *Cork Gazette* newspaper office) as receivers of subscriptions was quite usual. Dean Mahomed's inclusion of Mr Henry Field (d. 1799), Hairdresser and Perfumer, as a receiver of subscriptions for his book was highly unusual if not unique to publishing in this period.[50] This inclusion reveals a little about Dean Mahomed's social position, since for him to trust such a hairdresser and perfumer's establishment with receiv-ing subscriptions would seem to indicate that he dealt with Field regularly, either as a patron of Field's shop or as a companion of those who did so. Significantly, Dean Mahomed did not seem to have any shop or business office of his own where people could leave subscriptions. Further, he did not list his home on South Mall, perhaps because he did not want people bothering the Bakers at their residence. All this supports our location of Dean Mahomed as dependent on, and/or a manager of, the Baker household. His orientation remained to the Anglo-Irish elite rather than to Irish society in general.

## Dean Mahomed's Self-Location in *Travels*

Analyses of Dean Mahomed's word choice in his *Travels* reveals his self-presentation to his patrons. In the early part of *Travels*, Dean Mahomed located himself in a series of cultures. He used his Dedication and first letter to identify himself in 1794, as a 'native' of India living and writing among the Anglo-Irish of Cork. In contrast, in the next few letters, he placed himself with his birth family in Patna. He then described in moving terms his shift from his natal family to the military family of his Anglo-Irish patron, Baker. This was one of the few instances where he focused on himself and his transition in *Travels*. In the remainder of his work, he (often implicitly) wrote from the perspective of an associate of European officers of the Company Army. Never, however, did he show himself to be a member of any of these groups; he only located himself in their respective camps. While he changed the social context and status dramatically, he depicted an unchanging self experiencing these changes.

At the start of *Travels*, Dean Mahomed began to lay out a central theme about the fundamental distinctions between Indian and European cultures, and his own point of origin within the former. In Dean Mahomed's view, Indians (including himself) were essentially natural and artless, in his words 'ingenuous' and filled with 'sincerity', part of an ancient and innocent society. In contrast, he characterized European society as artful: epitomized by 'cultivated genius' (Dedication): sophisticated, highly refined philosophers and polished litterateurs. In many ways, these values reflected much late eighteenth-century European thought about the distinction between nature and art, which Dean Mahomed either internalized himself or else adopted for his Anglo-Irish audience.

While these initial characterizations romanticized and essentialized the two cultures, as he proceeded in *Travels*, he expanded on these characterizations to describe the less admirable extremes of these models. The sophistication of Europeans led some of them not only to 'boasting' but also to scepticism toward India's more sincere faith. He illustrated this with the incident of a scoffing European, contemptuously urinating on the grave of the revered saint of Pirpahar (VIII). We can only speculate about the response of Dean Mahomed's patrons to his inclusion of this incident showing the deceased Indian saint's power to strike a Protestant Christian dead.

In Dean Mahomed's account, Edenic India also contained less admirable extremes. Its naiveté tended among its less restrained people to savagery. He recounted repeatedly how the Company's Army had to ward off unwarranted attacks by 'merciless savages' (VI) and 'sanguinary and rapacious . . . lawless aggressors' (IX). Such bandits even tortured helpless animals. Nevertheless, such unrestrained people were not totally inhumane; he remarked upon the evidence of generosity even among them (VI, XV). The prevailing naiveté of most of India's people, however, made them victims of the overly sharp among them.

For Dean Mahomed, the essence of Indian society revealed itself through its holy men and ascetics. While he provided great detail about various of these seers and renouncers, he never identified them by religious community, sect, or name. Rather, they appeared as variations on a type, with superficial differences but an essentially identical message of serene detachment (VII). He asserted that Europeans failed to get past the superficial differences of dogma and practice to understand this inner core of meaning (XVII). In the depth and direction of his analysis of the internal divisions within Indian society, he differed from many of his European contemporaries.

While Dean Mahomed presented the bulk of his *Travels* from the perspective of the Company's army, he did occasionally adopt the viewpoint of the Anglo-Irish gentry and aristocracy who comprised the book's intended audience. In one example of this, he described an Indian palanquin being borne 'much in the same manner as our sedan chairs are carried in this country [Ireland]' (VI). In another instance, he wrote that a ghat in Benares was named 'Benegaut; as if we said, Sullivan's-quay, or French's-slip'—two wharves on the Cork riverfront (XVII). In contrast, he only referred to the Catholic farmers in Ireland from much the same distance as he did the villagers of India (III). Thus, he sometimes identified himself with his Anglo-Irish audience.

In late eighteenth-century Britain, the concept 'race' did not mean what it does today. Unlike later periods, in the late eighteenth century race had not yet solidified into a strong boundary in Britain. During this period, interracial marriages (to use today's terms) such as his were not common among people of the respectable classes (like his wife), although they seem to have been fairly frequent among servants.[51] Since neither Dean Mahomed nor his wife ever remarked upon their marriage, we can only speculate about their feelings about it.[52]

Dean Mahomed used the English term 'race' only thrice in *Travels*. In two instances, he referred to the descent groups of Indian rulers: his father 'descended from the same race as the' Nawabs of Bengal (I) and the Mughal Emperors stemmed from 'the race of the great Tamerlane' (XXII). In the third instance, he quoted a European commentator's gloss about 'Topasses—a tawney race' (XVI).

Dean Mahomed used the English terms 'White' and 'Black' only slightly more frequently. He classed as living in the 'White' section of Calcutta, 'the European Gentlemen, of every description', consisting of 'English, French, Dutch, Armenians, Abyssinians, and Jews' (X). While he uniformly identified himself as Indian, he never called himself 'Black'. Dean Mahomed published portraits of himself (illustrations 1 and 14) as quite dark in complexion yet he applied the term 'Black' only to others. When describing south India, Dean Mahomed frequently used the term 'Black' to refer generally to the local people, including poor fishermen, Indian soldiers and officers in the Company's Madras Army, and prosperous townsfolk (XXXVIII). In his depiction of Madras, however, he identified Armenians with Portuguese, as well as south Indians, as living in the 'black town' (XXXVIII). At one point, he did describe a Muslim bride marrying one of his relatives as a 'sable Dulcinea' (XIII), but his adding of colour to this literary allusion does not appear to suggest that he viewed himself as 'sable' or Black. During the course of his life, Dean Mahomed would have had to negotiate his own racial identity in light of the contemporary expectations of different classes in Ireland and England.

Dean Mahomed presupposed in *Travels* a world made up of

social groups and classes, in none of which did he fully belong. In analysing the sociological typology which he used both explicitly and implicitly, I argue that he is in each case representing a concept he grew up with: *qaum* ('nation' or 'ethnicity,' from his Persian/Urdu vocabulary). Qaum would have been used by his parents to identify the various 'nations' around them: Mughals, Iranians, Afghans, Hindus who had converted to Islam, Bengalis and other regionally-identified Indians, and each of the European nationalities. Also in common use among Dean Mahomed's natal culture would have been the term *jati*: a more Hindu concept, meaning 'genus' or 'birth' group, and often translated as 'caste'.[53] When he described churches and temples, he identified them not by a race or creed, but rather by the name of the nationality that patronized them.

By identifying himself occasionally with the perspective of Europeans, therefore, Dean Mahomed was not joining their qaum, but he was perhaps tying himself to their interests. The term *'asabiyat* ('group interest', a term so central to the classical sociology of the fourteenth century Muslim scholar, Ibn Khaldun) might reflect the concept that Dean Mahomed implicitly applied to his situation.[54] Therefore, his sociology used a person's birth but also a person's identification with the interests of a particular group (even a group that one was not born into) as the basis of its typology. Thus Dean Mahomed distanced himself from the qaum of his birth but associated himself with the European officers of the Company's army in India, and the European audience for his *Travels* in Ireland as well.

### The Genre Dean Mahomed Chose for His *Travels*

In the last half of 1793, in addition to soliciting subscribers, Dean Mahomed also finished writing *Travels*. He chose to write *Travels* very much in the fashionable English travel narrative genre. He accepted the definitions of authorial voice and content inherent in this genre (at the time) which favoured intertwining pleasure-giving depiction, useful and instructive description, and only limited and modest personal narration.[55] Further, his self-deprecating remarks about his own literary abilities reflected this convention's requirements and his own situation. This genre shaped his enterprise in distinctive ways, different from how genres produced by his natal culture would have done. Although he was probably familiar with Persian and Urdu literary forms of history-writing or travel literature current during his twenty-five years living in north India, little in *Travels* reflected those forms.[56] His clear understanding of, adherence to, and mastery over the conventions of this English literary genre thus provides evidence of his extensive study at a well-stocked and up-to-date library.

Nonetheless, Dean Mahomed's *Travels* clearly differed from most English travel literature in that he was a native of the lands he described. The conventional pattern of the genre—sad departure from home, exotic adventures, grateful return—applied only partially in his case. He began with his emotional parting from his parents and continued with a narrative of his adventures but, instead of a return, his book ended with a simple statement about his arrival in a new land. He did not recount his disembarkation, first impression of England, or particularly remark on his beginning of a new life in Ireland. His use of this genre, therefore, was apparently a deliberate effort to reach out to a literate, Anglophone audience in a specific way.

Dean Mahomed chose to use the epistolary form fashionable for fiction and travel literature in his day. England had produced some 800 epistolary novels by 1790; this form was especially strong in the 1750–1800 period, when approximately one out of every six works of fiction used it.[57] Like most contemporary authors of epistolary travel narratives, he used the fiction of pretending to have written his letters contemporaneously with the events they described. Unlike many other travel works of his day, however, he did not back-date these letters or devise a fictive dialogue with an imaginary correspondent. Although Dean Mahomed began each of the 38 letters in his book with 'Dear Sir', he did not seem to have any single real or imagined person as his intended audience throughout his book. While he occasionally responded to the expectations he imputed to his readers, he never even pretended to dialogue with his fictional correspondent. In part, the epistolary style enabled an author to write more intimately and confidently, to notionally address an (unnamed) friend, rather than a faceless world of unknown readers.

Scholars of the genre of English travel literature traced it back to Horace, yet the genre was continually redefined in the light of the culture of the day. During the eighteenth century, this increasingly popular genre had replaced its earlier 'romantic' style of idealized descriptions with a more factually accurate form that sought as its goal both edification and an artistically pleasing literary effect. Literary authorities including reviewers in such journals as *Monthly Review, Critical Review,* and *Analytical Review* critiqued or praised travel works to the extent that they conformed to, or advanced, these conventions. Until the 1780s, the author could appear only briefly in his or her narrative on pain of being condemned for 'hackneyed encomiums upon himself' or 'conceited egotisms'.[58] Indeed, it was conventional to attribute, as did Dean Mahomed, the impetus for writing the account to the author's friends and supporters, whom the author humbly obeyed (I).

That Dean Mahomed included in *Travels* only limited explicitly autobiographical material also reflected the British worldview of the time. The very term 'autobiography' had not yet been invented (it would first appear in English print in 1809). Weintraub argues that the concept of the individual as a historically minded being only started to develop as a significant cultural function in the West at this time; more recent scholarship has questioned his assertion as ethnocentric.[59] Lejeune defines autobiography as 'Retrospective prose narrative written by a real person concerning his own existence, where the focus is his individual life, in particular the story of his personality.'[60] Dean Mahomed rarely revealed a self-awareness of how he believed he was viewed by either Europeans or other Indians. The only exception was when he, as a boy, first encountered Europeans and described their and the sepoy guards' perceptions of him (II–IV). What few moral lessons he explicitly drew were either from the lives of others (his European patrons, Indian princes, Indian villagers) or else from abstract types (a courtesan, a sepoy). Since Dean Mahomed did not explicitly examine his inner self and, indeed, made his own life only a relatively minor theme in *Travels*, his work would thus qualify less as autobiography than as memoir. He described the outer world of the events, customs, and natural features he encountered. His apparent goals were to provide his readers with pleasure and edification, and also to shape his identity in their eyes. The stylistic requirement that the author must proclaim his own modesty therefore reinforced Dean Mahomed's particular self-location as an artless Indian writing for a sophisticated European audience.

Fortunately for our knowledge of Dean Mahomed's own life, just at the time that he determined to adopt this genre, it was undergoing a shift in its conventions that allowed some autobiographical elements and ethnographic description. Had he published much earlier, therefore, we might have read nothing about him personally in his *Travels*. As it is, we learn little about the details of his life, for example the food he ate or the clothes he wore. He organized his book around chronological and geographical structures but kept both subdued. Dean Mahomed, for instance, implicitly elided entire years. Ordinarily, he only described any particular area of India once; he passed over in silence his subsequent passages through that area, although his personal experiences there would presumably have varied from his earlier visit. Generally, once he had described a place, it had received the full treatment expected by the genre and any return to it would be classed by reviewers as repetitious.

We might view the very conventionality of *Travels* as reflecting Dean Mahomed's own remarkable capacity, and desire, to negotiate space for himself in Anglo-Irish, and later English, respectable society. While describing himself as a native of India, he had himself portrayed in formal English clothes (Illustration 1). Additionally, in order to impress his elite patrons in Ireland, he selected a formal, even Romantic and poetic, writing style. His use of classical quotations (for example, about shampooing) was a vestige of the conventions of travel literature of the earlier part of the century, like Joseph Addison's *Remarks on Several Parts of Italy* (1705). In this way, Dean Mahomed could display his knowledge of classical Latin, Biblical, and English literature. He also presupposed the recognition of his quotations and allusions by his elite audience.

One of the prerequisites of the travel narrative as it was understood by the Anglophone world at this time was veracity. Much fictional travel literature had been published throughout this period, including Robert Challes, *Journal d'un voyage fait aux Indes orientales* (1721), Daniel Defoe, *A New Voyage Around the World* (1725), and Tobias Smollett, *Travels in France and Italy* (1766). As a result, authors of 'true' travel literature had to prove their assertions by an appeal to the higher authority of their own lives. Yet, as Adams comments, 'Since any writer of travels other than pure guidebooks must . . . often approach the boundary between the existent and the uncertain, between facts for facts and facts for pleasure', much of this 'true' literature mixed 'the false with the fact.'[61] As Batton suggests: 'The autobiographical information in eighteenth-century travel accounts thus serves four main functions: it provides a principle of order, conveys entertainment, proves the author is accurate and truthful, and shows him to be the sort of man whose descriptions can be trusted.'[62] In part, Dean Mahomed's self-characterization as 'ingenuous' would thus validate the truth of his narrative.

Further, part of his Dedication pointed out that some of his audience had been present at the events he described: William Massey Baker, Bailie, and the other returned English Company officers who subscribed to his book. These eyewitnesses provided an 'armour of security' that should convince even the most 'judicious' among his readers of the accuracy of his words (Dedication). Thus, while he did enliven his account with some of his own adventures, he would necessarily have to stick to the established story about them as understood by his companions at the time. His most personal adventures (for example, being carried off in a palanquin by unsuspecting thieves or escaping from angry villagers with the Company's funds, VI, XXXI), must have been accepted by his audience then and later. The conventions of the genre suggest he described himself as a 'Native' in order to prove the authenticity of his account, not to marginalize or exoticize himself.

Dean Mahomed, however, did seek to construct an identity among his readers in Ireland. His self-presentation of material from his past was highly selective. He omitted some events and included others according to an agenda that would, presumably, demonstrate to his largely Anglo-Irish audience an identity of his own choosing. Spacks argues that, in the late eighteenth century, social change often appeared threatening: autobiographical writings and fiction both rewarded individuals who retained their essential nature unchanged.[63] Thus, he had to explain himself as retaining his proper social status despite his immigration. For example, he never mentioned his religious conversion, presenting himself as much the same man throughout his *Travels.*

In addition to the leading families of Ireland, Dean Mahomed may also have envisioned as his audience young men considering a career in, or a tour of, India. Soon after this time, English literary convention separated more technical descriptions from personal narrative. Dean Mahomed's delineating Indian cities, industries, geography, flora, and fauna heralded later utilitarian tour guides. The list of Persian terms which he inserted into his book, the duodecimo format (designed as two small volumes for easy portability), and the inclusion (without attribution) of factual descriptions of major cities which he did not himself visit indicate that he intended, at least in part, for his *Travels* to be a functional guide for future travellers in India.[64] Thus, like some early nineteenth century works—including Dean Mahomed's own later book, *Shampooing*—his *Travels* partly reflected the new belief in a more technical science, inappropriate for a purely literary travel narrative. On the other hand, his personal adventures and chronology foretold the largely entertaining travel book of the 'picturesque traveler'.[65] *Travels*, therefore, in its interposition of incidents from his own life, the adventures of others in which he did not appear, and the customs, objects, and scenes he observed all mark it as a multi-faceted example of travel literature in the last decade of the eighteenth century.

To understand Dean Mahomed's approach to this genre, it would be informative to compare his work with contemporary travel narratives written by Europeans. One European travel account comparable to *Travels* in time period and geographical setting was William Hodges, *Travels in India . . . 1780 . . . 1783* (1793). Hodges, an artist who had earlier gone with Captain Cook to the South Pacific, covered much the same territory as Dean Mahomed at some of the same times but he presented a distinctly different picture of India.[66] For example, Hodges and Dean Mahomed both described the island of Jangerah at about the same time. Hodges wrote: 'The situation this holy father has chosen is certainly proof of his taste and of his judgement; for, from the top, he has a most extensive prospect of the country and river; and in the summer heats it must be cooler than any situation in its neighbourhood.'[67] Hodge's artistic description differed considerably from Dean Mahomed's more human-centred one (VII). Hodges wrote nothing about the person of this 'Hindoo monk', which was Dean Mahomed's main focus in his description. Hodges received excellent reviews in the leading literary journals. They lauded Hodges as a man of taste who presented an informed view of India, a subject about which these journals lamented the 'dearth' of information.[68] Likewise, Thomas and William Daniell presented a picture of this same island in their *Antiquities of India* (1799), an image similar to Hodges but different from Dean Mahomed's.[69] The Daniells also received glowing reviews but Dean Mahomed's *Travels*, while known in London, was not even noticed.[70] While Dean Mahomed borrowed, without attribution, large parts of *Travels* from yet another European travel narrative, he retained his own voice throughout.

## Dean Mahomed's Use of Earlier Travels

When Dean Mahomed determined to write a travel narrative about India, he studied earlier travel narratives and paraphrased parts of them, including Jemima Kindersley's *Letters from the Island of Teneriffe . . . and the East Indies* (1777) and—most particularly—John Henry Grose's *Voyage to the East Indies* (1766).[71] Kindersley and Grose present unsympathetic pictures of India and Indians. Nonetheless, Dean Mahomed found aspects of their work worthy of emulation, since he paraphrased or directly lifted material from them without attribution (a practice today termed plagiarism). Grose's work found a popular audience but high literary critics condemned his egotistic violation of the conventions of the genre. Fashionable journals dismissed Grose as too limited in experience, base in character, and opinionated to produce fine literature or ethnography: 'a young man who does not pretend to have seen more than one or two sea-ports of an extensive continent . . . his remarks are often trite or frivolous.'[72] While Dean Mahomed took a number of words from Grose and Kindersley, significantly, he reconstructed them in his own way.

A close comparison of three specific examples will illustrate how Dean Mahomed used Grose's words without accepting his perspective or interpretation. I have italicized in both passages the words Dean Mahomed took from Grose. The first pair of passages described eating betel leaf, something Dean Mahomed knew well enough without having to rely on Grose, and yet he clearly did so:

| *Grose (vol. 1, p. 238)* | *Dean Mahomed (XXVII)* |
|---|---|
| *Another addition* too *they use* of what they call *Catchoo,* being *a blackish granulated perfumed* composition, of the size of a small shot, which they carry in little boxes on purpose. They are pleasingly tasted, and are reckoned *provocatives, when taken alone, which is not a small consideration with the Asiatics in general.* | *Another addition they use,* termed *catchoo,* is *a blackish, granulated, perfumed* substance; and a great *provocative, when taken alone, which is not a small consideration with the Asiatics in general.* |
| They pretend that this use of Betel sweetens the breath, fortifies *the stomach,* though the juice is rarely swallowed, *and preserves the teeth,* though it reddens them; but, I am apt to believe, that there is more of a vitious habit than any medicinal virtue in it, and that it is like *tobacco,* chiefly a matter of pleasure. | It is taken after meals, during a visit, and on the meeting and parting of friends or acquaintance; and most people here are confirmed in the opinion that it also strengthens *the stomach, and preserves the teeth* and gums. It is only used in smoking, with a mixture of *tobacco* and refined sugar, by the Nabobs and other great men, to whom this species of luxury is confined. |

Whereas Grose used this passage to indicate his scepticism about such vicious habits indulged in by natives, Dean Mahomed used some of the same words to describe a healthful and luxurious practice, conducive to polite social intercourse.

Similarly, in describing musicians and female dancers, Dean Mahomed took some of Grose's words but omitted his condemnations of these arts. We can only speculate about the relative personal familiarity of each man with the practitioners of such arts:

| *Grose (vol. 1, p. 139)* | *Dean Mahomed (XV)* |
|---|---|
| *These* dancing-girls *are generally recruited out of the people of all casts and denominations, though not without* especial regard *to beauty or agreeableness; yet even* | . . . *these* creatures, who *are generally recruited out of the people of all casts and denominations, though not without* a peculiar attention *to beauty or agreeableness;* |

the knowledge of their being so *common* cannot *with many* outbalance *their natural and acquired charms*, which will not appear incredible to those, who know how much the Operagirls in France were, and have not yet ceased to be, in fashion. Their dances however would hardly at first relish with Europeans, especially as they are accompanied with a *music* far from delightful, consisting *of* little *drums* they call Gum-gums, *cymbals*, and a sort of *fife*, which make a hideous din, and are played by men, whose effeminacy, grimaces, and uncouth shrivelled features, all-together, shock the eye, and torture the ear. However, by use we become reconciled to the noise, and may observe some not unpleasing airs; with which the dancers keep time: the words often express the matter of a *pantomime* dance, such *as a lover courting his mistress, a procuress* bringing a letter, and *endeavouring to seduce a woman from one gallant to another, a girl timorous and afraid of being caught in an intrigue. All these love-scenes*, the girls execute in character-dances, and with no despicable expression, if they are good proficients in their art; for then their *gestures, air, and steps*, are marking and *well adapted.*

*yet, even the knowledge of their being so common*, is *with many* totally forgotten in the ravishing display of *their natural and acquired charms.*

They dance to the *music of cymbals, fifes*, and *drums*, they term tum-tums,

and often represent in *pantomime* such scenes, *as a lover courting his mistress; a procuress, endeavouring to seduce a woman from one gallant to another;* and *a girl, timorous and afraid of being caught in an intrigue. All these love-scenes*, they perform, in *gestures, air, and steps*, with *well-adapted* expression.

The final pair of passages which I will present also described something which Dean Mahomed understood far more extensive-

ly than did Grose but decided to present largely in Grose's words:
the nature of Islam and the Prophet Muhammad. Once again,
much of the import of these parallel passages differed:

| Grose<br>*(vol. 1, pp. 175–6, 180)* | *Dean Mahomed (XIV)* |
|---|---|
| As to Mahomet himself, there is a faint reverence kept up for his name; which is, however, more more [sic] matter of habit than of devotion: neither was their superstitious regard for him ever pushed that length which is commonly imagined. That furious zeal of which the first Saracen conquerors made such a parade, and so successfully availed themselves, had not so much a *veneration for Mahomet* for its *object*, as *the unity of the Supreme Being*, in the invocation of which, if they joined the commemoration of his name, it was purely out of gratitude for his being *the missionary of that unity*, and *for* his *destroying* that *idol-worship, to which Arabia had continued so long under bondage.* For the rest they looked on him as a mere man, subject to all the failings and passions of one, and *so far from addressing him as a* saint, *that in their* moschs and *orisons, they do not pray to him but for him, recommending him to the divine mercy;* nor is there any such thing, as what has been vulgarly believed, of *pilgrimages to his tomb:* these being, *in a religious sense,* solely *directed to* | The Mahometans are strict adherents to the tenets of their religion, which does not, by any means, consist in that enthusiastic *veneration for Mahomet* so generally conceived: it considers much more, as its primary *object, the unity of the supreme Being,* under the name of Alla: Mahomet is only regarded in a secondary point of view, as *the missionary of that unity,*<br><br>merely *for destroying* the *idol worship, to which Arabia had continued so long under bondage.* and *so far from addressing him as a* deity, *that in their orisons, they do not pray to him, but for him recommending him to the divine mercy.* it is a mistaken, though a generally received opinion, that *pilgrimages* were made *to his tomb,* which, *in a religious sense, were only directed to what is called the cahabah or holy-house at Mecca, an idol temple dedicated by* him |

*[Grose, continued]*

what is called the Cahabah, or holy-house at Mecca; which, having long been *an idol-temple*, was *by* Mahomet *dedicated* to *the unity of God*, and wherein he retained, in compliance to the idolaters, the famous black-stone, which had been worshipped by them as representing Akbar their greatest god. The prophet's *tomb is at Medina, visited by the Mahometans, purely out of curiosity and reverence to his memory*; but the Indian Moors frequently return without ever seeing it at all, though it is so near Mecca . . .

In fact, *most of his* sectaries push *their veneration for the Supreme Being so far, as not only never to mention God* with the least irreverence; *but* they *think it* even *blasphemous to praise or define a Being, whom they* look on *as so infinitely* above *all praise, definition or comprehension*. They do not approve even of terming *him Good, Righteous, Merciful, or* the like; not only for *their thinking such epithets* just as *superfluous*, or even *impertinent, as if one* was *emphatically to say of a man that he had a head*, legs, arms, *or any other members* implied by the very name of man, and of whose having them no one could doubt; but as *they conceive it* is profaning the sacred Majesty *of the name of God, to* associate *it with human attributes* or conceptions, and that nothing fills the

*[Dean Mahomed, continued]*

to the unity of God. His *tomb is at Medina, visited by the Mahometans, purely out of curiosity and reverence to his memory.*

Most *of his* followers carry *their veneration for the supreme Being so far, as not only, never to mention* the word Alla or *God*, on any common occasion, *but think it* in some degree *blasphemous to praise or define a Being, whom they* consider *as so infinitely* transcendent to *all praise, definition or comprehension*. Thus, they carry their scrupulosity to such a length, as not even to approve of calling *him good, righteous, or merciful*, from their thinking such epithets superfluous and *impertinent; as if one* were *emphatically to say of a man that he had a head, or any other member* necessary to the human form: for *they conceive it* to be a profanation *of the name of God, to accompany it with human attributes*, and that no *idea* can be so acceptable *to that Being, as the name itself, a substantive*

| *[Grose, continued]* | *[Dean Mahomed, continued]* |
|---|---|
| idea due *to that Being* so well *as the name itself, a substantive* singularly and for ever above the company of an *adjective.* | infinitely superior and independent of the connexion of any *adjective* to give it the least degree of additional emphasis. |

While many of the words are the same, these two descriptions of Islam and the Prophet Muhammad differ in tone and emphasis.

Overall, Dean Mahomed took about 7 per cent of the words in *Travels* from Grose but only two paragraphs from Kindersley. Based on a careful analysis of these works, we can conclude that Dean Mahomed practised selective appropriation for two reasons. First, he used Grose's phrases for descriptions of topics which he did not know, most notably Surat and Bombay, and classical references by Seneca and Martial. These totalled about a quarter of his borrowings from Grose.

Second, Dean Mahomed deliberately took and reformed descriptions and phrases about topics which he knew well but apparently felt that Grose or Kindersley had stated more fluently or authoritatively for an Anglophone audience. Such topics included descriptions of Fort William in Calcutta, Allahabad architecture, the diet of Hindus, shampooing, coconut trees, jugglers and snake-charmers, the camel, elephant, and rhinoceros as well as the sections presented above on betel, Indian music and dance, and the Prophet Muhammad and Islam. Most extensively, Dean Mahomed used much of Grose's Glossary as his own 'Explanation of Persian and Indian Terms' (XVI). Dean Mahomed obviously knew the English meanings of these Indian terms but wished to rely on Grose's assessment of which terms a European audience would want defined. Of the 97 terms in Dean Mahomed's Glossary, he included only 6 terms that were unique or substantially different in definition from those of Grose: Bazar, Baudshaw, Baudshawjoddi, Codgi, Jemidar, and Mulna (all words of special interest to Dean Mahomed). He also altered 41 of Grose's definitions in some way, while he took exactly 50 from Grose. Dean Mahomed deliberately omitted 22 of the terms which Grose included, particularly terms not relevant to *Travels.*

We should also keep in mind that such extensive copying from earlier works remained quite common in the eighteenth century.

Indeed, Grose himself only added his Glossary in the later editions of his book, taking much of it from the 1761 travel narrative by Richard Cambridge, who himself copied parts of it from yet earlier works.[73] Robert Orme lifted entire sections of his authoritative *History* from an earlier account, without attribution.[74] Further, when Dean Mahomed cited the poetry of Goldsmith or Milton, he did indicate the author, if not always the source of the verses.[75] Dean Mahomed obviously made deliberate and selective use of Grose. When Grose made an error, Dean Mahomed did not automatically follow him. For example, he copied Grose's latitude and longitude for Calcutta but not for Surat (where Grose's error placed Surat as far north as Moscow).[76] Thus, Dean Mahomed retained his own voice, even if some of the words were those of Grose or Kindersley.

### The Issue of Voice

Although Dean Mahomed wrote *Travels* twenty-four years after the first events it narrated, and ten years after its point of termination, the specific details of names and places which he presented have proven quite precise. It is highly unlikely that Dean Mahomed himself took notes about all his adventures at the time (especially since they began at age eleven). He may have supplemented his memory (and perhaps any later notes) with material from the memories, diaries, or other papers of the Anglo-Irish officers then living in Cork who served with him in India. His account of the capture of Gwalior, for example, would seem to be based on another man's notes, since Dean Mahomed apparently never visited the city and copied the name as Ganlin. Nevertheless, *Travels* as a whole stands clearly as Dean Mahomed's own work. He orchestrated his various sources into his own narrative, as he understood and wished to present it to his Anglo-Irish patrons.

We can explore any possible particularly strong influences on the author by individual Europeans. First, we know that Godfrey Evan Baker had a tremendous influence on Dean Mahomed until 1786. When Dean Mahomed published *Travels*, however, Baker had been dead for over seven years. Further, while Dean Mahomed's relationship to Baker formed a core theme in *Travels*, this book was neither dedicated nor addressed to Baker or any of his relatives. All this would suggest that while Baker's notes or diary (if they existed) may have guided Dean Mahomed, Baker was himself not a direct 'voice' in *Travels*, although the lingering effects of his influence over Dean Mahomed's perceptions and forms of expression would presumably have continued after Baker's death. Baker's youngest brother, William Massey Baker, was in India until 1796, two years after Dean Mahomed published *Travels*. We know less about the relationship between the other Bakers and Dean Mahomed, but none had experience in India or appeared by name in the text. Thus, the Baker clan, while evidently supportive of Dean Mahomed, could not have directly contributed much to the content of *Travels*.

Another possibility is that Dean Mahomed's wife, Jane, might have guided the writing of *Travels*. They were married eight years before *Travels* came out. Internal evidence from *Travels*, however, indicates that Jane was neither his main intended audience nor apparently a determining voice in his narrative. At least in his first Letters, Dean Mahomed's ostensible correspondent was explicitly a man familiar with India. *Travels* lays heavy emphasis on military life in the field. In sharp contrast, European women writing about India at that time stressed domestic concerns or European life in urban India, subjects which Dean Mahomed gave limited attention to.[77]

The third possible influence on Dean Mahomed's narrative was William Annesley Bailie, to whom the book was dedicated. *Travels* praised Bailie extravagantly whenever his name appeared. Dean Mahomed addressed Bailie in the Dedication. As the book went on, however, he shifted away from addressing Bailie directly. Dean Mahomed's inclusion of lists of Indian terms and of the military ranks in the Company's army, with translations and definitions, would indicate that Bailie was not Dean Mahomed's main intended audience since he would already know all this. It is quite possible that Bailie gave direction to Dean Mahomed's work, but Bailie was present at very few of the actual incidents that Dean Mahomed described and therefore could not have determined their content. A further puzzling element that might discount Bailie's influence over *Travels* was Dean Mahomed's anomalous insertion of a brief description of a 'victory' by Colonel William A. Baillie in 1780 near Arcot (XXX). The wording of this insertion suggested that Dean Mahomed may have confused William A. Baillie with William A. Bailie. The wording Dean Mahomed used in both passages was nearly identical: 'Col. William Ann. Bailie . . . distinguished himself by his intrepid zeal and gallantry in this expedition' (XXI); 'The Colonel [William A. Baillie] as usual, distinguished himself on this occasion with great firmness and intrepidity' (XXX). Baillie's victory which Dean Mahomed mentioned was actually a severe defeat at the hands of Haidar Ali (involving as it did 3720 Company officers and men killed or captured, including Baillie, who died in one of Haidar Ali's prisons two years later). William A. Bailie was at that time fighting the Marathas near Bombay. Either Dean Mahomed gratuitously inserted an obvious falsehood—one not relevant to the events that provided its context in *Travels*—or else he had confused these two men. In the latter case, at least, Bailie would presumably have distinguished himself from the defeated Baillie, had he been directing Dean Mahomed's pen. In short, no single European seems, as an individual, to have been a major voice in *Travels*, although the book did respond to and reflect Dean Mahomed's presence in their society in Cork.

As with any autobiographical work, there must have been many reasons that Dean Mahomed wrote *Travels*, and wrote it in the way he did. He clearly intended that his readers should learn about his past as he presented it. As we shall see, his second autobiographical work, *Shampooing*, recast his life in very different ways, reflecting his social context at that point in his life. We can suppose that Dean Mahomed, located as he was as an Indian immigrant in Cork, also wished to answer questions in his own mind as to his identity.

### Dean Mahomed's Production of *Travels*

After he completed writing *Travels* on 15 January 1794, Dean Mahomed spent much of the rest of that year dealing with his printer. Like many authors of his day, Dean Mahomed published his own work. In England and Ireland both, books tended to be printed not by independent, established publishing houses, but rather by printers who were often booksellers as well. After he had received the advance cash instalments from his subscribers for 385 sets of *Travels*, totaling £104 5s. 5d., he could negotiate with Cork's four or more printers for the production of his work. Since the average press run, even in Dublin at this time, was 350–500 copies, he generated a respectable advance booking for his work.[78] In addition to the copies promised to subscribers, Dean Mahomed may have had another hundred or so copies printed for over-the-counter sales. He eventually contracted with John Connor, an established Cork printer, bookseller, and founder of a new lending library to set the type, supply the paper, print the signatures of, and bind *Travels*.

The economics of book publishing in Ireland at that time remained uncertain, even with such advance payments in hand. Many printers in Britain in those days cut costs by eliminating payments to authors: reprinting unauthorized editions of popular works. Irish printers proved particularly successful in using their lower labour costs to print inexpensive editions of works by English authors, which could then be exported to England, underselling English editions (even unauthorized editions). A continuing problem for Irish printers, however, was the supply of quality paper, which had to be imported. Dean Mahomed promised in his prospectus that his subscribers would receive 'fine paper' but at least some of the surviving copies of *Travels* (perhaps those sold over-the-counter instead of by subscription) had relatively coarse paper.

Once the signatures were ready late in 1794, Dean Mahomed probably had some of them bound and then personally saw both to their delivery to his subscribers and to the collection of the other half-crown each owed him. For non-subscribers who purchased the completed work from one of the several booksellers in Cork, the binding tended to express their personal taste. Even books written by famous authors would often be sold in signatures, unbound. The purchaser would then have the choice of binding—including calf-skin, boards, or paper—at a range of prices. For example, *Travels* was printed as two volumes but could be bound by the purchaser in one. The few copies of *Travels* that have survived reveal several different kinds of binding.

*Travels* made little impact on the London market. Although at least some literary figures in London read Dean Mahomed's work, none of the major journals reviewed it. This was not unusual for books written by Irish authors.

The Irish book trade at this time remained largely secondary to England's. This was especially true of publishing in Cork, which stood as secondary to Dublin. Lists of books available at booksellers in Cork, and Dublin as well, indicated a vast preponderance of English authors and English-produced books. In part, this is explained by the relatively smaller literate population in Ireland: not only fewer authors, but fewer book buyers and readers. Since bookselling often depended on economies of scale (i.e. amortizing the costs of setting and producing the book over large print runs), Ireland was not as attractive a market. Further, within the Anglo-Irish elite, many felt marginal to the world of London culture which lent prestige to English authors, even in Ireland.

At the price and apparent print-run of *Travels*, Dean Mahomed would apparently have obtained at best only a small profit, certainly not enough to retire on. He might have made about 1 shilling per book above his costs. At 400–500 copies, this equalled £20–25. Thus, he probably knew in advance that he wrote *Travels* for a social goal, not an economic one. We can presume that Dean Mahomed's successful completion of the project of writing, publishing, and delivering *Travels* enhanced his social position.


## Dean Mahomed and Jane in Cork (1794–*c.* 1807)

While Dean Mahomed and Jane seem to have lived fairly comfortably during their years in Cork, their sources of income are not known. Dean Mahomed may have brought some capital with him from India to Ireland. Godfrey Evan Baker may have helped establish Dean Mahomed in Cork, using money Baker had acquired in India, his family's extensive properties, or sums brought by his wealthy marriage into the Massey family. The wide range of commercial enterprises that the Baker clan managed would presumably have had room for Dean Mahomed somewhere. Jane Daly may also have brought property with her into their marriage; based on our estimate of her date of birth, she would have just turned 21 years old at the time Dean Mahomed began publishing his *Travels*. Unlike Dean Mahomed's later careers in England, however, he did not engage in an occupation in Cork that brought him into the public eye through newspaper advertisements or newsworthy activities.[79] Most plausibly, Dean Mahomed worked as the manager of the Baker household, probably not a servant in livery but not an independent gentleman either. He later claimed much experience in marketing and running a kitchen. As a manager, Dean Mahomed would have had some status in society but would have been dependent on his patrons, the Bakers.

Since Godfrey Evan Baker had died without a will in 1786, less than two years after he and Dean Mahomed arrived in Cork, Dean Mahomed could not have been dependent on him alone, as was the case for some of their time together in India. The father, Godfrey Baker, died in 1788 and with him much of the family's access to patronage in Cork city government. Godfrey Baker's surviving sons were Peter (died unmarried in 1797), Hugh Cossart (Captain, 27th Foot of the Royal Army, died in 1802), and William Massey Baker (in India until 1796 when he returned on leave).[80] Particularly following the quick remarriage of Godfrey Evan Baker's widow, the Honourable Margaret (1788) and the death of Godfrey Baker's widow, Elizabeth (1792), there would have been few of the immediate Baker family present in Cork with whom Dean Mahomed may have had close bonds, until William Massey Baker's return from India.[81]

The dedication of *Travels* to Bailie and inclusion of Edward Heard among the subscribers would indicate that Dean Mahomed's circle of social intercourse was wider than the Bakers alone, particularly among India-returned officers. Having drawn great wealth from India, such officers continued their bonds to it. At least two named their estates after places in India: 'Patna' (William Popham) and 'Fortwilliam' (Baker). Dean Mahomed apparently found a place for himself and his growing family within their society.

William Massey Baker, well known by Dean Mahomed from their time together in India, returned to Cork, on leave from the Company's army in 1796. This Baker had done extremely well financially in India, engaging in a variety of commercial activities, rather than depending on his Army salary alone.[82] It is not clear if he returned with his Anglo-Indian daughter, Eleanor, whom he baptized in Calcutta at the end of 1785.[83] Soon after his arrival in Cork, this Baker purchased—for a reported £2500—a large landholding a few miles from Cork and built a fine Georgian house, with all the latest conveniences, on the site.[84] His mansion, Fortwilliam, still stands today (Illustration 5).

Since William Massey Baker's only brother with an interest in the city, Peter, had died in 1797, he apparently saw no need to continue the family house on the South Mall in downtown Cork so he sold or let his interest in it in 1799.[85] Baker repeatedly extended his leave from the Company (until 1800). He also assumed his family's leading civic role, remaining particularly active in the maintenance of law and order and the pro-England movement that led up to the Act of Union of 1800.[86] When the Bakers shifted their household to Fortwilliam and give up their South Mall home, Dean Mahomed may have set up his own household on the estate. There, through a chain of remarkable conjunctions, Dean Mahomed met an Indian traveller in 1799.

A series of dignitaries from India, and elsewhere in Asia, made visits to Britain in the eighteenth and early nineteenth century.[87] Unlike Dean Mahomed, none settled there and none wrote books in English, directly for European audiences. Among these visiting dignitaries, Abu Talib Khan remains of particular relevance to us. Like Dean Mahomed, Abu Talib both claimed descent from immigrants to India from Iran and was related (by marriage) to the Nawabs of Bengal. Abu Talib had served several times in the administration of Awadh, each time forced to flee from that state by a change in factional alignments at court. He also had extensive service in several posts in the English Company, having secured the patronage of the Governor General of India, Cornwallis (1786–93) and other leading Company officials. Thus, he came from much the same Muslim service elite background as Dean Mahomed. He had, however, reached somewhat higher positions in it. By 1799, Abu Talib found himself unemployed but obtained the invitation of Captain David Richardson to accompany him to London as a self-proclaimed 'Persian Prince'.

At the end of a difficult sea-journey, adverse winds kept Abu Talib's ship from reaching London directly. His ship instead sought shelter in Cork's harbour. Tired of the sea and shipboard-fare, Abu Talib went ashore. He then decided to travel by land to Dublin, where he hoped to renew the patronage of Cornwallis, then viceroy of Ireland (1798–1801). While dining in Cork, Abu Talib fortuitously encountered William Massey Baker, whom he and Richardson had known in India. Baker invited Abu Talib to his estate outside of town, to show off its modern conveniences. While there, on 7 December 1799, Abu Talib met and chatted with Dean Mahomed. After Abu Talib's triumphant season in London's high society, he returned to Indian and unemployment. Thirteen years later, he wrote an (Persian language) account of his travels in Europe based on his notes of the trip. My complete translation from Abu Talib's Persian account of his chance meeting with Dean Mahomed provides many suggestions as to the latter's condition at this time:

### Mention of a Muslim named Dean Mahomed

Another person in the house of the aforementioned Captain [William Massey Baker] is named Dean Mahomed. He is from Murshidabad. A brother of Captain [William Massey] Baker raised him from childhood as a member of the family. He brought him to Cork and sent him to a school [*maktab*] where he learned to read and write English well. Dean Mahomed, after studying, ran off to another city with the daughter, known to be fair and beautiful, of a family of rank [*sharafi*] of Cork who was studying in the school [*madrasa*]. He then married [*nikah*] her and returned to Cork. He now has several beautiful children with her. He has a separate house and wealth [*khana 'ala 'hida o tamauwul*] and he wrote a book [*kitab*] containing some account of himself and some about the customs [*rusum*] of India [*Hind*].[88]

Abu Talib paid surprisingly limited attention to Dean Mahomed despite the incongruity of their meeting. This may indicate that the former considered himself socially superior and Dean Mahomed beneath extensive notice. Nevertheless, he states Dean Mahomed's social position provided him some independence in income and living arrangements, clearly not the status of a servant. Further, Abu Talib considered Dean Mahomed still a Muslim, at least by culture. In his writings and self-reported behaviour, Abu Talib showed a particular interest in sexual relationships between Indian men and European women, so he appears to have probed Dean Mahomed and the Bakers about Dean Mahomed's marriage and Jane's status. This extremely fortunate, but unfortunately brief, independent description of Dean Mahomed's life in Ireland at the end of the eighteenth century seems to confirm the sketchy internal evidence in *Travels* about his life there.

## The Departure of Dean Mahomed from Ireland (*c.* 1807)

Early in the eighteenth century, Dean Mahomed and his family decided to leave Ireland and move to London. We may never know the full reason, or combination of reasons, why they took this decision. A possible contributing cause might have been a degradation in their social or economic condition in Cork. By this time, many of their circle of people with Indian connections had died or left Ireland. Bailie had sold or let his Irish holdings and moved to England in 1799.[89] William Massey Baker, having delayed his return to India long enough to attain sufficient seniority for his promotion to Major, left Ireland for India in 1800.[90] Much later in his life, Dean Mahomed reportedly explained his coming to England as the result of a bank failure; perhaps his finances suffered a reverse at this time in Cork.[91] Other possibilities might include a personal tragedy in their family (although no deaths were reported in the newspapers).

The most probable cause of Dean Mahomed's departure would seem to have been a change in his relationship to the Bakers. Soon after Major William Massey Baker's second return from India to Ireland in 1806, he married (19 February 1807) Mary Towgood Davies, the well-born daughter of Reverend Richard Davies. We can speculate that her assumption of authority over the Fortwilliam household may have made Dean Mahomed's place there uncongenial, leading to his emigration. Whatever factors pushed him from Ireland or attracted him to London, Dean Mahomed was at this time nearly fifty, unusually late in life in that era to undertake such a radical change.

During his years in Ireland, Dean Mahomed learned much about European society and the ways to make himself a successful place within it. One business that he saw prospering around him in Cork, a business that he himself would soon take up, was exotic medicine. The Cork newspapers contained both attractive advertisements, and editorial praise, for a range of nostrums and health-aids, often with an oriental slant such as 'Oriental Tooth Powder' and 'Asiatic Tooth Powder'.[92] Dean Mahomed would himself later sell such tooth powder.

In addition, hot and cold sea bathing, as a health measure, burgeoned at spas in the Cork area, as they did elsewhere in Ireland and in England at this time. Medicinal springs scattered around the Cork area had long been popular.[93] From the 1790s in particular, several coastal towns established spas, as well as regular transportation from Cork city, for clients seeking health through salt-water and steam bathing.[94] Both these branches of medicine would prove essential in Dean Mahomed's final career, although no evidence suggests that he was aware of this as he and his family emigrated from Ireland to London around 1807.

## Notes

1. William J. Smyth, 'Social, Economic and Landscape Transformations', in Patrick O'Flanagan and Cornelius G. Buttimer, *Cork History and Society* (1993), pp. 655–98; Andy Bielenberg, *Cork's Industrial Revolution* (1991).
2. Edwards, *Cork Remembrancer*, p. 215.
3. See maps in the Cork Public Library including: Survey of the City and Suburbs of Cork, J. Rocque (1773); Plan of the City and Suburbs of Cork, William Beauford (1801) and Thomas Holt (1832).
4. Khan, *Travels* (1810), 1: 98.
5. de Latocnaye, *Frenchman's Walk*, tr. John Stevenson (1984 edition), p. 73. Other travellers concurred. E.g. Sir Richard Colt Hoare, *Journal* (1807), pp. 83–6.
6. CEP 18/11/1790. The city proper had a population at some 57,000 in 1796 and about 80,000 by the early nineteenth century.
7. CEP 18/11/1790
8. Mary Francis Cusack, *History of the City* (1875), p. 402.
9. D. Dodd, *Traveller's Director* (1801), p. 87. Indeed, tensions between Catholic tenants and Protestant landlords continued to rise; in about 1870 a relative of Baker, who had evicted some tenants from his estate in Tipperary, was killed. G. Locker Lampson, *Consideration* (1907), p. 337.
10. William Wilson, *Post-chaise Companion* (1784), pp. 138–9; Dodd, *Traveler's*, p. 86. Horatio Townsend, *Statistical Survey* (1810).
11. In 1748, he was at the centre of a medical controversy. C[harles] J.F. MacCarthy, 'Patrick Blair M.D.', *Journal of the Cork Historical and Archaeological Society*, 90, 249 (1985), pp. 104–19.
12. Townsend, *Statistical*, p. 695; Cork Corporation, *Council Book* (1876); Charles Smith, *Ancient and Present State* (1774).
13. Charles Bernard Gibson, *History of the County* (1861), 2: 217–18.
14. *Volunteer Journal* 19/5/1786.
15. Smith, *Ancient* 1: 407; William O'Sullivan, *Economic History* (1937), p. 208.
16. Many of the Baker clan were Freemen including Godfrey Baker's other

sons Peter (1784), Hugh Cossart Baker (1785), and William Massey Baker (1787). *Corporation Book, passim.*

17. He appeared as a patron of Captain Robert Parker, *Memoirs* (1746). Godfrey Baker's sons Godfrey Evan and William Massey served in the Company's Bengal Army. His second son, Hugh, became Captain in His Majesty's 27th Foot. Among grandsons, three became East India Company officers while four entered the Royal Army in the Royal Artillery, Royal Engineers, Fusiliers, and 51st Light Infantry respectively.

18: HC 27/2/1797.

19. CG 21/11/1792; HC 5/5/1796, 22/12/1796, 22/2/1798, 9/4/1798.

20. CEP 31/1/1788.

21. Marriages linked the Bakers of Cork to the Bomford, Cossart, Davies, Massey, Pope, Phipps, Swayne, and Wrixon families.

22. 'Index to Marriage Licence Bonds, Cashel and Emly Diocese', 1785, PRO Ireland, *Corporation Book.*

23. HC 4/2/1788.

24. Godfrey Evan Baker was survived by a son, Godfrey Hugh Massey Baker (1786/7–1877). Baker's widow remarried, in Dublin, to Captain Hugh Wheeler of Ballywire (Limerick), H.E.I.C.N.S. and had a son, Sir Hugh Massey Wheeler (1788/9–1857), Major General, K.C.B., also in the Company's service. 'Index to Prerogative Wills', Godfrey Evan Baker, Cork, Esq., deceased 1786 intestate, 'Index to Original Wills, Diocese of Dublin, 1800–1850', 'Marriage Licence, Godfrey Hugh Massey and Elizabeth Grace Baker, 1812, 272, T 238', and 'Attested Will of Godfrey Hugh Massey Baker of Grove Hill, Kent (1877)', PRO Ireland; John Bernard Burke, *Burke's Irish Family Records* (1976 edition), s.v. 'Baker'; Rosemary Ffolliott, *Biographical Notices* (1980).

25. 'Index to Marriage Licence Bonds, Cork and Ross Diocese, Deane Mahomet and Jane Daly, 1786', PRO Ireland. Khan, 'Masir', fols 97–8; Khan, *Travels* 1: 102–3. If we estimate a minimum age of 14 at the time of her marriage, she would have been born in 1772. This would make her 47 at the time she bore her last surviving child in 1819, a late—but biologically possible—age. Obituaries of two descendants suggest that Dean Mahomet may have remarried, to an Englishwoman from Bath, also named Jane. *Guy's Hospital Reports* (1885) 63: 1–10; BH August 4, 1888. No definitive evidence, however, has yet appeared to substantiate this possibility. Jane gave herself several dates of birth: the 1841 census has 1791; her gravestone (St Nicholas Church, Brighton) and her obituaries say 1780. BG January 2, 1851; BH January 4, 1851.

26. Marriage laws (dating from 1697) repressed the marriage of Protestants with non-Protestants. The even stricter Bills of 1743 and 1745 nullified any such intermarriages; later a penalty of death was attached by Parliament to violators of these marriage laws. Only from 1782 did the Catholic clergy obtain the right to celebrate marriages, although inter-religious marriages remained outlawed at the time of Dean Mahomed and Jane's wedding.

27. Dean Mahomed's list of subscribers for *Travels* includes only two named Daly. The first, 'Mr J. Daly', may have been Jeremiah Daly, a haberdasher and tailor, who had a shop on Cork's South Main Street in 1787. The second, 'Daly and Travers' (who subscribed for three sets of *Travels*), was a firm of booksellers, printers, and stationers in Cork headed by Eugene Daly (d. 1809). This Daly is also not a likely candidate for Jane's father, since his firm neither printed, nor received subscriptions, nor advertised *Travels*. Their subscription for three sets of *Travels* would thus probably indicate only a commercial, not a personal, interest in Dean Mahomed's work.

28. See Linda Colley, *Britons* (1992).

29. HC 20/6/1785.

30. CG 12/12/1795.

31. CG 20/7/1791.

32. CG 14/4/1792.

33. CG 17/8/1791.

34. CG 26/10/1791.

35. CG 25/2/1795.

36. Edward Gibbon, *Decline and Fall* (1776–86), Chapter 50. CG 11/6/1791.

37. Many saw the play as a veiled attack on the immorality of all office holders. This play was first performed in England in 1744 and remained quite popular through the end of the century. Citations from this work appeared repeatedly in the press. HC 20/11/1788, 24/3/1796, 11/2/1799.

38. CG 1/10/1791; HC 31/8/1804; CA 31/3/1807. Coincidently, the most popular actor who took this leading role on the London stage in 1796 was Mrs Jordan, long time mistress to the Prince Regent George, Dean Mahomed's future patron.

39. E.g. 'A Voyage to India, An Operatic Performance'. CA 16/7/1807.

40. Prabhu Guptara, *Black British Literature* (1986).

41. See Henry Louis Gates, Jr., 'James Gronniosaw', in James Olney, ed., *Studies in Autobiography* (1988), pp. 51–72. See also Homi Bhabha, 'Signs Taken for Wonders', in Henry Gates, ed. *'Race', Writing, and Difference* (1985), pp. 163–84.

42. Henry Louis Gates, Jr., ed., *Classic Slave Narratives* (1987). See also Angelo Costanzo, *Surprising Narrative* (1987); Paul Edwards and David Dabydeen, eds, *Black Writers* (1991).

43. For example, Hickey wrote about an Indian slave boy in London '. . . the boy in question . . . being now a Christian [his former owner] could no longer be justified, nor would the law permit him, to treat him as a slave.' Hickey, *Memoirs* 3: 150–1.

44. One grandson became a Church of England vicar, the Reverend James Dean Kerriman Mahomed (1853–1935). Only due to English hostility to the Ottoman Emperor during World War I did some of his great-grandchildren drop the name Mahomed and adopt that of Deane. J.

Stewart Cameron and Jackie Hicks, 'Frederick Akbar Mahomed', *International Kidney* (forthcoming).

45. CG 16/3/1793.

46. I could find this ad only in the *Cork Gazette* and not in the other papers of the day. This contrasted with his later lavish use of public advertising in newspapers in Brighton.

47. Personal communication from Sister Mary Hourigan, Librarian, Ursuline Convent, Blackrock 15/9/1994.

48. To CoD 7/12/1782, FTWM 9: 330. See Burke's *Landed Gentry of Ireland*, s.n. Bailie of Ringdufferin; V.P.C. Hodson, *List* (1927) 1: 71–2.

49. HC 29/8/1799.

50. Personal communication from Mary Pollard, 3/10/1994.

51. J. Jean Hecht, 'Continental and Colonial Servants', *Smith College Studies in History*, vol. 40 (1954).

52. For a European woman's view of her husband's Muslim family in the early nineteenth century see Ali, *Observations*.

53. For discussion of other 'native ethnographers' see Richard Burghart, 'Ethnographers', in Richard Fardon, *Localizing Strategies* (1990), 260–79.

54. See Ibn Khaldun, *Muqaddimah* tr. Franz Rosenthal (1967).

55. See Charles Batten, *Pleasurable Instruction* (1978).

56. One dominant form of 'Muslim travel literature' was the Rihla, another was accounts of the Haj. See Dale F. Eickelman and James Piscatori, *Muslim Travellers* (1990). For a later and quite different sort of travel account by a Muslim in Europe, see Muhammad As-Saffar, *Disorienting Encounters*, ed. and trans. Susan Gilson Miller (1991). See also Eric J. Leed, *Mind of the Traveler* (1991), Ibrahim Abu-Lughod, *Arab Rediscovery* (1963), Henri Pérès, 'Voyageurs Musulmans', in *Mémoires de l'Institut Français d'Archéologie Orientale du Caire*, LXVIII (1940), and Bernard Lewis, *Muslim Discovery* (1982), Mary Louise Pratt, 'Scratches', in Henry Louis Gates, Jr. ed., *'Race', Writing, and Difference* (1986), pp. 138–62. Carter states, 'The term "contact literatures" has been used to refer to creative writing by non-Western bilingual users of English in typical non-Western settings where English is primarily used as an institutionalized second language. Such literatures exhibit stylistic, ideological and discoursal characteristics which differ markedly from the traditional "canons" of English literature.' Ron Carter, 'A Question of Interpretation: An Overview of Some Recent Developments in Stylistics', in Theo D'hean, ed. *Linguistics and the Study of Literature* (1986), p. 18n.

57. See Percy G. Adams, *Travel Literature* (1983); Robert Adams Day, *Told in Letters* (1966); Frank G. Black, 'Technique', *Harvard Studies and Notes in Philology and Literature* XV (1933).

58. E.g. Review of Philip Thicknesse *Observations* in *Critical Review* 22 (1766), 434 and 25 (1768), 284 as cited in Batton, *Pleasurable*, p. 39.

59. Karl Weintraub, 'Autobiography', in *Critical Inquiry* 1, 4 (June 1975), pp. 821–48. For a discussion of a Mughal 'individualistic' autobiography see Stephen F. Dale, 'Steppe Humanism', *International Journal of Middle*

*East Studies*, vol. 22, no. 1 (February 1990), 37–58. Von Grunebaum argues that the pre-modern Islamic biographical tradition generated impersonal stereotypes rather than individual characters. Gustav E. Von Grunebaum, *Medieval Islam* (1953).

60.  See Philippe Lejeune, *On Autobiography*, tr. Katherine M. Leary (1989), p. 4; James Olney, ed. *Autobiography* (1980); Robert Folkenflik, ed., *Culture of Autobiography* (1993).

61.  Percy G. Adams, *Travelers* (1962).

62.  Batton, *Pleasurable*, p. 76.

63.  Patricia Meyer Spacks, *Imagining a Self* (1976).

64.  Batton, *Pleasurable*, pp. 84–5.

65.  E.g. Tobias Smollett, *Travels* (1949 reprint of 1766?), and William Gilpin, *Observations on the River Wye* (1782) and *Observations on the Western Parts of England* (1798). Batten, *Pleasurable*, pp. 29–30.

66.  See Barbara Maria Stafford, *Voyage into Substance* (1984).

67.  Hodges, *Travels*, p. 26.

68.  *Monthly Review*, 9 n.s. (May–August 1793): 133–8 and *Critical Review*, 7 n.s. (March 1793): 335–46.

69.  Thomas and William Daniell, *Antiquities* (1799) pl. 9, 'W.W. View of the Fakeer's Rock' and *Oriental Scenery* (1816), part 5, pls 9, 10. See Mildred G. Archer, *Early Views* (1980).

70.  *Willis' Current Notes* (1851), pp. 22–3.

71.  Jemima (Mrs Nathaniel Edward) Kindersley lived in Allahabad, 1767–68; two paragraphs in Dean Mahomet's Letter XIX paraphrase her pages 251–3. Grose first published his book in 1757 with expanded editions in 1766, 1767, and 1772; part appeared in John Knox, *New Collection* (1767), 2: 474–96.

72.  E.g. Review of first edition of Grose in *Monthly Review* 17 (July–December 1757): 301–6.

73.  Richard Owen Cambridge, *Account of the War* (1761), glossary of 'Indian and Persic Terms'.

74.  Orme borrowed from John Dalton, *Memoirs* (1886).

75.  Dean Mahomed cited: Oliver Goldsmith's 'The Hermit' (which Goldsmith himself quoted from Edward Young's 'The Complaint; or Night Thoughts', Night Four); John Milton, *Paradise Lost*, lines 1101–7; and *New Testament*, Mathew 25: 35.

76.  Letter XXV had Surat correctly at 21 degrees, 30 minutes north latitude, while Grose, 2: 320, had 52 degrees, 38 minutes north latitude.

77.  See Ali, *Observations;* Shade, *Narrative;* and Fay, *Original Letters.* See also Eliza Hamilton's fictional *Translation.*

78.  See M[ary] Pollard, *Dublin's Trade in Books* (1989), pp. 118ff; Robert Munter, *Dictionary of the Print Trade in Ireland* (1988).

79.  Extensive scrutiny of most of the surviving newspapers from Cork for the 1784–1808 period has failed to reveal any advertisements or mention of Dean Mahomed except relating to *Travels*.

80.  'Index to Prerogative Wills', Peter Baker, Cork, Gentleman, deceased

1797 and Hugh Cossart Baker, Cork, Esq., deceased 1802; T3681, 'Admonition of the Goods of Hugh Cossart Baker of Cork, deceased intestate 20 February 1802', PRO Ireland.

81. 'Index to Marriage Bonds, Cashel and Emly Diocese', Hugh Wheeler and Honorable Margaret Baker, 1788, PRO Ireland; CEP 2/4/1792; MS. 139, p. 78, Genealogical Society, Dublin.

82. BPbC 23/9/1785.

83. 'Baptisms in Calcutta,' *Bengal Past and Present,* 28 (1924): 199.

84. See Mark Bence-Jones, *Guide to Irish Country Houses* (1978), p. 126. Bengal Military Consultation Resolution 7/12/1795, FTWM 20: 610–11, Hoare, *Journal,* p. 84; Khan, 'Masir', ff. 97–8; Townsend, *Statistical,* pp. 700–2.

85. NCEP 22/4/1799; CA 20/7/1799.

86. HC 29/3/1798, 9/4/1798, 12/8/1799; NCEP 22/4/1799.

87. See Harihar Das, 'Early Indian Visitors', *Calcutta Review,* 3rd series, 13 (1924): 83–114 and Simon Digby, 'Eighteenth Century Narrative', in Christopher Shackle ed., *Urdu and Muslim South Asia* (1989), pp. 49–65.

88. Khan, 'Masir,' ff. 97–8.

89. HC 29/8/1799.

90. Minutes of CoD 11/7/1798, 18/7/1798, 28/11/1798, 5/12/1798, 10/4/1799, 26/3/1800, 28/3/1800, IOL; From CoD 11/6/1800, FTWM 21: 178.

91. Granville, who did not know about Dean Mahomed's decades in Ireland, attributes this failure to a bank in Calcutta but this may have been his own interpolation. A.B. Granville, *Spas of England* (1841) 2: 562–4.

92. HC 2/12/1799, 10/4/1800; CEP 4/4/1792.

93. Townsend, *Statistical,* p. 556; Wilson, *Post-chaise,* p. 139; Constantia Elizabeth Maxwell, *Country and Town* (1940), pp. 266ff.

94. For advertisements for baths at Youghal, Kinsale, and Passage see CEP 21/6/1790; HC 7/12/1804; CMC 5/12/1804; CA 15/5/1806, 5/6/1806, 5/5/1807.

# Chapter Six

# The World of London (c. 1807–13)

## Indian and Irish Immigrants in Cosmopolitan London

When Dean Mahomed and his family—including his ten year old son William and perhaps other children born in Cork—immigrated to London around 1807, they entered a cosmopolitan city quickly becoming the capital of an empire. London surpassed both Calcutta and Cork in scale and power. As the core of the capitalist world system, London drew its wealth from both England's industrializing economy and its colonies. Decisions made by London mercantile corporations, by Parliament, and by the British civil and military administration had profound effects on the people of India, Ireland, and the other colonies. At the same time, the actions of Indians and Irishmen and women powerfully affected the implementation of London's policies and the development of British society.

One result of British expansion was a counter-flow of ideas and peoples from the colonies coming to the metropolis, drawn by its wealth and contributing to it. London attracted many immigrants from Ireland. Several of Dean Mahomed's Anglo-Irish patrons had already moved to England; many of these absentee landlords would continue to draw rents from their Irish estates.[1] Numerous Irishmen and women entered the growing English economy, but they often found themselves in the bottom social and economic strata. As England developed its national identity, it largely did so over and against the Irish and other 'colonials'.[2] Even the Anglo-Irish often felt prejudiced against; Dean Mahomed never again referred in print to his many years in Ireland or his Anglo-Irish family.

Many immigrants from Asia also became part of the cosmopolitan society of the capital. British 'Nabobs' returned from

India with vast fortunes and tastes that distinguished them in—
and from—the established society of the capital.[3] These and less
successful Britons returning from India introduced new tastes
and practices in London. 'Eastern wisdom' (including medical
knowledge) and spices had always held an attraction for Europeans. By the early nineteenth century, the volume of exchange
had become such that the lands of Asia did not just provide
spices to flavour European foods, now whole new cuisines entered
the English palate. London had developed an insatiable appetite
for both luxury goods and health-producing agents. People believed that both could be drawn from India. Dean Mahomed
discovered in London that he could use his Indian identity to
offer health and pleasure.

Many more Indians worked to find places for themselves in the
capital.[4] Sections of London, especially around the dock-lands,
had become by the early nineteenth century the temporary abode
of up to two thousand Asian seamen—either between voyages or
marooned there. As the Directors of the English Company saw
it, the presence of indigent Indian servants and sailors in London
represented a financial burden. By law, the Company had the
responsibility (and financial obligation) to repatriate these Indians
rather than allow them to remain in London's slums. Grose
presented a typical description of the condition of unemployed
Indians in London:

> The public has here seen some of these miserable objects about the
> streets of London, begging charity, and exposed to all the distresses
> incident to persons so far remote from their native country, friendless,
> and abandoned, for want of knowing the laws and customs here,
> which joined to the thoughtlessness one would think natural to those
> of their rank on that element, rendered them a prey to all the little
> low designing people, amongst whom their station in life and mis-
> fortune had cast them away.[5]

Dean Mahomed never mentioned other Indians in England
and we cannot know the extent to which he either identified or
associated with them during his voyage or many years in Britain.
Nevertheless, he clearly stated throughout his life in England that
he obtained spices, herbs, and oils from India but, since he also
claimed proprietary access to these supplies, he never revealed his
means of procurement. We can only speculate that he may have

supplied himself through Indian sailors. (It is possible, however, that these items were also available from commercial exporters in India or importers in London.)

Though less numerous than sailors, other types of Indians also lived in London. The second largest group of Indians who had gone to Europe were servants or slaves.[6] Many hundreds of these people had accompanied their masters or mistresses back to Europe. London newspapers remained punctuated by personal advertisements both from Europeans seeking Indian servants and Indian servants seeking employers, either to remain in England or to find passage back to India. Again, Dean Mahomed must have known many such Indian servants, although he never mentioned them in print.

The third largest group of Indians comprised the wives, mistresses, and children of European men, who came back with them to Europe. A few of these appear briefly in history, on the margins of whatever social class the European man occupied. As we have seen, William Massey Baker had an Indian wife or mistress with whom he had a daughter. While English society admired the wealth so prominently displayed by these Nabobs, and their children of mixed ancestry, it also often marginalized them as of low birth. One 'satirical' work depicted such a family: 'Mind Old Pagoda the Nabob, with his piebald family. I wonder how much he will give [his daughters,] those dingy devils *set in diamonds* there. They'll doubtless fall to the lot of some dished guardsman.'[7] Significantly, despite this contempt, wealth and descent from the Indian aristocracy could place someone of mixed ancestry into the highest social circles.[8] Again, Dean Mahomed never mentioned in print other marriages which, like his own, fit into this category.

Lastly, a series of Indian ambassadors and noble visitors made the journey to England over the course of Dean Mahomed's life.[9] Dean Mahomed met with some of these men (we have already seen one of them, Abu Talib). While he may have tried to draw upon some of the prestige associated with these distinguished and fashionable visitors, he was clearly not of their class in society.

Significantly, and in accordance with their choices in Cork, Dean Mahomed and Jane did not make a home for themselves in the sections of London associated with the India trade, among either merchants doing business with India or Indian sailors.

Rather, they settled in the neighbourhood surrounding one of the most fashionable new centres of London society: Portman Square. The first evidence of Dean Mahomed and Jane's presence in this area is the record of the baptism of their daughter Amelia in St Marylebone Church (a few blocks north of Portman Square) on 11 June 1809.[10] On 6 January 1811, they baptized their next child, Henry Edwin, also in St Marylebone Church.[11] Thus, Dean Mahomed and Jane had settled in this parish and oriented themselves toward Portman Square.

Dean Mahomed apparently experimented with ways to represent himself in London. Hitherto, he had spelled his name variously Deen or Dean or Deane Mahomet. In England, he occasionally and then uniformly shifted the spelling of his name to Deen or Dean Mahomed (as I have consistently used throughout this book). In the birth register for Amelia (1809), he entered his name as William Dean Mahomed, apparently reflecting a brief Anglicization of his first name. From the next year onward, about when he turned fifty, he added to his name the honorific 'Sake' (*Shaikh*) meaning 'venerable-one'—often an epithet adopted by upwardly mobile communities of Muslims in India.

## Nabobs in Fashionable Portman Square

After his arrival in London, Dean Mahomed began to work with a rich and controversial nobleman, the Honourable Basil Cochrane (1753–1826), himself recently returned from India as one of the wealthiest of the Nabobs. Cochrane had developed a form of vapour cure while in India and now determined to improve London's lower classes, and his own reputation, by establishing a facility for their therapy at his plush home in fashionable Portman Square. He employed Dean Mahomed to assist in this vapour bath.

Cochrane, sixth son of the impoverished eighth Earl of Dundonald, proved throughout his life to be pugnacious, as well as determined, in his efforts to advance his own fortune and also to implement his own plans for the betterment of the world. He rose quickly in the Company's Madras civil service, from 'writer' (civil official) in 1769 (the same year as Godfrey Evan Baker) to 'senior merchant' by 1780.[12] When Dean Mahomed was passing through Madras, early in 1784, he may have heard of Cochrane's controversial trial for the murder of his Indian assistant. Although an all-British jury in Madras cleared Cochrane of this charge, the Company's Court of Directors remained convinced of his guilt and dismissed him. Only the powerful influence of Cochrane's family obtained his reinstatement.[13] Cochrane went on to establish his personal fortune through lucrative private trade and his profitable official appointments, including: 'Agent for the Management and Distribution of Spirituous Liquors for the Use of the Army' (1792–1806) and Paymaster to the civil and military establishments.[14] In addition, Cochrane embarked on a particularly promising avenue for self-enrichment when he secured the exclusive contract to supply the Royal Navy with food and equipment, as 'Contractor and Agent Victualler to His Majesty's Ships on the East India Station' (1792–1805).[15] In all, he billed the Navy some £1,418,236. On his return to London in April 1807, Cochrane triply demonstrated the vast wealth he acquired over his thirty-seven years in India by paying off the considerable 'debts, mortgages, annuities, etc.' of his eldest brother, the ninth Earl of Dundonald; by purchasing for himself the Barony of Auchterarder (County Perth, Scotland) and other landed estates; and by acquiring as his home the most expensive house on posh Portman Square.[16]

At this time, the fashionable set flocked to the Portman Square area of London. It contained mansions of no less than forty of the nobility and several wealthy Nabobs—topped by Cochrane's.[17] For a time, Prince George made Hertford House (in neighbouring Manchester Square) a second palace, and Lady Hertford the centre of his court and personal attentions. On Portman Square itself, the Ottoman Ambassador established an imposing residence about this time; Portman Square park boasted a mosque for the Turkish Ambassador's use.[18]

During his years in Portman Square, Cochrane maintained a high public profile, both for his heated defence of his honour and wealth (against the accusations of fraud by the Navy) and also for his public acts of beneficence, assisted by Dean Mahomed.[19] The main manifestation of this charity was Cochrane's new model vapour bath for the improvement of the health of the people of London, which he erected in one part of his vast Portman Square home early in 1808. Cochrane claimed that he hit upon the original idea of a vapour bath while he was in India. He attributed his inspiration not to Indian tradition, but rather to a British innovation which he encountered there: 'Mudge's Inhaler'.[20] A diagram (Illustration 6) which Cochrane published in 1809 shows that he simply fitted the end of a vaporizer tube to external parts of a patient's body.[21] Impressed with his own success, Cochrane then expanded his apparatus so that the vapour could cover the entire body. He first set up such a vapour bath in India and then, on his return to England, built another in his home in Portman Square. In particular, Cochrane experimented with the treatment of servants and other members of the lower classes.

In a work published later, Dean Mahomed's son, Horatio, acknowledged that the impetus for the establishment of the vapour bath in London had been Cochrane's, but then asserted the 'bath was fitted for' Cochrane by Dean Mahomed.[22] In fact, applying medicated steam to affected body parts was not an Indian tradition. Cochrane acknowledged the assistance mainly of his European pipe-fitter: 'the ingenious Mr Moser'.[23] Diagrams supplied and captioned by Cochrane showed the design he and his staff developed using flannel, whalebone, and metal pipefittings and boilers (Illustrations 7 and 8).[24]

Despite Cochrane's assertions, the practice of vapour bathing in London was not original to him. Institutions using a range of forms of such baths had existed for centuries. Hamams, or Turkish steam baths, had been established in London as early as in 1631 and would continue in various guises up to the present.[25] At the end of the seventeenth century, Sir John Colbatch (1670–1728) had begun to apply medicated vapour as a cure for a series of diseases.[26] Subsequently, a number of practitioners had established baths for medical and pleasurable uses in several English cities.[27] For example, Bartholomew de Dominiceti established substantial medicinal bath establishments first in Bristol (1754–64), and then in London (1764–71).[28] An Irishman, Dr Achmet, had established bath houses for medicinal purposes in Dublin by 1769, inspired by the work of Charles Lucas.[29] Achmet then himself inspired successors in Dublin and Cork. Further, portable or home models of vapour baths were 'invented' and advertised by a number of men including Playfair (1783) and Jones (1785).[30] Bath house proprietors associated with their vapour baths a range of medical treatments, some suggestive of another popular theme, orientalism.

Fads for Egyptian, Turkish, Indian, Chinese, and other oriental fashions had come and gone for centuries in Europe. British imperialist expansion in the eighteenth and nineteenth centuries, however, had introduced more varied and widespread patterns of such trends. Napoleon's invasion of Egypt (1798–1801) and the British conquest of India had brought ever larger numbers of Europeans into contact with—and power over—the 'east'. In terms of medicine and health treatments, the perception of the orient as exotic led to conflicting valuations. On one hand, Asia represented to many Europeans a largely unknown storehouse of wealth (including a wealth of medical knowledge, medicines, and practices). On the other hand, the growing conception among Europeans of Asians as essentially different people suggested that such medical knowledge and medicine might be specific to them and inapplicable or even hostile to Europeans, particularly to Europeans who had not been subjected to the environment of Asia.[31]

In London at that time, medical practice remained largely unregulated. Various individuals, often with no formal medical training, set themselves up as surgeons and dispensers of medicine. When Cochrane established his vapour bath to cure the people of London of a range of ills, he legitimized his practice not through any pretense of medical training but rather through his social prestige, and what he asserted was the inherent quality of his method. Over the years, Cochrane's wealth and social standing enabled him to enlist large numbers of the most prominent members of the medical establishment to observe and authenticate his innovation. Cochrane publicized his contribution to public health repeatedly and widely. Cochrane's most famous work, *An Improvement on the Mode of Administering the Vapour Bath* (1809), in many ways epitomized the self-promotional, quasi-medical literature of that era. Even established vapour bath house operators like Sir Arthur Clarke, M.D., and Edward Kentish, M.D., fell into line behind Cochrane's leadership; eventually, over seventy doctors and other formally-qualified medical men formally attested, in print, to the virtues of his method.[32]

While Cochrane's innovation had no particular Indian associations, Dean Mahomed apparently added to Cochrane's bath a practice that he would make famous in England as 'shampooing' (therapeutic massage). Cochrane only condescendingly conceded the benefit of this additional component in his vapour bath treatment. Cochrane admitted some patients

> . . . required friction, and in those cases my servants perform that operation according to the mode adopted in India, there called shampooing, and which might be learnt by any person, with great ease, in an hour. Having touched on shampooing I shall trespass to remark, that it is capable of more beneficial effects than will be imagined upon a slight consideration of a means so trifling in its seeming. The Indians hold it in the highest estimation and resort to it continually, both as a luxury and as a remedy.[33]

Cochrane thus grudgingly acknowledged the value of shampooing and, further, attributed the idea and practice of it to his servants (probably Dean Mahomed) and located its origin in India.

Dean Mahomed later claimed to have been practicing shampooing in Britain from 1784. Nevertheless, in *Travels* (XXV) Dean Mahomed gave an unflattering account of this art. From Grose's book, he borrowed Latin citations from Martial and Seneca giving derogatory descriptions of such a massage in imperial Rome. In the original context, Martial was castigating Zoilus, a sybarite who feasted surrounded by his catamite, concubine, slave boy, and female shampooer.[34] Similarly, Seneca stressed the immoral and emasculating nature of this Roman practice.[35] Further, in *Travels*, Dean Mahomed followed Grose in attributing the origin of this practice of shampooing to the Chinese. All this indicates that Dean Mahomed had little personal connection with shampooing in 1794; by the time he made himself a practitioner of shampooing in London (and later in Brighton), he had clearly changed his attitude toward it.

Shampooing (*champi*) and the related art, *malish*, was indeed widely practiced in India. As in Rome, however, many professional practitioners were servants or people of low status, both male and female. One of Dean Mahomed's contemporaries in Patna described a noble's attendants: 'one of his . . . favourite women . . . presented herself at the foot of his bed . . . whose office was to chuppy [shampoo] his limbs. . . . Within the seraglio, these . . . offices must be performed by women . . . they must be pretty, elegantly dressed, witty, and ready at repartees.'[36]

European commentators about India also described practitioners of this art of 'lulling to sleep in India . . . by the chuppy, a method of handling, from the feet upwards, all the members successively, opening the palm of the hand as if going to grip hard a handful of flesh, and yet grasping it so gently, as hardly to make any impression. The person that operates, is always a young one, and with long fingers, and a satined skin . . . '[37] Further, within a household, a wife or concubine might regularly shampoo the elders of the family or a child.

Following Dean Mahomed's work in Cochrane's famous establishment, the idea of shampooing for health quickly entered the jargon of the bath house profession. An established medical practitioner and 'Lecturer on Animated Nature and the Philosophy of the Animal Oeconomy' at the Royal Institute of Great Britain, Michael Este, wrote a medical textbook in 1811 which described the process of shampooing as new to England. While Este called shampooing 'a luxury of the Levant' that was also widely practised in India, he ascribed the introduction of this art into England to Cochrane.[38]

Within a year or so, advertisements for commercial bath houses included shampooing among their range of therapies offered. For example, in 1813, Mrs Clermont advertised a 'Turkish Vapour Bath', including 'champooine' (together with 'friction' and 'electricity') at her establishment at 5 Downing Street, Westminster.[39] In the unlicensed style of the time, she proclaimed her method as the 'sovereign remedy for all complaints in the human frame, without the use of medicine'. Her strategically located bath even boasted the patronage of the Royal family. Mrs Clermont published an extravagant testimonial from a satisfied client—improbably named Harriet Weaklin—whose deformed leg lengthened four inches during a brief series of treatments. Other equally hyperbolic advertisements for shampooing and vapour baths promising cure-all remedies appeared frequently in the newspapers of the day.[40] A reputation for medical innovation added even to Cochrane's social prestige. Dean Mahomed later used some of these same advertising methods in his own rise in society and the medical profession.

While Dean Mahomed and Jane located themselves around Portman Square, they did so not like Cochrane as part of elite society, but rather as part of its service economy. During the winter of 1808, Cochrane fell quite ill and his battles with the Admiralty over his finances took a temporary down-turn.[41] Possibly Dean Mahomed found Cochrane's patronage insufficient and sought other prospects for his growing family. In any case, by the end of 1809, Dean Mahomed felt himself ready to launch an independent business of his own, using his Indian identity as the calling card.

## The Hindostanee Coffee House (1810–12)

Based on his vision of what he could offer the British public, Dean Mahomed created an establishment which he named the 'Hindostanee Coffee House'. To distinguish this public house from the thousands of others then scattered across London, Dean Mahomed highlighted his Indian identity.[42] In the location, arrangement, and advertising for the Hindostanee Coffee House, Dean Mahomed clearly defined his target clientele. He sought to appeal and cater not to the numerous Indians then living in London but rather to the same type of men who had been his patrons in the past: Europeans who had worked or lived in India, men he called 'Indian gentlemen'. To this end, he located the establishment near Portman Square: on the corner of George and Charles Streets, two short blocks directly behind Cochrane's mansion.[43] In selecting 'coffee house' as the genre of his enterprise, he may have been evoking the oriental origins which Londoners continued to attribute to coffee. Like many other nominal coffee houses of the day, however, he did not feature coffee at all. Rather, he designed an eating house or restaurant, but one with a difference.

Unique among coffee houses, taverns, and other eating houses then found in London, the Hindostanee Coffee House provided what Dean Mahomed intended his European patrons to recognize as authentic Indian cuisine and ambiance. Dean Mahomed prepared a range of meat and vegetable dishes with Indian spices served with seasoned rice. He constructed bamboo-cane sofas and chairs on which the patrons would recline or sit. He adorned the walls with a range of paintings including Indian landscapes, Indians engaged in various social activities, and sporting scenes set in India. One observer reported 'Chinese pictures' as well, so he may have drawn upon Asia generally rather than India alone. In a separate *en suite* smoking room, he offered ornate hookas, with specially prepared tobacco blended with Indian herbs.[44]

Soon after he inaugurated their coffee house, Dean Mahomed presented his creation to the British public through a newspaper advertisement:

HINDOSTANEE COFFEE-HOUSE, No. 34 George-street, Portman square—MAHOMED, East-Indian, informs the Nobility and Gentry, he has fitted up the above house, neatly and elegantly, for the entertainment of Indian gentlemen, where they may enjoy the Hoakha, with real Chilm tobacco, and Indian dishes, in the highest perfection, and allowed by the greatest epicures to be unequalled to any curries ever made in England with choice wines, and every accommodation, and now looks up to them for their future patronage and support, and gratefully acknowledges himself indebted for their former favours, and trusts it will merit the highest satisfaction when made known to the public.[45]

This advertisement indicated Dean Mahomed's continuing public orientation towards Europeans who had traded or ruled in India, but also his effort to broaden his appeal to attract patronage from other segments of the British elite as well.

Neither did the starting nor did the running of this coffee house prove easy. The British Government had long identified both political unrest and morally licentious behaviour with coffee houses, taverns, and other public houses. This identification had led in 1753 to a tougher Licensing Act which stiffened the requirements for opening or running any such establishment.[46] Would-be publicans, including coffee house keepers, were required to have lived at least six months in the parish where they wished to operate. To prove this residence and their general moral fitness, they had to submit a certificate attesting to their 'good Fame, sober Life, and Conversation' signed by one clergyman (a parson, vicar, or curate) or else by 'the major part of the Churchwardens, Chapelwardens, and Overseers of the Poor', or else by 'eight inhabitant householders' of that parish. In addition, aspiring publicans had to engage in a £30 bond, and find a person willing to post an additional £20 bond as their 'Surety'. These bonds were 'To be levied upon their several Goods and Chattels, Lands and Testaments, by way of Recognizance to His Majesty's Use, his Heirs and Successors'. The wording of this recognizance, reflecting the legal terminology of the day, must have been daunting for Dean Mahomed:

Upon condition that the said Dean Mahomed do and shall keep the true Assize in uttering [offering] and selling Bread and other Victuals, Beer, Ale, and other Liquors, in his House, and shall not fraudulently dilute or adulterate the same, and shall not use in uttering or selling thereof any Pots or other Measures that are not of full Size; and shall not willfully or knowingly permit Drunkenness or Tippling, nor get Drunk, in his House or other Premises; nor knowingly suffer any gaming with Cards, Draughts, Dice, Bagatelle, or other sedentary Game in his House, any of the Outhouses, Appurtenances, or Easements thereto belonging by Journeymen, Labourers, Servants or Apprentices; nor knowingly introduce, permit, or suffer any Bull, Bear, or Badger Bating, Cock-fighting, or other such Sport or Amusements in any Part of his Premises; nor shall knowingly or designedly, and with a view to harbour and entertain such, permit or suffer Men or Women of notoriously bad Fame, or dissolute Girls and Boys, to assemble and meet together in his House or any of the Premises thereto belonging; nor shall keep open his House, nor permit or suffer any Drinking or Tippling in any Part of his Premises during the usual Hour of Divine Service on Sundays; nor shall keep open his House or other Premises during late hours of the Night, or early in the Morning, for any other Purpose than the Reception of Travellers; but do keep good Rule and Order therein; according to the Purport of a Licence granted for selling Ale, Beer, and other Liquors by Retail in the said House and Premises for one whole year, commencing on the Tenth Day of October last; then this Recognizance to be void, or else to remain in full Force.[47]

The bond had to be submitted, and then resubmitted annually, before two Justices of the Peace. Although women frequently ran public houses in their own names, only Dean Mahomed and not Jane appeared in the legal records for the Hindostanee Coffee House. Unfortunately for today's historians, the specific recognizance taken by Dean Mahomed has not survived and therefore we do not know the identity of the person who stood as surety for him. As his wife, Jane could not legally do so. It was, however, quite common for publicans to stand as reciprocal sureties (A for B and B for A), so perhaps a fellow publican entered into a bond for him. Alternatively, Cochrane may have supported his former shampooer in this way.

The Hindostanee Coffee House received a favourable reception in some quarters. During his first year as licensed victualler, Dean Mahomed expanded the enterprise into the neighbouring house.[48]

One connoisseur of fine dining later listed Dean Mahomed among the 'Artists who administer to the Wants and Enjoyment of the Table'.[49] To be economically successful, however, public houses either had to generate a loyal and substantial clientele or to have a prime location, drawing many occasional visitors. Some particularly successful London coffee houses had already made themselves into centres for a specialized activity (as had Lloyds Coffee House over the previous half century among ship insurers and owners).[50] By the time Dean Mahomed began his enterprise, however, the Jerusalem Coffee House (in Cornhill, far closer to the City of London financial centre) was already long established as the base for activity by merchants and veterans of the East Indies.[51] The elite of the Portman Square neighbourhood, including some wealthy Nabobs and other gentlemen who had returned from India, had their own private kitchens where their personal tastes would be catered to; they could easily hire Indian servants, or Europeans with experience in India, if they sought to eat in an Indian style regularly.[52] Therefore, the relatively exclusive location of the Hindostanee Coffee House and its novel and specialized cuisine and ambiance meant that its gestation time proved longer than Dean Mahomed's limited capital could support. After less than a year running the Hindostanee Coffee House on his own, he took in a partner, John Spencer, perhaps to infuse more cash into the business.[53] Spencer's partnership, however, proved either an inadequate recapitalization or simply a mistake, bringing with it even more financial difficulties. Less than a year after that (March 1812), Dean Mahomed (but not Spencer) had to petition for bankruptcy. As a regretful aficionado of the former house suggested: 'Mohammed's purse was not strong enough to stand the slow test of public encouragement.'[54] While the Hindostanee Coffee House apparently did eventually generate a loyal clientele and may have continued on the same site until as late as 1833, neither Dean Mahomed nor Jane held any further financial interest in it.[55]

## Bankruptcy (1812)

Dean Mahomed's bankruptcy proceeded smoothly according to the established regulations of that time. Nevertheless, it stripped him of his financial assets and kept him and his family enmeshed in complex legal processes for seventeen months. First, he engaged a solicitor, John Ireland (of Staple Inn, Holborn), to guide him through his bankruptcy. Then in addition to identifying himself as a 'Tavern-Keeper', Dean Mahomed had to declare himself a 'Dealer and Chapman', in order to come under the provisions of the current bankruptcy law. On 18 March 1812, Dean Mahomed petitioned for a Commission of Bankrupt to be assigned for him; the Crown awarded this five days later. This Commission then called on him to 'surrender himself' at the City of London Guildhall on three specified occasions over the next two months, both to face his creditors and also to 'make a full discovery and disclosure of his estate and effects'. The Commission publicized Dean Mahomed's bankrupt condition in the official legal organ, the *London Gazette.* Many of the other newspapers of the day (including the *Times* of London and most provincial newspapers, including those in Brighton, where Dean Mahomed and Jane would next move) republished his bankruptcy statement.

Fortunately for Dean Mahomed, his case was unexceptional.[56] By the end of June 1812, the Commission had satisfied itself that 'the said Dean Mahomet hath in all things conformed himself according to the directions of the several Acts of Parliament' and it allowed his Certificate of Bankrupt. The law permitted up to eighteen months for the remainder of the process to be concluded but thirteen months later (27 July 1813), the Commission ordered the public division and distribution of Dean Mahomed's property among his creditors in front of the Guildhall. Any creditor who had not by that date come forward and proved his claims against Dean Mahomed was thereafter excluded from any claim to his property.

While this bankruptcy left the fifty-four year old Dean Mahomed free to begin yet another career, it must have been an extremely difficult period for him and his growing family.[57] We can only imagine their pain, particularly since they were recent immigrants trying to establish themselves in a distinctly English society which relegated most Indians and Irish to the lower classes. Not surprisingly, Dean Mahomed soon excised all reference to his life in London from his subsequent autobiographical writings.

## Dean Mahomed Seeks Service (1812–13)

After receiving his 'Certificate of Bankrupt', but even before the division of his property, Dean Mahomed had to find a way to support himself and his family. In the fall of 1812, Dean Mahomed had to move his family out of the Hindostanee Coffee House to room in a boarding house on Paddington Street, in a less attractive neighbourhood a few blocks north. Their son William, in his mid-teens, may already have started working as a postman, an occupation he followed in London until his death.[58] The salary of a novice postman, however, could hardly have supported the rest of the family. Further, Dean Mahomed and Jane had a son, whom they named Deen Mahomed junior, about this time.

Dean Mahomed, lacking any other satisfactory employment, offered himself as an upper servant, hoping to revert to his earlier life running a household. His newspaper advertisement read: 'MAHOMED, late of HINDOSTANEE Coffee House, WANTS a SITUATION, as BUTLER, in a Gentleman's Family, or as Valet to a Single Gentleman; he is perfectly acquainted with marketing, and is capable of conducting the business of a kitchen; has no objections to town or country. Direct, post-paid, to D.M., 36, Paddington-street, Baker-street.'[59] Virtually unique for such 'Situations Wanted' advertisements in this period, Dean Mahomed gave his name and his previous situation. Most other such advertisements only provided the class, gender, general age, mailing address, and—often fictitious—initials of the applicant. Thus, Dean Mahomed must have still identified himself with his failed business and thought that he would be known to his potential employers as a named individual, not just a person with advertised skills.

The phrasing of Dean Mahomed's advertisement indicated his openness to any location and no hint of what he would soon develop as his next undertaking. Although Dean Mahomed sought a position as the major domo in a respectable household, based on his experience with the Bakers in India and Cork, he found employment in a bath house, probably based on his experience working for Cochrane. By 1814, he was established as a bath house manager in the burgeoning seaside resort of Brighton. There, his therapeutic skills and self-promotion as expert in the 'Indian Medicated Vapour Bath' and 'Shampooing Surgeon' would quickly lead to his most illustrious career.

## Notes

1. The son of Godfrey Evan Baker settled in England as such an absentee landlord. 'Attested Will of Godfrey Hugh Massey Baker of Grove Hill, Kent (1877)', PRO Ireland.
2. See Colley, *Britons.*
3. E.g. HC 15/6/1786.
4. For important studies of Asians in London, see Rozina Visram, *Ayahs, Lascars, and Princes* (1986) and Peter Fryer, *Staying Power* (1984).
5. Grose, *Voyage* (1757), pp. 176–7.
6. E.g. Hickey, *Memoirs* 3: 150–1.
7. A Pagoda was a south Indian coin; a 'dished guardsman' was a bankrupt officer in an elite military regiment. [Thomas Broun], *Brighton, or, The Steyne* (1818) 1: 232.
8. The fascinating case of David Octerlony Dyce Sombre, who married the daughter of Viscount St Vincent only to be declared insane, suggests the possibilities and limits of such intra-class but inter-racial marriages. *Dyce Sombre against Troup* (n.d.); *Mr Dyce Sombre's Refutation* (1849).
9. See Das, 'Early', pp. 83–114.
10. Amelia was born on 8 August 1808 but parents often delayed baptism. St Marylebone Parish Register, GLRO. If Dean Mahomed had indeed taken a second wife, also named Jane, they must have married between 1800 and 1807 (after Abu Talib met them in December 1799 and before Amelia's birth). Amelia died in 1894. Stewart, 'Frederick Akbar Mahomed'.
11. He was born 15 December 1810. St Marylebone Parish Register, GLRO. He died in 1823.
12. Henry Davison Love, *Vestiges* (1913), pp. 98, 555–6.
13. Letters Received from Madras, Select Committee 20/9/1784 Nos 16–17; Petition received 1/12/1783; CoD Resolution 26/4/1785; Dispatches of CoD to Fort St George 13, 19, 22/12/1786, 31/7/1787, 20/8/1788, 19/5/1790, 3/7/1795, 9/9/1801; Love, *Vestiges*, p. 379; Public Dispatches from England vol. 89, 22/12/1786; Minute of Governor Madras, Public Consultations vol. 143, 25/5/1787; Archibald Cochrane, *Memorial* (1786). Minutes of CoD 24/3/1786, 4/4/1786, 11/6/1788, 26/6/1788, 2/7/1788, 9/7/1788, 16/7/1788, 13/8/1788, 28/8/1788, 30/10/1788, 5/11/1788, 11/11/1788, 26/11/1788, 12/12/1788, 7/1/1789.
14. Letter of Basil Cochrane 23/1/1792, HMS 386 ff. 159–60.
15. So lucrative was Cochrane's private trade that, when the Directors forbade such trade by its servants, Cochrane resigned rather than relinquish it. Dispatches from CoD to Fort St George 26/8/1801, 9/9/1801,

28/4/1802, 23/10/1805; Public Consultation, vol. 243, 18/3/1800 cited in Love, *Vestiges*, p. 539. For Cochrane's financial accounts see Basil Cochrane, *Exposé* (1824).

16. Cochrane moved into 12 Portman Square in 1807 or early 1808. The assessed valuation of his house was £600 per year, matched by only one other property on Portman Square. Cochrane's widow continued there long after his death in 1826. Marylebone Rate Book (1810ff). *Gentleman's Magazine* 96, 2 (September 1826): 270.

17. Portman Square was constructed 1764–84; by 1806 it was rising to its peak. E.B. Chancellor, *History of the Squares* (1907), pp. 262–75. Other returned British officials of the Company stayed in the area. E.g. William Collin Jackson, *Memoir* (1809).

18. Thomas Smith, *Topographical* (1833), pp. 197–8.

19. Cochrane attacked his accusers vociferously for fifteen years and eventually 'proved' the Navy owed him £1282. Basil Cochrane, *Observations* (1822), *Inquiry* (1823), and *Historical Digest* (1824).

20. Cochrane, *Improvement*, pp. 1–2.

21. Cochrane, *Improvement*, Plate VII, Figure 4.

22. Horatio Mahomed, *The Bath* (1843), pp. 31–5.

23. Cochrane, *Improvement*, pp. 2–3.

24. Cochrane, *Improvement*, Plate III, Figure 2 and Plate VII, Figure 1.

25. In early nineteenth century London, the neighbouring Old and New Hummums provided baths, coffee, food, and lodging. For other examples, see the many directories of the day.

26. John Colbatch, *Physico Medical Essay* (1696). Horatio Mahomed lauded Colbatch as a pioneer in the vapour bath field. Horatio Mahomed, *Bath*, pp. 51–2.

27. Thomas Denman, *Letter* (1768); John Wynter, *Of bathing* (1728); John Symons, *Observations* (1766); Ralph Blegborough, *Facts and Observations* (1803).

28. Bartholomew de Dominiceti, *To the Public* (1764) and *Plan* (1771).

29. Charles Lucas, *Essay on Waters* (1756); Dr Achmet, *Theory and Uses of Baths* (1772) and 'To the Committee' (1773).

30. James Playfair, *Method of Construction* (1783); Philip Jones, *Portable Vapour Bath* (ca. 1785); Symons, *Observations*.

31. Personal communication from David Arnold, October 1994.

32. E.g., Arthur Clarke, *Essay on Warm, Cold, and Vapour Bathing* (1813; 1820); Edward Kentish, *Essay* (1809, 1813) and *Account of Baths* (ca. 1814); Robert James Culverwell, *Practical Treatise* (1829) pp. 39–40.

33. Cochrane, *Improvement*, pp. 5–6.

34. Martial, *Epigrams*, Book 3, Epigram 82.

35. Lucius Annaeus Seneca, *Epistles*, Letter 66.

36. Khan, *Seir* 2: 365.

37. Raymond in Khan, *Seir* ftnt 188. See also Forbes, *Oriental Memoirs* 1: 156, 350.

38. Michael Lambton Este, *Remarks on Baths* (1811). He also credited

Dr John Grosvenor with innovations in shampooing. See William Cleoburey, *Full Account of . . . Friction* (1825).

39.  *Times* 29/1/1813, 29/9/1813. [Mrs Clermont], *Observations on the Use of the Vapour* (1814); Samuel Leigh, *New Picture of London* (1824–25).

40.  E.g. *Times* 21/3/1814.

41.  Cochrane. *Exposé*, p. 20.

42.  Estimates range from about 2000 coffee houses to 5000 public houses in the London area. Ralph Nevill, *London Clubs* (1911), p. 3; Ellis Aytoun, *Penny Universities* (1956), p. xiv; Bryant Lillywhite, *London Coffee Houses* (1963); John Feltham, *Picture of London* (1810), p. 397.

43.  This establishment expanded from 34 George Street to include 35 George Street as well. Charles Street has been built over but a Japanese Restaurant, Yumi, currently stands near the site. Victualler's Licence (1810). Marylebone Rate Book (1810). *Holden's Directory* (1811).

44.  For a favourable review of the food and decor of Dean Mahomed's Hindostanee Coffee House see *Epicure's Almanack*, pp. 123–4. Dean Mahomed's house was known to one veteran of India, Charles Stewart, as the 'Hooka Club'. Mention of Dean Mahomed as the proprietor of this 'hooka club' appears in a footnote in the 1814 (but not the 1810) translation by Stewart of Khan, *Travels* 1: 124.

45.  *Times* 27/3/1811.

46.  26 George II c 31, revising 5 and 6 Edward II c 25.

47.  I have inserted Dean Mahomed's name in the text of a blank printed form for a Victualler's Licence from 1823, the closest year to his now lost licence. Victualler's Licence (1810–12).

48.  35 George Street, Marylebone Rate Book (1811).

49.  Significantly, a favourable review appeared even after the Hindostanee Coffee House had closed down, a tribute to its lingering impact in the culinary world of London. *Epicure's Almanack*, pp. 123–4.

50.  Lloyd's in the Royal Exchange continued to serve coffee and other simple fare at this time, but its shipping and insurance activities had come to predominate. Lillywhite, *London Coffee Houses*, pp. 330–5, 395–403.

51.  The Jerusalem Coffee House appeared in many newspaper advertisements at this time as a meeting place for ship owners and captains, merchants, travellers, and servants seeking business or passage to India. *Epicure's Almanack*, p. 31; Lillywhite, *London Coffee Houses*, pp. 289–94.

52.  E.g. Sarah Shade, the widow of a Sergeant, had lived for half a dozen years in India and then for a time in the late 1790s in London 'subsisted herself chiefly by making curry for different East Indian families [i.e. British "Nabobs"]—a dish for which she is famous.' Shade, *Narrative*, p. 27.

53.  Victualler's Licence (1811); Marylebone Rate Book (1812).

54.  *Epicure's Almanack*, pp. 123–4.

55.  Victualler's Licence (1812) listed the Hindostan Coffee House under the names George Spencer and Richard Burton. In subsequent years this set of records did not indicate any establishment of this name on the site.

Nevertheless, the annual issues of *British Imperial Calendar* and *Picture of London* identified the Hindoostanee Coffee House as continuing there from 1812–33. In his encyclopaedic work, Lillywhite missed the early years of the 'Hindoostance [sic] Coffee House', dating it 1819–33. Lillywhite, *London Coffee Houses*, p. 269. *Pigot's* and *Robinson's Directories* indicate that Joseph Cadney, Cheesemonger, Butter-dealer, and Dairyman was at 35 George Street *c.* 1819–40, so perhaps he ran this Coffee House.

56. Therefore the courts did not preserve the paper work of his case as they did more tendentious or sizable ones. Docket Book (B.4.31): Docquet 18 March 1812, case of Dean Mahomed, Tavern Keeper, George Street, PRO.

57. While Dean Mahomed never wrote explicitly about the trauma of his bankruptcy, a contemporary and later professional rival, Robert James Culverwell (1802–52), described his own bankruptcy in passionate terms. Robert James Culverwell, *Life* (1852), pp. 31–2.

58. William (1797–1833) had at least seven children. Parish Records, St Leonard's (Shoreditch), St Botolph-without-Aldergate, St Bartholomew the Great; Census of 1841.

59. *Times* 20/4/1813.

# Chapter Seven

# The World of Brighton (1813/14–51)

## The Resort of Brighton

For the half century prior to the arrival of Dean Mahomed and Jane in Brighton (1813/14), the town had been growing into a fashionable seaside spa, a resort for the British upper and middle classes. Sea-bathing on Brighton's shoreline grew in popularity as both a health-giving treatment and a social activity for the English elite. Additionally, Brighton had constructed indoor baths for luxury, hygiene, and medical therapy. The flamboyant presence of George IV (as Prince of Wales and then King), added a significant element of social prestige, and much income, to the expanding town. In the decades following Dean Mahomed's own arrival, Brighton developed all the more rapidly. Increased access from London by horse-drawn coaches and eventually by railway, and the enhanced reputation of Brighton itself, drew ever more visitors. George's imaginative Marine Pavilion (Illustrations 9, 10) and Dean Mahomed's own Indian offerings introduced an exotic oriental motif into Brighton's reputation.

Sea-bathing and the reputedly healthful marine environment first drew British public attention during the second half of the eighteenth century to what had been the small fishing village of Brighthelmstone. From 1750 onward, a series of medical texts asserted the health-giving nature of bathing in this town, renamed Brighton. In particular, Dr Richard Russell's influential work (first in Latin and then English) on the medicinal qualities of sea-water caught the attention of the literate public.[1] This model medical text—describing a range of diseases, providing analysis of particular cases, and advocating a course of treatment for them—would remain persuasive and popular for decades; Dean Mahomed himself adopted this genre in 1822, when he published a book to publicize his own medical methods.

Sea-bathing increased in popularity despite the fact that relatively few Englishmen or women actually knew how to swim. Further, the middle-classes who could afford, and felt they deserved, a holiday by the seashore were also developing a bourgeois mentality about revealing the physical body in public. To accommodate these interests and concerns, horse-drawn bathing machines sprang up along the Brighton shore that would convey the would-be bather into shallow water. Professional 'dippers' stood at the foot of these machines to encourage the (occasionally terrified) bathers, via the dipper's arms, into the shallow sea-water. As fourteen year old Thomas Babington Macaulay described his sister's descent into the sea: ' . . . Fanny was actually petrified and overwhelmed by horror and amazement at finding herself precipitated from the tremendous height of the stairs of the [bathing] machine . . . the sea-hearse, into the raging deep. The bathing woman, I am informed, animated and encouraged them to take the dreadful drop, by blandishments of a very remarkable kind . . . '[2]

For modesty's sake, the town fathers ordered women's bathing machines concentrated on one side of the shorefront, separated by some distance from the men's. Nonetheless, male 'gawkers' remained prevalent on the cliff-top promenades overlooking the shorefront, seeking to catch a glimpse of the female bathers below. In whichever fashionable direction bathing costumes evolved, the stress on the body that all this activity emphasized contributed the component of sexual interest that added to Brighton's attraction for a growing number of visitors.

In addition to outdoor sea bathing that drew people to Brighton (and to other seaside resorts), the town emerged as distinctive for its indoor activities as well. A series of medical publicists, most prominently Doctors Richard Russell and John Awsiter, popularized theories about the benefits of their particular water treatments. Russell asserted that, beyond bathing in the sea, drinking sea and mineral water held highly therapeutic powers for a broad range of maladies. Such treatments drew an increasing stream of eager patients to his home in Brighton. He further made Brighton's chalybeate spring into a health spa, modeled on the more well-established spas at Bath.

Building on the town's rising reputation, Dr Awsiter publicized his medicinal hot and cold salt-water baths. In 1769, he established his institution for such indoor bathing at the foot of the Steine (the open area that ran down the middle of Brighton).[3] Such institutions had the affluent as their target audience: a single cold shower bath cost 1s 6d while a single hot bath cost 4s. Seasonal subscribers paid £10 10s for three months of hot baths.

Other bathing establishments followed, varying this theme. In 1803, John Williams built a hot and cold bath institution near Awsiter's—the two were distinguished as the New and the Old Baths respectively. Nathan Smith developed his 'Air Pump Vapour Bath' (at a reputed cost of 1000 guineas and ten years of research) which he patented in 1798. This apparatus received the attention of Dr Ralph Blegborough, M.D., who touted it in letters to *The Medical and Physical Journal* (April 1802) and in his book: *Facts and Observations* (1803). Riding this publicity, Smith established his own 'Air Pump Vapour Bath' at Artillery Place on Brighton's West Cliff by 1806.[4] London entrepreneurs even sought to bypass Brighton by proposing an improbable scheme for piping sea-water directly from the coast to a grand bath at Lambeth.[5] Thus, long before Dean Mahomed and Jane's arrival in Brighton, a range of baths and bathing methods (with their attendant publicity) flourished there.

The resident population of Brighton grew about 65 per cent over the decade prior to Dean Mahomed's arrival, and then another 50 per cent during his first five years there. In addition, some 10,000–15,000 visitors came annually. By the time Dean Mahomed erected his magnificent Mahomed's Baths in 1821, the resident population of the town had doubled yet again to 24,429. The 1820s proved one of the most expansive periods in Brighton's development as various attractions for visitors (including the Chain Pier), hotels, and residential areas blossomed.

Ever broader segments of the British population found Brighton attractive, much to the disgust of some of the old elite. In 1819, one pillar of Brighton's high society (Mrs Fitzherbert, Prince George's morganatic wife) complained bitterly about the masses crowding Brighton: 'not a house [is] to be had [for lease]. I cannot boast of much good society which formerly we abounded with at this season. When I tell you that fifty-two public coaches go from hence to London every day and bring people down for six shillings, you will not be surprised at the sort of company we have . . . '6 The completion of the railway from London to Brighton in 1841 increased the number and broadened the class of visitors enormously. By the time of Dean Mahomed's death in 1851, the resident population reached 65,573; up to 74,000 visitors arrived in a single month.7 Thus, during the first half of the nineteenth century, ever larger numbers of Britons resorted to Brighton for a combination of health, holiday, and fashionably racy social intercourse.

George IV emerged as the single most notable among the growing body of patrons of both Brighton and Dean Mahomed. Prince George was not, however, the first member of the royal family who patronized Brighton. English royalty had been visiting Brighton since 1765. Indeed, George's first trip came in 1782/3 at the invitation of an uncle visiting there, the Duke of Cumberland.8 Nevertheless, over the years, George's almost unbridled expenditures and increasing notoriety focused attention on the resort. For example, in 1784, he dramatically demonstrated his own prowess and the accessibility of Brighton by riding horseback from Brighton to London and back in ten hours the same day.9

As Prince of Wales, George sought the independence Brighton offered from the social and moral restrictions of London and his father's court.10 From 1784, he rented an initially modest house. Over the years, he had this house remodeled by a series of fashionable architects (including Henry Holland, William Porden, Humphrey Repton, and John Nash) into the striking Brighton Marine Pavilion.11 Although George's allowance grew incrementally as he married, became Prince Regent on the incapacity of his father (George III), and then succeeded to the throne as King George IV, he felt he never had enough money. His indulgences and expenses—driven by his tastes and imagination—always surpassed his income—limited by Parliament. The Pavilion's furnishings and decoration alone cost some £100,000 above what the civil list allowed.12 As George developed his own imaginative style, the Pavilion mirrored it, being repeatedly transformed physically. Although George last visited the Pavilion in 1827, his brother and successor, William IV, continued royal patronage of Brighton on a more modest scale during his reign (1830–7).

Queen Victoria (1837–1901), however, found Brighton uncongenial, closed the Pavilion, stripped it of its furnishings, and sold it the year Dean Mahomed died (1851).

The major theme of the Pavilion was eclectic oriental exotica. The gift to George of Chinese wallpaper (*c.* 1802) led to extensive decoration and redecoration of the Pavilion in what George and his architects believed was eastern luxury. While Chinoiserie had been fashionable long before, a new amalgamation of putative 'Indian' themes made the Brighton Pavilion a striking expression of England's rapidly expanding eastern Empire, with India as its crown jewel.[13] The vast stable designed by William Porden went up (1803–5) in what architects of the day understood promiscuously as 'Hindu', 'Indian', or 'Turkish' style (what might be today called imitation Indo-Saracenic or Mughal style).

In that day, architects who had never been to India were just constructing such 'eastern' categories. Repton, who drew up plans in 1806 for the Pavilion in what he called 'Indian' style (plans that later informed his quondam partner Nash's reconstruction), explicitly argued in such loose terms about the styles he had considered for the Pavilion:

> The Turkish was objectionable, as being a corruption of the Grecian; the Moorish, as a bad model of the Gothic; the Egyptian as too cumbrous for the character of a villa; the Chinese too light and trifling for the outside, however it may be applied to the interior; and the specimens from Ava [Burma] were still more trifling and extravagant. Thus, if any known style were to be adopted, no alternative remained, but to combine from the Architecture of Hindustan such forms as might be applicable to the purpose . . . Under the name Indian Architecture may be included Hindustan, Gentoo, Chinese, or Turkish; which latter is a mixture of the other three.[14]

Repton and then Nash drew their inspiration from Thomas and William Daniell's paintings of India. Their composite design created a building whose style not even its patron's wife could clearly define or describe.[15]

Art critics—at the time and subsequently—have had similar difficulty coming to a consensus about the aesthetics of the Pavilion. William Hazlitt wrote in 1826: 'The Pavilion at Brighton is like a collection of stone pumpkins and pepper-boxes. It seems as if the genius of architecture had at once the dropsy and the *megrims.* Any thing more fantastical, with a greater durth of imagination, was never seen.'[16] Other contemporary commentators proved either impressed or bored, or both.[17] More sympathetic twentieth century art critics have seen the Pavilion as a striking epitome of its age and context: 'Indeed, the Pavilion contains . . . the seed of a British Empire style . . . proclaim[ing], perhaps rather loudly, that the Day of Empire is at Hand . . .'[18] Whatever its artistic value, its evolving presence added yet another attraction to Brighton for the growing number of nobility and gentry who resorted to it.

While Repton's plans preceded Dean Mahomed to Brighton, the actual reconstruction of the Pavilion into its current form took place under John Nash, from 1815–23, subsequent to Dean Mahomed's arrival. Dean Mahomed's appearance in Brighton proved timely, since he gave Brighton a further fillip of Indianness. Conversely, Brighton proved more receptive to his Indian offerings than London had been. Thus, even as Dean Mahomed cast around in London for employment as a butler or valet in 1813, many of the elements of what he would soon make his new career were already present in Brighton: medical bathing, royal patronage, and orientalism. During their more than thirty-five years in Brighton, Dean Mahomed and Jane would refine these elements and put them to use by emphasizing his Indian medical treatments and representational arts.

### Dean Mahomed and Jane Move to Brighton (1813/14)

When Dean Mahomed printed his 'situation wanted' advertisement in April 1813, he evidently had no intention of going to Brighton as a bath housekeeper. Nevertheless, by September 1814, Dean Mahomed and Jane were established in such a position, on the edge of that growing town.[19] The bath house which Dean Mahomed and Jane came to manage, 11 Devonshire Place (near St James Street and New Steine), stood some way up the hill from the Prince Regent's Marine Pavilion. Dean Mahomed, stripped of his assets by the previous year's bankruptcy, could not personally have had the capital to rent or equip this bath house. The identity of the owner of this bath house is not clear, but it was apparently attached to W.R. Mott's New Steyne Hotel.[20]

In this Devonshire Place bath house, Dean Mahomed and Jane offered a range of exotic luxuries, just as they had in their Hindostanee Coffee House. Dean Mahomed advertised some of their Indian wares in the local newspapers:

> MAHOMED has on sale INDIAN TOOTH POWDER, which possesses extraordinary excellence. It is the first ever offered to the public in this country. He has also just introduced from India, the celebrated CULEFF [*kalaf,* Persian for red-black hair dye], for changing the Hair, of whatever colour it might be, to a beautiful glossy permanent BLACKNESS, which will ever remain unaffected by the attacks of time.[21]

Such advertisements show that Dean Mahomed and Jane were clearly casting around for ways to trade on his Indian identity. Soon they dropped the advertisement of these substances to concentrate on selling Indian medicated baths and shampooing.

At this Devonshire Place house, Dean Mahomed and Jane distinguished their form of the therapeutic bath from others by adding medical herbs and other substances to the vapour and calling it 'the Indian Medicated Vapour Bath'. Further, Dean Mahomed had already made 'shampooing' his distinctive speciality. As Dean Mahomed later explained his entry into the bath house business, his initial 'Indian' treatments were 'gratuitous', performed when other remedies had failed.[22] Perhaps some people came to him for an ordinary vapour bath; he tried shampooing them and it cured their complaint.

While Dean Mahomed and Jane gained some public recognition of their distinctive offerings, the British public clearly had its own ways of perceiving the 'east'. The first popular guidebook (1815) to note their bath praised their offerings but presented their identity in its own frame of reference as 'Turkish':

> Mahomed's Baths, near the New Steyne. These baths are kept by a native of Turkey, and combine all the luxuries of the baths of the east. They are adapted either for ladies or gentlemen, and the system is highly salutary in many diseases, independently of the gratification it affords, particularly to those who have resided in the east.[23]

For Dean Mahomed and Jane to broaden their appeal, they had to make clear both that their methods were unique to their bath and also that these methods cured not only Europeans whose constitution had been affected by their residence in Asia, but rather all people and a broad range of complaints.

Dean Mahomed featured shampooing using 'Indian oils' as his special contribution. Dean Mahomed's son (and successor as a professional shampooer), explained this process:

> To describe this operation [shampooing] is a matter of no ordinary difficulty, as it consists of a series of manipulations which can only be understood by repeatedly witnessing them, and only acquired by dint of long practice. They may be likened to the fingering of the violinist in the execution of rapid passages of music, requiring great gentleness through firmness of touch, administered with rapidity and precision.
>
> This process consists of friction and extention of the ligaments, tendons, &c., of the body, the operation commencing by briskly administering gentle friction gradually increasing the pressure, along the whole course of the muscles; imperceptibly squeezing the flesh at the same moment: the operator then grasps the muscles with both hands whilst he kneads it with his fingers; this is succeeded by a light friction of the whole surface of the body . . .
>
> When shampooing is applied for any specific affection of any particular part, as lumbago, sciatica, &c . . . the hand is then anointed with a medicated oil, which is applied with friction, the muscles are then gently pounded with the thick muscle of the hand below the thumb . . . [24]

This later description, if it accorded with Dean Mahomed and Jane's practice at the start of their careers as shampooers, seems to indicate a conventional massage, although the exact nature of their proprietary 'Indian oils' remains unknown.

However nascent their career in Brighton, it clearly developed quickly. A bath house (like a coffee house) required a large and steady volume of clients in order to be economically successful. Seeking to expand his clientele among the public in general, Dean Mahomed took out what would be a long series of ambitious paid advertisements to announce his and his wife's professional services at the Devonshire Place establishment. In these advertisements (starting early in 1815), he publicly declared that he had treated members of 'the Nobility with the happiest results'.[25] Dean Mahomed's hyperbolic advertisements asserted that his combined treatments comprised a virtual panacea:

No. 11, Devonshire-Place, Brighton.

Mahomed's Steam and Vapour Sea Water Medicated BATHS, upon reasonable Terms.

They are far superior to the common Baths, as they promote copious perspiration, and never fail in giving relief when every thing else has been tried in vain, to cure many Diseases, particularly Rheumatic and Paralytic Affections of the extremities, stiff joints, old sprains, lameness, eruptions, and scurf on the skin, which it renders quite smooth; also diseases arising from the abuse of mercury, consumption, white swellings, aches and pains in the joints; in short, in all cases where the circulation is languid, or the nervous energy debilitated, as is well known to many professional gentlemen and others in this country.—Mr M. has attended several of the Nobility with the happiest results, can give most satisfactory references.

N.B. Board and Lodgings in his House, if required.

— Mr and Mrs MAHOMED Possess the Art of SHAMPOOING.[26]

In format and broad claims, these early advertisements differed little from other aspiring practitioners of other panaceas; in their featuring an 'Indian' element of shampooing, however, they were distinctive, although later imitated.

Dean Mahomed and Jane learned quickly to stress his Indian identity. Their newspaper advertisements continued and developed over time, revealing shifts in the way they presented him to the public. Their advertising copy later in 1815 seemed to respond to the growing moral niceties of the nineteenth century, and also perhaps Jane's continued and active role in the business, by adding the assurance of sexual segregation: 'N.B. Ladies attended by Mrs MAHOMED'. (See Illustration 11 for the only known surviving portrait of Mrs Jane Mahomed.) This second round of advertisements highlighted India by moving shampooing to a more featured place in the text and adding: 'The above pleasant and soothing mode of practice in the East, is well known to many professional gentlemen and others in this country, and the art is possessed to an eminent degree by MAHOMED, a native of India.'

They also shifted from advertising a conventional vapour bath to stressing their uniquely 'Indian' form of bath. These later advertisements replaced 'on reasonable terms' (from the earlier advertisements) with 'upon the Indian Construction' as its primary identification. To create his 'Indian Medicated Vapour Bath', Dean Mahomed apparently simply modified the apparatus described in Cochrane's vapour bath with the addition of alleged Indian elements (Illustrations 7, 8). Dean Mahomed used a wooden framework, painted to resemble bamboo, in place of Cochrane's whalebone. Into the vapourizing chamber, Dean Mahomed placed various substances which he identified as exotic 'Indian herbs', known and obtained from India exclusively by himself. Otherwise, he used the same type of conventional white flannel cloth, chair with foot stool, thermometers, and 'flesh-and bath-brushes', that several other bath house keepers routinely employed.[27]

Further, Dean Mahomed marshalled the conventional sources of support for bath house keepers. He announced that he had on display numerous written testimonials from the nobility and gentry as 'proof of the efficacy of his unrivalled practice'.[28] Dean Mahomed's publication of specific names of his patients (with their permission), their conditions, and a description of his successful treatment enhanced the celebrity of his patients and also allowed him to capitalize on that celebrity. Finally, he offered to take in patients, adding to the level of their care and his own income: 'Patients, either Ladies or Gentlemen, may, if wished, be accommodated with Board and Lodging in the house, where probably he would be enabled to pay a more scrupulous attention to their respective complaints than he could do elsewhere.'

Their success and their family grew. Jane bore their daughter, Rosanna, in mid-1815.[29] After only a year or so, Dean Mahomed and Jane outgrew the Devonshire Place baths and moved on to a grander establishment.

## Mahomed's Battery House Baths (1815–20)

The publicity and the method deployed by Dean Mahomed and Jane clearly met with an extremely favourable response. He claimed (perhaps with exaggeration) by 1815 to have treated 'a thousand Cases'.[30] Further, by December 1815, they had shifted from Devonshire Place to a more prominent location: the Battery House, overlooking the sea, at the bottom of East-Street, and near the old, established White-horse Inn. The British Board of Ordinance still owned the Battery House, which had previously held four large cannon.[31] The vibrations from cannon-fire and the erosion from the sea, however, had combined to weaken this building's foundations and the cliff beneath. As a result, the Board of Ordinance removed the cannon and rented out the building. Dean Mahomed retained his baths in this building, and lived there with his growing family, through 1819.[32] Their sons Horatio, Frederick, and Arthur Ackber were born here during these years and were baptized at St Nicholas parish church; here as well, their two year old daughter, Rosanna, died.[33]

Increasingly, publicists who touted Brighton and its growing health care industry made his the featured Bath House in Brighton in their guidebooks. They further backed Dean Mahomed's extravagant claims for his method. One asserted:

> The use of [Mahomed's Battery House] baths have proved an infallible cure to many afflicted and diseased patients, of which variety of interesting cases may be seen at the bathing-house.
>
> The unafflicted, in the enjoyment of these baths insure continued freedom from disease, and revel in an innocent luxury before untasted . . . [In Mahomed's] surgical skill and practice in the act of Shampooing . . . the universal remedy, as a panacea, has at length been discovered.[34]

In addition to a growing body of loyal and distinguished clients, they also developed a personal history that presented him to his clients in a suitable manner.

From about 1818, Dean Mahomed began to publicize the title he apparently invented for himself: 'Shampooing Surgeon'. In 1820, Dean Mahomed extended his publicity campaign by publishing a book containing both descriptions of many of the cases he had treated and glowing testimonials from his grateful patients, including many from prominent members of high society. This work was to demonstrate to the world the extent of his medical successes and create a bandwagon effect; such tracts, while expensive to produce, were a frequent vehicle for bath house advertising.[35] He entitled the work: *Cases Cured by Sake Deen Mahomed, Shampooing Surgeon, And Inventor of the Indian Medicated Vapour and Sea-Water Baths, Written by the Patients Themselves* (1820). He modestly attributed the impulse to publish this book to his distinguished patients: 'By the pressing desires of many of the Nobility, and others of the first consideration, Sake Deen Mahomed has caused the few cases, herein presented to the public, to be printed. He would, indeed, be wanting in gratitude, did he not acknowledge that he feels pride and pleasure in acquiescing with the wishes of those whom he considers not only his own personal friends, but the friends of the human race.' In his brief opening 'Address' (pp. v–vi), he represented his life in only general terms, excising any time in Ireland or London: 'S.D. MAHOMED has been too long before the world, to need to trust his character to any assurances of his own in favour of his professional Art, which he invented while on his travels through Asia and Europe, and which he has practiced for more than fifty years, but is content to leave his pretensions to the decision of those whom disease has introduced to his attention and care.' This statement implied that he had been doing shampooing since 1780. By 1822, he had begun to assert that he was 'Inventor of the Indian Medicated Vapour Baths . . . by whom the Art of Shampooing was first introduced into England in 1784.'[36] These statements—and Dean Mahomed's consistent excision while in Brighton of his previous careers in Ireland and London—have led most later writers who mention or discuss Dean Mahomed to date his arrival in Brighton erroneously as 1784 or soon thereafter.[37]

During Dean Mahomed's years in the Battery House bath, the entire industry continued to expand dramatically. Numbers of baths sprang up across Britain, using a variety of vapours, chemicals, electrical charges, and other fluids as their healing medium. Each type of bath had its inventor, publicist(s), and grateful patients. Like Dean Mahomed, the proprietors or promoters of these baths published a substantial number of tracts, pamphlets, and books promoting these baths as universal remedies.[38] Therefore, in order to prosper, Dean Mahomed had to create a special niche for himself in the medical industry and in Brighton.

Since the Battery House building in which he located his bathing and shampooing apparatus proved limiting, Dean Mahomed designed a magnificent, purpose-built bath house on the cliff-top nearby. At the same time, the Brighton Town Council was developing the shore-front by building Kings' Road past that site. During the period when the construction of this road disrupted traffic and commerce and/or while his new baths were under construction, Dean Mahomed shifted temporarily (1820–1) to a cross-town location on West Cliff.[39]

The arrangements in his West Cliff establishment may not have been fully satisfactory. It was here in 1820 that two distressing incidents occurred which could have ruined Dean Mahomed's budding career. In the first incident, John Claudius Loudon, a promising landscape gardener, took treatment at Mahomed's bath for a badly rheumatic right arm. The shampooers working under Dean Mahomed misjudged the brittleness of Loudon's humerus and, through excessive pressure, snapped that bone close to the shoulder. This bone never healed properly. For years, Loudon had to wear an iron case over it. When the bone broke again, Loudon was compelled to have it amputated.[40] In the second incident, an elderly gentleman of means, Mr Spode, died while undergoing a shower at Mahomed's West Cliff baths. According to a newspaper report, Spode 'ordered a shower bath, when he was ready, the water was, in the usual manner, discharged upon him, when, shocking to relate, he fell instantly dead. His death is supposed to have been produced by the shock being too severe for a frame already much debilitated, or from apoplexy. The coroner's verdict was—*Died by the visitation of God*'.[41] Despite these untoward incidents, the town of Brighton stood behind Dean Mahomed and his career continued to flourish. The Kings' Road officially opened on New Years Day 1822 and Mahomed's Baths opened for business about the same time.

## Mahomed's Baths (1821–43)

Mahomed's Baths stood as the most concrete expression of Dean Mahomed's professional success. Dean Mahomed, Jane, and a wealthy London backer, Thomas Brown, constructed the magnificent baths at a particularly striking location, just down the Steine from the Brighton Pavilion, and perched on a prominent vantage point overhanging the shore on the new main seaside road.[42] (Illustration 12). This building first opened when Dean Mahomed had already turned 62 years old. Its location, imposing form, and elaborate internal decoration stood as testimony to the prominence he and Jane had reached in the community and in the bath house profession. It is well worth expanding on the design and ornamentation of Mahomed's Baths, based on a composite of several descriptions from the time of its glory.[43] These descriptions conveyed the elements which Dean Mahomed combined in the minds of his patients: oriental and classical Grecian exotica, almost religious faith in his method, his scientific medical professionalism, and the patronage of the elite. This combination made Dean Mahomed's Baths the epitome of fashion in Brighton for nearly two decades.

Mahomed's Baths opened for its visitors with a splendid vestibule, on the north of the building, off the fashionable Kings' Road. Dean Mahomed directed that the walls of this entrance room be covered with a mural of 'Moguls and Janissaries . . . represented in rich dresses, and the Muses, as they should be, in plain Grecian attire'. Over the years, Dean Mahomed further festooned the walls of this entry with relics, what a visitor called his 'trophies in the shape of crutches, spine-stretchers, leg-irons, head-strainers, bump-dressers, and club-foot reformers . . . [bestowed by] former martyrs to rheumatism, sciatica, and lumbago. Mahomed's vigorous and scientific shampooing having restored them to health'.

In this entry-way as well, Dean Mahomed kept his 'visitor's books', open for testimonials from his distinguished guests. Dean Mahomed divided his patients by sex and class: reserving one book, for example, for 'Ladies of the Nobility'. Dean Mahomed later mined these visitor's books, selecting particularly important people or glowing tributes for his publicity.

From this entry-room, ladies mounted the stairs to their floor above, while gentlemen proceeded directly ahead down a corridor through the centre of the building. A description of the gentlemen's corridor written by a naturalist has survived: On the walls, a 'profusion of trees laden with their fruits and rich foliage, meet the eye on every side, and description of the Duranta Plumina, the Chinese Limodoron, the large flowing sensitiloe plant or mimosa grandiflora, the rencalmina nutens or nodding grandiflora, the bouvardia versicolor, the bright rencalmis, is given with a correctness that is delightful. Birds of the gayest colours are represented also winging their rapid flight through sylvan groves, and Hebe [Greek goddess of health] is seen reclining on the ambent air, and strewing the earth with flowers, symbolical of the efficacy of the Medicated Baths, which are prepared in a peculiar manner from herbs, etc. the growth of India.'

Awaiting their time in the baths on separate floors, ladies and gentlemen amused themselves in reading rooms furnished with a variety of local and metropolitan newspapers and journals (which Jane and Dean Mahomed selected for the expected interests of their respective genders). These rooms faced south, overlooking the sea and, to the east and west, the Brighton seashore and open-air sea bathing machines. The walls of these reading rooms 'were beautifully painted in the most glowing colours, with Indian landscapes, from designs of Mr Mahomed himself. On one side is seen a superb pagoda, surrounded by a variety of figures in the costume of the country, making their profound salams. On another is a gorgeous temple, beneath which is represented an enormous idol, the object of idolatrous worship. Here is the celebrated car of Jaggernaut, and here a messenger just dispatched on a distant journey, on his camel, and armed as they are seen in India. On one side is a Rajah's mausoleum, and on another a group of Brahmins, and on a third a group of native musicians sitting beneath the umbrageous trees of that prolific soil. Here is a lake whose liquid surface is lost beneath the rising bosom of those distant mountains whilst the swan, swelling with pride, gently breaks the monotonous stillness of the scene and the rich plumage of the Balearic and Numidian cranes.' In addition, ladies had a 'boudoir' and gentlemen a 'private parlour' in which to wait their turn in the baths. Elevated balconies surrounded the building, including 'an elegant sun screen' room.

Arranged symmetrically off each of the central corridors stood the bathing rooms themselves, four on each floor. All the bathing rooms '[are] fitted with a marble bath, and have the means of giving in the same room hot water, cold water, shower, and douche baths. Four of them are also fitted with the Indian vapour or shampooing baths, two of which are appropriated for ladies and two for gentlemen.' Above, five bedrooms awaited any invalid or other guest who desired to remain for more extended treatment. Dean Mahomed located water closets discretely at various places within the building.

Unseen by the guests, but essential to the functioning of the Baths, were a basement with 'a large coal and store cellars, breakfast room, a manservant's room, kitchens, scullery, and other offices. A spacious area, in which is the steam engine room, surrounds the west and south sides of the house, enclosed with an iron fence, which is a most important benefit to the comfort and security of the building.' This steam engine pumped the large volume of sea and fresh water used by the establishment. To give a visual sense of the structure and apparatus of Mahomed's Baths, we can examine Illustration 13.[44]

As servants and bath attendants, Dean Mahomed and Jane employed two men and three women who lived on the premises and perhaps others who lived elsewhere in town. No one on the staff, except Dean Mahomed, was Indian. Adjacent to the Baths stood a comfortable house where Dean Mahomed, Jane, and their growing family lived.[45] To accompany this new Mahomed's Baths, Dean Mahomed developed a new public persona for himself.

## Dean Mahomed's Shifting Self-Presentations in *Shampooing*

Following the opening of his grand Mahomed's Baths, Dean Mahomed's fame and popularity grew dramatically. He enhanced this growth through frequent self-promotional publicity, projecting himself and his method as the latest in medical science and exotic fashion. In addition to his continuing newspaper advertisements, he expanded his book: *Cases Cured by Sake Deen Mahomed* (1820) into a full medical case book. Dean Mahomed followed this popular case book genre by organizing his book around a quasi-scientific analysis of diseases, symptoms, methods, cures, and testimonials. He named it: *Shampooing, or, Benefits Resulting From the use of The Indian Medicated Vapour Bath, As introduced into this country by S.D. Mahomed (A Native of India); containing a brief but comprehensive view of the effects produced by the use of The Warm Bath, in comparison with Steam Or Vapour Bathing. Also A detailed account of the various Cases to which this healing remedy may be applied; its general efficacy in peculiar diseases, and its success in innumerable instances, when all other remedies have been ineffectual. To which is subjoined An Alphabetical List Of Names (Many of the very first consequence,) Subscribed in testimony of the important use and general approval of The Indian Method of Shampooing*. In all, Dean Mahomed published three editions of this book: in 1822, 1826, 1838. Each edition expanded the previous one, adding another layer to his identity to reflect the self-image he wished to project at that time (see Illustration 14).

This work received serious attention in at least one leading literary journal.[46]

In the first edition of *Shampooing* (1822), Dean Mahomed created formal medical credentials for himself. In an age when each medical faculty (Physicians, Surgeons, and Apothecaries) was gradually organizing itself into a Royal College, with standards of formal training required for admission, Dean Mahomed clearly felt the need to qualify himself.[47] In the 1820s, the standards for such medical qualifications were still in the process of formulation; decisive legislation to regulate the medical profession did not pass in Parliament until 1858. In this entrepreneurial environment of the early nineteenth century, a range of self-proclaimed experts made fortunes selling medicine and medical treatments to the public.[48] Dean Mahomed, therefore, remained well within the bounds of medical and advertising ethics of the day.

In *Shampooing*, Dean Mahomed modified his autobiography considerably from that in *Travels*. As we have already seen, he had lopped off his thirty years in Ireland and London, at first by tacit omission and later by explicit statement. In *Shampooing*, he provided himself with ten years of medical training in India, prior to his entry into the Company's Army:

> The humble author of these sheets, is a native of India; and was born in the year 1749, at Patna, the capital of Bihar, in Hindoostan, about 290 miles N.W. of Calcutta. I was educated to the profession of, and served in the Company's Service, as a Surgeon, which capacity I afterwards relinquished, and acted in a military character, exclusively for nearly fifteen years. In the year 1780, I was appointed to a company under General, then Major Popham; and the commencement of the year 1784, left the service and came to Europe, where I have resided ever since.[49]

Thus in Brighton, Dean Mahomed increased his official age by a decade.

Later family traditions among Dean Mahomed's descendants attributed to him medical training in the Calcutta Hospital and such medical success that he received his promotion to Subedar as a result of them: 'Of Mahomed's early life in India it is definitely known that he was a medical student at the hospital in Calcutta. He had much success in treating cholera in the 27th Regiment of Native Infantry; in grateful recognition of this the

Colonel appointed him Soobahdar of the Regiment.'[50] This family tradition, including that Dean Mahomed served in the 27th Native Infantry, is not supported either by East India Company records or *Travels*. Rather, Captain Hugh Cossart Baker, with whom Dean Mahomed lived for a time in Cork, was an officer in the 27th Regiment of the Royal Army. Other descendants of Dean Mahomed explained the decade-wide discrepancy in the date he gave for his birth as due to the 'difficulty' of conversion from the Muslim Hijri calendar to the Christian calendar.[51] While Dean Mahomed may have given this implausible explanation to the curious and his descendants, the 1759 date of birth he stated in *Travels* accords perfectly with existing records and the chronology of the events of his life, while the 1749 date he asserted in *Shampooing* does not.

In the next edition of *Shampooing* (1826), Dean Mahomed further enhanced the amount of scientific medical development that had gone into his 'invention'. He repeated how he developed his 'hypothesis' about the properties of his vapour and shampooing. Echoing a scientific paper, he continued: '[I] sedulously applied myself, when I arrived here, in trying such preliminary experiments' on a range of medical conditions. He deduced that this process 'which in India is used as a restorative luxury, would, with certain improvements, operate in this country also, as a most surprising and powerful remedy for many cases of disease. I felt justified in publishing to the world the discovery I had made, a discovery supported by proof the most flattering and convincing'.[52] He further recounted the empirical evaluation by impartial (and initially sceptical) men of science who tested and proved his method:

> Since the publication of the first edition of this work [*Shampooing*], public attention has been excited; medical men of the first professional reputation did not think it beneath their dignity, to investigate the merits of my discovery, to apply the power of reasoning to account for causes and effects; and soon were convinced of the salutary and invigorating power of the Indian Vapour Baths combined with Shampooing, if judiciously applied. Upwards of a hundred medical gentlemen have since tried the experiment on themselves; most of them were invalids, but many were merely prompted by an honourable desire to ascertain truth. By those means the Faculty in general, even on the Continent, have had their attention drawn towards my humble

discovery. I feel this flattering distinction, and am in return most grateful and happy—I might add proud—when names like the following have thought proper to send patients to me.

He then named twenty-one physicians and surgeons who had referred patients to him, and continued:

I have had recommendations from two of the first Physicians at Paris; several German Physicians have visited my establishment and honoured it with their approbation. Under such auspices, it is not to be wondered at, when I assert that I could easily swell this edition with many hundreds of additional cases: but I shall only select a few which are peculiar and important. To the Public in general, and to the Faculty in particular, who with a candour worthy of their enlightened pursuits, not only appreciated the value of the invention, but at once grasped at the full capability of it, by pointing out diseases, the cure of which had not been contemplated, such as incipient pleurisy, putrid sore throat, etc. where the curative process depends principally on inhaling the warm steam;—to all I return my most grateful thanks, and I shall, by perseverance, prove myself worthy of such signal patronage.[53]

Thus, by this time, Dean Mahomed had located his medical discoveries within the European scientific discourse.

In addition to 'modern' medicine, Dean Mahomed also drew upon the European classical tradition to support his method. He pointed (albeit vaguely) to laudatory references to medical bathing in Greek literature:

BATHING is coevil with the remotest periods of antiquity. Homer mentions the use of private baths, which baths possessed medicinal properties, and were enriched by the most fragrant perfumes. In the eastern part of the world, it has ever been known and esteemed, and is continued in a variety of forms, to the present period. It is not distinctly stated by any author, I believe, that the Romans directed their attention in particular to the actual cure of disease by impregnated waters, nor did they, that I can collect, imagine any virtue to result from steam immersions, or any thing beyond the simple application of water.

This passage contrasted strikingly with the more specific, and scathing, classical references to it by Martial and Seneca that Dean Mahomed published in *Travels* (XXV).

Dean Mahomed further took authority for his method from

ancient Hindu practice: 'To the Hindoos, who are the cleanest and finest people in the East, we are principally indebted for the Medicated Bath, in cases of disease and bodily infirmity. Many complaints to which we are subject, arise from languid circulation, and for an inactive state of the animal functions, and which in many instances resist the use of medicine, and beget consequences the most protracted and fatal; the native practitioners of India are aware of this, and Shampooing has always proved a most salutary and effective remedy with them.' Dean Mahomed thus presented himself as building on Hindu traditions, somewhat broadening his personal identification from that which he advanced in *Travels.* Many among the British public never understood the distinction between Hindu and Muslim, or Dean Mahomed's relationship to either religious community, even after he had lived in Britain for well over half a century.[54]

Dean Mahomed also selectively appropriated European descriptions of the 'oriental' practice of shampooing. For example, in the course of showing the extent of the practice, he republished an account by the illustrious British traveller, Sir R.K. Porter, about shampooing in Persia.[55] Dean Mahomed, however, made no effort to link himself to the Muslim practitioners whom Porter described, nor to Islamic Persia. His inclusion of this westerner's description appeared as just another justification for the practice.

Nowhere, indeed, did Dean Mahomed specify his own training in his methods, or any family tradition, that would have prepared him for this career. His very self-identification as a 'native' of India thus would seem to have qualified him as a master of 'eastern' knowledge generally. Familiar as we now are with his earlier years, we can understand how, although he came to this career in his mid-fifties, he sought to indicate to his patients and potential patients a far longer commitment to the profession.

As Dean Mahomed retrospectively (1826) represented his start in Brighton, he revealed his image of the difficulties which he initially faced. He described himself as an innovative, but doubted, medical practitioner whose empirically derived method eventually triumphed over prejudice. This prejudice, however, appeared in his words to the British public not so much against him on racial grounds, but rather against him as an innovator with a better method, a challenge and rival to more established and conventional medical practitioners:

On my arrival in Brighton, I was not immediately enabled to promul-
gate the decided advantages which my method had over the common
Warm-bathing; I was fortunate however, in several gratuitous cures,
after every other attempt had been made and failed; cures which soon
gained circulation among those who were ignorant of the virtues of
my Bath, and adducing the most positive and convincing evidence
of the great superiority of Shampooing over every other description
of treatment, in peculiar cases. It is not in the power of any individual
to give unqualified satisfaction, or attempt to establish a new opinion
without the risk of incurring the ridicule, as well as censure, of some
portion of mankind. So it was with me: in the face of indisputable
evidence, I had to struggle with doubts and objections raised and
circulated against my Bath, which, but for the repeated and numerous
cures effected by it, would long since have shared the common fate
of most innovations in science. Fortunately, however, I have lived to
see my Bath survive the vituperations of the weak and the aspersions
of the [in]credulous.[56]

Here he explained clearly how the value and virtues of his methods
ultimately vindicated him.

## Dean Mahomed's Proprietary Claim to the Indian Method

Through the rest of his career, Dean Mahomed increasingly wove
together the identities of his method and himself, since each went
to legitimize the other. Alone among his rival bath house keepers,
he could point to his identity as an Indian and therefore to his
proprietary right to his India-derived method. Nevertheless, as
Dean Mahomed's fame grew, various competitors sought to ap-
propriate the terms and methods of 'Indian Medicated Bath' and
'Shampooing' for themselves. By the 1820s, both these terms had
became generic labels for a variety of methods found in many
baths. Dean Mahomed himself broadened Indian to mean Asian
generally. Further, Dean Mahomed also enhanced his stress on
the primacy of his practice as the 'original', drawing upon seniority
as well as ethnicity to legitimize his status.

As his success led to imitation by rivals, Dean Mahomed increasingly attributed to himself exclusive links and access to India.
One of his most competitive rivals, John Molineux, opened a bath
house similar to Mahomed's Baths (but somewhat smaller and
less elegant), two doors down on East Cliff in 1821.[57] In clear

imitation of Mahomed's shampooing and Indian medicated vapour baths, Molineux offered first 'affriction' and then, in an effort to shift the origin of this method away from Dean Mahomed's area of expertise: 'TURKISH MEDICATED SEA-WATER, VAPOUR, AND SHAMPOOING BATHS . . . the soothing mode of pressing the muscles and joints, which process is performed whilst in the vapour, and is called in TURKEY, and other parts, SHAMPOOING.'[58] Much to Dean Mahomed's disgust, many patrons and guidebooks conflated the two baths, so similar were they in advertisement, location, and operation.[59]

In response to this situation, from June 1821 onward, Dean Mahomed ran a series of front-page newspaper advertisements warning the public not to be fooled by such false imitators:

> In consequence of the many IMITATIONS of and the repeated attempts to rival his celebrated Indian Bath, [Dean Mahomed] thinks it necessary to assure the public that the art of SHAMPOOING, as practiced in India, is exclusively confined to himself in Brighton. The well known efficacy of HIS Bath, and the numerous cures performed by him (a book of which may be had at his house) will, he feels confident, save from reproach this invaluable remedy, should error result from a SPURIOUS and IMITATIVE process, or the application be attended with less favourable effects than have been witnessed in most cases where the GENUINE INDIAN method of SHAMPOOING has been administered. HIS BATH is well known to the faculty, and is recommended in all cases of Gout, Rheumatism, Paralysis, old Sprains, Colds, Hurts of various kinds, and many other diseases to which the human frame is subject. It is simple in its operation and therefore more easily imitated, but though the outward appearance may be copied, the EFFICACY of it defies competition.
>
> To avoid mistake the public are particularly requested to enquire for MAHOMED'S BATHS, No. 39, EAST CLIFF.[60]

Molineux replied directly in his own series of public announcements, impugning Dean Mahomed's motives and medical training:

> J. MOLINEUX thinks it his duty in answer to an advertizement that appeared in last week's Gazette, which endeavoured to insinuate into the minds of the public his want of ability in what he professes to say, that although he dislikes the idea of imitations or quackery, *references* may be had at his baths, which will expose the unhandsome and unmanly allusions which have been put forth, and convince the public of their falsehood.

J.M. Does not, in the vulgar term, wish to *gull* the public by saying, that he was the first person that introduced Shampooing into this country, but, with the greatest confidence, he can say he understands it equal to any one who practices it, having, for the last eighteen years, been constantly employed therein, under the directions of the FIRST MEDICAL MEN IN THE WORLD, and thereby obtained a necessary knowledge of the human frame. And his study will ever be to relieve all diseases in which Shampooing is so eminently successful, which he flatters himself will be confirmed by most of the medical gentlemen in Brighton, to whom he returns his sincere thanks for the great support he has received during the eight years he has been in Brighton; and he begs to assure the public also, that he will pursue that line of conduct which has hitherto, he is proud to say, secured him their confidence. 'Let man live without envy.'[61]

Even as Dean Mahomed and Molineux battled over the provenance of Shampooing (Turkey or India) and similarly the legitimacy of Dean Mahomed's claim as an Indian or Molineux' claim as a professional medical man, other bath proprietors also sought to capitalize on Dean Mahomed's reputation. In 1823, the oldest bath house in Brighton, the 'Royal Original Hot, Cold and Improved Shower Baths' (founded by Awsiter in 1769), revised the treatment it featured to 'Improved Indian Medicated Vapour and Shampooing'. The initial advertisement for this 'new' method featured the term 'improved' six times and 'Indian' four times.[62] Eventually, however, these rivals gave up their direct imitation of Dean Mahomed's special methods. Nonetheless, Dean Mahomed had made the terms 'shampooing' and 'Indian medicated bath' widespread in the field (at least temporarily), consequently losing monopolistic control over their use.

As an illustration of the shift in authority among bath house keepers to Dean Mahomed's method, we have the case of William Seaman. In Seaman's series of advertisements in 1830, he claimed his establishment offered Continental and Turkish features:

Shampooing Turkish Medicated Vapour, humid sulfur vapour, Barège, and other artificial baths, plain, warm, cold, and shower baths. This establishment is conducted by Mr W. Seaman, and is the most complete in London. The baths are of marble, and every possible attention is shown to those who frequent them. The humid sulfur vapour baths in imitation of those at Baia, Tritole, St Germano, etc. were invented by Mr S.[63]

Five years later, Seaman altered his pitch to tout both his connections to an early Italian keeper of a Turkish bath house and also his own putative experience in India:

> [These] Shampooing, Turkish Medicated Vapour . . . Baths, being the first and only ones in England for above fifty years, were introduced by B. Dominicetti, M.D., from Turkey, in 1764, and are now conducted on the same principles by Mr William Seaman, whose experience in India enables him to unite all the advantages of the Indian and Turkish methods of Vapour Bathing and Shampooing, which sets it above competition . . . [64]

Thus, a number of Dean Mahomed's rivals both accepted that a connection to India carried authority and also claimed that connection for themselves. Dean Mahomed was therefore not alone in revising and inflating his qualifications.

The need to distinguish his treatment from those of others led Dean Mahomed to highlight his special status as an Indian, something that none of his rivals could claim as convincingly. As Dean Mahomed put it: 'The herbs and essential oils with which my Baths are impregnated, are brought expressly from India, and undergo a certain process known only to myself, before they are fit for use.'[65] Since he reported never having personally returned to India, one wonders how he arranged the importation of these special herbs and oils without rivals gaining access to them.

Further, as used by Dean Mahomed, and by his British audience, 'eastern' remained a loosely defined concept. Although Dean Mahomed most frequently used the term 'India', he also deployed 'the East' and 'the Eastern parts of the world' virtually interchangeably.[66] In addition, he advertised a range of treatments: courses of 'vegetable pills' (compounded from an undisclosed formula), 'Paste or Wooptong baths', 'electuaries', 'dry cupping', and 'electrification'—none of which were traditional in India.[67] On at least one occasion, Dean Mahomed displayed at his baths a model of an alleged freak of nature from China:

> a most extraordinary *Lusus Naturae*,—a native of China now living in that country. A most singular protuberance, bearing a close resemblance to the human shape, grows from his body, and which is so sensitive that on a finger being merely touched, a sensible motion is, we are assured, immediately perceived in the excrescence. He was,

we understand, born in this state, and it does not prevent his moving and walking around.[68]

Thus, to attract broad-based attention, legitimacy, and patronage, Dean Mahomed did not restrict his publicity or methods to 'Indian' tradition alone.

At the height of his career, London as well as Brighton newspapers featured extensive and laudatory, if not always precise, items in their news and editorial sections about his 'astonishing' cures.[69] Sometimes newspapers published 'news items' that they openly referred to as 'puffs' (at least in part, as a quid pro quo for Dean Mahomed's paid advertisements in their pages):

> The Shampooing and Indian Medicated Bath Establishment of Sake Dun [sic] Mahomed . . . is daily thronged, not only with the ailing, but the hale . . . the powerful efficacy of which have brought foreigners to him from all quarters of the World; and the advantages derived to them from his treatment have furnished him with testimonials to that effect from most of the Courts of Europe. Shampooing has now become common in most Bathing Establishments, from discoveries . . . made from the practice of Sake Dun . . . [70]

This puff appeared on the same day as the first of a series of paid advertisements by Dean Mahomed in this paper so the publisher may have been rewarding Dean Mahomed for advertising revenues.

Other times, these news reports seem to have resulted from genuine news interest with no apparent payoff from Dean Mahomed. Some of the stories simply paraphrased Dean Mahomed's own advertising copy. Others presented as 'news', fashionable society items extremely favourable to Dean Mahomed's business, for example: 'There are at this moment [1825] under Mr Mahomed's care no less than seven ladies of title, all of whom have experienced great benefit from his Medicated Vapour Baths. These baths are the weekly and daily resort of invalids from every part of the kingdom, attracted hither by the celebrity of Mr Mahomed.'[71] Since Mahomed's Baths stood as one of Brighton's main attractions, the local newspapers boosted the town's reputation by boosting his.

Even as Dean Mahomed's reputation spread back to the metropolis, his old patron, Basil Cochrane, threw his continued influence and reputation as the instigator of the vapour bath behind his rivals. Cochrane announced his conviction that Captain Edward Jekyll, Royal Navy, had invented a portable vapour bath apparatus far superior in convenience to fixed baths like Dean Mahomed's. Cochrane even appeared in print in 1825 as referring patients disappointed with the shampooing baths of Brighton to the London baths of Jonathan Green, a retired Royal Navy surgeon. Green's bath house in the club district of St James employed Jekyll's apparatus.[72] Green himself published a work deriding extravagant advertisements by his rivals (including, by implication, Dean Mahomed) and offering shampooing (which he stated, however, was of only limited benefit).[73]

Numbers of other bath keepers also published books proclaiming their distinctive methods.[74] Nevertheless, Dean Mahomed rose out of this welter of claims and counter-claims in a large measure because his undeniable identity as an Indian distinguished him in the eyes of his patrons: the British gentry and nobility. His most conspicuous support came Brighton's most prominent patrons, the English Royal family.

## Dean Mahomed as Shampooing Surgeon to Royalty

One of Brighton's most celebrated attractions, and sources of patronage, remained the English Royal family. In particular, George—as Prince, Prince Regent, and King—did much to embellish Brighton's reputation for fashionable and risqué society life. After the erection of Mahomed's Baths, Dean Mahomed received patronage from Kings George and William, and their courtiers, which did much to dignify his reputation.

During George's early visits to Brighton, he participated in outdoor sea-bathing which was Brighton's initial attraction. His changing public persona and health, however, led him to give up such a public activity from about 1806 onward and bath only in private. To indulge his tastes, he had a vast white marble bath constructed in his private bathroom in the Pavilion (in the northwest corner, just off his private bedroom) at a cost of some £600. This bath held over 7000 gallons of salt-water pumped in from the sea and heated to the high temperature he preferred.[75]

George occasionally entrusted his body to Dean Mahomed, who provided George with shampooing and vapour bath treatments.

Pleased with this treatment, in 1822 the King bestowed a Royal Warrant upon him: 'Admit . . . Sake Deen Mahomed, Esq., Shampooing Surgeon, Brighton . . . into the Place and Quality in Ordinary to His Majesty . . .'[76] Denominated both 'Shampooing Surgeon' and 'Esquire' by Royalty did much to elevate Dean Mahomed socially and economically.

On his part, Dean Mahomed capitalized on this Royal Warrant by inserting George IV's coat of arms in his newspaper advertisements (March 1822 onward). In 1825, Dean Mahomed installed (or perhaps reinstalled) an 'Indian Vapour Bath' apparatus in the Pavilion's royal bathroom, at a cost to the Royal household of £25.[77] He continued to sell bathing gowns of twilled calico and swanskin flannel, flesh- and bath-brushes, and other bathing gear to the Pavilion over the years.[78] Dean Mahomed's visits to the Pavilion to supervise his vapour bath apparatus excited the fascinated gossip of Brighton society, in part because he received advanced word of the King's arrival in town.[79]

While it is not clear how many baths George himself actually received from Dean Mahomed, the Pavilion account books reveal that members of the Royal household regularly bathed under Dean Mahomed's care, and under that of other bath house keepers as well. Each courtier had a favourite bathing method.[80] The most frequent patron of Mahomed's Baths (1822–37) remained J. Whiting, Page of the Back-stairs. Thus, Dean Mahomed entered marginally into the inner world of the Royal court, but even that access distinguished him in the eyes of Brighton society.

For Dean Mahomed, King William IV proved even more regular a patron than his brother and predecessor, George IV. Very soon after King William's coronation, he came to Brighton, issued his Royal Warrant appointing Dean Mahomed his 'Shampooing Surgeon', and took a course of treatment under him: 18 shampooing and vapour baths over the period 1–21 September 1830.[81] Significantly, King William took at least some of these baths by going to Dean Mahomed's own bath establishment—rather than simply summoning him to the Pavilion.[82]

In response to a royal summons later in 1830, Dean Mahomed hurriedly made up a special set of bathing equipment for the Pavilion (for which he charged handsomely): a 'Spanish Mahogany chair, covered with crimson velvet; Seat and cushion to match £5; Cain stool mahogany legs 15 shillings; 5 Bathing cloaks, making, etc. 5 guineas; Bath stool, 1 guinea; 2 Thermometers £1 14 shillings; 3 yards white cassimere £1 7 shillings; 1 box Eau de Carmes £1 4 shillings; 2 brushes 8 shillings; a pail 3 shillings 6 pence; Bath cloths 5 shillings; Flannel for Bath 15 shillings.'[83] In 1832, Dean Mahomed again treated King William and sold him more bathing gear: 'For the Vapour Bath: 22 yards superfine white cloth £22; Making ditto as a cover to fit bath 1 guinea; For His Majesty: Making a superfine flannel gown including flannel binding etc., £2/8/3; grand total £25 9 shillings 3 pence.'[84] While Dean Mahomed continued to shampoo and insert 'Indian' substances in his vapour bath, there was nothing particularly Indian about most materials he sold to the King.

Nevertheless, Dean Mahomed did retain an Indian identity in the royal court. His official court costume was visibly modelled on the Mughal imperial court dress. In portraits of him in this dress, Dean Mahomed's own ambivalent status was clear from his English neck-cloth (and presumably other English undergarments) worn beneath these green and gold silk court robes. He reportedly wore these robes to the horse racing track.[85] (See Illustration 15.)

In addition to Kings George and William, other members of the Royal family, both male and female, also patronized Dean Mahomed. In 1830, for instance, he treated the Landgravine of Hesse-Homburg; the next year he treated Princess Louise of Saxe-Weimar (Queen Adelaide's fourteen-year-old niece).[86] Dean Mahomed also treated other continental royalty, including Princess Poniatowska (Comtesse Tyszkiewicz).[87] For attendance on such noble patients, he charged a royal rate of 1 guinea each for a shampoo and vapour bath. Even more valuable to Dean Mahomed than his fees was the attention among the general public that such royal patronage brought him and his baths.

Dean Mahomed did much to make visible and emphasize his connection to the British Royal family through fervent expressions of loyalty to the royal house. He dedicated his book *Shampooing* to King George. Further, Dean Mahomed adopted a small, but for him unusual, public role in Brighton politics, when he placed himself among the inhabitants calling publicly for a town meeting to organize a reception for the newly-crowned King William IV.[88]

On each celebration of the arrival in Brighton, birthday, marriage, or birth of a Royal family member, Dean Mahomed highlighted his Baths with a prominent display, often illuminating them with the newly-available gas-lamps. Such expressions were duly noted in the Brighton newspapers. A typical newspaper notice detailed how Dean Mahomed placed:

> on the balcony facing the sea, portraits of the King and Queen [with the] motto 'Welcome to Your People'. Under the portrait of the King was written 'King William, Neptune's Favourite Son', and under that of Her Majesty 'Queen Adelaide, Patroness of Every Virtue'. The balcony was also hung with variegated Chinese lanterns. In front of the house: W. IV R., surmounted by a crown of gas, on the left side of which was a transparency, representing Fame crowning William IV, Britannia supporting the portrait.[89]

In another exhibit celebrating the anniversary of their coronation, Dean Mahomed used much the same iconography (apparently reusing the portraits, lanterns, and gas fittings) but added occasional verses (reminiscent of the verses in *Travels*):

> All England's love had crowned them long before,
> With homage rooted in the heart's sound core.[90]

For the newly crowned Victoria's first visit to Brighton, Dean Mahomed displayed:

> a transparency of large dimensions, representing Her Majesty walking into Brighton, preceded by a number of damsels strewing flowers before her; in the distance, a view of the sea, with the chain pier, etc. It attracted great attention . . . Also two others, one representing Britannia, with a portrait of Her Majesty, crowned by Fame; the other, a column, with the inscription 'Welcome to your People'. Also V.R. and crown in gas.[91]

Dean Mahomed's public display of loyalty to the Royal family was not unusual among entrepreneurs in Brighton, where Royal patronage bestowed the greatest cachet and attracted the attention of a less elevated but more broad-based market. Nevertheless, Dean Mahomed's arrays were repeatedly among the grandest.

Over the late 1830s, however, Dean Mahomed's connection to the British Royal family faded. Royal favour changed to other baths, making them more fashionable. For instance, early in 1835, King William turned his patronage to the rival German Spa, which then basked for a time in Royal favour.[92] Queen Victoria, despite Dean Mahomed's effusive expressions of loyalty, never graced his baths during her Royal visits to Brighton (1837–44); no evidence reveals that she ever submitted herself to a bath or shampoo at his or Jane's hands. Instead, while in Brighton, she bestowed her patronage on William's Royal Baths.[93] Nevertheless, Dean Mahomed's transient entry into the circle of attendants on the Royal family did much to draw the attention of society to him and his mode of treatment.

## Dean Mahomed's Social Position in Brighton

Dean Mahomed's rise and then decline in Royal favour paralleled his reputation in Brighton society generally. Through the 1820s and early 1830s, Dean Mahomed placed his name prominently before the public as a patron of worthy causes, donating up to £5 at a time. He particularly participated in supporting the Sussex County Hospital and General Sea-Bathing Infirmary, making generous donations from 1825 (even before its inauguration) through the early 1830s, most regularly and visibly as an official Steward for its Annual Charity Ball.[94] Such an association with the medical establishment, particularly in the role of patron, must have enhanced Dean Mahomed's professional image in society. Dean Mahomed also prominently donated for the relief of the destitute, subscribing to a fund to supply them with free soup and coal. He further offered his medical treatment gratis to the deserving poor, as his advertisements and the press noted.[95] Although Dean Mahomed had a reputation as a poor judge of horses, he contributed handsomely to the Brighton Race Fund through the 1820s, thus locating himself among the patrons of this sport of kings.[96] Such public acts of benevolence, however, cost money; each one of his £5 donations represented the gross income from sixteen Indian vapour baths (with shampooing).

Dean Mahomed and Jane's lives had been uneven financially prior to arriving in Brighton, and this continued during their years there. On a good day, Mahomed's Baths could provide twelve Indian Medicated Vapour baths and thirty hot water baths. In theory, this worked out to be nearly £8 per day. Such an income, however, would rarely be sustained. Because his bath rooms were dedicated by sex and type of bath, the operation had little flexibility. To run at full efficiency, Mahomed's Baths required an exact balance of female and male patients arriving evenly throughout the day, seeking precisely the type of treatment available at that moment. In contrast, his fixed expenses remained high: rental to the building's owner, salaries to the attendants, expenses including coal and laundry, subscriptions to many newspapers, advertising costs, and taxes. Given the seasonal nature of resort life in Brighton, long periods of little or no business would have to be expected. Nevertheless, in flush times, there would be a handsome income, no doubt enhanced with tips.

In 1825, only a few years after the establishment of his grand Mahomed's Baths, Brighton's leading architectural and construction firm, Wilds and Busby, proposed building him yet another, even more lavish bath house. This striking building would be located on the cliff perched above the sea-shore, at the central focal point of the vast Lewes Crescent of attached residential houses just east of Brighton.[97] While the interior of the existing Mahomed's Baths exhibited oriental themes, its exterior (while dramatically sited) followed a more conventional British pattern. The promoters of this new Mahomed's Baths announced that its 'style of architecture will be in strict accordance with the purest examples of Indian composition . . . '[98] While we cannot know exactly what the architect had in mind as pure 'Indian', it may have resembled the Brighton Pavilion. Indeed, Pavilionesque homes arose in several places in Brighton in this period.[99] Unfortunately, Wilds and Busby split up later that very year and this second product of Dean Mahomed's vision never materialized.[100] Nevertheless, Dean Mahomed's public image, only partly under his control, emerged from a number of writings by visitors to Brighton.

## Other People's Representations of Dean Mahomed

Most of the pen portraits of Dean Mahomed through the 1820s and 1830s tended to paint him in sympathetic but eccentric terms, as an established Brighton 'character'. During this period, his identification by the British public with India and Islam led not to its dismissal of him but to its grudging respect for what he had overcome. Some of his supporters lauded his medical accomplishments as bringing the best that the 'east' and Islam could offer. Others identified him in the forefront of modern medical innovation. Yet others regarded him as a society fashion which one was obliged to undergo while in Brighton. Among his detractors, the most consistent theme remained that his self-promotional advertising and his fashionable reputation were out of proportion to the medical benefits of his method.

A resort town such as Brighton spawned a genre of literature designed to amuse visitors by parodying its outstanding features, including Dean Mahomed. Despite the humorous intent, some of the associations made in this literature suggested the underlying presuppositions of the society that produced it. In this vein, the humorist Horace Smith identified Dean Mahomed with Islam and located him in European demonology about the Prophet Muhammad, yet in a way that praised Dean Mahomed's accomplishments despite this background:

> O thou dark sage . . .
> Sprung, doubtless, from Abdallah's son, [Prophet Muhammad]
> Thy miracles thy sire's outrun,
> Thy cures his deaths outnumber . . .
> Go, bid that turban'd Mussulman
> Give up his Mosch [mosque], his Ramadam,
> And choak his well of Zemzem
> Thy bath, whose magic steam can fling
> On winter's cheek the rose of Spring,
> To Lethe's Gulf condemns 'em . . .
> While Turkish dome and minaret
> In compliment to Mahomed,
> O'ertop the King's Pavilion.[101]

This poet explicitly placed Dean Mahomed in the lineage, both biological and moral, of the Prophet Muhammad. Nevertheless, in the poet's eyes, Dean Mahomed compensated for Muhammad's (alleged) killings by healing many more. This poet's identification of Dean Mahomed as an exotic being, linked to the exotic Brighton Pavilion, proved a frequent motif among such commentators. Dean Mahomed himself found this 'Ode to Mahomed, the Brighton Shampooing Surgeon' favourable enough to republish as a testimonial.

Other writers also counterpointed Dean Mahomed with the

Prophet Muhammad, playing the positive features of the former off against a popular British stereotype (usually negative) of the latter. For example, Cruikshank wrote:

> *Mahomed,* were here, O fie!
> Has worshippers no few;
> And less than half a crown will buy
> His heaven of *Shampoo.*[102]

Later, a reputed wit published a poem, the burden of which was that it was ironic that Dean Mahomed drank alcohol since someone named after the Prophet would not be supposed to do so.[103]

Other 'comic' works about Brighton, parodying its well-known people, mentioned his background but stressed his method in their lampoon. For example, Charles Malloy Wesmacott published a sketch of Dean Mahomed in 1825:

> A dingy empiric has invented a new system of humbug, which is in great repute here, and is called shampooing; a sort of stewing alive by steam, sweetened by being forced through odoriferous herbs, and undergoing the pleasant sensation of being dabbed all the while with pads of flannels through holes in the wet blankets that surround you, until the cartilaginous substances of your joints are made as pliable as the ligaments of boiled calves' feet, your whole system relaxed and unnerved, and your trembling legs as useless in supporting your body as a pair of boots would be without the usual quantity of flesh and bone within them.[104]

Dean Mahomed became so widely known that he even appeared as the 'straight man' in mocking anecdotes about other Brighton characters. One anecdote ridiculed a rustic and ethnocentric Brighton horse-dealer, called 'Buckhorse', for applying the terms 'savage Hingeon [Indian]', 'canibal', 'nigger wagabones', and 'black 'Ottenpot [Hottentot]' to both Dean Mahomed (who cured him) and Molyneux (who did not). The overall point of this story was that Buckhorse remained so fixed in his nature that he could not sell a used horse honestly. Although Buckhorse was extremely grateful to Dean Mahomed for curing his ills, he could not prevent himself from later cheating Dean Mahomed in the sale of an expensive but broken-down horse.[105]

In contrast, more sincere tributes to Dean Mahomed located

him among the innovators making use of modern steam-power. One former patient, John Hills, attempted verse:

> Though steam may drive the loom and wheel,
> Impress the bullion coin,
> 'Gainst wind and tide, impel the keel,
> Or drain the darksome mines,
> Yet thine is the noblest end
> For which it is employ'd . . . [106]

Over the years, Brighton newspapers contained a series of such well-meaning doggerel and prose items in praise of this Brighton luminary.[107]

During the 1820s and 1830s, the visiting British, continental, and Asian social elite came to see a course of treatment from Dean Mahomed as de rigeur for their stay in Brighton. Foreign dignitaries went with their English hosts to partake of this highlight of a visit to Brighton. We can only imagine the conversation as Dean Mahomed explained his 'Indian medicated bath' to his Indian visitors.[108] In 1833, for example, several among the Duke of Wellington's set, including the Duke himself, came to Brighton expressly to partake of his fashionable cure.[109] In 1823, the future Lord Seaford demonstrated his compliance with this fashion to his aunt, Lady Erne:

> I have I think given the Muscleman [Muslim] Doctor a fair trial for I have missed but two days since I came [to Brighton], and I have let him vapour my leg or my whole person just as he pleased, and shampoo me, and dry cup me—in short I have let him play his whole game; and as he cured Lady Louisa Cornwallis with three Baths, & General Capel with two, if he does not do me any good in fifteen he will have less right to complain than I shall. But I shall not complain much, for I have been mending . . . [I] pay some visits, and write my name Courtier like in our Royal master's sick list, and then be vapoured & shampood, which will occupy the rest of my morning . . . [110]

The imprimatur of the elite thus put Dean Mahomed on the visitor's map of Brighton.

Even decades later, Dean Mahomed remained an unusual figure, but one remembered fondly. One raconteur recalled Dean Mahomed as:

a truly worthy East Indian, whom I remember in my earliest childhood as a proprietor of some baths at Brighton, associated with which was a shampooing department . . . The shampooer was, I think, an eccentric; and, in his moments of unbending, used to sing to some Oriental tune, swaying his body to and fro meanwhile, a song of which I can only remember the first line, and the refrain—

'The ducks and the geese have all come over,
Sakerdeen Mahomed, Sakerdeen Mahomed!'

Whence the ducks and geese had come, and whether they had emigrated for the purpose of being shampooed by the excellent Sakerdeen Mahomed, I have no means of ascertaining.[111]

Even Dickens presumed his audience already knew about shampooing when he described a visitor to Brighton: 'Miss Pankey (a mild little blue-eyed morsel of a child, who was shampoo'd every morning, and seemed in danger of being rubbed away altogether).'[112] In a British traveller's description of medical practices in Turkey, he used Mahomed's Baths as the comparison that he presumed would be familiar to his British readers.[113]

Except for Dean Mahomed's competitors, few accused him of malpractice. Nevertheless, his extravagant advertising, and his free use of the names of his patients in those advertisements, seemed ridiculous to some. Horace Smith pointed out to a friend how the friend's 'miraculous' recovery had become part of Dean Mahomed's pitch: 'To put you in good humour again, I must tell you that Mahommed yesterday pointed out to a friend of mine a suspended crutch, which he averred to have been yours, and that he had enabled you to throw it away by shampooing you! There! if this assurance of your recovered equigravity does not restore your equanimity, nothing will!'[114] Thus, at least some believed that their medical history should not become part of Dean Mahomed's publicity without their permission. Nevertheless, at the height of his career, Dean Mahomed had inserted 'shampooing', and, to an extent himself, into English popular culture as exotically attractive.

## The Changing Environment of Mahomed's Baths

From the 1820s onward, the Brighton Town Commissioners determined on several massive redevelopment projects for the town's shore-front. The crumbling cliff had always in the past proved a hazard to the town's control over its shoreline. Thus, at vast expense (over £100,000), the town built broad sea-walls in front of the cliff and filled in the intervening space eventually to create a wide, 'Grand Junction Road' and esplanade. Lady Wharn-cliffe rhapsodized in 1840 about this newly completed road and promenade, built on the sea-wall up to 60 feet high and 23 feet broad.[115]

Beyond any financial losses incurred by this disruptive construction, Dean Mahomed had to pay for part of the costs.[116] Further, the pipes and pumping arrangement that brought sea-water to Mahomed's Baths had to be reconstructed due to the new wall.[117] While the ultimate result was a more secure foundation for Mahomed's Baths, the noise and debris of construction must have brought discomfort to anyone seeking a bath in his house. In addition, at various times, access to the house was precluded or made difficult due to the workmen, equipment, and diverted traffic. Complaints by Dean Mahomed in 1837 to the Town Commissioners about inadequate lighting and disruption met with little satisfaction.[118] Perhaps to compensate for obstructed access to his Baths, in 1838 Dean Mahomed advertised a mobile bath service. He had a purpose-built carriage constructed, which he dispatched with attendants and vapour bath apparatus to the patron's rooms.[119] Certainly the ambiance of Mahomed's Baths, much of the attraction of his business, would be diminished by this extended construction outside its door and windows.

Further, all this construction isolated Mahomed's Baths from the sea-shore. Instead of a prominent (if perhaps insecure) location on the cliff-top, Mahomed's Baths by about 1830 had become land-locked. As we can see from Illustration 16, strollers now looked in at eye-level to both the ground-floor gentlemen's bath rooms and also the lowest level of the balcony, one of Mahomed's Baths most attractive architectural features.

Dean Mahomed's influence with the Brighton Town Commissioners seems always to have been limited. He periodically ran into confrontations with them over the physical operation of his Baths.[120] Despite his premier reputation within his branch of the town's health-care industry, Dean Mahomed never appeared among its civic leaders. Rather, he remained on the margins of town government and society. Part of this may have been by his own choice rather than by any legal restrictions on him. For example, while Dean Mahomed was a registered voter from 1841 on, he did not actually vote in Parliamentary elections until 1847.[121]

## Branches of the Family Business

Dean Mahomed had so identified himself with his method, that he found passing it on to the next generation quite difficult. The rhetoric of his advertisements accorded him a monopoly over the esoteric knowledge of his method. Only as an addendum could he try to make an exception to this monopoly for a son. As one news item (echoing one of Dean Mahomed's advertisements) put it: 'Shampooing has now become common in most Bathing Establishments . . . but it is irrational to suppose that he would suffer the chief secrets of his art to be torn from him, or rest with any person living besides himself and his son.'[122]

Over the years, Dean Mahomed and Jane proved very interested in preparing for his succession by their sons living with them in Brighton. Their elder son William, who remained in London as a postman, died in 1833. Dean Mahomed and Jane provided three of their younger sons with the 'modern' western medical training which he lacked. Yet, these sons thereby lost the proprietary claims to his 'Indian' methods.

Dean Mahomed and Jane first prepared their eldest son living with them, Deen, to be his successor as 'Shampooing Surgeon'. After their arrival in Brighton, they apprenticed Deen to Thomas Mapleton, 'Cupper to the King'. Cupping (i.e. bleeding) a patient was highly fashionable at the time. Unlike Dean Mahomed, Mapleton was salaried as part of the Crown's civil list. Since Molineux, Dean Mahomed's main competitor in Brighton, had also been apprenticed to Mapleton, Dean Mahomed may have been trying to match or surpass this competitor's qualifications, at least in the next generation.

For a time, Deen Mahomed junior worked hard to establish himself as a 'cupper' in Brighton. He ran a series of copious advertisements (1828–9), modelled on his father's publicity.[123] Deen's profession as a cupper, however, derived no special advantage from his Islamic name (or his distinctive identity as an

Indian) in the eyes of many of his potential clients. Until mid-1830, Deen also served as a shampooer in support of his father in Mahomed's Baths.[124]

Later in 1830, Dean Mahomed established a bath house for Deen in a fashionable district of London: at 11 St James Place, quite near both St James Palace and also the numerous gentlemen's clubs that clustered there. Having remodelled the house, adding the necessary apparatus for a range of bath services and shampooing, Deen entered into his new life.[125] Four years after having established himself in London, Deen married Mary Ann Malthus at St James Church, Westminster.[126] Unfortunately, however, it seems Deen died sometime in 1836.[127] Although Dean Mahomed arranged for another bather (Susan Whittaker) to temporarily manage the establishment, within a year this bath house went to a rival, George Fry.[128]

Fry, after making his own alterations, reopened this establishment, baldly exploiting Dean Mahomed's hard won reputation. Fry called his business 'The Genuine Indian Medical Vapour Bath' and then, even more blatantly, 'Mahomed's Baths'. Dean Mahomed felt he could not allow this crude infringement on his reputation to go unchallenged. Since the law courts offered him no copyright or trademark protection, Dean Mahomed responded by opening his own bath house at 7 Little Ryder Street, a few blocks from Fry. Although a smaller house and in a less desirable location than St James Place, this Ryder Street establishment boasted one advantage that Fry could not match: Dean Mahomed himself.

When he opened his Ryder Street Baths early in 1838, Dean Mahomed was nearly eighty years old and admitted to a reluctance to take on this new operation. Nevertheless, he publicized his new enterprise among his established clients at Brighton (many of whom resided in London) and made himself available there to 'be personally consulted'.[129] He promised this bathing establishment would offer the same quality services as that in Brighton. He further warned people against Fry's rival business 'carried on in [Dean Mahomed's] name, [but] with which he has not, nor ever had the slightest connection'. Fry, however, lasted until 1842. By 1844, the St James Place house had been taken over by an established surgeon, George Alfred Walker, who continued it as a bathing establishment but without infringing upon Dean Mahomed's name, calling it the less imitative 'Steam Bath Company' and 'Polythermal Institution'.[130] Having beaten off his imitator, Dean Mahomed gradually withdrew from active involvement with the Ryder Street Baths, leaving them to his eldest surviving son, Horatio, to manage. Horatio took over their operation almost entirely from about 1843 onward.

Horatio, like his late elder brother Deen, had received the 'modern' medical education valued in the profession. As Dean Mahomed publicly proclaimed in 1833 (when Horatio was 17 years old):

> he [Dean Mahomed] has not only imparted to his Son the fullest instruction in the Indian Art, but in order to render him conversant with its important duties, he has placed him under the most eminent Anatomical Instructors in London, for the purpose of obtaining a correct knowledge of the human frame; and having completed his various studies as house pupil to Mr Millard, and at Graingers School of Anatomy, Webb Street, Boro', during which he attended all the lectures and demonstrations etc., become perpetual pupil, he will be in constant attendance at the Baths, in order to receive the instructions of, and correctly apply the Baths according to the directions of the Medical Profession, to which the most implicit attention will be given. He also begs to state that his son has closely applied himself to the study of Cupping at St Thomas's Hospital, having been receiving the instruction of Mr Hill, Cupper to that establishment, which art he also purposes following in all its various branches.[131]

Despite these encomiums on his son Horatio, in this public announcement Dean Mahomed did not actually mention Horatio's name, only his relationship to Dean Mahomed himself. Thus, Dean Mahomed apparently found it hard to give up his personal identification with his method. Nevertheless, Horatio gradually established himself as a shampooer and bath house keeper in London.

Back in Brighton, Dean Mahomed and Jane looked to their two youngest sons. Frederick never seems to have participated in the family business. Rather, he developed an enthusiasm, and a career, as a dancer and then a fencer. Broadening from this central interest, he established himself in Brighton as a teacher of gymnastics for men and 'hygeinics' for women. From the mid-1840s, Frederick ran his own gymnasium and carried on with success in this profession.

Dean Mahomed and Jane's youngest son, Arthur Ackber Mahomed, proved not so great as their heir apparent. As the reputation of Mahomed's Baths in Brighton seemed to flag in the late 1830s, Arthur apparently did little to enhance the family name. By 1839, Dean Mahomed and Jane felt compelled to publicly advertise their repudiation of Arthur's debts: 'Mr and Mrs S.D. MAHOMED find themselves under the painful necessity of cautioning their Friends, and the Public generally, against giving Credit to their youngest son, ARTHUR ACKBER MAHOMED, who is a minor, and has no means of paying any Debts improvidently contracted.'[132] Nevertheless, Arthur continued to live with his parents as they were forced into retirement and carried on their reduced bathing establishment in Brighton for many years after their deaths.

## Dean Mahomed Loses Mahomed's Baths (1841–51)

Despite Dean Mahomed's distinguished reputation, he did not have full control over his career. While the town of Brighton continued to grow and develop, Mahomed's Baths began to lose its prominence from the end of the 1830s. Queen Victoria did not continue her royal uncles' patronage of Mahomed's Baths. Already into his eighties, Dean Mahomed may have found life as an innovative entrepreneur exhausting.

Instead of being fresh and innovative, Mahomed's Baths became somewhat stodgy in the eyes of Brighton society. Reviewers of bath houses in the late 1830s began to criticize Mahomed's Baths as having become something of a 'museum', lacking 'the air of freshness and sweet atmosphere' found in its rival bath houses. While his baths appeared passé, Dean Mahomed personally remained 'One of the greatest curiosities at Brighton'. Nevertheless, even he had become something of a fossil, his anecdotes all too familiar:

SAKE DEEN MAHOMED, who is nearly as old as his more holy name-sake and prophet, who stands before you to tell his own story and panegyric, and narrates it erect, hale, firm, and without tremulousness of any sort, at the age of ninety-two! Out of pure respect for this quasi-century on two legs, one listens attentively to all he has to say. How he first entered the Indian army, and fought in all the battles on the banks of the Ganges and Brahmapootra, and was at the siege of Chunarghur and Mirzapoor, and Heavens knows what other sieges, and got a commission, and found himself penniless by the breaking of his banker in Calcutta (no uncommon thing, by the bye, in that region), and how he came to Europe to work out the skill he had acquired by a few years' service in the *medical department*, to do good to suffering humanity, and become a very celebrated character.[133]

After a quarter century in Brighton, Dean Mahomed found it difficult to generate the feeling of novelty within his audience. Nevertheless, he could still retain their attention as a 'character'.

An unfortunate financial blow hit Dean Mahomed in 1841. Mahomed's Baths remained owned by a silent partner, Thomas Brown. When that partner died, Brown's executors determined to sell Mahomed's Baths. Despite twenty years of flourishing practice, Dean Mahomed himself did not have enough capital to purchase Mahomed's Baths. Thus, Brown's executors offered Mahomed's Baths by public auction.

In the auction notice, Dean Mahomed's reputation featured as the establishment's greatest asset. Dean Mahomed, however embarrassing this open advertisement of his dependence may have been, offered in the auction announcement to lease Mahomed's Baths from whomever made the highest bid. To add to this public embarrassment, the first auction (16 October 1841) failed, since no one was willing to meet the reserve price. Mahomed's Baths were not worth in a public market what the owners expected. Almost two years later (12 August 1843), Brown's executors once again offered Mahomed's Baths at a public auction, this time with no bottom price. Dean Mahomed, Jane, and their youngest son Arthur moved to a far more modest rented establishment on 2 Black Lion Street.[134]

The purchaser of Mahomed's Baths, William Furner (a solicitor of the firm Furner and Hill, perhaps acting with a client's money) leased Mahomed's Baths not to Dean Mahomed but rather to a long-standing rival, William Knight. Knight entered on a five year lease, at only £210 annually for the building.[135] While Dean Mahomed and Jane sought to revive their fortunes in their smaller and more obscure house on Black Lion Street, Knight capitalized on Dean Mahomed's lingering reputation. Knight hired the same bath attendants and servants who had worked for Dean Mahomed. Further, he advertised the Baths almost exactly as had Dean Mahomed:

> Original Indian Medicated Vapour and Shampooing Baths . . . known as MAHOMED'S BATHS, the CELEBRATED INDIAN MEDICATED VAPOUR AND SHAMPOOING BATHS (first introduced into England at this Establishment) as well as Water Baths of every description, are still to be had in precisely the same way, *and with every attention* to comfort as originally. The same attendants who have for many years lived in the house and given such universal satisfaction, being retained by W.K.[136]

In response to this marketing of his name and claim to primacy, Dean Mahomed took out counter-advertisements announcing he had no connection with his former establishment and now practised the profession in his home on Black Lion Street. Interestingly, in these later years (1844–5), Jane's name resurfaced in their announcements, from whence it had faded since the initial advertisements of 1815: 'The Ladies Bath is under the entire personal administration of Mrs Mahomed.'[137] Indeed, Dean Mahomed and Jane continued to advertise in newspapers for clients at least until late in 1845, and local directories listed him as active until just before his death, although their son Arthur may have been doing much of the actual shampooing.[138] Thus, when the railway opened between London and Brighton (in 1841), leading to a new boom for the town, Dean Mahomed was already moving toward a somewhat inglorious retirement.

By the time Jane and Dean Mahomed died (26 December 1850 and 24 February 1851 respectively), they had largely faded from public attention. Newspaper obituaries uniformly took the tone that Dean Mahomed, once so important to the town's development, had largely been forgotten. They presented him as too innocent to be a successful entrepreneur: 'That a man who was so [generously] disposed and little conversant with 'business' should, as age grew upon him, have encountered reverses, is not calculated to excite surprise but it may be a satisfaction to all who knew this philanthropist in the brilliant phases of his career to learn that his declining years were rendered comfortable and cheerful by the untiring attention and care of a dutiful son [Frederick].'[139] His reputation had been such that several London periodicals eulogized him.[140] Thus, as prominent as he had made himself through entrepreneurial and medical innovation, Dean Mahomed remained ultimately dependent on the fickle patronage of British society.

## Notes

1. Richard Russell, *Dissertation on . . . Sea-Water* (1752). See also Anthony Relhan, *Short History* (1762, 1829).
2. Thomas Babington Macaulay, *Letters*, ed. Thomas Pinney (1974) letter dated 11/8/1814, 1: 48–9.
3. John George Bishop, *Peep into the Past* (1892), pp. 225–6; Hot and cold baths were established in Margate by 1760s, Scarborough by 1798, and Weymouth by 1785. Sue Farrant, *Georgian Brighton* (1980), p. 15.
4. John Feltham, *Guide* (1806), p. 85.
5. *Picture of London* (1808), p. 18.
6. Mrs Fitzherbert to Creevey 28/12/1819 in Thomas Creevey, *Creevey's Life and Times*, ed. John Gore (1934), p. 115.
7. Census figures cited in Henry Martin, *History of Brighton* (1871), p. 26 and Farrant, *Georgian Brighton*, pp. 3, 23.
8. Thomas Walker Horsfield, *History* (1835), 1: 127.
9. Edward Brayley in John Nash, *Illustrations* (1838), p. 1.
10. For popular images of George in Brighton see: Humphrey Hedgehog, *Pavilion* (1817) and Anonymous, *Peep at the P\*v\*\*\*\*n* (1820).
11. See Sue Farrant, 'Physical Development of the Royal Pavilion' (1992), pp. 171–84 and Henry D. Roberts, *History of the Royal Pavilion* (1959).
12. Brayley in Nash, *Illustrations*, p. 4.
13. Osbert Sitwell, *Discursions* (1925), p. 38.
14. H. Repton, *Designs for the Pavilion* (1808), pp. v, 27.
15. Mrs Fitzherbert called it 'the building which it is impossible for me, or indeed any one else, to describe'. Mrs Fitzherbert letter 28/12/1819 in Creevey, *Life*, p. 115.
16. William Hazlitt, *Notes on a Journey* (1826), pp. 3–4.
17. E.g. Charles Grenville, *Grenville Diary*, ed. Philip Whitwell Wilson, (1927) 18/12/1821, 1: 113
18. Sitwell, *Discursions*, p. 38.
19. Dean Mahomed published testimonials in Brighton dated September 1814 from grateful patients living there, whom he named, and therefore are unlikely to be forgeries. He may have come to Brighton a little earlier but none of his testimonials date from before September 1814 or come from anywhere except Brighton.
20. A testimonial (10/11/1814) jointly thanked and tipped Dean Mahomed and a waiter at New Steyne Hotel. S.D. Mahomed, *Cased Cured* (1820), pp. 28–9. Mott's New Steyne Hotel featured baths from at least 1815, see Feltham, *Guide*, pp. 117–18. In 1818, a bath house on nearby

Devonshire Street owned by W.R. Mott discharged dirty water downhill, polluting wells and undermining the street below. Brighton Commissioners, 'Minute Books' 4/2/1818.

21. No date but early in 1815, in John Ackerson Erredge, *History of Brighton* (Grangerized copy) 4: 149.

22. Mahomed, *Shampooing* (1822), Preface.

23. Feltham, *Guide* (1815), p. 118. For example, H.R. Atree, *Topography of Brighton* (1809) did not mention Dean Mahomed.

24. Mahomed, *Bath*, pp. 54–8.

25. Significantly, Dean Mahomed never mentioned Cochrane among the nobility whom he had treated.

26. See identical advertisements in SWA, 17, 24/4/1815, 1, 8, 15, 22, 29/5/1815.

27. For an inventory of equipment Dean Mahomed sold to the King see: LC/11/49: 10/10/1825, 5/1/1828, PRO.

28. SWA 9/10/1815.

29. Baptized 26/3/1815 at St Nicholas Parish Church.

30. Advertizement ca. 1815 in Erredge, *History* (Grangerized) 4: 149.

31. Atree, *Topography*, p. 62; John Bruce, *History of Brighton* (1833), pp. 43, 91; Brighton Commissioners, 'Minute Books' 10/9/1823; WO 55/1578(7) Minutes 17/2/1827, PRO Kew.

32. Dean Mahomed's financial backer for his Battery House Baths remained a silent partner. Such arrangements were quite usual. The newspapers of the day frequently held advertisements both from capitalists willing to invest as silent partners in promising ventures and also from entrepreneurs seeking such investments.

33. Born 17 November 1816, 2 August 1818, and 28 December 1819 respectively; Rosanna died 7 January 1818. St Nicholas Church baptismal and burial certificates.

34. C. Wright, *Brighton Ambulator* (1818), pp. 137–9.

35. Culverwell, *Life*, pp. 26–38.

36. Mahomed, *Shampooing* (1822), Preface; *British Traveller* (London) 6/1/1823; *Morning Advertiser* (London) 11/9/1828; and BG 17/11/1831.

37. E.g. D. Robert Elleray, *Brighton* (1987), n.p.; Sir Evan Cotton, 'Sake Deen Mahomed', *Sussex County Magazine*, 13 (1939): 746–50; Farrant, *Georgian*, p. 18; Clifford Musgrove, *Life in Brighton* (1970, 1981), pp. 203–5; Frederick Harrison and James Sharp North, *Old Brighton* (1937), p. 111.

38. E.g. John Aldini, *General Views* (1819); John G. Coffin, *Discourses* (1818, 1826); M. La Beaume, *Observations* (1818); Charles Gower, *Auxiliaries* (1819); Theodore Hart, *Treatise* (1819); William Scott, *Proposal* (1820); Andre Louis Gosse, *Account* (1820).

39. Dean Mahomed announced his new Bath on East Cliff as opened in February 1821 but must have temporarily shifted to West Cliff during the final stages of the construction of the Kings' Road late that year. See advertisement for his West Cliff establishment, BG 27/12/1821.

40. John Gloag, *Mr Loudon's England* (1970), pp. 200–1.
41. Newspaper clipping from 1821 in Erredge, *History* (Grangerized), 4: 148.
42. Thomas Brown, a largely silent partner, submitted the original plan for the Bath but left its management to Dean Mahomed. E.g. Brighton Commissioners, 'Minute Books', 19/3/1823, 2/4/1823, 11/11/1829, ESRO.
43. The sources for this composite are: Letter to the Editor from A. Monsieur, Dieppe, 12/5/1826, BG 1/6/1826; Granville, *Spas* 2: 562–4; Advertisements for the auction of the property, BH 18/9–16/10/1841, 8–29/7/1843, 5–12/8/1843, 24/4/1847–8/5/1847 and BG 16/9–14/10/1841, 2,9/8/1843.
44. The plan comes from Cochrane's *Improvement.* The basement, pipes, and bathing arrangements (for Middlesex Hospital) seem to be similar to Mahomed's Baths, although the latter had two floors of baths, no consulting room, and no 'Russian' baths.
45. Surviving Brighton Land Tax records, ESRO, listed Dean Mahomed as the proprietor and occupier of this house from 1822 until (the records end in) 1831. From July 1839 onward, Dean Mahomed and Jane used 2 Black Lion Street as their address. The Census of 6/6/1841, however, located them as having spent the previous night at Kings' Road. Perhaps they had moved back temporarily so as to install baths in their Black Lion Street home. In October 1841 and August 1843, other people lived in the Kings' Road house. From September 1844 until their death, Dean Mahomed and Jane lived on Black Lion Street.
46. E.g. *Gentleman's Magazine*, 93, 2 (August 1823), p. 162
47. See M[ildred] Jeanne Peterson, *Medical Profession* (1978); John Gibney, *Treatise* (1825), pp. 84–5.
48. See F.B. Smith, *People's Health* (1979), especially pp. 333–45.
49. Mahomed, *Shampooing* (1822), Preface. Popham, whom Dean Mahomed had almost certainly known in Cork, had died in 1821.
50. Cotton cites his interview with a grandson, Reverend James Mahomed (who died in 1935). Cotton, 'Sake Deen Mahomed'. Cotton may not be fully responsible for this article since the magazine published it posthumously.
51. George Mahomed, 'Sake Deen Mahomed', p. 42.
52. Mahomed, *Shampooing* (1826), pp. viii–x.
53. Mahomed, *Shampooing* (1826), pp. xi–xiii.
54. For example, in 1841 Granville referred to Dean Mahomed both as 'the Hindoo' and a Muslim in the same passage. *Spas* 2: 562–4. Dean Mahomed's own son Horatio recalled in 1843 that sceptics called shampooing 'a cheat and a Hindoo juggle'. *The Bath*, p. 57.
55. Mahomed, *Shampooing* (1826), pp. 94–5 selectively citing Robert Ker Porter, *Travels* (1821) 1: 230–3.
56. Mahomed, *Shampooing* (1826), pp. ix–x. C.f. Visram, *Ayahs*, p. 66.
57. Molineux moved his existing baths to this site from 15 Broad Street, Brighton. Mahomed's Baths was rated about 25–30 per cent higher in

assessed valuation than Molineux's. *Brighton Town Rate Books*, 1824, 1827, BRL; *Rate Books* DB/B65/1 (1826) ESRO.

58. E.g. BG 14/6/1821, 10/1/1822.
59. E.g. E. Wallis, *Brighton Townsman* (*ca.* 1826), p. 61 and Charles Marsh, *Clubs of London* (1828), 1: 168ff.
60. E.g. BG 27/12/1821, 28/3/1822, 4/4/1822.
61. BG 10/1/1822.
62. BG 25/9/1823.
63. *New Picture of London* (1830) and Pigot's *Directory* (1832).
64. *St James Chronicle* 12–28/3/1835.
65. Mahomed, *Shampooing* (1826), pp. viii, 17.
66. E.g. SWA and BG 22/2/1821.
67. BG 27/12/1821; Mahomed, *Shampooing* (1838), pp. 138–9; Mahomed, *Shampooing* (1826), pp. 49, 55.
68. BG 27/10/1825.
69. *British Traveller*, 6 January 1823.
70. *Morning Advertiser* (London) 11/9/1828.
71. BG 27/10/1825.
72. Basil Cochrane, *Vapour Bath* (1825).
73. Jonathan Green, *Short Illustration* (1825).
74. Examples subsequent to Dean Mahomed's *Shampooing* include: Robert James Culverwell, *Few Practical Observations* (n.d.), *Practical Treatise*, and *Life*; William Saunders, *Treatise* (1805); Charles Whitlaw, *Scriptural Code of Health* (1838) and *Treatise* (1831); Henry Weekes, *Warm Water Remedy* (1844); Thomas John Graham, *Account* (1829), especially p. 235; and Horatio Mahomed, *The Bath* and *Short Hints*.
75. Letter 19/8/1822 in *Grenville Diary* 1: 114; Brayley in Nash, *Illustrations*, p. 14; John Morley, *Making of the Royal Pavilion* (1984), p. 228.
76. Warrant from William IV. LC/3/69 Warrants and Appointments, 161a) 20/9/1830, PRO. The somewhat disordered records of George IV apparently do not include his warrant.
77. LC/11/49, 10/10/1825, PRO.
78. E.g. LC/11/49, 5/1/1828, PRO.
79. BG 28/12/1826, 4/1/1827. Musgrove expanded on this incident but gives the wrong year, *Life*, p. 171.
80. E.g. Dean Mahomed's bill for 22 baths to 4 members of staff @ 6 shillings LC/11/49, 10/10/1825; LC/11/49, 5/1/1828, PRO.
81. LC/3/69, September 1830; LC/11/69, 10/10/1830, PRO; BG 8–10/9/1830.
82. In the early days of their reign, William and Adelaide tried to brave the crowds of gapers who crowded around the Royal couple whenever they ventured unceremoniously among the public. Soon, however, they had to give up this practice since it created chaos wherever they went. E.g. when Queen Adelaide tried to go to William's Bath in 1831, the press of the crowd dissuaded her from entering it. BG 22/9/1831.
83. LC/11/69 quarter ending 10/10/1830, PRO.

84. 'Ordered 6 November, delivered 10 November.' LC/11/78, 31/12/1832, PRO.
85. BH August 4, 1888.
86. 23, 25/9/1830, LC/11/69, 10/10/1831, PRO; Lady Bedingfeld (Woman of the Bedchamber to Queen Adelide) recorded the medical treatment of Princess Louise of Saxe-Weimar and herself by courses of Vapour Baths and 'rubbing' in the Pavilion, September–November 1831. Lady Jerningham, *Jerningham Letters*, ed. Egerton Castle (1896) 2: 348–50.
87. Visitor's Book, BRL.
88. BG 19/8/1830.
89. BG 2/9/1830.
90. BG 15/9/1831; see BG 17/8/1826 for Dean Mahomed's tribute to King George IV.
91. BG 7/10/1837.
92. See G.S. Jenks, *Medical Observations* (1840); Edmund W. Gilbert, *Brighton* (1954), p. 73. Nevertheless, some members of the Royal Household continued to patronize Dean Mahomed's Baths: LC/11/87, 102: 31/3/1835 for two members of His Majesty's household: 9 vapour baths @ 8s.; one water bath @ 3s.; grand total £3/15; 31/12/1838 5 vapour baths for Mr Whiting @ 8s plus attendance 5s; grand total £2/5/0, PRO.

   Lady Wharncliffe asserted that Queen Adelaide favoured a German homeopathic doctor and German lotions, *First Lady Wharncliffe*, ed. Caroline Grosvenor and Charles Beilby (1927) 2: 126, 206.
93. BH 25 August 1849.
94. BG 24/3/1825, 10/2/1831, 9/2/1832, 11/1/1834.
95. BG 19/12/1833 7, 21, 28/12/1833, 18/1/1834, 15/2/1834; *Brighton Guardian* 26/2/1851.
96. Marsh, *Clubs* 1: 171–7; BG and BH, *passim.*
97. Lewes Crescent (begun 1823) was itself a copy of the innovative Royal Crescent in Bath. The developer of the Lewes Crescent in Kemp Town, Thomas Read Kemp, was one of Dean Mahomed's patients. Mahomed, *Shampooing* (1826), p. 51.
98. BG 7/4/1825.
99. Thomas Read Kemp built a house for himself with a dome, called 'The Temple'. In 1833 Amon Henry Wilds designed for himself a small oriental residence, the 'Western Pavilion'. Elleray, *Brighton*, caption to plate 111.
100. See Neil Bingham, *C.A. Busby* (1991), especially pp. 75–6. John and Jill Ford, *Images* (1981), p. 111. John Harris, 'Busby at Brighton', *Apollo* 135, 355 (September 1991), pp. 197–8.
101. Mahomed, *Shampooing* (1826), p. 88–90. Also in Horace Smith, ed. *Comic Miscellanies* (1841), 1: 330–3.
102. [Isaac] Robert Cruikshank, *Brighton!* (1830), p. 13, stanza xix.
103. 'Brighton Misnomers' by Bernard Blackmantle [Charles Malloy Wesmacott] in BG 27/4/1826.
104. Bernard Blackmantle, *English Spy* (1825) 1: 345.

105. Marsh on 'A Brighton Oddity', in *Clubs*, 1: 168ff.
106. Cited by Dean Mahomed in *Shampooing*, (1838), pp. 124–7.
107. E.g. John Shaw, Letter to the Editor BG 13/12/1821; Mahomed, *Shampooing* (1826), pp. 68–77.
108. Nevertheless, one such visitor, Deenshah Firamgee, probably a Parsi from Bombay, approved of the cure. Mahomed's Visitors' Book (*ca.* January 1827), BRL.
109. Alexander Finlay to Wellington 16/10/1833; James Dacre to Finlay 14/10/1833 in Arthur Wellesley, *Prime Minister's Papers*, eds John Brooks and Julia Gardy (1975), 1: 341, 343. See Visitor's Books, BRL.
110. Letter 10/4/1823, in Wharncliffe, *First Lady* 1: 315.
111. George Augustus Sala, *Life and Adventures* (1895) 1: 201–2.
112. Charles Dickens, *Dombey and Son* (1846–8) n. p.
113. Richard R. Madden, *Travels* (1829) 1: 64–5.
114. Horace Smith to Charles Mathews (1828) quoted in Arthur H. Beavan, *James and Horace Smith* (1899), p. 280.
115. Letter 16/8/1840 in Wharncliffe, *First Lady* 2: 307.
116. In order to subsidize the cost of the sea-wall, the Town Council assessed householders along its route for part of the expense. Anthony Dale, *Brighton Town* (1976), p. 199.
117. Brighton Commissioner's Minute Book, 27/8/1828.
118. For Dean Mahomed's complaints and the Commissioners' negative response see BH 23/9/1837.
119. BH 17/3/1838.
120. Brighton Commissioner's Minute Books 27/8/1828, 18/3/1829, 11/11/1829, 3/11/1830, 29/8/1832, 19/9/1832, ESRO.
121. Brighton, East Sussex, and Sussex Poll Books 1820–47.
122. *Morning Advertiser* (London) 11/9/1828.
123. BG 3/4/1828. These repeated irregularly through 3/12/1829.
124. Mahomed, *Shampooing* (1838), pp. 138–9.
125. Westminster Rate Books 1830–5, WPL.
126. St James, Westminster Parish Records 25/12/1834.
127. Deen apparently died prior to the national registration of births, deaths, and marriages instituted in 1837.
128. The Westminister Rate Books 1836, 1837 show this transition. Susan Whittaker went on to run a 'vapour and shampooing bath' in the City of London for many years.
129. BH 30/6/1838 and end matter in Mahomed, *Shampooing* (1838).
130. Westminister Rate Books, Post Office, Boyle's Court Guide (1844), and various other Directories. It lasted until the establishment burned out in 1854.
131. BG 7/12/1833, repeated irregularly until 15/2/1834.
132. BH 6/7/1839.
133. Granville, *Spas* 2: 562–4.
134. Jane Page was the owner. Brighton Valuation Registers 1846, 1848, Brighton Town Rate Book 1851, BRL.

135. Brighton Valuation Register 1846; Furner managed to get the assessed valuation of Mahomed's Baths building reduced by one fourth (from £214 to £160), BRL.
136. BH 5–19/10/1844.
137. BH 28/9/1844, 5/10/1844, 12/10/1844, 18/10/1845.
138. E.g. BH 18/10/1845. They also had two live-in English servants, 1841 census.
139. Brighton Guardian 26/2/1851; BG 27/2/1851.
140. Gentleman's Magazine April 1851, p. 444b. Willis' Current Notes (March 1851), pp. 22–3.

## Chapter Eight

# The Legacies of Dean Mahomed

### Dean Mahomed's Life and Works

Dean Mahomed accomplished much during his long life, and left many marks of his passing. He lived and wrote within a series of contact zones of unequal power relationships: as subaltern in the Bengal Army and then as an immigrant to colonial Ireland and then to England. In each context, he adapted himself to the dominant culture but also retained his own voice. He never lost the culture of his birth nor assimilated fully into that which he entered. Rather, he continued to reshape a series of distinctive identities for himself through negotiations with his Anglo-Irish and English audience. Nevertheless, there often remained a gap between the self-identities he projected and the perceptions held by the members of the dominant culture around him.[1]

In India, people like him who served the English East India Company shaped the development of colonialism. Although the British located Indians almost exclusively in subordinate roles, Indians nevertheless vastly outnumbered Europeans in the colonial army and administration and did much to determine how they functioned.

By writing his *Travels*, Dean Mahomed uniquely represented Indian society and the role of the English Company directly to the British society around him. Further, while many European sources for the history of the vital transitional period from Mughal imperial rule to English Company administration have survived, Dean Mahomed's *Travels* remains the only Indian description of this period composed in English. Indeed, only relatively few Indian accounts of life within the Bengal Army are available today in any language. Thus, to understand the history of India during a formative period of colonialism, his life-story (and that of others of his class) and his first autobiographical book prove particularly important.

Dean Mahomed's place among the Anglo-Irish highlights the complexity of the expanding British empire. The city of Cork thrived on the commerce among Ireland, India, the various other colonies, and England. His writings (and, indeed, his very presence) established a dialogue with the images of India and Islam then prevalent in Ireland. Further for a man of Dean Mahomed's background to marry and live relatively harmoniously among the Anglo-Irish elite for nearly a quarter century tells us much about the cosmopolitan nature of the empire.

During his two-thirds of a century in England, Dean Mahomed redefined and represented himself repeatedly, within a changing social and economic environment. His initial service as a shampooer for a Scottish nobleman and Nabob, Basil Cochrane, suggests London's social and cultural diversity as it developed into the core of a world-empire. His enterprise in purveying Indian cuisine to the English elite met only with mixed success. While restaurant critics applauded his sophisticated offerings, he proved unable to mobilize sufficient patronage to sustain his business. A century later, Indian restaurants would become a significant part of London's culinary world.

In Brighton, Dean Mahomed's marketing of his Indian identity and medical expertise finally brought him prominence. As Shampooing Surgeon, he made a place for himself in both the Royal court and also the thriving economy of this sea-side resort. Nevertheless, Dean Mahomed never secured sufficient capital to attain financial security. During his later years, Victorian English society once again moved him to the margins. He died dependent on his children.

## Dean Mahomed's Legacy in Brighton: His Baths and His Sons

Dean Mahomed and Jane left several kinds of reminders of their presence in Brighton. Their last years had been far from pleasant, after their ouster from their famous Mahomed's Baths. This building as well had a disappointing history. Their successor, William Knight, apparently failed to sustain its earlier glory. From their modest establishment on Black Lion Street, Dean Mahomed and Jane watched as the new owners once again put the baths up for auction in May 1847. Once again, the bidders failed to meet the reserve price of £4000, despite the fact that 'the auctioneer spared no pains to do justice to their merits either in their present shape or as a building speculation'.[2] When Knight's lease ended the next year, he left and took over as manager of the Royal Baths from his father-in-law, John Banister, who had himself been in financial difficulties. An established swimming bath company, Brill, took possession of Mahomed's Baths, refurbished and renamed it the Brill's Shampooing Baths, and ran it as a subsidiary establishment until 1870 when Markwell's hotel took over the site. Markwell's was itself later absorbed into the Queen's Hotel in 1908, which remains there today.

As Brighton continued to expand, it cast Dean Mahomed into the role of an eccentric founder of its bathing industry. The growing body of local histories located him among the earliest of the bath house keepers: accepting his later anachronistic implications that he arrived in Brighton in 1784, coinciding with that of the town's even more celebrated attraction, Prince George. Local histories have particularly emphasized the links among Dean Mahomed, the Prince Regent, and the Pavilion, at the cost of his more complex relationship to Brighton society. Some local histories picture Dean Mahomed lowering the portly Prince into the Pavilion's vast marble bath by means of a pulley apparatus.[3] Further, Dean Mahomed has been crudely commercialized. For example, the hotel now located on the site of his former Mahomed's Baths advertised (in the 1970s) its 'Sake Dene Cocktail Lounge'.

Dean Mahomed and Jane's youngest son, Arthur Ackber Mahomed, inherited their direct legacy: the operation of their shampooing and bathing establishment. At their rented Black Lion Street home, and later a few blocks away (64 West Street, opposite St Paul's Church), Arthur continued in this profession, apparently until his death in 1872. Like his mother, Arthur's wife, Amelia, attended to their female patrons.

As an entrepreneur, however, Arthur lacked his father's charisma and lived in a different era. Arthur's newspaper advertisements only echoed his father's, highlighting Dean Mahomed's superannuated royal warrants, but said virtually nothing new about himself.[4] In some English eyes, he could not justly claim Indian 'authenticity' since his distance from India diminished his proprietary claims to the Indian methods of his father. In fact, Arthur's British clients who had actually lived in India suggested his was only a modest imitation of the authentic Indian shampoo, of which they were expert connoisseurs; John Carnac Morris (late of the Madras Civil Service) explained that he had 'considerable experience' with shampooing in India and therefore he could judge Arthur's work against that standard.[5] At the same time, however, some English also excluded him from their society on racial grounds. In both Victorian England and the British Empire generally, racial discrimination intensified. Morris went on to identify Arthur with 'jettee' [Black] natives of India. Following the end of Arthur's career, his reputation faded quickly, leaving no legacy comparable to Dean Mahomed's in Brighton's local histories.

Dean Mahomed and Jane's second youngest son, Frederick, proved far more successful than Arthur, but in a different field. His entrepreneurial efforts made his gymnasium the centre for the exercise of the fashionable young of middle-class Brighton. Schools, ladies' seminaries, and private families appointed him to instruct their pupils in 'Orthopaedics', 'Hygenian Exercises', gymnastics, and fencing.[6] The fencing and gymnastic exhibitions which he arranged for his graduating class each year remained significant events in the Brighton social calendar.[7] He apparently prospered financially and provided shelter and care to his parents in their final illnesses.[8] He also appeared as a man about town in the distinguished gentlemen's clubs of London.[9] Further, continuing his family tradition of medical innovation, Frederick advertised a 'Portable Gymnasium' and an 'Orthopaedic Couch . . . to overcome that lateral curvature of the spine'.[10] While Frederick merged into middle class British society and never referred in his public advertisements to his partly Indian background, he nevertheless retained part of his father's heritage. Frederick and his wife, Sarah Hodgkinson, gave most of their sons at least one Islamic given name, in addition to their surname Mahomed: Frederick Henry Horatio Akbar (later a noted physician), James Deen Kerriman (a Church of England Vicar), Omar Said (an architect), Arthur George Sulieman (a physician), and Henry (or Herbert) Abdulla Salim.[11] Their daughters followed their maternal heritage with 'English' names: Florence Gertrude, Marcia Madeline, Adeline Alice Bertha.

## Dean Mahomed's Legacy in London: Horatio and His Bath

Dean Mahomed established his son Horatio in the Ryder Street Baths in London's clubland. Like Arthur, Horatio sought to sustain the legacy established by their father as a shampooer and bath house proprietor. Indeed, over his years in London, Horatio made a reputation in his own right. His second marriage in 1848 received a notice in the *Gentleman's Magazine*.[12] He drew the patronage of various distinguished members of London society, including the controversial David Octerlony Dyce Sombre who gave Horatio a £1000 tip (later disallowed on the grounds of the patron's insanity).[13]

Following in his father's footsteps, Horatio published two books publicizing both the practice of bathing as an ancient and healthful tradition and also his own Ryder Street establishment. The prolix titles, as in the case of his father's works, indicated the substance of his presentation. The more general work he called: *The Bath: A Concise History of Bathing, As Practiced by the Nations of the Ancient and Modern World, Including a Brief Exposition of the Medical Efficacy and Salubrity of the Warm, Medicated, Vapour, Shampooing, Shower, and Douche Baths, with Remarks on the Moral and Sanative influence of Bathing* (1843). In his more specific book, published the next year, Horatio aimed more pointedly at promoting his Ryder Street establishment: *Short Hints on Bathing, With Special Reference to the use of the Indian Medicated Vapour Bath, with the Operation of Shampooing, Being the Result of the Experience of the Author and his Father, Sake Deen Mahomet, During a Period of Fifty Years.* Although Horatio dedicated his books to his father, he made virtually no mention of India as a model or source. Rather, he acknowledged Basil Cochrane's innovations in the field. Further, in an ambitious scheme, Horatio proposed a chain of Mahomed's Bath Houses in each 'of the principal towns in England' and claimed that 'a large body of the most respectable inhabitants of Yarmouth' had already begun establishing a bath on Dean Mahomed's design.[14]

As in the case of his father, however, Horatio lacked the

financial resources to sustain a leading place in their profession. Horatio's small establishment succumbed to a far more heavily capitalized corporation: the Metropolitan Bath Company, Ltd. In 1858, this company hired him briefly as its 'Resident Manager'. But the next year, Horatio went back into business for himself. He returned to his parents' old neighbourhood near Portman Square and opened a small operation at his home: 42 Somerset Street where he remained until his death in 1873.[15]

## The Appropriation of the Vapour Bath

Dean Mahomed's concept of Shampooing and the Indian Medicated Vapour Bath also merged into British society. By the mid-nineteenth century, however, a growing sense of British imperial supremacy meant that Britons sought control over this 'oriental' practice. No longer did the people of the 'East' have much of an audience in Britain. Rather, Britons took control of explaining the nature of the 'East' to Britons, and to Asians as well. Thus, while the techniques developed and made famous by Dean Mahomed persisted in England, Britons appropriated them.

Most influential, the celebrated British traveller to the eastern Mediterranean, David Urquhart, claimed to represent the 'East' to Britain. In a book published years after Dean Mahomed's death, Urquhart argued that hot baths had no Indian or Turkish origin at all but rather had initially 'belonged to the Celtic races', and had been adopted from them by the Romans and subsequently by Turks.[16] Despite the opposition of the Prophet Muhammad, Muslims adopted vapour bathing but used it almost exclusively as a sensual luxury. Thus, he argued, while vapour bathing died out in the West, it was preserved in the 'East'.

Urquhart asserted his authority over the practice by claiming that he was the first ever to realize the method's full and precise medicinal benefits. When he returned to Ireland in the mid-nineteenth century, he inspired a new generation of bath keepers, first in the region around Cork and then in Dublin and England. In so doing, Urquhart and his apostles ignored the earlier bath houses which had existed for a century in Ireland and England. Urquhart went on to assert that the Turks, recognizing the improvements he had made, subsequently copied his British therapeutic form of the baths.[17] Thus, by a convoluted argument, Urquhart claimed the 'Turkish Bath' as an aboriginal British tradition and took an authoritative leadership role in the medical-bathing profession.[18]

As the nineteenth century proceeded, Turkish Baths became an established industry in England. For example, in 1862 the London and Provincial Turkish Bath Company erected a massive bath complex on Jermyn Street (near the site of Dean Mahomed's Ryder Street baths), designed by the noted architect George Somers Clarke. An account from 1873 about these Baths reveals that British public opinion had settled on a classical Roman identification for them, rather than Indian: ' . . . the plan of the old Roman bath is strictly followed. There is the Tepidarium, the Sudatorium . . . and the Calidarium . . . Next to this is the Lavatorium, in which the washing and shampooing process is carried on.'[19] While Turkish baths continued to offer 'shampooing' into the twentieth century, the actual practitioners of this art held the status only of relatively high paid servants, often spoiled by association with men above their station.[20] The claims of Dean Mahomed and his sons for the primacy of their Indian vapour bath became lost in this welter of assertions.

### Dean Mahomed and the Asian Community in Britain

Over the century since Dean Mahomed's death, English attitudes toward Indians hardened. While Dean Mahomed and Jane's 'inter-racial' marriage apparently excited no comment during their lifetimes, their descendants continued to be marked as different by the English around them. Many English contemporaries of these descendants continued to remark upon their alien features: 'dark and typically Eastern', with an 'Oriental strain . . . to [their] looks and character'.[21]

As the British Empire developed during the years after Dean Mahomed's death, English society altered its attitudes toward an 'oriental' identity. Dean Mahomed marketed his Indian birth, costume, and medical methods as attractive features of his medical persona. He used his 'oriental' identity to elevate him above his rivals. English identification of his descendants as 'oriental' did not preclude their rising in their careers—

particularly in the medical profession—but it apparently did not help them either.

During the late twentieth century, members of the Asian community in Britain have regained a public voice and been drawing attention to the achievements of early Indian immigrants. Coming out of the context of deep racial tensions in post-World War II Britain, their words are beginning to be heard within the wider British community. Some among them have pointed to Dean Mahomed as an early Asian professional in England, making him a symbol of early 'Black' contributions to British society. In recognizing Dean Mahomed's achievements, we should ensure that his image is not again divorced from his own deeds and writings.[22]

Soon after Dean Mahomed's death, British society absorbed each of his accomplishments, with only a limited recognition of their significance. Most histories of British colonial rule in India or in Ireland have overlooked his book *Travels*. His life in London, like that of the thousands of other Asians living there, has likewise not received much attention until recently. In Brighton, the town continues to celebrate him as a local eccentric character, but according to its own perspective on his life and works. Dean Mahomed and his writings and life deserve to be remembered and understood on their own terms, allowing us access to these transitional years in the history of India, Ireland, and England within the burgeoning British Empire.

## Notes

1. Pratt uses 'transculturation' to 'describe how subordinated or marginal groups select and invent from materials transmitted to them by a dominant or metropolitan culture. While subjugated peoples cannot readily control what emanates from the dominant culture, they do determine to varying extents what they absorb into their own, and what they use it for. Transculturation is a phenomenon of the contact zone', *Imperial eyes*, p. 6.
2. BH 15/5/1847.
3. Musgrove, *Life* pp. 104–5.
4. Advertisement (*ca.* 1853) in Visitor's Book, BRL.
5. Testimonial 30/10/1854, Visitor's Book, BRL.
6. BH 13/7/1839 and *passim.*

7. BH 17/6/1848; BG 8/6/1848.
8. Frederick owned several properties, including 49 Preston Street and 1 Palace Place and rented others. Brighton Valuation Book 1846, 1848, BRL. Richard Thornburgh, *Mahomed's Royal Gymnasium* (1980).
9. Sala, *Life* 1: 201–2.
10. BH 19/9/1840, 27/1/1844, 3/2/1844.
11. *Dictionary of National Biography*, s.v. 'Frederick Akbar Mahomed', *British Medical Journal* (1884), pp. 1099, 1165, 1206–7, 1261–2 (1885), p. 386; *Guy's Hospital Reports* 42 (1886): 1–10; G.H. Brown, *Lives of the Fellows* (1955), p. 276; H.C. Cameron, *Mr Guy's Hospital* (1954), pp. 212, 242–5; F.A. Mahomed, 'Contribution', *Practitioner* 15 (July–December 1876), pp. 21–36; Cameron, 'Frederick Akbar Mahomed'. George Mahomed, *Treatment of the Bournemouth Mont Dore* (1889); Horace Dobbel, *On the Mont Dore Cure* (1881).
12. *Gentleman's Magazine* June 1848, p. 656.
13. Codicil dated 26/5/1843 to an unattested will dated 10/5/1843, *Dyce Sombre against Troup*, p. 45.
14. Horatio Mahomed, *Bath*, p. 81.
15. Westminster Rate Books, 1859–73, Westminster Public Library.
16. Significantly, Urquhart did not make this argument in his first famous book, *Pillars of Hercules* (1850), but he developed it later in *Turkish Bath* (1856), pp. 6, 27. See also his *Manual of the Turkish Bath*, ed. Sir John Fife (1865). Charles Bartholomew accepted Urquhart's lead, *Turkish Bath . . . Evidence* (1871).
17. In support of this last claim, he cited articles in the *Turkish Medical Gazette* by Dr Millengen, Physician to the Ottoman Sultan lauding Urquhart's method.
18. Rival medical innovators, including Doctors Richard Barton and Richard Madden, competed with Urquhart for precedence and primacy in this reinvented Turkish Bath tradition. For various positions on the debate about the origins of the Turkish Bath in Britain see: Diogenes [pseudonym], *Life in a Tub* (1858 3rd ed); Photophilus [pseudonym], *New Irish Bath* (1860); Madden, *Travels*; Richard Beamish, *Lecture* (1859); James Lawrie, *Roman or Turkish Bath* (1864).
19. Edward Walford, *Old and New London* (1873) 4: 206.
20. Arthur L. Baxter, 'Extra Service', in Charles Booth, ed. *Life and Labour*, second series, *Industry* (1903) 4: 252–88.
21. Edith Ohlson, letter to editor, *Sussex County Magazine* 9 (January–December 1935), p. 331; Samuel Wilks, *Biographical History of Guy's Hospital* (1892), pp. 306–11.
22. Dean Mahomed appears, for example, in a visual presentation at Liverpool's Trans-Atlantic Slave Trade Museum although he had nothing to do with slavery or its abolition.

# Sources Cited

## Published Books and Articles

ABUL Fazl Allami, *Ain-i Akbari*, H.S. Jarrett, tr., Jadunath Sarkar, ed. (New Delhi: Crown Publications, 1988 reprint).

ACHMET, Dr, *Theory and Uses of Baths* (Dublin: J. Potts, 1772).

—— *To the Committee of Physicians and Surgeons* (Dublin: The Author, 1773).

ADAMS, Percy G., *Travel Literature and the Evolution of the Novel* (Lexington: University Press of Kentucky, 1983).

—— *Travellers and Travel Liars, 1660–1800* (Berkeley: University of California Press, 1962).

ALAVI, Seema, 'Company Army and Rural Society: The Invalid Thanah 1780–1830', *Modern Asian Studies*, 27, 1 (1993): 147–78.

—— 'Makings of Company Power: James Skinner in the Ceded and Conquered Provinces, 1802–40', *The Indian Economic and Social History Review*, 30, 4 (October 1993), pp. 437–59.

ALDINI, John, *General Views on the Application of Galvanism to Medical Purposes* (London: J. Callow, 1819).

ALI, Mrs Meer Hassan, *Observations on the Mussulmauns of India*, 2 vols (London: Parbury, Allen, 1832).

ARNOLD, David, *Police Power and Colonial Rule, Madras, 1859–1947* (Delhi: Oxford University Press, 1986).

AS-SAFFAR, Muhammad, *Disorienting Encounters*, Susan Gilson Miller, ed. and tr. (Berkeley: University of California Press, 1991).

ATREE, H.R., *Atree's Topography of Brighton* (Brighton: The Author, 1809).

AYTOUN, Ellis, *The Penny Universities: A History of the Coffee-Houses* (London: Secker and Warburg, 1956).

'Baptisms in Calcutta', *Bengal Past and Present*, 28 (1924): 199.

BARAT, Amiya, *The Bengal Native Infantry, Its Organization and Discipline, 1796–1852* (Calcutta: Firma K.L. Mukhopadhyay, 1962).

BARNETT, Richard B., *North India Between Empires* (Berkeley: University of California Press, 1980).

BARTHOLOMEW, Charles, *The Turkish Bath . . . Evidence*, 6th edition (Bristol: The Author, 1871).

BATTEN, Charles, *Pleasurable Instruction: Form and Convention in Eighteenth-century Travel Literature* (Berkeley: University of California Press, 1978).

BAXTER, Arthur L., 'Extra Service', in Charles Booth ed., *Life and Labour of the People of London*, second series, vol. 4, *Industry* (London: Macmillan, 1903), pp. 252–88.

BAYLY, C.A., *Indian Society and the Making of the British Empire* (Cambridge: Cambridge University Press, 1988).

BEAMISH, Richard, *Lecture, Delivered . . . with Special Reference to the Improved Turkish Bath* (London: H. Bailliers, 1859).

BEAVAN, Arthur H., *James and Horace Smith* (London: Hurst and Blackett, 1899).

BENCE-JONES, Mark, *A Guide to Irish Country Houses* (London: Constable, 1978).

BERTHOU and Georges, *Album de Brighton* (Brighton: Berthou and Georges, 1838).

BHABHA, Homi, 'Signs Taken for Wonders', in Henry Gates ed., *'Race', Writing, and Difference* (Chicago: University of Chicago, 1985).

BICKERSTAFF, Isaac, *The Sultan; or, a Peep into a Seraglio* (London: Theatre Royal, 1785).

BIELENBERG, Andy, *Cork's Industrial Revolution 1780–1880* (Cork: Cork University Press, 1991).

BINGHAM, Neil, *C.A. Busby, the Regency Architect of Brighton and Hove* (Brighton: RIBA Gallery, 1991).

BISHOP, John George, *Peep into the Past: Brighton in the Olden Time* (Brighton: J.G. Bishop, 1892).

BLACK, Frank G., 'The Technique of Letter Fiction Writing in English from 1740 to 1800', *Harvard Studies and Notes in Philology and Literature*, 15 (1933).

BLAGDON, Edward, *A Cadetship in the Honourable East India Company's Service* (Oxford: University Press, 1931).

BLEGBOROUGH, Ralph, *Facts and Observations Respecting the Air-Pump Vapour Bath in Gout . . . and Other Diseases* (London: Lackington, Allen, 1803).

BOND, E.A., ed. *Speeches of the Managers and Counsel in the Trial of Warren Hastings*, 4 vols (London: Longman, Brown, Green, Longmans and Roberts, 1859).

BROOME, Arthur, *History of the Rise and Progress of the Bengal Army* (Calcutta: W. Thacker, 1850).

[BROUN, Thomas], *Brighton, or, They Steyne: A Satirical Novel*, 3 vols, 2nd edition (London: The Author, 1818).

BROWN, G.H., *Lives of the Fellows of the Royal College of Physicians of London, 1825–1925* (London: The College, 1955).

BRUCE, John, *History of Brighton* (Brighton: John Bruce, 1833; 1835).

BRYANT, Gerald, 'Officers of the East India Company's Army in the Days of Clive and Hastings', *Journal of Imperial and Commonwealth History*, 4 (1977–8): 203–27.

—— 'Pacification in the Early British Raj, 1755–85', *Journal of Imperial and Commonwealth History*, 14 (1985): 3–19.

BUCKLE, E., *Memoir of the Services of the Bengal Artillery*, J.W. Kaye ed. (London: William H. Allen, 1852).

BURGHART, Richard, 'Ethnographers and their Local Counterparts in India', in Richard Fardon ed., *Localizing Strategies; Regional Traditions of Ethnographic Writing* (Edinburgh: Scottish Academy Press, 1990), pp. 260–79.

BURKE, John Bernard, *Burke's Irish Family Records* (London: Burke's Peerage, 1976 edition).

—— *Burke's Irish Peerage* (London: Burke's Peerage, 1976 edition).

BUSTEED, H.E., *Echoes from Old Calcutta; being chiefly reminiscences of the days of Warren Hastings, Francis, and Impey*, 4th edition (London: W. Thacker, 1908).

CALLAHAN, Raymond, *The East India Company and Army Reform, 1783–98*, Harvard Historical Monographs 67 (Cambridge: Harvard University Press, 1972).

CAMBRIDGE, Richard Owen, *An Account of the War in India Between the English and French* (London: T. Jefferys, 1761).

CAMERON, H.C., *Mr Guy's Hospital* (Longmans, Green, 1954).

CARACCIOLI, Charles, *Life of Robert, Lord Clive, Baron Plassey*, 4 vols (London: T. Bell, 1775–77).

CARDEW, Francis Gordon, *A Sketch of the Services of the Bengal Native Army to the Year 1895* (Calcutta: Superintendent of Government Printing, 1903).

CARTER, Ron, 'A Question of Interpretation: An Overview of Some Recent Developments in Stylistics', in Theo D'hean ed., *Linguistics and the Study of Literature* (Amsterdam: Rodopi, 1986), pp. 7–26.

CHAKRABARTI, Shubhra, 'Collaboration and Resistance: Bengal Merchants and the English East India Company, 1757–1833', *Studies in History* 10, 1 n.s. (1994), 105–29.

CHANCELLOR, E.B., *History of the Squares of London* (London: K. Paul, Trench and Trubner, 1907).

CHATTERJI, Nandlal, *Mir Qasim, Nawab of Bengal, 1760–63* (Allahabad: Indian Press, 1935).

CLARKE, Sir Arthur, *An Essay on Warm, Cold, and Vapour Bathing*, 5th edition (London: Henry Colburn, 1820).

CLEOBUREY, William, *A Full Account of the System of Friction*, 3rd edition (Oxford: Munday and Slatter, 1825).

[CLERMONT, Mrs], *Observations on the Use of the Vapour, Tepid, and Other Baths* (London: The Author, 1814).

COCHRANE, Archibald, Earl of Dundonald, *Memorial and Petition to the Honourable the Court of Directors of the East India Company* (London: The Author, 1786).

COCHRANE, Basil, *An Exposé of the Conduct of the Victualling Board* (London: J. Davy, 1824).

—— *An Historical Digest of the Reports of the Commissioners* (London: The Author, 1824).

—— *An Improvement on the Mode of Administering the Vapour Bath* (London: John Booth, 1809).

—— *An Inquiry into the Conduct of the Commissioners for Victualling His Majesty's Navy* (London: J. Davy, 1823).

—— *Observations upon the System Pursued by the Victualling Department* (London: The Author, 1822).

—— *The Vapour Bath in Miniature* (London: T.C. Hansard, 1825).

COFFIN, John G., *Discourses on Cold and Warm Bathing* (Boston: John Eliot, 1818; 1826).

COHEN, Stephan P., *The Indian Army* (Delhi: Oxford University Press, 1990).

COLBATCH, Sir John, *Physico Medical Essay* (London: Dan. Browne, 1696).

COLE, Juan R.I., 'Invisible Occidentalism: Eighteenth-Century Indo-Persian Constructions of the West', *Iranian Studies*, 25, 3–4 (1992): 3–16.

COLLEY, Linda, *Britons* (New Haven: Yale University Press, 1992).

CORK Corporation, *Council Book of the Corporation of the City of Cork* (Cork: J. Billing and Sons, 1876).

COSTANZO, Angelo, *Surprizing Narrative: Olaudah Equiano and the Beginnings of Black Autobiography* (New York: Greenwood, 1987).

COTTON, Sir Evan, '"Sake Deen Mahomed" of Brighton', *Sussex County Magazine*, 13 (1939): 746–50.

CREEVEY, Thomas, *Creevey's Life and Times*, John Gore, ed. (London: John Murray, 1934).

CROWELL, Lorenzo M., 'Military Professionalism in a Colonial Context: The Madras Army *circa* 1832', *Modern Asian Studies*, 24 (1990): 249–74.

CRUIKSHANK, [Isaac] Robert, *Brighton! A Comic Sketch* (London: William Kidd, 1830).

CULVERWELL, Robert James, *A Few Practical Observations on Warm, Vapour, Shampooing, Sulphur-Fumigating, and Medicated Bathing* (London: The Author, n.d.).

—— *A Practical Treatise on Bathing; with Observations on Cold, Warm, Shampooing, Vapour, Sulfur, Harrowgate, and Other Baths* (London: The Author, 1829).

—— *The Life of Dr Culverwell, Written by Himself* (London: The Author, 1852).

CUSACK, Mary Francis, *A History of the City and County of Cork* (Cork: McGlashan and Gill, 1875).

DALE, Antony, *Brighton Town and Brighton People* (London: Phillamore, 1976).

DALE, Stephan F., 'Steppe Humanism: The Autobiographical Writing of Zahir al-Din Muhammad Babur', *International Journal of Middle East Studies*, vol. 22, no. 1 (February 1990), 37–58.

DALTON, John, *Memoirs of Captain Dalton*, Charles Dalton, ed. (London: W.H. Allen, 1886).

DANIELL, Thomas and William, *Antiquities of India* (London: Daniell, 1799).

—— *Oriental Scenery: One Hundred and Fifty Views* (London: T. and W. Daniell, 1816).

DAS, Harihar, 'The Early Indian Visitors to England', *Calcutta Review*, 3rd series, 13 (1924): 83–114.

DATTA, Kalikinkar, *Shah Alam II and the East India Company* (Calcutta: World Press, 1965).

DAY, Robert Adams, *Told in Letters, Epistolary Fiction* (Ann Arbor: University of Michigan Press, 1966).

DENMAN, Thomas, *Letter to Dr Richard Huck, on the Construction and Method of Using Vapour Baths* (London: The Author, 1768).

DICKENS, Charles, *Dombey and Son* (London: Bradbury and Evans, 1846–8).

*Dictionary of National Biography.*

DIGBY, Simon, 'An eighteenth century narrative of a journey from Bengal to England: Munshi Isma'il's "New History"', *Urdu and Muslim South Asia: Studies in honour of Ralph Russell*, Christopher

Shackle, ed. (London: School of Oriental and African Studies, University of London, 1989), pp. 49–65.

DIOGENES [pseudonym], *Life in a Tub, with a Description of the Turkish Bath*, 3rd edition (Dublin: William McGee, 1858).

DOBBEL, Horace, *On the Mont Dore Cure and the Proper Way to Use It* (London: J and A Churchill, 1881).

DODD, J.D., *The Traveller's Director through Ireland* (Dublin: J. Stockdale, 1801).

DODWELL, Henry, *Sepoy Recruitment in the Old Madras Army* (Calcutta: Superintendent Government Printing, 1922).

DOMINICETI, Bartholomew de, *Plan for Extending the Use of Artificial Water Baths, Pumps, Vaporous and Dry Baths* (London: The Author, 1771).

—— *To the Public, Tract* (London: The Author, 1764).

DYCE SOMBRE, David Octerlony, *Dyce Sombre against Troup, Solaroli (Intervening) and Prinsep and the Hon. East India Company (also Intervening) . . . In the Perogative Court of Canterbury* (London: Henry Hansard, n.d.).

—— *Refutation of the Charges of Lunacy in the Court of Chancery* (Paris: Dyce Sombre, 1849).

East India Company, *List of the Company's Civil Servants* (London: East India Company, 1771).

EDWARDS, Anthony, *Cork Remembrancer: or Tablet of Memory* (Cork: Anthony Edwards, 1792).

EDWARDS, Paul and David Dabydeen, eds, *Black Writers in Britain 1760–1890* (Edinburgh: Edinburgh University Press, 1991).

EICKELMAN, Dale F. and James Piscatori, *Muslim Travellers: Pilgrimage, Migrations, and the Religious Imagination* (Berkeley: University of California Press, 1990).

ELLERAY, D. Robert, A.L.A., *Brighton, A Pictorial History* (Chicester: Phillimore, 1987).

EMIN, Joseph, *The Life and Adventures of Joseph Emin, An Armenian, Written in English by Himself* (London: The Author, 1792); 2nd edition, A. Apcar ed. (Calcutta: Asiatic Society of Bengal, 1918).

*Epicure's Almanack; or, Calendar of Good Living Containing A Directory of the Taverns, Coffee-Houses, Inns, Eating houses, and Other Places of Alimentary Resort . . . A Review of Artists who administer to the Wants and Enjoyment of the Table* (London: Longman, Hurst, Rees, Orme, and Brown, 1815).

EQUIANO, Olaudah, *The Interesting Narrative of the Life of Olaudah Equiano, or Gustavus Vassa, the African. Written by Himself* (Leeds: James Nichols, 1814).

ERREDGE, John Ackerson, *History of Brighthelmston* (Brighton: E. Lewis, 1862; grangerized copy in BRL).

ESTE, Michael Lambton, *Remarks on Baths: Water, Swimming, Shampooing, Heat, Hot, Cold, and Vapor Baths* (London: J. Ridgway, 1811; 1812; 1845).

FARRANT, Sue, *Georgian Brighton, 1740–1820*, University of Sussex Centre for Continuing Education Occasional Papers 13 (Lewes: University of Sussex, 1980).

—— 'The Physical Development of the Royal Pavilion Estate and Its Influence on Brighton (E. Sussex) 1785–1823', *Sussex Archaeological Collections* 130 (1992): 171–84.

FAY, Eliza, *Original Letters from India (1779–1815)*, E.M. Forster, ed. (New York: Harcourt Brace, 1925).

FELDBAEK, Ole, 'Danish East India Trade 1772–1807', *Scandinavian Economic History Review* 26, 2 (1978): 128–44.

—— *India Trade under the Danish Flag, 1772–1808* (Copenhagen: Studentlitteratur, 1969).

FELTHAM, John, *Guide to all the Watering and Sea Bathing Places* (London: Longman, Hurst, Rees, Orme, and Brown, 1806; 1815).

—— *Picture of London* (London: Longman, Hurst, Rees, Orme, Browne and Green, 1806–32).

[FENTON, Albert], 'Bengalee', *Memoirs of a Cadet* (London: Saunders and Otley, 1839).

FFOLLIOTT, Rosemary, *Biographical Notices . . . 1756–1827* (Fethard, Tipperary: Glebe House, 1980).

FISHER, Michael H., *Indirect Rule in India: Residents and the Residency System* (New Delhi: Oxford University Press, 1991).

—— ed., *Politics of the British Annexation of India* (Delhi: Oxford University Press, 1993).

FOLKENFLIK, Robert, ed., *Culture of Autobiography* (Stanford: Stanford University Press, 1993).

FORBES, James, *Oriental Memoirs*, 2 vols (London: Richard Bentley, 1834 edition).

FORD, John and Jill, *Images of Brighton* (Richmond-upon-Thames: Saint Helena Press, 1981).

FORREST, George William, *Life of Lord Clive*, 2 vols (London: Cassell, 1918).

—— *Selections from the State Papers of the Governors-General of India*, 4 vols (London: Constable, 1910–26).

FOSTER, George, *Journey from Bengal to England*, 2 vols (London: R. Faulder, 1798).

Fox, Richard G., *Kin, Clan, Raja, Rule* (Berkeley: University of California Press, 1971).

Fryer, Peter, *Staying Power: The History of Black People in Britain* (London: Pluto, 1984).

Furber, Holden, *John Company at Work* (Cambridge: Harvard University Press, 1948).

Gates, Henry Louis, Jr., ed., *The Classic Slave Narratives* (New York: Mentor, 1987).

—— 'James Gronniosaw and the Trope of the Talking Book', in James Olney, ed., *Studies in Autobiography* (New York: Oxford University Press, 1988), pp. 51–72.

Ghosh, Suresh Chandra, *Social Condition of the British Community in Bengal, 1757–1800* (Leiden: Brill, 1970).

Gibbon, Edward, *The Decline and Fall of the Roman Empire* (London: The Author, 1776–86).

Gibney, John, *Treatise on the Properties and Medical Application of the Vapour Bath* (London: Knight and Lacey, 1825).

Gibson, Charles Bernard, *The History of the County and City of Cork*, 2 vols (London: T.C. Newby, 1861).

Gilbert, Arthur N., 'Recruitment and Reform in the East India Company Army, 1760–1800', *Journal of British Studies*, 15 (1975): 89–111.

Gilbert, Edmund W., *Brighton, Old Ocean's Bauble* (London: Methuen, 1954; 1975).

Gilpin, William, *Observations on the River Wye* (London: The Author, 1782).

—— *Observations on the Western Parts of England* (London: The Author, 1798).

Gloag, John, *Mr Loudon's England* (Newcastle: Oriel, 1970).

Gosse, Andre Louis, *Account of a Visit Made to the Baths of St Filippo in Tuscany* (Edinburgh: A. Constable, 1820).

Gower, Charles, *Auxiliaries to Medicine* (London: J. Hubbard, 1819).

Grace, Henry, *The Code of Military Standing Regulations of the Bengal Establishment* (Calcutta: Cooper and Upjohn, 1791).

[Graham, Thomas John], 'A Physician,' *Account of Persons Remarkable for their Health and Longevity* (London: The Author, 1829).

Granville, A.B., *The Spas of England, and Principal Sea Bathing Places*, 2 vols (London: Henry Colburn, 1841).

Great Britain, Parliament, 'An Account of the Number of Non-Commissioned Officers and Private Men Sent to the East Indies from

September 1762 to September 1772', *Eighth Report from the Committee of Secrecy* (25 May 1773).

GREEN, Jonathan, *Short Illustration of the Advantages Derived by the Use of Sulphurous Fumigating, Hot Air and Vapour Baths* (London: The Author, 1825).

[GREGG, Hilda] 'Grier, S.C.', 'Some Fresh Light on the Second Mrs Hastings and Her Family', *Bengal Past and Present,* 5 (1910): 333–4.

GRENVILLE, Charles, *The Grenville Diary,* 2 vols, Philip Whitwell Wilson, ed. (London: William Heineman, 1927).

GROSE, John Henry, *A Voyage to the East Indies with Observations* (London: S. Hooper and A. Morley, 1757; 1766; 1772).

GUPTARA, Prabhu, *Black British Literature: An Annotated Bibliography* (Sidney: Dangaroo Press, 1986).

HAMILTON, Charles, *An Historical Relation of the Origin, Progress, and Final Dissolution of the Rohilla Afghans* (London: K. Keersley, 1787).

HAMILTON, Eliza, *Translation of the Letters of a Hindoo Rajah,* 2 vols (London: G.G. and J. Robinson, 1796; 1811).

HARRIS, John, 'Busby at Brighton: An Unrecognized Regency Architect', *Apollo* 135, 355 (September 1991): 197–8.

HARRISON, Frederick and James Sharp North, *Old Brighton, Old Preston, Old Hove* (Hassocks: Flare, 1974; reprint of 1937).

HART, Theodore, *Treatise on the Dry Sulphuric Baths* (London: George Taylor, 1819).

HASTINGS, Warren, *Memoirs of the Life of . . . Warren Hastings,* 3 vols, G.R. Gleig, ed. (London: Richard Bentley, 1841).

—— *A Narrative of the Insurrection Which Happened in the Zemeedary of Banaris* (Calcutta: The Author, 1782).

HAZLITT, William, *Notes on a Journey Through France and Italy* (London: Hunt and Clarke, 1826).

HEATHCOTE, T.A., *The Military in British India . . . 1600–1947* (Manchester: Manchester University Press, 1995).

HECHT, J. Jean, 'Continental and Colonial Servants in Eighteenth Century England', *Smith College Studies in History* 40 (1954).

HEDGEHOG, Humphrey, *The Pavilion, or, A Month in Brighton,* 3 vols (London: J. Johnson, 1817).

HERVEY, Albert, *Soldier of the Company, Life of an Indian Ensign, 1833–43,* Charles Allen, ed. (London: Michael Joseph, 1988).

HICKEY, William, *Memoirs of William Hickey,* 4 vols, 3rd edition, Alfred Spencer, ed. (London: Hurst and Blackett, 1919–25).

HILL, S.C., 'The Old Sepoy Officer', *English Historical Review* (April, July 1913), pp. 260–91, 496–514.

HILL, S.C., *Yusuf Khan, The Rebel Commandant* (London: Longmans, Green, 1914).

HOARE, Sir Richard Colt, *Journal of a Tour in Ireland, AD 1806* (London: W. Miller, 1807).

HODGES, William, *Travels in India . . . 1780 . . . 1783* (London: The Author, 1793).

HODSON, V.P.C., *List of the Officers of the Bengal Army 1758–1834*, 4 vols (London: Constable and Phillimore, 1927–47).

HOLZMAN, James Mayer, *Nabobs in England . . . the Returned Anglo-Indian, 1760–85* (New York: The Author, 1926).

HORSFIELD, Thomas Walker, *History, Antiquities, and Topography of the County of Sussex*, 2 vols (Sussex: Lewes Press, 1835).

HUSAIN, Iqbal, *Rise and Decline of the Ruhela Chieftaincies in 18th Century India* (Delhi: Oxford University Press, 1994).

IBN Khaldun, *Muqaddimah*, Franz Rosenthal, tr. (Princeton: Princeton University Press, 1967).

India, Imperial Record Department, *Calendar of Persian Correspondence* (Calcutta: Superintendent Government Printing, 1911; 1970).

India, National Archives of India, *Fort William-India House Correspondence*, 21 vols (New Delhi: National Archives of India, 1949–85).

JACKSON, William Collin, *Memoir of the Public Conduct and Services* (London: The Author, 1809).

JENKS, G.S., *Medical Observations or the Factitious German Mineral Waters, at Brighton* (Brighton: The Author, 1840).

JERNINGHAM, Lady, *The Jerningham Letters (1780–1843)*, 2 vols, Egerton Castle, ed. (London: Richard Bentley, 1896).

JONES, M.E. Monckton, *Warren Hastings in Bengal*, Oxford Historical and Literary Studies, vol. 9 (Oxford: Clarendon Press, 1918).

JONES, Philip, *Portable Vapour Bath* (London: The Author, 1785).

KENTISH, Edward, *Account of Baths and of a Maderia-House at Bristol* (London: Longman, Hurst, Rees, Orme, and Brown, 1814).

—— *Essay on Warm and Vapour Bathing* (London: Joseph Mawman, 1809; 1813).

KHAN, Abu Taleb, *Travels of Mirza Abu Taleb Khan . . . 1799 . . . 1803; Written by Himself in . . . Persian*, 2 vols, Charles Stewart, tr. (London: Longman, Hurst, Rees, and Orme, 1810; 1814).

KHAN, Sayid Ghulam Husain, *The Seir Mutaqherin*, 4 vols, M. Raymond, tr. (Calcutta: T.D. Chatterjee, 1902 reprint).

KINDERSLEY, [Jemima], *Letters from the Island of Teneriffe . . . and the East Indies* (London: Norse, 1777).

KNOX, John, *A New Collection of Voyages, Discoveries and Travels* (London: John Knox, 1767).

KOLFF, Dirk H.A., *Naukar, Rajput and Sepoy: The Ethnohistory of the Military Labour Market in Hindustan, 1450–1850* (Cambridge: Cambridge University Press, 1990).

LA BEAUME, M., *Observations on the Properties of the Air-Pump Vapour-Bath* (London: The Author, 1818).

LAMPSON, G. Locker, *Consideration of the State of Ireland* (London: Archibald Constable, 1907).

LATOCNAYE, de, *A Frenchman's Walk through Ireland 1796–97*, John Stevenson, tr. (Belfast: Blackstaff Press, 1984).

LAWRIE, James, *The Roman or Turkish Bath: Together with Barege, Medicated, Galvanic, and Hydropathic Baths* (Edinburgh: Maclachlan and Stewart, 1864).

LEED, Eric J., *The Mind of the Traveller: From Gilgamesh to Global Tourism* (New York: Basic Books, 1991).

LEIGH, Samuel, *New Picture of London* (London: S. Leigh, 1824–34).

LEJEUNE, Philippe, *On Autobiography*, Katherine M. Leary, tr. (Minneapolis: University of Minnesota Press, 1989).

LENMAN, Bruce P., 'The Weapons of War in Eighteenth-Century India', *Journal of the Society for Army Historical Research* 36 (1968): 33–43.

—— 'The Transition to European Military Ascendancy in India, 1600–1800', in *Tools of War*, John Lynn, ed. (Bloomington: University of Indiana, 1990).

LEWIS, Bernard, *The Muslim Discovery of Europe* (London: Weidesfeld and Nicolson, 1982).

LILLYWHITE, Bryant, *London Coffee Houses* (London: G. Allen and Unwin, 1963).

LOCKWOOD, Edward, *Natural History, Sport, and Travel* (London: William H. Allen, 1878).

LONG, J., *Selections from Unpublished Records of Government for the Years 1748 to 1767*, vol. 1 (Calcutta: Superintendent Government Printing, 1869).

LOVE, Henry Davison, *Vestiges of Old Madras (1640–1800)*, Indian Records Series, vol. 3 (London: John Murray, 1913).

LUCAS, Charles, *Essay on Waters*, 3 vols (London: A. Millar, 1756).

LUTFULLAH, *Autobiography*, Edward B. Eastwick, ed. (New Delhi: International Writer's Emporium, 1987; reprint of 1857).

MACAULAY Thomas Babington, *Letters*, 6 vols, Thomas Pinney, ed. (Cambridge: Cambridge University Press, 1974).

MACCARTHY, C.J.F., 'Patrick Blair'. *Journal of the Cork Historical and Archaeological Society*, 90, 249 (1985): 104–19.

MACPHERSON, William Charles, ed. *Soldiering in India, 1764–87* (Edinburgh: William Blackwell, 1928).

MADDEN, R[ichard] R., *Travels in Turkey, Egypt, Arabia, and Palestine in 1824 . . . 1827*, 2 vols (London: Whittaker and Treacher, 1829; 1833).

MAHOMED, F.A., 'A Contribution to the Clinical History of Scarletinal Convelescence', *The Practitioner*, 15 (July–December 1876): 21–36.

MAHOMED, George S., 'Sake Deen Mahomed', *Sussex County Magazine* 14 (1940): 42.

MAHOMED, George, *The Treatment of the Bournemouth Mont Dore* (London: Bailliere, Trudall, and Cox, 1889).

MAHOMED, Horatio, *The Bath: A Concise History of Bathing* (London: Smith, Elder, 1843).

—— *Short Hints on Bathing* (London: The Author, 1844).

MAHOMED, S.D., *Cases Cured by Sake Deen Mahomed, Shampooing Surgeon, And Inventor of the Indian Medicated Vapour and Sea-Water Baths* (Brighton: The Author, 1820).

—— *Shampooing, or, Benefits Resulting from the Use of the Indian Medicated Vapour Bath* (Brighton: The Author, 1822; 1826; 1838).

MARSH, Charles, *Clubs of London*, 2 vols (London: H. Colburn, 1828).

MARSHALL, P[eter] J., *East Indian Fortunes: The British in Bengal* (Oxford: Clarendon, 1976).

MARTIN, Henry, *The History of Brighton and Environs* (Brighton: John Beal, 1871).

MASON, Philip, *A Matter of Honour; An Account of the Indian Army* (New York: Holt, Rinehart and Winston, 1974).

MAXWELL, Constantia Elizabeth, *Country and Town in Ireland under the Georges* (London: G.G. Harrap, 1940).

MONTESQUIEU, Charles de Secondat, *Lettres persanes*, 2 vols (Cologne: Chez Pierre Marteau, 1744).

MOODIE, John, *History of the Military Operations in Hindustan, 1744–84*, 2 vols (London: The Author, 1788).

—— *Remarks on the Most Important Military Operations of the English Forces* (London: Logographic Press, 1788).

MORIER, James, *Adventures of Hajji Baba of Ispahan*, 3 vols (London: John Murray, 1824).

MORLEY, John, *The Making of the Royal Pavilion, Brighton* (London: Sotheby, 1984).

MUNRO, Innes, *Narrative of Military Operations against the French, Dutch, and Hyder Ally Cawn, 1780–84* (London: The Author, 1789).

MUNTER, Robert, *Dictionary of the Print Trade in Ireland* (New York: Fordham, 1988).

MUSGROVE, Clifford, *Life in Brighton* (London: Faber, 1970; 1981).

NAOROJI, Dadabhai, *Poverty and Un-British Rule in India* (London: Sonnenschien, 1901).

NASH, John, *Illustrations of Her Majesty's Palace at Brighton, Formerly the Pavilion*, Edward Wedlake Brayley, ed.(London: J.B. Nichols and Son, 1838).

NESS, Gayl D. and William Stahl, 'Western Imperialist Armies in Asia', *Comparative Studies in Society and History*, 19 (1977), 2–29.

NEVILL, Ralph Henry, *London Clubs, Their History and Treasures* (London: Chatto and Windus, 1911).

Obituary of Frederick Akbar Mahomed, *Guy's Hospital Reports*, 43 (1886): 1–10.

OLNEY, James, ed., *Autobiography: Essays Theoretical and Critical* (Princeton: Princeton University Press, 1980), pp. 3–27.

O'MALLEY, L.S.S., *Bengal District Gazetters: Monghyr* (Calcutta: Bengal Secretariat Book Depot, 1909).

OMISSI, David, *The Sepoy and the Raj . . . 1860–1940* (London: Macmillan, 1994).

ORME, Robert, *History of the Military Transactions of the British Nation in India*, 2 vols (London: The Author, 1780).

O'SULLIVAN, William, *Economic History of Cork City . . . to the Act of Union* (Cork: Cork University Press, 1937).

*Oxford English Dictionary*

PARKER, *The History of the War in India* (London: The Author, 1789).

PARKER, Robert, *Memoirs of the Most Remarkable Military Transactions . . . to 1718* (Dublin: His Son, 1746).

PEARSE, Thomas Deane, 'Memoir of Colonel Thomas Deane Pearse of the Bengal Artillery', *Bengal Past and Present* 2–7 (1908–11).

*Peep at the P\*v\*\*\*\*n; or, Boiled Mutton with Caper Sauce, at the Temple of Joss; A Satirical Poem* (London: E. Wilson, 1820).

PEERS, Douglas M., *Between Mars and Mammon: Colonial Armies and the Garrison State in 19th-century India* (London: I.B. Tauris, 1995).

—— '"The Habitual Nobility of Being"; British Officers and the Social

Construction of the Bengal Army in the Early Nineteenth Century,' *Modern Asian Studies* 25, 3 (1991), 545–69.

—— 'War and Public Finance in Early Nineteenth-Century British India', *International History Review*, 11, 4 (November 1989), 628–47.

HENRI Pérès, 'Voyaguers Musulmans en Europe aux XIXe et Xxe siècles', in *Mémoires de l'Institut Français d'Archéologie Orientale du Caire*, LXVIII (1940).

PETERSON, M[ildred] Jeanne, *Medical Profession in Mid-Victorian London* (Berkeley: University of California Press, 1978).

PHOTOPHILUS [pseudonym], *The New Irish Bath Versus the Old Turkish Bath* (Dublin: William McGee, 1860).

PLAYFAIR, James, *A Method of Construction of Vapour Baths* (London: John Murray, 1783).

*Poll Books*: Brighton, 1835, 1841, 1847, 1852, 1857, 1859; East Sussex 1832, 1837; Sussex 1820, 1832, 1837, 1841; Westminster 1841, 1851–2.

POLLARD, M[ary], *Dublin's Trade in Books, 1550–1800* (Oxford: Clarendon Press, 1989).

PORTER, Sir Robert Ker, *Travels though Georgia, Persia, Armenia, Ancient Babylon . . . 1817 . . . 1820*, 2 [3] vols (London: Longman Hurst, Rees, Orme and Brown, 1821).

PRATT, Mary Louise, *Imperial Eyes: Travel Writing and Transculturation* (London: Routledge, 1992).

—— 'Scratches on the Face of the Country', in Henry Louis Gates, Jr. ed., *'Race', Writing, and Difference* (Chicago: University of Chicago, 1986), pp. 138–62.

RAYE, N.N., *The Annals of the Early English Settlement in Bihar* (Calcutta: Kamala Book Depot, 1927).

RAZZELL, P.E., 'Social Origins of Officers in the Indian and British Home Army: 1758–1962,' *British Journal of Sociology*, 14, 3 (September 1963): 248–60.

RELHAN, Anthony, *Short History of Brighthelmstone* (Brighton: Philanthropic Society, 1829, reprint of 1761).

RENNELL, James, *Journals*, T.D. LaTouche, ed. (Asiatic Society of Bengal, 1910).

—— *Marches of the British Army in . . . India . . . 1790 . . . 1791*, 2nd edition (London: The Author, 1792).

REPTON, H., *Designs for the Pavillion at Brighton* (London: J.C. Sadler, 1808).

Review of S.D. Mahomed, *Shampooing* in *Gentleman's Magazine*, 93, 2 (August 1823): 162.

RICHARDS, J.F., 'Norms of Comportment Mughal Officers,' in *Moral Conduct and Authority*, Barbara Daly Metcalf, ed. (Berkeley: University of California Press, 1984), pp. 255–89.

ROBERTS, Henry D., *A History of the Royal Pavilion Brighton* (London: Country Life, 1959).

RUSSELL, Richard, *A Dissertation on the use of Sea-Water in the Diseases of the Glands* (London: The Translator, 1752).

SALA, George Augustus, *The Life and Adventures*, 2 vols (London: Cassell, 1895).

SALIM ALLAH, *Narrative of the Transactions in Bengal*, Francis Gladwin, tr. (Calcutta: Stuart and Cooper, 1788).

SAUNDERS, William, *Treatise on the Chemical History and Medical Powers of Some of the Most Celebrated Mineral Waters*, 2nd edition (London: Phillips and Fardon, 1805).

SCHWARTZBERG, Joseph, *A Historical Atlas of South Asia* (Chicago: University of Chicago Press, 1978).

SCOTT, Richard, 'Journal', *Naval and Military Magazine*, 1–4 (1827–28).

SCOTT, William, *Proposal for Establishing in Edinburgh . . . a Newly Improved Apparatus for the application of the Vapour of Water* (Edinburgh: Waugh and Innes, 1820).

SHADE, Sarah, *Narrative of the Life of Sarah Shade* (London: Knight and Compton, 1801).

SHIPP, John, *Memoirs of the Extraordinary Militiary Career*, 3 vols (London: T.F. Unwin, 1890 reprint of 1829).

SHURREEF, Jaffur, *Qanoon-e-Islam*, G.A. Herklots, tr. (Delhi: Oriental Reprints, 1972 reprint of 1832).

SITA RAM, *Sepoy to Subedar*, J. Norgate, ed. and tr. (Calcutta: Baptist Mission Press, 1911 reprint of 1873).

SITWELL, Osbert, *Discursions on Travel, Art, and Life* (London: Grant Richards, 1925).

SMITH, Charles, *Ancient and Present State of the County and City of Cork*, 2 vols, 2nd edition (Dublin: W. Wilson, 1774).

SMITH, F.B., *The People's Health, 1830–1910* (New York: Holmes and Meier, 1979).

SMITH, Horace, ed. *Comic Miscellanies in Prose and Verse of the Late James Smith Esq.*, 2 vols, 2nd edition (London: Henry Colburn, 1841).

SMITH, Thomas, *A Topographical and Historical Account of the Parish of St Mary-le-bone* (London: John Smith, 1833).

SMYTH, William J., 'Social, Economic and Landscape Transformations in County Cork', in *Cork History and Society*, Patrick O'Flanagan and Cornelius G. Buttimer, eds. (Dublin: Geography, 1993), pp. 655–98.

SPACKS, Patricia Meyer, *Imagining a Self: Autobiography and Novel in Eighteenth-century England* (Cambridge: Harvard University Press, 1976).

STABLES, W. Gordon, *Turkish and other Baths* (London: The Author, 1882).

STAFFORD, Barbara Maria, *Voyage into Substance: Art, Science, Nature, and the Illustrated Travel Account, 1760–1840* (Cambridge: MIT Press, 1984).

STEWART, J. Cameron, 'Frederick Akbar Mahomed', *International Kidney* (forthcoming).

STRACHEY, John, *Hastings and the Rohilla War* (New Delhi: Prabha, 1985; reprint of 1892).

STRACHEY, Henry, *Narrative of the Mutiny of the Officers of the Army in Bengal in the Year 1766* (London: The Author, 1773).

STUBBS, Francis W., *History of the Organization, Equipment, and War Services of the Regiment of Bengal Artillery*, 2 vols (London: Henry S. King, 1877).

SUTHERLAND, Lucy S., *The East India Company in Eighteenth Century Politics* (Oxford: Oxford University Press, 1952).

SYMONS, John, *Observations on Vapour-Bathing and its Effects* (Bristol: The Author, 1766).

THORNBURGH, Richard, *Mahomed's Royal Gymnasium* (Brighton: The Author, 1980).

TOWNSEND, Horatio, *Statistical Survey of the County of Cork* (Dublin: Graisberry and Campbell, 1810).

URQUHART, David, *Manual of the Turkish Bath*, Sir John Fife, ed. (London: John Churchill and Sons, 1865).

—— *Pillars of Hercules*, 2 vols (London: Richard Bentley, 1850).

—— *The Turkish Bath with a View to its Introduction into the British Dominions* (London: David Bryce, 1856).

VANSITTART, Henry, *A Narrative of the Transactions in Bengal 1760–64*, Anil Chandra Banerjee and Bimal Kanti Ghosh, eds. (Calcutta: K.P. Bagchi, 1976; reprint of 1766).

VERELST, Harry, *View of the Rise, Progress, and Present State of the English Government in Bengal* (London: J. Nourse, 1772).

VISRAM, Rozina, *Ayahs, Lascars and Princes: Indians in Britain 1700–1947* (London: Pluto Press, 1986).

VOLTAIRE, Francois, *Mahomet, The Impostor: A Tragedy*, Reverend James Miller, tr. (London: The Translator, 1778).

VON GRUNEBAUM, Gustav E., *Medieval Islam* (Chicago: University of Chicago Press, 1953).

WALFORD, Edward, *Old and New London*, vol. 4, *Westminster and the Western Suburbs* (London: Cassell, 1873).

WALLIS, E. *Brighton Townsman and Visitor's Directory* (Brighton: E. Wallis, *ca.* 1826).

WEEKES, Henry, *Warm Water Remedy* (London: Edwards and Hughes, 1844).

WEINTRAUB, Karl, 'Autobiography and Historical Consciousness', *Critical Inquiry*, 1, 4 (June 1975): 821–48.

WELLESLEY, Arthur, *Prime Minister's Papers*, vol. 1, John Brooks and Julia Gardy, eds. (London: HMSO, 1975).

[WESMACOTT, Charles Malloy] Bernard Blackmantle, *The English Spy*, 2 vols (London: Sherwood, Jones, 1825).

WHARNCLIFFE, Lady, *The First Lady Wharncliffe and Her Family (1779–1856)*, 2 vols, Caroline Grosvenor and Charles Beilby, eds. (London: William Heineman, 1927).

WHITLAW, Charles, *The Scriptural Code of Health* (London: The Author, 1838).

Whitlaw, Charles, *A Treatise* (London: The Author, 1831).

WILKS, Samuel, *Biographical History of Guy's Hospital* (London: Ward, Lock, Bowden, 1892).

WILLIAMS, John, *Historical Account of the Rise and Progress of the Bengal Native Infantry* (London: John Murray, 1817; 1970).

WILLIAMSON, Thomas, *The East Indian Vade Mecum* (London: Black, Parry, and Kingsbury, 1810).

WILLIS, G., *Current Notes* (Covent Garden: G. Willis, 1851).

WILSON, C.R. and W.H. Carey, *Glimpses of the Olden Times*, Amarendranath Mookerji ed. (Calcutta: Eastlight, 1968 reprint).

WILSON, William, *The Post-chaise Companion* (Dublin: W. Wilson, 1784).

WRIGHT, C., *The Brighton Ambulator* (London: C. Wright, 1818).

WYLLY, H.C., *Life of Lieutenant-General Sir Eyre Coote* (Oxford: Clarendon Press, 1922).

WYNTER, John, *Of bathing in the Hot-baths, at Bathe* (London: W. Innys, 1728).

YULE, Henry and A.C. Burnell, *Hobson-Jobson*, William Crooke, ed. (New Delhi: Muhshiram Manoharlal, 1968 reprint of 1903).

*Manuscripts and Record Series Cited (with Abbreviations)*

Abu Talib Khan, 'Masir Talibi fi Bilad Afranji', 3 vols, BM Add 8145–47, IOL.

BMC  Bengal Military Consultations, IOL.

BMCG  Bengal Military Consultations, General Department, NAI.

Board of Ordinance, Minutes, PRO (Kew).

BPbC  Bengal Public Consultations, IOL.

BPOC  Bengal Public Original Consultation, NAI.

Brighton Commissioners, Minute Books, ESRO.

Brighton Land Tax Records, ESRO.

Brighton Rate Books, ESRO.

Brighton Town Rate Books, BRL.

Brighton Valuation Registers, BRL.

BSC  Bengal Secret Consultations, IOL.

BSMC  Bengal Secret and Military Consultations, IOL.

Census of England, 1841, 1851, 1861, 1871, 1881, 1891, PRO.

Docket Book (B.4.31), PRO.

Foreign Department Consultations, IOL.

Foreign Secret, Original Consultations, NAI.

GOCC  General Orders of the Commander-in-Chief, NAI.

Great Britain, Census 1841, 1851, PRO.

GRT  General Return of Troops, Fort William, NAI.

HMS  Home Miscellaneous Series, IOL.

HPC  Home Public Consultations, NAI

Index to Marriage Licence Bonds, PRO Ireland.

Kinlock, George, 'Journal of Captain George Kinlock in the Expedition to Nepal', MS Eur F.128/40, IOL.

Lord Chamberlain's Accounts, PRO.

Madras Military Consultations, IOL.

Mahomed's Visitor's Books, BRL.

'Manuscript Documents', MS 7410–192 1–7, National Army Museum.

'Manuscript Notebook', MS 6709/38, National Army Museum.

Marylebone Parish Register, GLRO.

Military Consultations, NAI.

Minutes of the CoD, IOL.

Patna Factory Records, IOL.

Persian Correspondence, Translations of Issues, NAI.

Rate Books for Marylebone, MPL.

St Bartholomew the Great Parish Records, Guildhall.
St Botolph-without-Aldergate Parish Records, Guildhall.
St James (Westminster) Parish Records, WPL.
St Leonard's (Shoreditch) Parish Records, Guildhall.
St Nicholas (Brighton) Parish Records, ESRO.
Victualler's Licence Register of all the Innkeepers' and Alehouse Keepers'
    Recognizances within . . . Holborn, GLRO.
Westminster Rate Books, 1830–35, WPL.

## Periodicals Cited (with Abbreviations)

BG    *Brighton Gazette*
BH    *Brighton Herald*
*Boyle's Court Guide*
*Brighton Directories*
*Brighton Guardian*
*British Imperial Calendar*
*British Medical Journal*
*British Traveller* (London)
CA    *Cork Advertizer or Commercial Advertizer*
CEP    *Cork Evening Post*
CG    *Cork Gazette*
CMC    *Cork Merchantile Chronicle*
*Cork Courier*
*Cork Herald*
*Critical Review*
*Gentleman's Magazine*
*Guy's Hospital Reports*
HC    *Hibernian Chronicle*
*Hibernian Telegraph*
*Holden's Directory*
*Illustrated Times*
*Journal of the Cork Historical and Archaeological Society*
*London Gazette*
*Monthly Review*
*Morning Advertiser*
NCEP    *New Cork Evening Post*
*New Picture of London*
*Picture of London*

*Pigot's Directories*
*Post Office Directories*
*Robinson's Directories*
*St James Chronicle*
*Sussex County Magazine*
SWA    *Sussex Weekly Advertizer*
*Times* (London)
*Volunteer Journal*
*Willis' Current Notes*

## List of Other Abbreviations

| | |
|---|---|
| BRL | Brighton Reference Library |
| CinC | Commander in Chief |
| CoD | Court of Directors of the English East India Company |
| CPC | Calendar of Persian Correspondence |
| ESRO | East Sussex Record Office |
| FTWM | Fort William-India House Correspondence |
| GLRO | Greater London Record Office |
| IOL | Oriental and India Office Collections |
| MPL | Marylebone Public Library |
| NAI | National Archives of India |
| PRO Ireland | Public Record Office of Ireland (Dublin) |
| PRO | Public Record Office of England (Chancery Lane) |
| PRO (Kew) | Public Record Office of England (Kew) |
| WPL | Westminster Public Library |

# Glossary and Index